World Military Guide
France

Compiled by
Pandora Ruff

Scribbles

Year of Publication 2018

ISBN : 9789352979080

Book Published by

Scribbles

(An Imprint of Alpha Editions)

email - alphaedis@gmail.com

Produced by: PediaPress GmbH
Limburg an der Lahn
Germany
http://pediapress.com/

The content within this book was generated collaboratively by volunteers. Please be advised that nothing found here has necessarily been reviewed by people with the expertise required to provide you with complete, accurate or reliable information. Some information in this book may be misleading or simply wrong. Alpha Editions and PediaPress does not guarantee the validity of the information found here. If you need specific advice (for example, medical, legal, financial, or risk management) please seek a professional who is licensed or knowledgeable in that area.

Sources, licenses and contributors of the articles and images are listed in the section entitled "References". Parts of the books may be licensed under the GNU Free Documentation License. A copy of this license is included in the section entitled "GNU Free Documentation License"

The views and characters expressed in the book are those of the contributors and his/her imagination and do not represent the views of the Publisher.

Contents

Articles 1

Introduction 1
    French Armed Forces 1

History 13
    Military history of France 13
    French Army in World War I 51
    Military history of France during World War II 72
    History of the French Navy 154

French Army 181
    French Army 181
    French Foreign Legion 203

Modern Military 273
    Modern equipment of the French Army 273
    France and weapons of mass destruction 283

White Paper 297
    2008 French White Paper on Defence and National Security 297
    2013 French White Paper on Defence and National Security 298

French Air Force   **303**

   History of the Armée de l'Air (1909–1942) 303

   History of the Armée de l'Air in the colonies (1939–62) 321

   French Air Force 332

French Navy   **359**

   French Navy 359

National Gendarmerie   **379**

   National Gendarmerie 379

National Guard   **405**

   National Guard (France) 405

Appendix   **415**

   References 415

   Article Sources and Contributors 428

   Image Sources, Licenses and Contributors 430

Article Licenses   **439**

Index   **441**

Introduction

French Armed Forces

French Armed Forces	
Forces armées françaises	
Logo of the French Armed Forces	
Founded	1792
Service branches	French Army *(Armée de terre)* French Navy *(Marine Nationale)* French Air Force *(Armée de l'Air)* National Gendarmerie *(Gendarmerie nationale)* National Guard *(Garde nationale)*
Headquarters	Paris
Leadership	
Commander-in-Chief	President Emmanuel Macron
Minister of the Armed Forces	Florence Parly

Chief of the Defence Staff	François Lecointre
Manpower	
Military age	17.5
Conscription	None
Active personnel	265,458 (2016)
Reserve personnel	71,472 reserve (2017) (Gendarmerie included)
Deployed personnel	17,000+
Expenditures	
Budget	€40.5 billion (2017)[1] Note: Incl. Gendarmerie budget
Percent of GDP	1.81% (2018)
Industry	
Foreign suppliers	Austria Belgium Germany Italy Sweden United Kingdom United States
Related articles	
History	Military history of France
Ranks	Army ranks Navy ranks Air force ranks

The **French Armed Forces** (French: *Forces armées françaises*) encompass the Army, the Navy, the Air Force, the National Guard and the Gendarmerie of the French Republic. The President of France heads the armed forces as *chef des armées*.

France maintains the sixth largest defence budget in the world and the largest armed forces in size in the European Union (EU). France also maintains the world's third-largest nuclear deterrent (behind Russia and the United States).

History

The military history of France encompasses an immense panorama of conflicts and struggles extending for more than 2,000 years across areas including modern France, greater Europe, and French territorial possessions overseas. According to the British historian Niall Ferguson, France has participated in 50 of the 125 major European wars fought since 1495, and in 168 battles fought since 387 BC, they have won 109, drawn 10 and lost 49: this makes

Figure 1: *Free French Foreign Legionnaires at the Battle of Bir Hakeim (1942).*

France the most successful military power in European history—in terms of number of fought and won.

The Gallo-Roman conflict predominated from 60 BC to 50 BC, with the Romans emerging victorious in the conquest of Gaul by Julius Caesar. After the decline of the Roman Empire, a Germanic tribe known as the Franks took control of Gaul by defeating competing tribes. The "land of Francia," from which France gets its name, had high points of expansion under kings Clovis I and Charlemagne. In the Middle Ages, rivalries with England and the Holy Roman Empire prompted major conflicts such as the Norman Conquest and the Hundred Years' War. With an increasingly centralized monarchy, the first standing army since Roman times, and the use of artillery, France expelled the English from its territory and came out of the Middle Ages as the most powerful nation in Europe, only to lose that status to Spain following defeat in the Italian Wars. The Wars of Religion crippled France in the late 16th century, but a major victory over Spain in the Thirty Years' War made France the most powerful nation on the continent once more. In parallel, France developed its first colonial empire in Asia, Africa, and in the Americas. Under Louis XIV, France achieved military supremacy over its rivals, but escalating conflicts against increasingly powerful enemy coalitions checked French ambitions and left the kingdom bankrupt at the opening of the 18th century.

Resurgent French armies secured victories in dynastic conflicts against the Spanish, Polish, and Austrian crowns. At the same time, France was fending off attacks on its colonies. As the 18th century advanced, global competition with Great Britain led to the Seven Years' War, where France lost its North American holdings. Consolation came in the form of dominance in Europe and the American Revolutionary War, where extensive French aid in the form of money and arms, and the direct participation of its army and navy led to America's independence.[2] Internal political upheaval eventually led to 23 years of nearly continuous conflict in the French Revolutionary Wars and the Napoleonic Wars. France reached the zenith of its power during this period, dominating the European continent in an unprecedented fashion under Napoleon Bonaparte, but by 1815 it had been restored to its pre-Revolutionary borders. The rest of the 19th century witnessed the growth of the Second French colonial empire as well as French interventions in Belgium, Spain, and Mexico. Other major wars were fought against Russia in the Crimea, Austria in Italy, and Prussia within France itself.

Following defeat in the Franco-Prussian War, Franco-German rivalry erupted again in the First World War. France and its allies were victorious this time. Social, political, and economic upheaval in the wake of the conflict led to the Second World War, in which the Allies were defeated in the Battle of France and the French government surrendered and was replaced with an authoritarian regime. The Allies, including the government in exile's Free French Forces and later a liberated French nation, eventually emerged victorious over the Axis powers. As a result, France secured an occupation zone in Germany and a permanent seat on the United Nations Security Council. The imperative of avoiding a third Franco-German conflict on the scale of those of two world wars paved the way for European integration starting in the 1950s. France became a nuclear power and since the 1990s its military action is most often seen in cooperation with NATO and its European partners.

International stance today

Today, French military doctrine is based on the concepts of national independence, nuclear deterrence (*see Force de frappe*), and military self-sufficiency. France is a charter member of NATO, and has worked actively with its allies to adapt NATO—internally and externally—to the post-Cold War environment. In December 1995, France announced that it would increase its participation in NATO's military wing, including the Military Committee (France withdrew from NATO's military bodies in 1966 whilst remaining full participants in the Organisation's political Councils). France remains a firm supporter of the Organisation for Security and Co-operation in Europe and other cooperative efforts. Paris hosted the May 1997 NATO-Russia Summit which sought the signing of the Founding Act on Mutual Relations, Cooperation and Security. Outside of NATO, France has actively and heavily participated in both coalition and unilateral peacekeeping efforts in Africa, the Middle East, and the Balkans, frequently taking a lead role in these operations. France has undertaken a major restructuring to develop a professional military that will be smaller, more rapidly deployable, and better tailored for operations outside of mainland France. Key elements of the restructuring include: reducing personnel, bases and headquarters, and rationalistion of equipment and the armaments industry.

Since the end of the Cold War, France has placed a high priority on arms control and non-proliferation. French Nuclear testing in the Pacific, and the sinking of the *Rainbow Warrior* strained French relations with its Allies, South Pacific states (namely New Zealand), and world opinion. France agreed to the Nuclear Non-Proliferation Treaty in 1992 and supported its indefinite extension in 1995. After conducting a controversial final series of six nuclear tests on Mururoa in the South Pacific, the French signed the Comprehensive Test Ban Treaty in 1996. Since then, France has implemented a moratorium on the production, export, and use of anti-personnel landmines and supports negotiations leading toward a universal ban. The French are key players in the adaptation of the Treaty on Conventional Armed Forces in Europe to the new strategic environment. France remains an active participant in: the major programs to restrict the transfer of technologies that could lead to the proliferation of weapons of mass destruction: the Nuclear Suppliers Group, the Australia Group (for chemical and biological weapons), and the Missile Technology Control Regime. France has also signed and ratified the Chemical Weapons Convention.

2008 White Paper

On 31 July 2007, President Nicolas Sarkozy ordered M. Jean-Claude Mallet, a member of the Council of State, to head up a thirty-five member commission charged with a wide-ranging review of French defence. The commission issued its White Paper in early 2008.[3] Acting upon its recommendations, President Sarkozy began making radical changes in French defense policy and structures starting in the summer of 2008. In keeping with post-Cold War changes in European politics and power structures, the French military's traditional focus on territorial defence will be redirected to meet the challenges of a global threat environment. Under the reorganisation, the identification and destruction of terrorist networks both in metropolitan France and in francophone Africa will be the primary task of the French military. Redundant military bases will be closed and new weapons systems projects put on hold to finance the restructuring and global deployment of intervention forces. In

Figure 2:
France
French military interventions since 2001: Afghanistan; Ivory Coast; Chad; Libya; Somalia; Mali; Central African Republic; Syria; Iraq.

a historic change, Sarkozy furthermore has declared that France "will now participate fully in NATO," four decades after former French president General Charles de Gaulle withdrew from the alliance's command structure and ordered American troops off French soil.[4]

Recent operations

There are currently 36,000 French troops deployed in foreign territories—such operations are known as "OPEX" for *Opérations Extérieures* ("External Operations"). Among other countries, France provides troops for the United Nations force stationed in Haiti following the 2004 Haiti rebellion. France has sent troops, especially special forces, into Afghanistan to help the United States and NATO forces fight the remains of the Taliban and Al Qaeda. In Opération Licorne a force of a few thousand French soldiers is stationed in Ivory Coast on a UN peacekeeping mission. These troops were initially sent under the terms of a mutual protection pact between France and the Ivory Coast, but the mission has since evolved into the current UN peacekeeping operation. The French Armed Forces have also played a leading role in the ongoing UN peacekeeping mission along the Lebanon-Israel border as part of the cease-fire agreement that brought the 2006 Lebanon War to an end. Currently, France has 2,000 army personnel deployed along the border, including infantry, armour, artillery and air defence. There are also naval and air personnel deployed offshore.

The French Joint Force and Training Headquarters (État-Major Interarmées de Force et d'Entraînement) at Air Base 110 near Creil maintains the ability to command a medium or large-scale international operation, and runs exercises. In 2011, from 19 March, France participated in the enforcement of a no-fly zone over northern Libya, during the Libyan Civil war, in order to prevent forces loyal to Muammar Gaddafi from carrying out air attacks on Anti-Gaddafi forces. This operation was known as Opération Harmattan and was part of France's involvement in the conflict in the NATO-led coalition, enforcing UN Security Council Resolution 1973. On 11 January 2013 France begun Operation Serval to fight Islamists in Mali with African support but without NATO involvement.

2013 White Paper

In May 2014, high ranking defence chiefs of the French Armed Forces threatened to resign if the defence budget received further cuts on top of those already announced in the 2013 White Paper. They warned that further cuts would leave the armed forces unable to support operations abroad.

Personnel

The head of the French armed forces is the President of the Republic, in his role as *chef des armées*. However, the Constitution puts civil and military government forces at the disposal of the *gouvernement* (the executive cabinet of ministers chaired by the Prime Minister, who are not necessarily of the same political side as the president). The Minister of the Armed Forces (as of 2017, the incumbent Florence Parly) oversees the military's funding, procurement and operations. Historically, France relied a great deal on conscription to provide manpower for its military, in addition to a minority of professional career soldiers. Following the Algerian War, the use of non-volunteer draftees in foreign operations was ended; if their unit was called up for duty in war zones, draftees were offered the choice between requesting a transfer to another unit or volunteering for the active mission. In 1996, President Jacques Chirac's government announced the end of conscription and in 2001, conscription formally was ended. Young people must still, however, register for possible conscription (should the situation call for it). As of 2017 the French Armed Forces have a reported strength of 265,458 active personnel.

It breaks down as follows (2015):

- The French Army; 111,628 personnel.
- The French Air Force; 43,597 personnel.
- The French Navy; 36,044 personnel.
- Tri-service DHS, SEA, and DGA; 17,647 personnel in medical, support and administrative roles, and in the acquisition of weapon systems.

Figure 3: *AMX 56 Leclerc Tank of Armée de terre.*

The reserve element of the French Armed Forces consists of two structures; the Operational Reserve and the Citizens Reserve. As of 2015 the strength of the Operational Reserve is 27,785 personnel.

Apart from the three main service branches, the French Armed Forces also includes a fourth paramilitary branch called the National Gendarmerie. It had a reported strength of 98,155 personnel in 2011.[5] They are used in everyday law enforcement, and also form a coast guard formation under the command of the French Navy. There are however some elements of the Gendarmerie that participate in French external operations, providing specialised law enforcement and supporting roles.

Historically the National Guard functioned as the Army's reserve national defense and law enforcement militia. After 145 years since its disbandment, due to the risk of terrorist attacks in the country, the Guard was officially reactivated, this time as a service branch of the Armed Forces, on 12 October 2016.

Organisation and service branches

The French armed forces are divided into five service branches:

Figure 4: *The Charles de Gaulle, the nuclear aircraft carrier of Marine nationale.*

French Army (*Armée de terre*)

- Special Forces
- Airborne Units
- Infantry (*Infanterie*)
- Armoured Cavalry (*Arme blindée cavalerie*)
- Artillery (*Artillerie*)
- French Foreign Legion (*Légion étrangère*)
- Troupes de Marine
- French Army Light Aviation (*Aviation légére de l'armée de terre, ALAT*)
- Engineers (*Génie*)
- Paris Fire Brigade (brigade des sapeurs-pompiers de Paris)
- Signals (*Transmissions*)
- Transport and logistics (*Train*)
- Supply (*Matériel*)
- Intelligence (*Renseignement*)

French Navy (*Marine nationale*)

- Parachute Units of the French Navy
    - Naval Infantry and Naval Commandos (*Fusiliers Marins*)
- Naval Air Arm (*Aviation navale*)

Figure 5: *Dassault Rafale of Armée de l'Air.*

- Submarine Force (*Forces sous-marines*)
- Naval Action Force (*Force d'action navale*)
- The Marseille Marine Fire Battalion

In addition, the National Gendarmerie form a Coast Guard force called the Gendarmerie Maritime which is commanded by the French Navy.

French Air Force (*Armée de l'Air*)

- Parachute Units of the French Air Force
  - Air force ground troops (*Fusiliers Commandos de l'Air*)
  - Paratroopers/Special forces (*Commando parachutiste de l'air*)
- Territorial Air Defence

National Gendarmerie (*Gendarmerie nationale*)

- Parachute Units of the National Gendarmerie
- Gendarmerie Départementale (GD) - Is a territorial police force.
- Gendarmerie Mobile (GM) - Is an anti-riot unit and counter-terrorism group (GIGN).
- Garde républicaine - Is the republican guard of France.
- Gendarmerie des Transports Aériens - Is an airport security force.
- Gendarmerie de l'Air - Used for Air Force security.
- Gendarmerie Maritime - Is a coast guard unit.
- Provost Gendarmerie - Provides military police services to French Armed Forces personnel in deployments outside France.

The National Gendarmerie is primarily a military and airborne capable police force which serves as a rural and general purpose police force.

National Guard (*Garde nationale*)

Reactivated in 2016, the National Guard serves as the official primary military and police reserve service of the Armed Forces. It also doubles as a force multiplier for law enforcement personnel during contingencies and to reinforce military personnel whenever being deployed within France and abroad.

External links

- Official site of the French Ministry of Defence[6]
- French Military Strategy and NATO Reintegration[7]—Council on Foreign Relations
- French Army rank insignia[8]

History

Military history of France

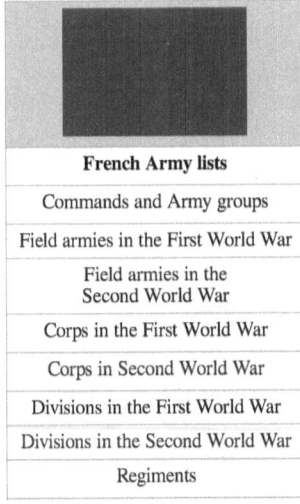

French Army lists
Commands and Army groups
Field armies in the First World War
Field armies in the Second World War
Corps in the First World War
Corps in Second World War
Divisions in the First World War
Divisions in the Second World War
Regiments

The **military history of France** encompasses an immense panorama of conflicts and struggles extending for more than 2,000 years across areas including modern France, the European continent, and a variety of regions throughout the world.

According to historian Niall Ferguson: "of the 125 major European wars fought since 1495, the French have participated in 50 – more than Austria (47) and England (43). Out of 168 battles fought since 387BC, they have won 109, lost 49 and drawn 10."

The first major recorded wars in the territory of modern-day France itself revolved around the Gallo-Roman conflict that predominated from 60 BC to 50 BC. The Romans eventually emerged victorious through the campaigns of

Figure 6: *In July 1453, a French army crushed its English opponents at the Battle of Castillon, the last major engagement of the Hundred Years War. The decisive victory at Castillon showcased the power of artillery against charging masses of infantry and allowed the French to capture Bordeaux a few months later. The English subsequently lost their major remaining possessions on the European continent.*

Julius Caesar. After the decline of the Roman Empire, a Germanic tribe known as the Franks took control of Gaul by defeating competing tribes. The "land of Francia," from which France gets its name, had high points of expansion under kings Clovis I and Charlemagne, who established the nucleus of the future French state. In the Middle Ages, rivalries with England prompted major conflicts such as the Norman Conquest and the Hundred Years' War. With an increasingly centralized monarchy, the first standing army since Roman times, and the use of artillery, France expelled the English from its territory and came out of the Middle Ages as the most powerful nation in Europe, only to lose that status to the Holy Roman Empire and Spain following defeat in the Italian Wars. The Wars of Religion crippled France in the late 16th century, but a major victory over Spain in the Thirty Years' War made France the most powerful nation on the continent once more. In parallel, France developed its first colonial empire in Asia, Africa, and in the Americas. Under Louis XIV France achieved military supremacy over its rivals, but escalating conflicts against increasingly powerful enemy coalitions checked French ambitions and left the kingdom bankrupt at the opening of the 18th century.

Resurgent French armies secured victories in dynastic conflicts against the Spanish, Polish, and Austrian crowns. At the same time, France was fending off attacks on its colonies. As the 18th century advanced, global competition with Great Britain led to the Seven Years' War, where France lost its North American holdings. Consolation came in the form of dominance in Europe and the American Revolutionary War, where extensive French aid in the form of money and arms, and the direct participation of its army and navy led to America's independence.[9] Internal political upheaval eventually led to 23 years of nearly continuous conflict in the French Revolutionary Wars and the Napoleonic Wars. France reached the zenith of its power during this period, dominating the European continent in an unprecedented fashion under Napoleon Bonaparte. By 1815, however, it had been restored to the same borders it controlled before the Revolution. The rest of the 19th century witnessed the growth of the Second French colonial empire as well as French interventions in Belgium, Spain, and Mexico. Other major wars were fought against Russia in the Crimea, Austria in Italy, and Prussia within France itself.

Following defeat in the Franco-Prussian War, Franco–German rivalry erupted again in the First World War. France and its allies were victorious this time. Social, political, and economic upheaval in the wake of the conflict led to the Second World War, in which the Allies were defeated in the Battle of France and the French government signed an armistice with Germany. The Allies, including the Free French Forces led by a government in exile, eventually emerged victorious over the Axis Powers. As a result, France secured an occupation zone in Germany and a permanent seat on the United Nations Security Council. The imperative of avoiding a third Franco-German conflict on the scale of the first two world wars paved the way for European integration starting in the 1950s. France became a nuclear power and, since the late 20th century, has cooperated closely with NATO and its European partners.

Dominant themes

In the last few centuries, French strategic thinking has sometimes been driven by the need to attain or preserve the so-called "natural frontiers," which are the Pyrenees to the southwest, the Alps to the southeast, and the Rhine River to the east.[10] Starting with Clovis, 1,500 years of warfare and diplomacy has witnessed the accomplishment of most of these objectives. Warfare with other European powers was not always determined by these considerations, and often rulers of France extended their continental authority far beyond these barriers, most notably under Charlemagne, Louis XIV, and Napoleon.[11] These periods of incessant conflict were characterized by their own standards and

Figure 7: *Animated map of French territory in continental Europe over time. After centuries of warfare and diplomacy, France has the largest territory of any nation in Western Europe.*

conventions, but all required strong central leadership in order to permit the extension of French rule.[12] Important military rivalries in human history have come about as a result of conflict between French peoples and other European powers. Anglo-French rivalry, for prestige in Europe and around the world, continued for centuries, while the more recent Franco-German rivalry required two world wars to stabilize.[13]

Starting in the early 16th century, much of France's military efforts were dedicated to securing its overseas possessions and putting down dissent among both French colonists and native populations. French troops were spread all across its empire, primarily to deal with the local population. The French colonial empire ultimately disintegrated after the failed attempt to subdue Algerian nationalists in the late 1950s, a failure that led to the collapse of the Fourth Republic.[14] Since World War II, France's efforts have been directed at maintaining its status as a great power and its influence on the UN Security Council. France has also been instrumental in attempting to unite the armed forces of Europe for their own defense in order to both balance the power of Russia and to lessen European military dependence on the United States. For example, France withdrew from NATO in 1966 over complaints that its role in the organization was being subordinated to the demands of the United States.[15]

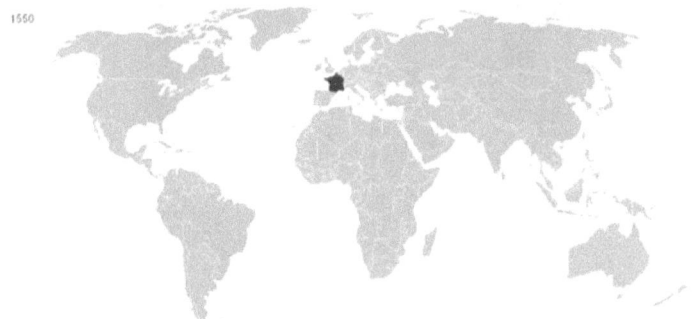

Figure 8: *Animated map showing growth and decline of the French colonial empire.*

French objectives in this era have undergone major shifts. Unencumbered by continental wars or intricate alliances, France now deploys its military forces as part of international peacekeeping operations, security enforcers in former colonies, or maintains them combat ready and mobilized to respond to threats from rogue states. France is a nuclear power with the largest nuclear arsenal in Europe, and its nuclear capabilities, just like its conventional forces, have been restructured to rapidly deal with emerging threats.[16]

Early period

Around 390 BC, the Gallic chieftain Brennus made his own way through the Alps, defeated the Romans in the Battle of the Allia and sacked Rome for several months. The Gallic invasion left Rome weakened and encouraged several subdued Italian tribes to rebel. One by one, over the course of the next 50 years, these tribes were defeated and brought back under Roman dominion. Meanwhile, the Gauls would continue to harass the region until 345 BC, when they entered into a formal treaty with Rome. But Romans and Gauls would maintain an adversarial relationship for the next several centuries and the Gauls would remain a threat in Italia.

Around 125 BC, the south of France is conquered by the Romans who called this region *Provincia Romana* ("Roman Province"), which evolved into the name Provence in French. Brennus' sack of Rome was still remembered by Romans, when Julius Caesar conquered the remainder of Gaul. Initially Caesar met with little Gallic resistance: the 60 or so tribes that made up Gaul were unable to unite and defeat the Roman army, something Caesar exploited by pitting one tribe against another. In 58 BC, Caesar defeated the Germanic tribe of the Suebi, which was led by Ariovistus. The following year he conquered

Figure 9: *Brennus and the sack of Rome as imagined in the 19th century*

the Belgian Gauls after claiming that they were conspiring against Rome. The string of victories continued in a naval triumph against the Veneti in 56 BC. In 53 BC, a united Gallic resistance movement under Vercingetorix emerged for the first time. Caesar laid siege to the fortified city of Avaricum (Bourges) and broke through the defenses after 25 days, with only 800 out of the 40,000 inhabitants managing to escape.[17] He then besieged Gergovia, Vercingetorix's home town, and suffered one of the worst defeats in his career when he had to retreat to suppress a revolt in another part of Gaul. After returning, Caesar surrounded Vercingetorix at Alesia in 52 BC. The townspeople were starved into submission and Caesar's unique defensive earthworks, protruding towards the city and away from it in order to stop a massive Gallic relief force,[18] eventually forced Vercingetorix to surrender. The Gallic Wars were over.

Gallo-Roman culture settled over the region in the next few centuries, but as Roman power weakened in the 4th and 5th centuries AD, a Germanic tribe, the Franks, overran large areas that today form modern France. Under King Clovis I in the late 5th and early 6th centuries, Frankish dominions quadrupled as they managed to defeat successive opponents for control of Gaul. In 486 the Frankish armies under Clovis triumphed over Syagrius, the last Roman official in Northern Gaul, at the Battle of Soissons.[19] In 491 Clovis defeated Thuringians east of his territories. In 496 he overcame the Alamanni at the Battle of Tolbiac. In 507 he scored the most impressive victory in his career,

Figure 10: *Frankish expansion from the early Clovis I' kingdom (481) to the divisions of Charlemagne's Empire (843/870).*

prevailing at the Battle of Vouillé against the Visigoths, who were led by Alaric II, the conqueror of Spain.[20]

Following Clovis, territorial divisions in the Frankish domain sparked intense rivalry between the western part of the kingdom, Neustria, and the eastern part, Austrasia. The two were sometimes united under one king, but from the 6th to the 8th centuries they often warred against each other. Early in the 8th century, the Franks were preoccupied with Islamic invasions across the Pyrenees and up the Rhone Valley. Two key battles during this period were the Battle of Toulouse and the Battle of Tours, both won by the Franks, and both instrumental in slowing Islamic incursions.

Under Charlemagne the Franks reached the height of their power. After campaigns against Lombards, Avars, Saxons, and Basques, the resulting Carolingian Empire stretched from the Pyrenees to Central Germany, from the North Sea to the Adriatic. In 800 the Pope made Charlemagne Emperor of the West in return for protection of the Church. The Carolingian Empire was a conscious effort to recreate a central administration modeled on that of the Roman Empire,[21] but the motivations behind military expansion differed. Charlemagne hoped to provide his nobles an incentive to fight by encouraging looting on campaign. Plunder and spoils of war were stronger temptations than imperial expansion, and several regions were invaded over and over in order

Figure 11: *A section of the Bayeux Tapestry chronicling the Norman victory at Hastings.*

to bolster the coffers of Frankish nobility.[22] Cavalry dominated the battlefields, and while the high costs associated with equipping horses and horseriders helped limit their numbers, Carolingian armies maintained an average size of 20,000 by recruiting infantry from imperial territories near theaters of operation.[23] The Empire lasted from 800 to 843, when, following Frankish tradition, it was split between the sons of Louis the Pious by the Treaty of Verdun.

Middle Ages

Military history during this period paralleled the rise and eventual fall of the armored knight. Following Charlemagne, there was a great increase in the proportion of cavalry supplemented by improvement in armor: leather and steel, steel helmets, coats of mail, and even full armor added to the defensive capabilities of mounted forces.[24] Cavalry eventually grew to be the most important component of armies from French territories,[25] with the shock charge they provided becoming the standard tactic on the battlefield when it was invented in the 11th century.[26] At the same time, the development of agricultural techniques allowed the nations of Western Europe to radically increase

Figure 12: *Castles were the most important defensive structures during the Middle Ages, making them a valuable target for any invading army.*

food production, facilitating the growth of a particularly large aristocracy under Capetian France. The rise of castles, which began in France during the 10th century, was partly caused by the inability of centralized authorities to control these emerging dukes and aristocrats.[27] After campaigns designed for plundering, attacking and defending castles became the dominant feature of medieval warfare.[28]

During the Crusades, there were in fact too many armored knights in France for the land to support. Some scholars believe that one of the driving forces behind the Crusades was an attempt by such landless knights to find land overseas, without causing the type of internecine warfare that would largely damage France's increasing military strength.[29] However, such historiographical work on the Crusades is being challenged and rejected by a large part of the historical community. The ultimate motivation or motivations for any one individual are difficult to know, but regardless, nobles and knights from France generally formed very sizeable contingents of crusading expeditions.[30] Crusaders were so predominantely French that the word "crusader" in the Arabic language is simply known as *Al-Franj* or "The Franks" and Old French became the lingua franca of the Kingdom of Jerusalem.

In the 11th century, French knights wore knee-length mail and carried long lances and swords. The Norman knights fielded at the Battle of Hastings were

Figure 13: *The advent of artillery, like these bombards at the Mont-Saint-Michel, greatly changed the techniques of warfare in the late Middle Ages.*

more than a match for English forces, and their victory simply cemented their power and influence. Between 1202 and 1343, France reduced England's holdings on the continent to a few small provinces through a series of conflicts including the Bouvines Campaign (1202-1214), the Saintonge War (1242) and the War of Saint-Sardos (1324). Improvements in armor over the centuries led to the establishment of plate armor by the 14th century, which was further developed more rigorously in the 15th century.[31] However, by the late 14th century and the early 15th century, French military power declined during the first part of the Hundred Years' War. New weapons, including artillery, and tactics seemingly made the knight more of a sitting target than an effective battle force, but the often-praised longbowmen had little to do with the English success.[32] Poor coordination or rough terrain led to bungled French assaults.[33] The slaughter of knights at the Battle of Agincourt best exemplified this carnage. The French were able to field a much larger army of men-at-arms than their English counterparts, who had many longbowmen. Despite this, the French suffered about 6,000 casualties[34] compared to a few hundred for the English because the narrow terrain prevented the tactical envelopments envisioned in recently discovered French plans for the battle.[35] The French suffered a similar defeat at the Battle of the Golden Spurs against Flemish militia in 1302. When knights were allowed to effectively deploy, however, they could be more useful, as at Cassel in 1328 or, even more decisively, at Bouvines in 1214 and Patay in 1429.

Figure 14: *Francis I at the Battle of Marignan (1515).*

Popular conceptions of the final stages of the Hundred Years War are often dominated by the exploits of Joan of Arc, but French resurgence was rooted in multiple factors. A major step was taken by King Charles VII, who created the *Compagnies d'ordonnance*—cavalry units with 20 companies of 600 men each[36]—and launched the first standing army for a dynastic state in the Western world.[37] The *Compagnies* gave the French a considerable edge in professionalism and discipline. Strong French counterattacks turned the tide of the war. The important victories of Orléans, Patay, Formigny and Castillon allowed the French to win back all English continental territories, except Calais, which was later captured by the French.

Ancien Régime

The French Renaissance and the beginning of the *Ancien Régime*, normally marked by the reign of Francis I, saw the nation become far more unified under the monarch. The power of the nobles was diminished as a national army was created. With England expelled from the continent and being consumed by the Wars of the Roses, France's main rival was the Holy Roman Empire. This threat to France became alarming in 1516 when Charles V became the king of Spain, and grew worse when Charles was also elected Holy Roman Emperor in 1519. France was all but surrounded as Germany, Spain,

Figure 15: *The Battle of Rocroi in (1643).*

and the Low Countries were controlled by the Habsburgs. The lengthy Italian Wars that took place during this period resulted in defeat for France and established Catholic Spain, which formed a branch of the Habsburg holdings, as the most powerful nation in Europe. Later in the 16th century, France was weakened internally by the Wars of Religion. As nobles managed to raise their own private armies, these conflicts between Huguenots and Catholics all but demolished centralization and monarchical authority, precluding France from remaining a powerful force in European affairs.[38] On the battlefield, the religious conflicts highlighted the influence of the gendarmes, heavy cavalry units that comprised the majority of cavalrymen attached to the main field armies.[39] The pride of the royal cavalry, gendarme companies were often attached to the main royal army in hopes of inflicting a decisive defeat on Huguenot forces, although secondary detachments were also used for scouting and intercepting enemy troops.[40]

After the Wars of Religion, France could do little to challenge the dominance of the Holy Roman Empire, although the empire itself faced several problems. From the east it was severely endangered by the Ottoman Empire, with which France formed an alliance.[41] The vast Habsburg empire also proved impossible to manage effectively, and the crown was soon divided between the Spanish and Austrian holdings. In 1568, the Dutch declared independence, launching

Figure 16: *The Battle of Fontenoy (1745), during the War of the Austrian Succession.*

a war that would last for decades and would illustrate the weaknesses of Habsburg power. In the 17th century, the religious violence that had beset France a century earlier began to tear the empire apart. At first France sat on the sidelines, but under Cardinal Richelieu it saw an opportunity to advance its own interests at the expense of the Habsburgs. Despite France's staunch Catholicism, it intervened on the side of the Protestants. The Thirty Years' War was long and extremely bloody, but France and its allies came out victorious. After their victory, France emerged as the sole dominant European power under the reign of Louis XIV. In parallel, French explorers, such as Jacques Cartier or Samuel de Champlain, claimed lands in the Americas for France, paving the way for the expansion of the French colonial empire.

The long reign of Louis XIV saw a series of conflicts: the War of Devolution, the Franco-Dutch War, the War of the Reunions, the Nine Years War, and the War of the Spanish Succession. Few of these wars were either clear victories or definite defeats, but French borders expanded steadily anyway. The west bank of the Rhine, much of the Spanish Netherlands, and a good deal of Luxembourg were annexed while the War of the Spanish Succession saw the grandson of Louis placed on the throne of Spain. The French strategic situation, however, changed decisively with the Glorious Revolution in England, which replaced a pro-French king with an enemy of Louis, the Dutch William of Orange. After a period of two centuries seeing only rare hostilities with France, England now became a consistent enemy again, and remained

Figure 17: *Surrender of Lord Cornwallis to French troops (left) and American troops (right), at Yorktown (1781).*

so until the 19th century. To stop French advances, England formed coalitions with several other European powers, most notably the Habsburgs. While these armies had difficulties against the French on land, the British Royal Navy dominated the seas, and France lost many of its colonial holdings. The British economy also became Europe's most powerful, and British money funded the campaigns of their continental allies.

Wars in this era consisted mostly of sieges and movements that were rarely decisive, prompting the French military engineer Vauban to design an intricate network of fortifications for the defense of France.[42] The armies of Louis XIV were some of the most impressive in French history, their quality reflecting militaristic as well political developments. In the mid-17th century, royal power reasserted itself and the army became a tool through which the King could wield authority, replacing older systems of mercenary units and the private forces of recalcitrant nobles.[11] Military administration also made gigantic progress as food supply, clothing, equipment, and armaments were provided in a regularity never before equaled.[43] In fact, the French embedded this standardization by becoming the first army to give their soldiers national uniforms in the 1680s and 1690s.[44]

The 18th century saw France remain the dominant power in Europe, but begin to falter largely because of internal problems. The country engaged in a long

Figure 18: *The armies of the Revolution at Jemappes in 1792. With chaos internally and enemies on the borders, the French were in a jittery state in 1792. By 1797, however, they had exported their ideology (and the army that followed it) to the Low Countries and Northern Italy.*

series of wars, such as the War of the Quadruple Alliance, the War of the Polish Succession, and the War of the Austrian Succession, but these conflicts gained France little. Meanwhile, Britain's power steadily increased, and a new force, Prussia, became a major threat. This change in the balance of power led to the Diplomatic Revolution of 1756, when France and the Habsburgs forged an alliance after centuries of animosity.[45] This alliance proved less than effective in the Seven Years' War, but in the American Revolutionary War, the French helped inflict a major defeat on the British.

Revolutionary France

The French Revolution, true to its name, revolutionized nearly all aspects of French and European life. The powerful sociopolitical forces unleashed by a people seeking liberté, égalité, and fraternité made certain that even warfare was not spared this upheaval. 18th-century armies—with their rigid protocols, static operational strategy, unenthusiastic soldiers, and aristocratic officer classes—underwent massive remodeling as the French monarchy and nobility

Figure 19: *An episode (Battle of Entrames) of the civil war between republicans and royalists during the French Revolutionary Wars*

gave way to liberal assemblies obsessed with external threats. The fundamental shifts in warfare that occurred during the period have prompted scholars to identify the era as the beginning of "modern war".[46]

In 1791 the Legislative Assembly passed the "Drill-Book" legislation, implementing a series of infantry doctrines created by French theorists because of their defeat by the Prussians in the Seven Years' War.[47] The new developments hoped to exploit the intrinsic bravery of the French soldier, made even more powerful by the explosive nationalist forces of the Revolution. The changes also placed a faith on the ordinary soldier that would be completely unacceptable in earlier times; French troops were expected to harass the enemy and remain loyal enough to not desert, a benefit other Ancien Régime armies did not have. Following the declaration of war in 1792, an imposing array of enemies converging on French borders prompted the government in Paris to adopt radical measures. August 23, 1793, would become a historic day in military history; on that date the National Convention called a levée en masse, or mass conscription, for the first time in human history.[48] By summer of the following year, conscription made some 500,000 men available for service and the French began to deal blows to their European enemies.[49]

Armies during the Revolution became noticeably larger than their Holy Roman counterparts, and combined with the new enthusiasm of the troops, the tactical and strategic opportunities became profound. By 1797 the French had defeated the First Coalition, occupied the Low Countries, the west bank of the Rhine, and Northern Italy, objectives which had defied the Valois and Bourbon dynasties for centuries. Unsatisfied with the results, many European powers formed a Second Coalition, but by 1801 this too had been decisively beaten. Another key aspect of French success was the changes wrought in the officer classes. Traditionally, European armies left major command positions to those who could be trusted, namely, the aristocracy. The hectic nature of the French Revolution, however, tore apart France's old army, meaning new men were required to become officers and commanders.[50]

Besides opening a flood of tactical and strategic opportunities, the Revolutionary Wars also laid the foundation for modern military theory. Later authors that wrote about "nations in arms" drew inspiration from the French Revolution, in which dire circumstances seemingly mobilized the entire French nation for war and incorporated nationalism into the fabric of military history.[51] Although the reality of war in the France of 1795 would be different from that in the France of 1915, conceptions and mentalities of war evolved significantly. Clausewitz correctly analyzed the Revolutionary and Napoleonic eras to give posterity a thorough and complete theory of war that emphasized struggles between nations occurring everywhere, from the battlefield to the legislative assemblies, and to the very way that people think.[52] War now emerged as a vast panorama of physical and psychological forces heading for victory or defeat.

See also: List of French Revolutionary wars and battles, French Revolutionary Army

Napoleonic France

The Napoleonic Era saw French power and influence reach immense heights, even though the period of domination was relatively brief. In the century and a half preceding the Revolutionary Era, France had transformed demographic leverage to military and political weight; the French population was 19 million in 1700,[53] but this had grown to over 29 million in 1800, much higher than that of most other European powers.[54] These numbers permitted France to raise armies at a rapid pace should the need arise. Furthermore, military innovations carried out during the Revolution and the Consulate, evidenced by improvements in artillery and cavalry capabilities on top of better army and staff organization, gave the French army a decisive advantage in the initial stages of the Napoleonic Wars. Another ingredient of success was Napoleon Bonaparte himself—intelligent, charismatic, and a military genius, Napoleon

Figure 20: *Napoleon and the Grande Armée receive the surrender of Austrian General Mack after the Battle of Ulm in October 1805. The decisive finale of the Ulm Campaign raised the tally of captured Austrian soldiers to 60,000. With the Austrian army destroyed, Vienna would fall to the French in November.*

Figure 21: *Napoleon I at the battle of Iena (1806) which led to the occupation of Prussia.*

Figure 22: *Napoleonic Empire, 1811. The French Empire is in dark blue while the "Grand Empire" includes areas under French military control (light blue) and the allies of France.*

absorbed the latest military theories of the day and applied them in the battlefield with deadly effect.

Napoleon inherited an army that was based on conscription and used huge masses of poorly trained troops, which could usually be readily replaced.[55] By 1805 the French Army was a truly lethal force, with many in its ranks veterans of the French Revolutionary Wars. Two years of constant drilling for an invasion of England helped to build a well-trained, well-led army. The Imperial Guard served as an example for the rest of the army and consisted of Napoleon's best handpicked soldiers. Napoleon's huge losses suffered during the disastrous Russian campaign would have destroyed any professional commander of the day, but those losses were quickly replaced with new draftees. After Napoleon, nations planned for huge armies with professional leadership and a constant supply of new soldiers, which had huge human costs when improved weapons like the rifled musket replaced the inaccurate muskets of Napoleon's day during the American Civil War.

This large size came at a cost, as the logistics of feeding a huge army made them especially dependent on supplies. Most armies of the day relied on the supply-convoy system established during the Thirty Years' War by Gustavus

Adolphus. This limited mobility, since the soldiers had to wait for the convoys, but it did keep possibly mutinous troops from deserting, and thus helped preserve an army's composure. However, Napoleon's armies were so large that feeding them using the old method proved ineffective, and consequently, French troops were allowed to live off the land. Infused with new concepts of nation and service. Napoleon often attempted to wage decisive, quick campaigns so that he could allow his men to live off the land. The French army did use a convoy system, but it was stocked with very few days worth of food; Napoleon's troops were expected to march quickly, effect a decision on the battlefield, then disperse to feed. For the Russian campaign, the French did store 24 days' worth of food before beginning active operations, but this campaign was the exception, not the rule.[56]

Napoleon's biggest influence in the military sphere was in the conduct of warfare. Weapons and technology remained largely static through the Revolutionary and Napoleonic eras, but 18th-century operational strategy underwent massive restructuring. Sieges became infrequent to the point of near-irrelevance, a new emphasis arose towards the destruction of enemy armies as well as their outmaneuvering, and invasions of enemy territory occurred over broader fronts, thus introducing a plethora of strategic opportunities that made wars costlier and, just as importantly, more decisive.[57] Defeat for a European power now meant much more than losing isolated enclaves. Near-Carthaginian treaties intertwined whole national efforts—social, political, economic, and militaristic—into gargantuan collisions that severely upset international conventions as understood at the time. Napoleon's initial success sowed the seeds for his downfall. Not used to such catastrophic defeats in the rigid power system of 18th-century Europe, many nations found existence under the French yoke difficult, sparking revolts, wars, and general instability that plagued the continent until 1815, when the forces of reaction finally triumphed at the Battle of Waterloo.[58]

> See also: List of Napoleonic wars and battles, History of La Grande Armée

French colonial empire

The history of French colonial imperialism can be divided in two major eras: the first from the early 17th century to the middle of the 18th century, and the second from the early 19th century to the middle of the 20th century. In the first phase of expansion, France concentrated its efforts mainly in North America, the Caribbean and India, setting up commercial ventures that were backed by military force. Following defeat in the Seven Years' War, France

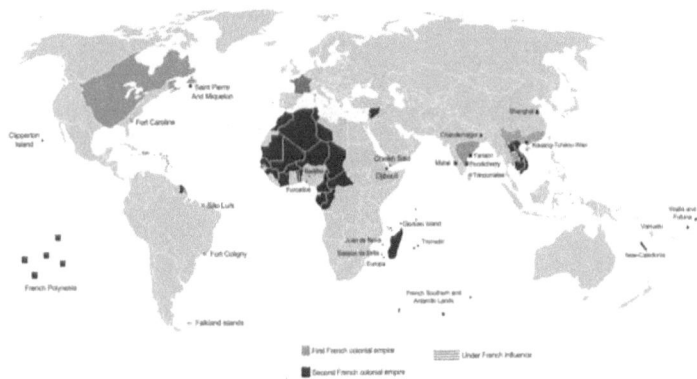

Figure 23: *Map of the first (green) and second (blue) French colonial empires*

lost its possessions in North America and India, but it did manage to keep the wealthy Caribbean islands of Saint-Domingue, Guadeloupe, and Martinique.

The second stage began with the conquest of Algeria in 1830, then with the establishment of French Indochina (covering modern Vietnam, Laos, and Cambodia) and a string of military victories in the Scramble for Africa, where it established control over regions covering much of West Africa, Central Africa and Maghreb. In 1914 France had an empire stretching over 13,000,000 km² (6,000,000 mile²) of land and about 110 million people.[59] Following victory in World War I, Togo and most of Cameroon were also added to the French possessions, and Syria and Lebanon became French mandates. For most of the period from 1870 to 1945, France was territorially the third largest nation on Earth, after Britain and Russia (later the Soviet Union), and had the most overseas possessions following Britain. Following the Second World War, France struggled to preserve French territories but wound up losing the First Indochina War (the precursor to the Vietnam War) and granting independence to Algeria after a long war. Today, France still maintains a number of overseas territories, but their collective size is barely a shadow of the old French colonial empire.

See also: List of French colonial wars and battles, French Colonial Forces, Army of Africa

Figure 24: *French Zouaves during the Franco-Austrian War (1859).*

From 1815

After the exile of Napoleon, the freshly restored Bourbon monarchy helped the absolute Bourbon king of Spain to recover his throne during the French intervention in Spain. To restore the prestige of the French monarchy, disputed by the Revolution and the First Empire, Charles X engaged in the military conquest of Algeria in 1830. This marked the beginning of a new expansion of the French colonial empire throughout the 19th century. In that century, France remained a major force in continental affairs. After the July Revolution, the liberal king Louis Philippe I victoriously supported the Spanish and Belgian liberals. The French later inflicted a defeat on the Habsburgs in the Franco-Austrian War of 1859, a victory which led to the unification of Italy in 1861, after having triumphed over Russia with other allies in the Crimean War. Detrimentally, however, the French army emerged from these victories in an overconfident and complacent state.[60] France's defeat in the Franco-Prussian War led to the loss of Alsace-Lorraine and the creation of a united German Empire, both results representing major failures in long-term French foreign policy and sparking a vengeful, nationalist revanchism meant to earn back former territories.[61] The Dreyfus Affair, however, mitigated these nationalist tendencies by prompting public skepticism about the competence of the military.[62]

Figure 25: *French soldiers in a trench, during the Battle of Verdun (1916).*

First World War

In World War I, the French, with their allies, managed to hold the Western front and to counterattack on the Eastern front and in the colonies until the final defeat of the Central Powers and their allies. After major conflicts such as the Battle of the Frontiers, the First Battle of the Marne, the Battle of Verdun, and the Second Battle of the Aisne—the latter resulting in tremendous loss of life and mutiny within the army—the French proved to be enough of a cohesive fighting force to counterattack and defeat the Germans at the Second Battle of the Marne, the first in what would become a string of Allied victories that ended the war.[63] The Treaty of Versailles eventually returned Alsace-Lorraine to France. The French military, civilian and material losses during the First World War were huge. With more than 1.3 million military fatalities and more than 4.6 million wounded, France suffered the second highest Allied losses, after Russia. As a result, France was adamant on the payment of reparations by Germany. The organised failure of the Weimar Republic to pay reparations led to the Occupation of the Ruhr by French and Belgian forces.

Figure 26: *Free French Foreign Legionnaires at the Battle of Bir Hakeim (1942)*

Second World War

A variety of factors—ranging from inexperienced conscripts and a smaller industrial base to low population growth and obsolete military doctrines—crippled the French effort at the outset of World War II. The Germans won the Battle of France in 1940 despite the French often having better equipment than their opponents. Prior to the Battle of France, there were sentiments among many Allied soldiers, French and British, of pointless repetition; they viewed the war with dread since they had already beaten the Germans once, and images of that first major conflict were still poignant in military circles.[64] The costs of World War I along with the now stale doctrine employed by the French Army (while the Germans were developing a doctrine which stressed initiative from junior commanders and combining different arms, the French sought to minimize casualties through a rigorously controlled type of battle and a top down command structure) forced the French to look for more defensive measures. The Maginot Line was the result of these deliberations: the French originally allocated three billion francs for the project, but by 1935 seven billion had been spent.[65] The Maginot Line succeeded in holding off the German attack.[66] However, while the French thought that the main weight of the German attack would arrive through central Belgium, and accordingly deployed their forces here, the assault actually came further south in the Ardennes forest.[67] The Third Republic collapsed in the ensuing conflict.

Figure 27: *An ERC 90 Sagaie of the 1st Parachute Hussar Regiment in Côte d'Ivoire in 2003.*

After the defeat, Vichy France cooperated with the Axis powers until 1944. While Charles de Gaulle exhorted the French people to join the allied armies, French Vichy forces participated in direct action against Allied forces, inflicting casualties in some cases. The Normandy landings in that year were the first step towards the eventual liberation of France. The Free French Forces, under de Gaulle, had participated widely throughout previous campaigns, and their large size made them notable at the end of the war. As early as the winter of 1943, the French already had nearly 260,000 soldiers,[68] and these numbers only grew as the war progressed. At the end of the conflict, France was given one of four occupation zones in Germany and in Berlin and Austria.

Post-1945 warfare

Following the 1939–45 war, decolonization spread through the former European empires.

Following the First Indochina War, they withdrew from Vietnam, Laos and Cambodia. The military also tried to keep control of Algeria during the Algerian War, when French forces attempted to defeat the Algerian rebels. Despite its military victory, France granted independence to Algerians. French Algeria was home to over a million of settlers (known as Pieds-Noirs), de Gaulle's decision to grant independence to Algeria, almost led to a civil war, supported by various Pied-Noir, Harki and nationalist factions, including the FAF and the OAS.

By 1960 France had lost its direct military influence over all of its former colonies in Africa and Indochina. Nonetheless, several colonies in the Pacific, Caribbean, Indian Oceans and South America remain French territory to this day and France kept a form of indirect political influence in Africa colloquially known as the *Françafrique*.

As President of the French Republic, Charles de Gaulle oversaw the development of French atomic weapons and promoted a foreign policy independent of U.S. influence. He also withdrew France from the NATO military command in 1966—although remaining a member of the western alliance. The effect of withdrawal was reduced by continued cooperation between the French military and NATO, though France did not formally rejoin the NATO military command until 2009.

France intervened in various post-colonial conflicts, supporting former colonies (Western Sahara War, Shaba II, Chadian–Libyan conflict, Djiboutian Civil War), NATO peacekeeping missions in war-torn countries (UNPROFOR, KFOR, UNAMIR) and many humanitarian missions.

As a nuclear power and having some of the best trained and best equipped forces in the world, the French military has now met some of its primary objectives which are the defense of national territory, the protection of French interests abroad, and the maintenance of global stability. Conflicts indicative of these objectives are the Gulf War in 1991—when France sent 18,000 troops, 60 combat aircraft, 120 helicopters, and 40 tanks[69]—and Mission Héraclès in the War in Afghanistan, along with recent interventions in Africa.

African interventions during the early 21st century include peacekeeping actions in Côte d'Ivoire, which involved brief direct fighting between the French and Ivorian armies in 2004; French forces returned to Côte d'Ivoire in 2011 to remove the Ivorian president. In the same year, France played a pivotal role in the 2011 military intervention in Libya against Muammar Gaddafi. The year after, France intervened in Mali during that country's civil war, as Islamist militants appeared to threaten the south after seizing control of the arid north. Changes in the government of France, including Socialist François Hollande becoming president in 2012 after years of center-right governance, have done little to alter Paris' foreign policy in Africa.

Hollande also proposed French military involvement in the Syrian civil war in the wake of chemical attacks French intelligence reports linked to the forces of President Bashar al-Assad in mid-2013.

France has encouraged military cooperation at an EU level, starting with the formation of the Franco-German Brigade in 1987 and Eurocorps in 1992, based in Strasbourg. In 2009 a battalion of German light infantry was moved to Alsace, the first time German troops had been stationed in France since the Nazi occupation of World War II. This process has not been immune to budget cuts – in October 2013 France announced the closure of her last infantry regiment in Germany, thus marking the end of a major presence across the Rhine although both countries will maintain around 500 troops on each other's territory. As fellow members of the UN Security Council with many interests and problems in common, the UK and France have a long history of bilateral collaboration. This has occurred both at government level and in industrial programmes like the SEPECAT Jaguar whilst corporate mergers have seen Thales and MBDA emerge as major defence companies spanning both countries. The financial crisis of 2007–08 led to renewed pressure on military budgets and the "austerity alliance" enshrined in the Lancaster House Treaties of 2010. These promised close integration in both procurement and at an operational level, reaching into the most sensitive areas such as nuclear warheads.

Topical subjects

French Air Force

The Armée de l'Air became one of the first professional air forces in the world when it was founded in 1909. The French took active interest in developing their air force and had the first fighter pilots of World War I. During the interwar years, however, particularly in the 1930s, the technical quality fell when compared with the Luftwaffe, which crushed both the French and British air forces during the Battle of France. In the post–World War II era, the French made a concerted and successful effort to develop a homegrown aircraft industry. Dassault Aviation led the way forward with their unique and effective delta-wing designs, which formed the basis for the famous Mirage series of jet fighters. The Mirage repeatedly demonstrated its deadly abilities in the Six-Day War and the Gulf War, becoming one of the most popular and well-sold aircraft in the history of military aviation along the way.[71] Currently, the French are awaiting the A400M military transport aircraft, which is still in developmental stages, and the integration of the new Rafale multi-role jet fighter, whose first squadron of 20 aircraft became operational in 2006 at Saint-Dizier.[72]

Figure 28: *The Tricolore cockade of the French Air Force was the first roundel used on combat aircraft*[70]

French Navy

Medieval fleets, in France as elsewhere, were almost entirely composed of merchant ships enlisted into naval service in time of war, but the early beginnings of the French naval history goes back to that era. The first battle of the French Navy was the battle of Arnemuiden (23 September 1338), where it defeated the English Navy.[73] The battle of Arnemuiden was also the first naval battle using artillery.[74] It was later defeated by an Anglo-Flemish fleet at the Battle of Sluys and, with Castilian help, managed to beat the English at La Rochelle—both battles playing a crucial role in the development of the Hundred Years War. However, the navy did not become a consistent instrument of national power until the 17th century with Louis XIV. Under the tutelage of the "Sun King," the French Navy was well financed and equipped, managing to resoundingly defeat a combined Spanish-Dutch fleet at the Battle of Palermo in 1676 during the Franco-Dutch War, although, along with the English navy, it suffered several strategic reversals against the Dutch, who were led by the brilliant Michiel de Ruyter. It scored several early victories in the Nine Years War against the Royal Navy and the Dutch Navy. Financial difficulties, however, allowed the English and the Dutch to regain the initiative at sea.

Figure 29: *The French ships engage the British navy (right) in the Battle of Chesapeake.*

Figure 30: *The Charles de Gaulle, the first nuclear-powered aircraft carrier in Europe.*

A perennial problem for the French Navy was the strategic priorities of France, which were first and foremost tied to its European ambitions. This reality meant that the army was often treated better than the navy, and as a result, the latter suffered in training and operational performance.[75] The 18th century saw the beginning of the Royal Navy's domination, which managed to inflict a number of significant defeats on the French. However, in a very impressive effort, a French fleet under de Grasse managed to defeat a British fleet at the Battle of the Chesapeake in 1781, ensuring that the Franco-American ground forces would win the ongoing Siege of Yorktown. Beyond that, and Suffren's impressive campaigns against the British in India, there was not much more good news. The French Revolution all but crippled the French Navy, and efforts to make it into a powerful force under Napoleon were dashed at the Battle of Trafalgar in 1805, where the British all but annihilated a combined Franco-Spanish fleet. The disaster guaranteed British naval domination until the end of the Napoleonic wars.

Later in the 19th century, the navy recovered and became the second finest in the world after the Royal Navy. It conducted a successful blockade of Mexico in the Pastry War of 1838 and obliterated the Chinese navy at the Battle of Foochow in 1884. It also served as an effective link between the growing parts of the French empire. The navy performed well during World War I, in which it mainly protected the naval lanes in the Mediterranean Sea. At the onset of the war, the French—with 16 battleships, 6 cruisers, and 24 destroyers—had the largest fleet in the Mediterranean.[76] French defeats in the early stages of World War II, however, forced the British to destroy the French navy at Mers-el-Kebir in order to prevent its fall to the Germans. Currently, French naval doctrine calls for two aircraft carriers, but the French currently only have one, the *Charles de Gaulle*, due to restructuring. The navy is in the midst of some technological and procurement changes; newer submarines are under construction and Rafale aircraft (the naval version) are currently replacing older aircraft.

French Foreign Legion

The French Foreign Legion was created in 1831 by French king Louis-Philippe. Over the past century and a half, it has gone on to become one of the most recognizable and lauded military units in the world. The Legion had a very difficult start; there were few non-commissioned officers, many of the soldiers could not speak French, and pay was often irregular.[77] The Legion was soon transferred to fight in Algeria, performing moderately successfully given its condition. On August 17, 1835, the commander of the Legion, Colonel Joseph Bernelle, decided to amalgamate all the battalions so that no nationality was exclusively confined to a particular battalion; this helped ensure that the Legion did not fragment into factions.[78]

Figure 31: *Légionnaires in dress uniform. Note the red epaulettes and the distinctive white kepi. They carry the standard assault rifle, the FAMAS.*

Following participation in Africa and in the Carlist Wars in Spain, the Legion fought in the Crimean War and the Franco-Austrian War, where they performed heroically at the Battle of Magenta, before earning even more glory during the French intervention in Mexico. On April 30, 1863, a company of 65 legionnaires was ambushed by 2,000 Mexican troops at the Hacienda Camarón; in the resulting Battle of Camarón, the legionnaires resisted bravely for several hours and inflicted 300–500 casualties on the Mexicans while 62 of them died and three were captured.[79] One of the Mexican commanders, impressed by the memorable intransigence he had just witnessed, characterized the Legion in a way they've been known ever since, "These are not men, but devils!"[80]

In World War I, the Legion demonstrated that it was a highly capable unit in modern warfare. It suffered 11,000 casualties in the Western Front while conducting brilliant defenses and spirited counter-attacks.[81] Following the debacle in the Battle of France in 1940, the Legion was split between those who supported the Vichy government and those who joined the Free French under de Gaulle. At the Battle of Bir Hakeim in 1942, the Free French 13th Legion Demi-Brigade doggedly defended its positions against a combined Italian-German offensive and seriously delayed Rommel's attacks towards Tobruk.

The Legion eventually returned to Europe and fought until the end of the Second World War in 1945. It later fought in the First Indochina War against the Viet Minh. At the climatic Battle of Dien Bien Phu in 1954, French forces, many of them legionnaires, were completely surrounded by a large Vietnamese army and were defeated after two months of tenacious fighting. French withdrawal from Algeria led to the collapse of the French colonial empire. The legionnaires were mostly used in colonial interventions, so the destruction of the empire prompted questions about their status. Ultimately, the Legion was allowed to exist and participated as a rapid reaction force in many places throughout Africa and around the world.[82]

Notes

<templatestyles src="Template:Refbegin/styles.css" />

1. ^ Richard Brooks (editor), *Atlas of World Military History*. p. 101. "*Washington's success in keeping the army together deprived the British of victory, but French intervention won the war.*"
2. ^ William Roosen, *The age of Louis XIV: the rise of modern diplomacy*. p. 55
3. ^ Richard Brooks (editor), *Atlas of World Military History*. pp. 46–7, 84–5, 108–9.
4. ^ Brooks pp. 46–7, 84–5, 108–9.
5. ^ William Thompson, *Great power rivalries*. p. 104
6. ^ Richard Brooks (editor), *Atlas of World Military History*. p. 234
7. ^ Kay, Sean. *NATO and the future of European security*. p. 43
8. ^ Jolyon Howorth and Patricia Chilton, *Defence and dissent in contemporary France*. p. 153
9. ^ Alfred Bradford and Pamela Bradford, *With arrow, sword, and spear: a history of warfare in the ancient world*. p. 213
10. ^ Richard Brooks (editor), *Atlas of World Military History*. p. 31. In De Bello Gallico, Caesar claims a Gallic relief force of 250,000 men, but the logistical requirements for such a huge army were beyond anything the Gauls could procure. It is likely that Caesar inflated the figures to make his victory seem more impressive.
11. ^ Jim Bradbury, *The Routledge companion to medieval warfare*. p. 109
12. ^ Jim Bradbury, *The Routledge companion to medieval warfare*. p. 110
13. ^ Robert Cowley, *What If? Eminent Historians Imagine What Might Have Been*. p. 73, p. 87. The latter page carries an account by historian Edward Gibbon: "*A victorious line of march had been prolonged above a thousand miles from the rock of Gibraltar to the banks of the Loire; the repetition of an equal space would have carried the Saracens to the confines of Poland and the Highlands of Scotland: the Rhine is not more*

impassable than the Nile or Euphrates, and the Arabian fleet might have sailed without a naval combat into the mouth of the Thames. Perhaps the interpretation of the Koran would now be taught in the schools of Oxford, and her pulpits might demonstrate to a circumcised people the sanctity and truth of the revelation of Mahomet."

14. ^ Richard Brooks (editor), *Atlas of World Military History.* p. 43. The above claims seem to be more rhetoric than possible historical reality. No contemporaries viewed the battle as decisive and Arab raids continued for much longer after the Battle of Tours. What is indisputable is the battle's huge symbolic significance, since in one of the first major fights between the Christian West and Islam, the former managed to prevail.
15. ^ J. M. Roberts, *History of the World.* p. 384
16. ^ Brooks, Richard (editor), *Atlas of World Military History.* p. 46
17. ^ Brooks p. 47
18. ^ French Medieval Armies and Navies[83], Xenophon Group. Accessed March 20, 2006
19. ^ French Medieval Armies and Navies[83], Xenophon Group. Accessed March 20, 2006
20. ^ Richard Brooks (editor), *Atlas of World Military History.* p. 53
21. ^ Brooks p. 50
22. ^ Brooks p. 50
23. ^ Andrew Jotischky, *Crusading and the Crusader States.* p. 37. The theory that argues for sociological and economic rather than spiritual motivation provides regional examples where noble fathers would give their lands to the oldest surviving son, meaning younger sons would be left landless and looking for somewhere to go (the Crusades, in this case). Problems with the theory include, but are not limited to, the fact that there is no proof that younger sons formed the majority of the crusaders, the response to the crusading movement was just as strong in areas with equitable inheritance systems, and, since they were in many ways bound to the wishes and the decisions of their nobles, knights often had little individual choice in whether they would participate in a crusade.
24. ^ Jotischky p. 37
25. ^ David Eltis, *The military revolution in sixteenth-century Europe.* p. 12
26. ^ Richard Brooks (editor), *Atlas of World Military History.* p. 59. *"Much has been made of the success of the English longbow. However, it was not a war-winning weapon. Reliance on this defensive weapon on the battlefield gave the initiative to the French.."*
27. ^ Brooks p. 59. (continuing from last comment) *"...its victories also depended on the French bungling their attack. The English were fortunate that their opponent failed to get it right three times in a 70-year period."*
28. ^ Trevor Dupuy, *Harper Encyclopedia of Military History.* p. 450

29. ^ Richard Brooks (editor), *Atlas of World Military History*. p. 59. "*The major defeats of the French by the English boosted French military thought. A recently discovered document of the French battle plan for the Agincourt campaign shows how carefully the French thought about ways of defeating the English. In the event, the plan could not be fully executed because the battlefield at Agincourt was too narrow for the French forces to fully deploy.*"
30. ^ Brooks p. 58
31. ^ French Medieval Armies and Navies[83], Xenophon Group. Accessed March 20, 2006
32. ^ Jeremy Black, *Cambridge illustrated atlas, warfare: Renaissance to revolution, 1492-1792*. p. 49
33. ^ Jeff Kinard, *Artillery: an illustrated history of its impact*. pp. 61–2
34. ^ John A. Lynn, *The Wars of Louis XIV*. p. 8
35. ^ James Wood, *The King's Army*. p. 131
36. ^ Wood p. 132
37. ^ Kemal Karpat, *The Ottoman state and its place in world history*. p. 52
38. ^ Jamel Ostwald, *Vauban under siege*. p. 7
39. ^ John A. Lynn, *Giant of the Grand Siècle: The French Army, 1610–1715*. p. 16 (preface)
40. ^ Lynn p. 16 (preface)
41. ^ Richard Brooks (editor), *Atlas of World Military History*. p. 84
42. ^ Jackson Spielvogel, *Western Civilization: Since 1500*. p. 551
43. ^ Lester Kurtz and Jennifer Turpin, *Encyclopedia of violence, peace and conflict, Volume 2*. p. 425
44. ^ David G. Chandler, *The Campaigns of Napoleon*. p. 136
45. ^ John R. Elting, *Swords Around a Throne: Napoleon's Grande Armée*. p. 35. The opening words are mundane, but they helped pave the way for a new era in human history, one where militarism became entrenched in national culture: "*From this moment until our enemies shall have been driven from the territory of the Republic, all Frenchmen are permanently requisitioned for the service of the armies.*"
46. ^ T. C. W. Blanning, *The French Revolutionary Wars*. p. 109
47. ^ John R. Elting, *Swords Around a Throne: Napoleon's Grande Armée*. p. 28–29. Aristocratic officers deserted gradually, not suddenly. Furthermore, desertion rates depended upon the service: cavalry officers were more likely to leave the army than their artillery counterparts.
48. ^ Parker, Geoffrey. *The Cambridge history of warfare*. p. 189
49. ^ Peter Paret, *Clausewitz and the State*. p. 332
50. ^ John A. Lynn, *The Wars of Louis XIV*. p. 28
51. ^ Martyn Lyons, *Napoleon Bonaparte and the Legacy of the French Revolution*. p. 43. Lyons writes, *France had a large population by Euro-*

pean standards, numbering over 29 million in 1800. This was more than the population of the Habsburg Empire (20 million), more than double the population of England (about 12 million), and more than four times the population of Prussia (6 million).

52. ^ Lester Kurtz and Jennifer Turpin, *Encyclopedia of violence, peace and conflict, Volume 2.* p. 425
53. ^ Lester Kurtz and Jennifer Turpin, *Encyclopedia of violence, peace and conflict, Volume 2.* p. 425
54. ^ David G. Chandler, *The Campaigns of Napoleon.* p. 758
55. ^ Chandler p. 162
56. ^ Todd Fisher & Gregory Fremont-Barnes, *The Napoleonic Wars: The Rise and Fall of an Empire.* p. 186. "*Up to 1792,...conflicts were, of course, those of kings, and followed the pattern of eighteenth-century warfare: sovereigns sought limited objectives and entertained no desire to overthrow their adversaries' ruling (and indeed usually ancient) dynasty. The outbreak of the French Revolution in 1789 altered this pattern forever and international relations underwent some radical changes as a result.*"
57. ^ Conrad Phillip Kottak, *Cultural Anthropology.* p. 331
58. ^ Richard Brooks (editor), *Atlas of World Military History.* p. 129
59. ^ Paul Marie de la Gorce, *The French Army: A Military-Political History* p. 48. Following the Franco-Prussian War and the loss of Alsace-Lorraine, revanchism in French politics made certain that the army was carefully nurtured and well-treated because it was viewed as the only instrument through which France could overcome the humiliations of 1870.
60. ^ de la Gorce p. 48
61. ^ Hew Strachan, *The Oxford Illustrated History of the First World War.* p. 280
62. ^ John Keegan, *The Second World War.* p. 64
63. ^ Keegan p. 61
64. ^ Boyce, *French Foreign and Defence Policy.* p. 185
65. ^ Boyce p. 185
66. ^ F. Roy Willis, *France, Germany, and the New Europe, 1945-1967.* p. 9
67. ^ Charles Hauss, *Politics in France.* p. 194
68. ^ Shlomo Aloni, *Israeli Mirage and Nesher Aces.* p. 6
69. ^ French airforce adds home-grown fighter plane to its arsenal[84] Agence-France Presse. Accessed November 7, 2006
70. ^ Russell Weigley, *The age of battles: the quest for decisive warfare from Breitenfeld to Waterloo.* pp. 158–9
71. ^ Barbara Tuchman, *The Guns of August.* p. 166

72. ^ David Jordan, *The History of the French Foreign Legion*. p. 10
73. ^ Jordan p. 14
74. ^ Byron Farwell, *The encyclopedia of nineteenth-century land warfare*. p. 155
75. ^ David Jordan, *The History of the French Foreign Legion*. p. 34
76. ^ Jordan p. 67
77. ^ Jordan p. 94

Further reading

<templatestyles src="Template:Refbegin/styles.css" />

- Aloni, Shlomo. *Israeli Mirage and Nesher Aces*. Oxford: Osprey Publishing, 2004. ISBN 1-84176-653-4
- Black, Jeremy. *Cambridge illustrated atlas of warfare: Renaissance to revolution, 1492-1792*. Cambridge: Cambridge University Press, 1996. ISBN 0-521-47033-1
- Blanning, T.C.W. *The French Revolutionary Wars*. London: Hodder Headline Group, 1996. ISBN 0-340-56911-5
- Boyce, Robert. *French Foreign and Defence Policy, 1918-1940*. Oxford: CRC Press, 1998. ISBN 0-203-97922-2
- Bradbury, Jim. *The Routledge companion to medieval warfare*. New York: Routledge, 2004. ISBN 0-415-22126-9
- Bradford, Alfred and Pamela. *With arrow, sword, and spear: a history of warfare in the ancient world*. Westport: Greenwood Publishing Group, 2001. ISBN 0-275-95259-2
- Brooks, Richard (editor). *Atlas of World Military History*. London: HarperCollins, 2000. ISBN 0-7607-2025-8
- Chandler, David G. *The Campaigns of Napoleon*. New York: Simon & Schuster, 1995. ISBN 0-02-523660-1
- Chilton, Patricia and Howorth, Jolyon Howorth. *Defence and dissent in contemporary France* Oxford: Taylor & Francis, 1984. ISBN 0-7099-1280-3
- Clayton, Anthony. Paths of glory: the French Army 1914-18. London: Cassell, 2003.
- Cowley, Robert (editor). *What If? Eminent Historians Imagine What Might Have Been*. New York: Penguin Group, 1999. ISBN 0-399-15238-5
- Doughty, Robert A. *Pyrrhic Victory: French Strategy and Operations in the Great War* (2008), 592pp; excerpt and text search[85]
- Dupuy, Trevor N., *Harper Encyclopedia of Military History*. New York: HarperCollins, 1993. ISBN 0-06-270056-1

- Elting, John R. *Swords Around a Throne: Napoleon's Grande Armée*. New York: Da Capo Press Inc., 1988. ISBN 0-306-80757-2
- Eltis, David. *The military revolution in sixteenth-century Europe*. New York: I. B. Tauris, 1998. ISBN 1-86064-352-3
- Farwell, Byron. *The encyclopedia of nineteenth-century land warfare*. New York: W. W. Norton & Company, 2001. ISBN 0-393-04770-9
- Fisher, Todd & Fremont-Barnes, Gregory. *The Napoleonic Wars: The Rise and Fall of an Empire*. Oxford: Osprey Publishing Ltd., 2004. ISBN 1-84176-831-6
- de la Gorce, Paul Marie. *The French Army: A Military-Political History*. New York: George Braziller, Inc., 1963.
- Greenhalgh, Elizabeth. *The French Army and the First World War* (2014), 486 pages; comprehensive scholarly history.
- Hauss, Charles. *Politics in France*. Washington, DC: CQ Press, 2007. ISBN 1-56802-670-6
- Jordan, David. *The History of the French Foreign Legion*. Spellmount Limited, 2005. ISBN 1-86227-295-6
- Jotischky, Andrew. *Crusading and the Crusader States*. Pearson Education Limited, 2004. ISBN 0-582-41851-8
- Karpat, Kemal. *The Ottoman state and its place in world history*. Leiden: BRILL, 1974. ISBN 90-04-03945-7
- Kay, Sean. *NATO and the future of European security*. Lanham: Rowman & Littlefield, 1998. ISBN 0-8476-9001-6
- Keegan, John. *The Second World War*. New York: Penguin Group, 1989. ISBN 0-670-82359-7
- Kinard, Jeff. *Artillery: an illustrated history of its impact*. Santa Barbara: ABC-CLIO, 2007. ISBN 1-85109-556-X
- Kottak, Conrad. *Cultural Anthropology*. Columbus: McGraw-Hill Higher Education, 2005. ISBN 0-07-295250-4
- Kurtz, Lester and Turpin, Jennifer. *Encyclopedia of violence, peace and conflict, Volume 2*. New York: Academic Press, 1999. ISBN 0-12-227010-X
- Lyons, Martyn. *Napoleon Bonaparte and the Legacy of the French Revolution*. New York: St. Martin's Press, Inc., 1994. ISBN 0-312-12123-7
- Lynn, John A. *Giant of the Grand Siècle: The French Army, 1610–1715*. New York: Cambridge University Press, 1997. ISBN 0-521-57273-8
- Lynn, John A. *The Wars of Louis XIV*. London: Longman, 1999. ISBN 0-582-05629-2
- Ostwald, Jamel. *Vauban under siege*. Leiden: BRILL, 2007. ISBN 90-04-15489-2
- Paret, Peter. *Clausewitz and the State*. Princeton: Princeton University Press, 2007. ISBN 0-691-13130-9

- Parker, Geoffrey. *The Cambridge history of warfare*. Cambridge: Cambridge University Press, 2005. ISBN 0-521-85359-1
- Porch, Douglas. *The March to the Marne: The French Army 1871-1914* Cambridge University Press (2003) ISBN 978-0521545921
- Roberts, J.M. *History of the World*. New York: Penguin Group, 1992. ISBN 0-19-521043-3
- Roosen, William . *The age of Louis XIV: the rise of modern diplomacy*. Edison: Transaction Publishers, 1976. ISBN 0-87073-581-0
- Spielvogel, Jackson. *Western Civilization: Since 1500*. Florence: Cengage Learning, 2008. ISBN 0-495-50287-1
- Strachan, Hew. *The Oxford Illustrated History of the First World War*. Oxford: Oxford University Press, 1998. ISBN 0-19-289325-4
- Thompson, William. *Great power rivalries*. Columbia: University of South Carolina Press, 1999. ISBN 1-57003-279-3
- Tuchman W., Barbara. *The Guns of August*. New York: Random House, 1962. ISBN 0-345-38623-X
- Weigley, Russell. *The age of battles: the quest for decisive warfare from Breitenfeld to Waterloo*. Bloomington: Indiana University Press, 2004. ISBN 0-253-21707-5
- Willis, F. Roy. *France, Germany, and the New Europe, 1945-1967*. Palo Alto: Stanford University Press, 1968. ISBN 0-8047-0241-1
- Wood, James. *The King's Army*. Cambridge: Cambridge University Press, 2002. ISBN 0-521-52513-6

Historiography

- Messenger, Charles, ed. *Reader's Guide to Military History* (2001) 948pp; Evaluation of thousands of books on military history, many of them involving France.

In French

- Bertaud, Jean-Paul, and William Serman. *Nouvelle histoire militaire de la France, 1789-1919* (Paris, Fayard: 1998); 855pp

External links

 Wikimedia Commons has media related to *Military of France*.

- French Military Terms Adopted by the English Language[86]
- French military participation from 1800 to 1999[87]
- The French Army: Royal, Revolutionary and Imperial[88]
- An excellent guide to French Medieval warfare[89]
- France in the American Revolution[90]
- French Army from Revolution to the First Empire, Illustrations by [[Hippolyte Bellangé[91]] from the book P.-M. Laurent de L'Ardeche «Histoire de Napoleon», 1843]
- The French Military in Africa[92] (2008) - Council on Foreign Relations

French Army in World War I

This article is about the **French Army in World War I**. During World War I, France was one of the Triple Entente powers allied against the Central Powers. Although fighting occurred worldwide, the bulk of the fighting in Europe occurred in Belgium, Luxembourg, France and Alsace-Lorraine along what came to be known as the Western Front, which consisted mainly of trench warfare. Specific operational, tactical, and strategic decisions by the high command on both sides of the conflict led to shifts in organizational capacity, as the French Army tried to respond to day-to-day fighting and long-term strategic and operational agendas. In particular, many problems caused the French high command to re-evaluate standard procedures, revise its command structures, re-equip the army, and to develop different tactical approaches.

Background

France had been the major power in Europe for most of the Early Modern Era: Louis XIV, in the seventeenth century, and Napoleon I in the nineteenth, had extended French power over most of Europe through skillful diplomacy and military prowess. The Treaty of Vienna in 1815 confirmed France as a European power broker. By the early 1850s, Prussian Chancellor Otto von Bismarck started a system of alliances designed to assert Prussian dominance over Central Europe. Bismarck's diplomatic maneuvering, and France's maladroit response to such crises as the Ems Dispatch and the Hohenzollern Candidature led to the French declaration of war in 1870. France's subsequent

Figure 32: *French poilus (soldiers) posing in a trench, 16 June 1917.*

Figure 33: *French army during the Franco-Prussian War of 1870–71*

defeat in the Franco-Prussian War, including the loss of its army and the capture of its emperor at Sedan, the loss of territory, including Alsace-Lorraine, and the payment of heavy indemnities, left the French seething and placed the reacquisition of lost territory as a primary goal at the end of the 19th century; the defeat also ended French preeminence in Europe. Following German Unification, Bismarck attempted to isolate France diplomatically by befriending Austria–Hungary, Russia, Britain, and Italy.

After 1870, the European powers began gaining settlements in Africa, with colonialism on that continent hitting its peak between 1895 and 1905. However, colonial disputes were only a minor cause of World War I, as most had been settled by 1914. Economic rivalry was not only a source for some of the colonial conflicts but also a minor cause for the start of World War I. For France the rivalry was mostly with the rapidly industrializing Germany, which had seized the coal-rich region of Alsace-Lorraine in 1870, and later struggled with France over mineral-rich Morocco.

Another cause of World War I was growing militarism which led to an arms race between the powers. As a result of the arms race, all European powers were ready for war.

France was bound by treaty to defend Russia. Austria–Hungary had declared war on Serbia due to the Black Hand's assassination of Archduke Ferdinand, which acted as the immediate cause of the war. France was brought into the war by a German declaration of war on August 3, 1914.

The Pre-War Army and mobilization

In common with most other continental European powers, the French Army was organised on the basis of universal conscription. Each year, the "class" of men turning twenty-one in the upcoming year would be inducted into the French Army and spend three years in active service. After leaving active service they would progress through various stages of reserves, each of which involved a lower degree of commitment.

- Active Army (20–23)
- Reserve of the Active Army (24–34)
- Territorial Army (35–41)
- Reserve of the Territorial Army (42–48)

The peacetime army consisted of 173 infantry regiments, 89 cavalry regiments and 87 artillery regiments. All were substantially under strength and would be filled out on mobilization by the first three classes of the Reserve (that is, men between 24 and 26). Each regiment would also leave behind a cadre of training personnel to conduct refresher courses for the older reservists, who

Figure 34: *Photograph shows reservists and crowd at the Gare de Paris-Est, Paris during the beginning of World War I*

were organized into 201 Reserve Regiments and 145 Territorial Regiments. Above the regimental level, France was divided into 22 Military Regions, each of which would become an Army Corps on mobilization.

At the apex of the French Army was the General Staff, since 1911 under the leadership of General Joseph Joffre. The General Staff was responsible for drawing up the plan for mobilization, known as Plan XVII. Using the railroad network, the Army would be shifted from their peacetime garrisons throughout France to the eastern border with Germany.

The order for mobilization was given on 1 August, the same day that Germany declared war on Russia.

Organization during the war

Upon mobilization, Joffre became Commander-in-Chief of the French Army. Most of his forces were concentrated in the north east of France, both to attack Alsace-Lorraine and to meet the expected German offensive through the Low Countries.

- First Army (7th, 8th, 13th, 14th, and 21st Army Corps), with the objective of capturing Mulhouse and Sarrebourg.

French Army in World War I

Figure 35: *French soldiers at the beginning of World War I. They retain the peacetime blue coats and red trousers worn during the early months of the war*

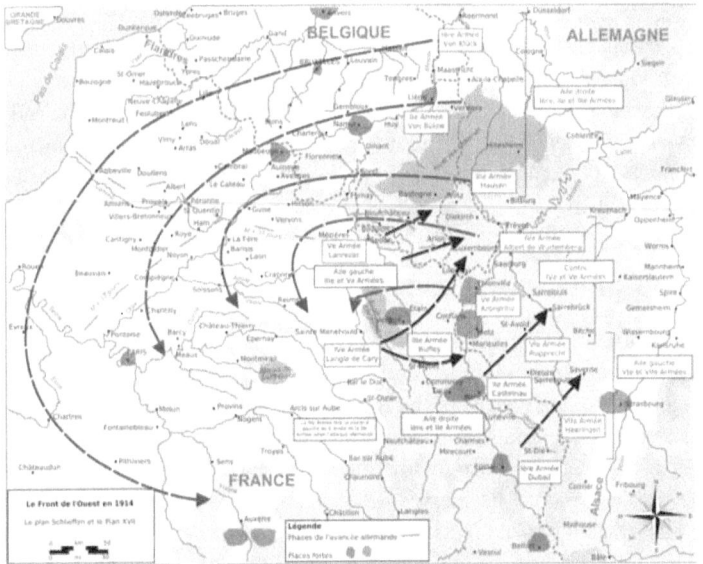

Figure 36: *Obsolete map of the Schlieffen Plan and the French offensives of Plan XVII*

- Second Army (9th, 15th, 16th, 18th and 20th Army Corps), with the objective of capturing Morhange.
- Third Army (4th, 5th and 6th Army Corps), defending the region around Metz.
- Fourth Army (12th, 17th and Colonial Army Corps) held in reserve around the Forest of Argonne
- Fifth Army (1st, 2nd, 3rd, 10th and 11th Army Corps), defending the Ardennes.

Over the course of the First World War another five field armies would be raised. The war scare led to another 2.9 million men being mobilized in the summer of 1914 and the costly battles on the Western Front forced France to conscript men up to the age of 45. This was done by the mobilization in 1914 of the Territorial Army and its reserves; comprising men who had completed their peacetime service with the active and reserve armies (ages 20–34).[93]

In June 1915, the Allied countries met in the first inter-Allied conference. Britain, France, Belgium, Italy, Serbia and Russia agreed to coordinate their attacks but the attempts were frustrated by German offensives on the Eastern Front and spoiling offensives at Ypres and in the hills west of Verdun.

By 1918, towards the end of the war, the composition and structure of the French army had changed. Forty percent of all French soldiers on the Western Front were operating artillery and 850,000 French troops were infantry in 1918, compared to 1.5 million in 1915. Causes for the drop in infantry include increased machine gun, armored car and tank usage, as well as the increasing significance of the French air force, the Service Aéronautique. At the end of the war on November 11, 1918, the French had called up 8,317,000 men, including 475,000 colonial troops. France suffered over 4.2 million casualties, with 1.3 million dead.

Commanders in Chief

Joseph Joffre was Commander-in-Chief, a position for which he had been designated since 1911. While serving in this position, Joffre was responsible for development of the Plan XVII the mobilisation and concentration plan for the offensive strategy against Germany, which proved a costly failure. Joffre was thought to be the 'Savior of France' due to his serenity and a refusal to admit defeat, valuable at the beginning of the war, along with his regrouping of retreating Allied forces at the Battle of the Marne. Joffre was effectively relieved of his duties on December 13, 1916, following the heavy human losses at the Battle of Verdun and the Somme, and the defeat of Romania, which appeared for a time to put the Salonika Bridgehead in jeopardy. Due to his popularity,

Figure 37: *A photograph of Joseph Joffre, Commander-in-Chief for most of the war, taken before 1918.*

it was not presented to the public as a dismissal when he was promoted to Marshal of France on the same day.

Robert Nivelle, who began the war as a regimental colonel, was appointed Commander-in-Chief. However, after the failure of the Nivelle Offensive in April 1917 he was removed from his position and appointed Commander-in-Chief in North Africa.

On May 15, 1917, Philippe Pétain was made Commander-in-Chief after a few weeks as Army Chief of Staff. The French Army Mutinies had begun during that period, and he restored the fighting capability of the French troops by improving front line living conditions, and conducting only limited offensives. In the Third Battle of the Aisne, fought in May 1918, French positions collapsed due to the local commander General Duchene's defiance of Pétain's recommendation of defence in depth, and Petain's pessimism saw him subordinated to the Supreme Allied Commander Ferdinand Foch.

Figure 38: *Soldiers of the 87th Regiment, 6th Division at Côte 304 (Hill 304), northwest of Verdun, in 1916*

Western Front

Germany marched through neutral Belgium as part of the Schlieffen Plan to invade France, and by August 23 had reached the French border town of Maubeuge, whose true significance lay within its forts. Maubeuge was a major railway junction and was consequently a protected city. It had 15 forts and gun batteries, totaling 435 guns, along with a permanent garrison of 35,000 troops, a number enhanced by the British Expeditionary Force. The BEF and the French Fifth Army retreated on August 23, and the town was besieged by German heavy artillery starting on August 25. The fortress was surrendered on September 7 by General Fournier, who was later court-martialed, but exonerated, for the capitulation.

The Battle of Guise, launched on August 29, was an attempt by the Fifth Army to capture Guise, they succeeded, but later withdrew on August 30. This delayed the German Second Army's invasion of France, but also hurt Lanrezac's already damaged reputation. The First Battle of the Marne was fought between September 6 and September 12. It started when retreating French forces (the Fifth and Sixth armies), stopped south of the Marne River. Victory seemed close, the First German Army was given orders to surround Paris, unaware the French government had already fled to Bordeaux. The First Battle of the Marne was a French victory, but was a bloody one: the French suffered 250,000 casualties, of which 80,000 died, with similar numbers believed for the Germans, and over 12,700 for the British. The German retreat after the First Battle of the Marne halted at the Aisne River, and the Allies soon caught up, starting the First Battle of the Aisne on September 12. It lasted until September 28, it was indecisive, partially due to machine guns beating back infantry sent to capture enemy positions. In the Battle of Le Cateau, fought on August 26–27, the French Sixth Army prevented the British from being outflanked. The first major Allied attack against German forces since the incarnation of trench warfare on the Western Front, the First Battle of Champagne, lasting from December 20, 1914, until March 17, 1915; it was a German victory, due in part to their machine gun battalions and the well-entrenched German forces.

The indecisive Second Battle of Ypres, from April 22 – May 25, was the site of the first German chlorine gas attack and the only major German offensive on the Western Front in 1915. Ypres was devastated after the battle. The Second Battle of Artois, from May 9 – June 18, the most important part of the Allied spring offensive of 1915, was successful for the Germans, allowing them to advance rather than retreat as the Allies had planned, and Artois would not be in Allied hands again until 1917. The Second Battle of Champagne, from September 25 – November 6, was a general failure, with the French only advancing about 4 kilometres (2.5 mi), and not capturing the German's second line. France suffered over 140,000 casualties, while the Germans suffered over 80,000.

The Battle of the Somme, fought along a 30 kilometres (19 mi) front from north of the Somme River between Arras and Albert. It was fought between July 1 and November 18 and involved over 2 million men. The French suffered 200,000 casualties. Little territory was gained, only 12 kilometres (7.5 mi) at the deepest points.

Battle of the Frontiers

The Battle of the Frontiers consisted of five offensives, commanded and planned by French Commander-in-Chief Joseph Joffre and German Chief-of-Staff Helmuth von Moltke. It was fought in August 1914. These five offensives, Mulhouse, Lorraine, Ardennes, Charleroi, and Mons, were launched almost simultaneously. They were the result of the French XVII and the German plans colliding. The Battle of Mulhouse, on August 7–10, 1914, was envisioned by Joffre to anchor the French recapture of Alsace, but resulted in Joffre holding General Louis Bonneau responsible for its failure and replacing him with General Paul Pau. The Battle of Lorraine, August 14–25, was

Figure 39: *Bayonet charge in 1914*

an indecisive French invasion of that region by General Pau and his Army of Alsace. The Battle of the Ardennes, fought between August 21 and 23 in the Ardennes forests, was sparked by unsuspecting French and German forces meeting, and resulted in a French defeat, forfeiting to the Germans a source of iron-ore. The Battle of Charleroi, which started on August 20 and ended on August 23, was a key battle on the Western Front, and a German victory. General Charles Lanrezac's retreat probably saved the French Army, but Joffre blamed him for the failure of Plan XVII, even though the withdrawal had been permitted.

Race to the Sea

The First Battle of Albert was the first battle in the so-called 'Race to the Sea', so-called because the campaign was attempting to reach the English Channel in an effort to outflank the German army. The First Battle of Albert was fought on September 25–29, 1914, after the First Battle of the Marne and the First Battle of the Aisne. It occurred after both sides realized that a breakthrough was not possible. It was evident that both the French Plan XVII and the German Schlieffen Plan had failed. Both sides then proceeded to attempt to outmaneuver the other, and the battle ended indecisively. The Battle of Arras, which was another attempt on the part of the French to outflank the Germans, was started on October 1. Despite heavy attacks by three corps from the First,

Figure 40: *French reserve troops crossing a river on their way to Verdun*

Second, and Seventh armies, the French held on to Arras, albeit losing Lens on October 4. The Battle of the Yser, fought between October 18 and November 30, was the northernmost battle in the 'Race to the Sea'. The battle was a German victory, and fighting continued along the Yser River until the final Allied advance that won the war. The last of the 'Race to the Sea' battles, the First Battle of Ypres, started on October 19, marked the formation of a bond between the British and French armies. The battle was an Allied victory and ended, according to France, Britain, and Germany, on November 13, 22, or 30 respectively.

Battle of Verdun

The Battle of Verdun was the longest of the war, lasting from February 21, 1916 until December 18 of the same year. The battle started after a plan by German General Erich von Falkenhayn to capture Verdun was executed, but after a few weeks, the battle had become a series of local actions. For the French, the battle signified the strength and fortitude of the French Armed Forces. Many military historians consider Verdun the "most demanding" and the "greatest" battle in history.

The German attack on Verdun began with one million troops, led by Crown Prince Wilhelm, facing only about 200,000 French soldiers. The following day, the French were forced to withdraw to the second line of trenches, and on February 24, they were pushed back to the third line, only 8 kilometres (5.0 mi) from Verdun. The newly appointed commander of the Verdun sector, General Philippe Pétain, stated that there would be no more withdrawals, and had every French soldier that was available fighting in the Verdun sector, eventually involving 259 out of 330 infantry regiments. A single road had remained open for trucks, enabling a continual flow of supplies to the defenders.

The German attacking forces were not able to enter the city of Verdun itself and by December 1916 had been forced back beyond the original French trench lines of February. The sector became again a relatively inactive one as the allied focus shifted to the Somme and the Germans adopted a defensive stance. While generally regarded as a tactical victory for the French, the battle had caused massive losses on both sides. French casualties had been higher but the original German objective: of taking Verdun while destroying the defending army through a battle of attrition in a restricted area, had not succeeded.[94]

Nivelle Offensive

In October 1916, troops under Robert Nivelle's command captured Douaumont and other Verdun forts, making him a national hero. Nivelle formulated a plan using his "creeping barrage" tactics that would supposedly end the war in 48 hours with only 10,000 casualties. War Minister Hubert Lyautey, General Philippe Pétain and Sir Douglas Haig were all opposed to the plan, although Aristide Briand supported the "Nivelle Offensive". Lyautey resigned after being shouted down in the Chamber of Deputies for refusing to discuss military aviation secrets. For the offensive in April 1917, one million French soldiers were deployed on a front between Royle and Reims.

The main action of the Nivelle Offensive, the Second Battle of the Aisne, started on April 16, 1917, with the French suffering 40,000 casualties on the first day. By the time the battle was over on May 9, the French had suffered 187,000 casualties, while the Germans suffered 168,000. The Allies eventually suffered over 350,000 casualties fighting the Nivelle Offensive.

Mutinies

In the spring of 1917, after the failed Nivelle Offensive, there were a series of mutinies in the French army. The mutinies started on April 17, the day after the failed Nivelle Offensive, and ended on June 30. Over 35,000 soldiers were involved with 68 out of 112 divisions affected, but fewer than 3,000 men were punished. Following a series of court-martials, there were 49 documented executions and 2,878 sentences to penal servitude with hard labour. Of the 68 divisions affected by mutinies, 5 had been "profoundly affected" 6 had been

Figure 41: *Execution reportedly at Verdun at the time of the mutinies. The original French text accompanying this photograph notes however that the uniforms are those of 1914/15 and that the execution may be that of a spy at the beginning of the war*

"very seriously affected", 15 had been "seriously affected", 25 were affected by "repeated incidents" and 17 had been affected by "one incident only", according to statistics compiled by French military historian Guy Pedroncini.

Mutinies began in April 1917 after the failure of the Second Battle of the Aisne, the main action in the Nivelle Offensive. They involved units from nearly half of the French infantry divisions stationed on the western front. The mutinies were kept secret at the time, and their full extent and intensity were not revealed for a half century. The more serious episodes involved only a few units; the mutinies did not threaten complete military collapse, but did make the high command reluctant to call another offensive. The popular cry was to wait for the arrival of millions of fresh U.S. troops. The mutinous soldiers were motivated by despair, not by politics or pacifism. They feared that mass infantry offensives would never prevail over machine guns and artillery. General Pétain restored morale through a combination of rest rotations for front-line units, furloughs home, and stricter discipline.[95] However, Smith has argued that the mutinies were akin to labour strikes and can be considered political. The soldiers demanded not only peace, leave, and better food, and objected to the use of colonial workers on the home front; they were also concerned about the welfare of their families. The courts-martial were merely symbolic, designed to demonstrate the absolute authority of the high command.[96] The

Figure 42: *The 114th infantry in Paris, 14th July 1917.*

British government was alarmed, for it interpreted the mutinies as a sign of deep malaise in French society, and tried to reinvigorate French morale by launching the Third Battle of Ypres, or Passchendaele.[97]

Kaiserschlacht

The French army was heavily involved in the defence of the allies' line of defense during the final German offensives in spring 1918. When the British troops were attacked during operation Michael, 40 French divisions were sent to help them. Those troops finally took part in the battle. Then, the third German offensive was launched against French positions in Champagne. The French troops began to lose ground but eventually, the Germans were stopped by a counterattack led by General Charles Mangin.

In July, a last German assault was launched against the French on the Marne. The German troops were crushed by about 40 French divisions helped by British and American troops. This was a turning point in the war on the western front.

Figure 43: *French troops going to Gallipoli in 1915*

The Grand Offensive

During the summer of 1918, General Ferdinand Foch was appointed supreme commander of the allied forces. After the decisive defeat of the Germans at the second Battle of the Marne, Foch ordered an offensive against Amiens. Some French units participated in this battle. Then, a general offensive was launched against the German positions in France. The French First Army helped the British troops in the north, while eight French field armies formed the center of the offensive. An additional army was sent to help the Americans. The French forces were the most numerous of all the allied troops, and during the last stage of the war, they took about 140,000 prisoners. British troops spearheaded the main attack by attacking in Flanders and Western Belgium where they first smashed the Hindenburg line. Meanwhile, the more exhausted French army managed to liberate most of northern France and to enter Belgian territory.

These numerous offensives left the German army on the verge of disaster and when Germany sought for an armistice, British, French and American troops were ready to launch an important offensive in Lorraine, where the Germans were collapsing.

Figure 44: *A French 75 in action at Cape Helles in 1915*

Other campaigns

While the French Army's main commitment was inevitably to the Western Front, significant forces were deployed in other theatres of war. These included the occupation of the German colonies of Togo and Kamerun in West Africa, participation in the Dardanelles and Palestinian campaigns against the Ottoman Empire and a diversionary offensive in the Balkans carried out in conjunction with other Allied forces. The bulk of the French troops utilized in these campaigns were North African and colonial units, both European and indigenous. However the French reinforcements sent to the Italian Front in 1917 following the Battle of Caporetto were drawn from metropolitan French units, marking a diversion of resources from the Western Front.

Equipment

At the outset of the war, the primary French field gun was the French 75, (75mm caliber, entered service in 1897). The French had about 4,000 of these guns, an adequate number, but despite accuracy, quick firing, and lethality against infantry, German howitzers outranged the French 75, which had a range of 7 kilometres (4.3 mi), by 3 kilometres (1.9 mi), and used heavier shells, inflicting more damage than the French guns. In 1913, General Joseph

Joffre authorized the limited adoption of the Rimailho Model 1904TR, a howitzer with a range of over 10 kilometres (6.2 mi).

When war broke out in August 1914, the German Army had about 12,000 machine guns, while the British and French armies had a few hundred. French models of machine gun used during the war included the Hotchkiss M1914, the Chauchat, and the St. Étienne Mle 1907.

The first tank was ready for combat by January 1916. Unaware of the British tank development programme, Colonel Jean Baptiste Eugène Estienne persuaded Joffre to begin production of French tanks. An order for 400 Schneider CA1s and 400 Saint-Chamonds was soon placed. The French deployed 128 tanks in April 1917 as part of the Second Battle of the Aisne, but they were unreliable. However, the Renault FT proved more worthy, and the French produced a total of 3,870 tanks by the end of the war.

Grenades came to the attention of German military planners as a result of the Russo-Japanese war of 1904–1905, and by the beginning of the Great War, the Germans had 106,000 rifle grenades and 70,000 hand grenades. The French and Russian armies were better prepared than the British, expecting to find themselves besieging German fortresses, a task suited to the grenade. The French, along with the British, persisted in the use of rifle grenades (they used a special cup for launching) throughout the war, increasing their range from 180 and 200 metres (590 and 660 ft) to 400 metres (1,300 ft).

The mortar also interested the Germans, for a specific use: an invasion of France's eastern front. The advantage of a mortar was that it could be fired from the relative safety of a trench, unlike artillery. At the beginning of World War I, the German Army had a stockpile of 150 mortars, which was a surprise to the French and British. The French were able to use the century-old Coehorn mortars from the Napoleonic Wars. Subsequently, the French borrowed the design of the British Stokes Mortar, and collaborated on mortar designs with the British throughout the war. Eventually, large mortars could throw bombs 2 kilometres (1.2 mi).

Despite the technological advances in grenades, machine guns, and mortars, the rifle remained the primary infantry weapon, in large part because other weapons were too cumbersome and unwieldy for an infantryman, and remained the weapon of choice for snipers. Rifles remained virtually the same during the war years, mostly because research tended to be focused on larger weapons and poison gas. The average range of a rifle throughout World War I was 1,400 metres (4,600 ft), but most were only accurate to 600 metres (2,000 ft). The French rifle of choice was the Lebel Model 1886, officially styled the Fusil Modèle 1886-M93, from 1886. Its major design flaw was its eight-round tubular magazine which could cause explosions when the nose of

Figure 45: *French machine gunners defend a ruined cathedral, late in the war*

one cartridge was forced onto the base of another. In 1916, the Berthier rifle, officially titled the Fusil d'Infanterie Modele 1907, Transforme 1915, was issued as an improvement; it was clip-loaded. The original, produced in 1907, only held three rounds. Later versions in 1915 introduced the use of spitzer bullets and 1916 increased the clip size to five rounds, and a carbine version of the Berthier, dubbed the Berthier carbine but titled Mousqueton modele 1916, was released in 1916. The carbine was preferred over a 'normal' rifle because of the advantages in handling in a confined space, such as a trench, and was one of the few significant advances in rifle technology, although periscopes and tripods were produced for trench warfare.

Contrary to popular belief, the first country to use chemical warfare in World War I was not Germany, but France, who used tear gas grenades against the German army in August 1914; however, the Germans were the first to seriously research chemical warfare. Poison gas (chlorine) was first used on April 22, 1915, at the Second Battle of Ypres, by the German army. April 1915 saw the first innovation in protection against chemical warfare: a cotton pad dipped in bicarbonate of soda, but by 1918, troops on both sides had charcoal respirators. By November 11, 1918, France had suffered 190,000 chemical warfare casualties, including 8,000 dead.

Figure 46: *French cuirassiers on their way to the front in August 1914*

Uniforms

At the outbreak of war the French Army retained the colourful traditional uniforms of the nineteenth century for active service wear. These included conspicuous features such as blue coats and red trousers for the infantry and cavalry. The French cuirassiers wore plumed helmets and breastplates almost unchanged from the Napoleonic period.[98] From 1903 on several attempts had been made to introduce a more practical field dress but these had been opposed by conservative opinion both within the army and amongst the public at large. In particular, the red trousers worn by the infantry became a political debating point. Adolphe Messimy who was briefly Minister of War in 1911-1912 stated that "This stupid blind attachment to the most visible of colours will have cruel consequences"; however, in the following year, one of his successors, Eugène Étienne, declared "Abolish red trousers? Never!"[99]

In order to appease traditionalists, a new cloth was devised woven from red, white and blue threads, known as "Tricolour cloth", resulting in a drab purple-brown colour. Unfortunately the red thread could only be produced with a dye made in Germany, so only the blue and white threads were used. The adoption of the blue-grey uniform (known as "horizon-blue" because it was thought to prevent soldiers from standing out against the skyline) had been approved by

Figure 47: *Test uniforms created in 1912 by Edouard Detaille for the line infantry. They were never adopted, but the blue-grey coats and the burgonet-style leather helmets influenced later uniforms*

the French Government in June 1914 but new issues had not been possible before the outbreak of war a few weeks later.[100]

The very heavy French losses during the Battle of the Frontiers can be attributed in part to the high visibility of the French uniforms, combined with peacetime training which placed emphasis on attacking in massed formations.[101] The shortcomings of the uniforms were quickly realized and during the first quarter of 1915 general distribution of horizon-blue clothing in simplified patterns had been undertaken. The long established infantry practice of wearing greatcoats for field service, buttoned back when on the march, was continued in the trenches. British-style puttees were issued in place of leather gaiters from October 1914.[102] The French Army was the first to introduce steel helmets for protection against shrapnel, and by December 1915 more than three million "Adrian" helmets had been manufactured.[103]

The horizon-blue uniform and Adrian helmet proved sufficiently practical to be retained unchanged for the remainder of the war, although khaki of a shade described as "mustard" was introduced after December 1914 for the North African and colonial troops serving in France.

Further reading

- Arnold, Joseph C, "French tactical doctrine 1870-1914", *Military Affairs: The Journal of Military History, Including Theory and Technology*. (1978): 61-67, doi: 10.2307/1987399[104]. Link[105] in JSTOR

- Clayton, Anthony. *Paths of glory: the French Army 1914-18*, London: Cassell, 2003
- Delvert, Charles (translator Ian Sumner). *From Marne to Verdun: A French Officer's Diary*, Pen & Sword Military (2016) ISBN 978-1473823792
- Doughty, Robert A. *Pyrrhic Victory: French Strategy and Operations in the Great War* (2008), 592pp; excerpt and text search[106]
- Fogarty, Richard S. *Race and war in France: Colonial subjects in the French army, 1914–1918* (Johns Hopkins University Press, 2008)
- Gilbert, Bentley B. and Bernard, Paul P. "The French Army Mutinies of 1917"[107], *The Historian* (1959) Volume 22 Issue 1, pp 24–41, doi: 10.1111/j.1540-6563.1959.tb01641.x[108]
- Horne, Alistair. *The French Army and Politics, 1870-1970*, Basingstoke: Macmillan, 1984
- Porch, Douglas. *The March to the Marne: The French Army 1871-1914*, Cambridge University Press (2003) ISBN 978-0521545921
- Sumner, Ian. *The First Battle of the Marne: The French 'Miracle' Halts the Germans (Campaign)*, Osprey Publishing (2010) ISBN 978-1846035029
- Sumner, Ian. *The French Army: 1914-18*, Osprey Publishing (1995) ISBN 1-85532-516-0
- Sumner, Ian. *The French Army at Verdun* (Images of War), Pen & Sword Military (2016) ISBN 978-1473856158
- Sumner, Ian. *The French Army in the First World War* (Images of War), Pen & Sword Military (2016) ISBN 978-1473856196
- Sumner, Ian. *French Poilu 1914-18* (Warrior), Osprey Publishing (2009) ISBN 978-1846033322
- Sumner, Ian. *They Shall Not Pass: The French Army on the Western Front 1914-1918*, Pen & Sword Military (2012) ISBN 978-1848842090

Military history of France during World War II

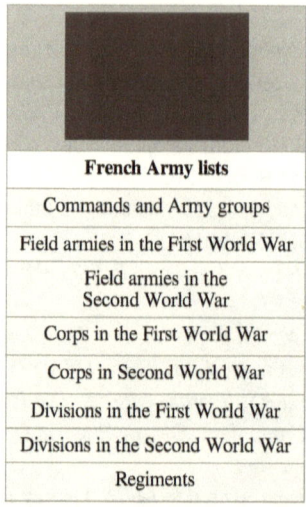

French Army lists
Commands and Army groups
Field armies in the First World War
Field armies in the Second World War
Corps in the First World War
Corps in Second World War
Divisions in the First World War
Divisions in the Second World War
Regiments

The **military history of France during World War II** covers three periods. From 1939 until 1940, which witnessed a war against Germany by the French Third Republic. The period from 1940 until 1945, which saw competition between Vichy France and the Free French Forces under General Charles de Gaulle for control of the overseas empire. And 1944, witnessing the landings of the Allies in France (Normandy, Provence), expelling the German Army and putting an end to Vichy Regime.

France and Britain declared war on Germany when they invaded Poland in September 1939. After the Phoney War from 1939 to 1940, within seven weeks, the Germans invaded and defeated France and forced the British off the continent. France formally surrendered to Germany.

In August 1943, the de Gaulle and Giraud forces merged in a single chain of command subordinated to Anglo-American leadership, meanwhile opposing French forces on the Eastern Front were subordinated to Soviet or German leaderships. This in-exile French force together with the French Forces of the Interior (FFI) played a variable-scale role in the eventual liberation of France by the Western Allies and the defeat of Vichy France, Fascist Italy, Nazi Germany, and the Japanese empire. Vichy France fought for control over the French overseas empire with the Free French forces, which were aided by Britain and the U.S. By 1943, all of the colonies, except for Indochina, had joined the Free French life.[109]

The number of Free French troops grew with Allied success in North Africa and subsequent rallying of the Army of Africa which pursued the fight against the Axis fighting in many campaigns and eventually invading Italy, occupied France and Germany from 1944 to 1945 by demanding unconditional surrender to the Axis Powers in the Casablanca Conference. On October 23, 1944, Britain, the United States, and the Soviet Union officially recognized de Gaulle's regime as the Provisional Government of the French Republic (GPRF) which replaced the in-exile Vichy French State (its government having fled to Sigmaringen in western Germany) and preceded the Fourth Republic (1946).

Recruitment in liberated France led to enlargements of the French armies. By the end of the war in Europe in May 1945, France had 1,250,000 troops, 10 divisions of which were fighting in Germany. An expeditionary corps was created to liberate French Indochina then occupied by the Japanese. During the course of the war, French military losses totaled 212,000 dead, of which 92,000 were killed through the end of the campaign of 1940, 58,000 from 1940 to 1945 in other campaigns, 24,000 lost while serving in the French resistance, and a further 38,000 lost while serving with the German Army (including 32,000 "malgré-nous").[110]

Military forces of France during World War II

France had several regular and irregular army forces during World War II; this was partially due to a major geopolitical change. Following the lost Battle of France in 1940, the country switched from a democratic republican regime fighting with the Allies to an authoritarian regime collaborating with Germany and opposing the Allies in several campaigns. These complex opposing forces were called, in a simplistic manner, Vichy French forces and Free French forces. They fought battles all over the world from 1940 to 1945, and sometimes fighting against each other. These forces were composite, made of rebel factions and colonial troops; France controlled a large colonial empire, only second to the British empire.

The military participation of the French ground armies, navies and air forces on the Allied side in each theater of World War II (1939–1945) before, during and after the Battle of France, even though it was on various degrees, secured France's acknowledgment as a World War II victor and allowed its evasion from the US-planned AMGOT; even though after World War II USAF bases were maintained in France until their evacuation in 1967, due to de Gaulle's rejection of NATO. As a result, Free French General François Sevez signed the first German Instrument of Surrender, as witness, on 7 May 1945 (Rheims,

Figure 48: *Vichy French's Légion des Volontaires Français World War II battle honor (Russian front in 1941–43).*

Figure 49: *Free French 3rd SAS World War II battle honor (Crete, Libya, Tunisia, France, Belgium, Netherlands in 1942–45).*

Figure 50: *French Army of Africa's 7e RCA World War II battle honor (Italy, France and Germany in 1944–45).*

France), French 1st Army General Jean de Lattre de Tassigny signed the second declaration on 8 May 1945 (Berlin, Germany), also as witness, and French General Philippe Leclerc de Hauteclocque signed the Japanese Instrument of Surrender on behalf of the Provisional Government of the French Republic on 15 August 1945 (Tokyo bay, Japan).

The complex and ambiguous situation of France from 1939 to 1945, since its military forces fought on both sides under French, British, German, Soviet, US or without uniform – often subordinated to Allied or Axis command – led to some criticism *vis-à-vis* its actual role and allegiance, much like with Sweden during World War II.

French Army (1939–40)

File:France location map-Regions and departements-2016.svg

French divisions on 1 Sep 1939

Figure 51: *General Charles de Gaulle and British Prime Minister Winston Churchill in 1944.*

The French Army on the eve of the German attack in 1940 was commanded by General Maurice Gamelin with its headquarters in Vincennes, on the outskirts of Paris. It consisted of 117 divisions with 94 committed to the North-Eastern front of operations. The North-Eastern Front Command was held by its Commander-in-Chief, General Alphonse Georges, at La Ferte-sous-Jouarre. The French air force was commanded by General Joseph Vuillemin, whose headquarters was located in Coulommiers.[111]

Prisoners of war

After the French armies surrendered, Germany seized 2 million French prisoners of war and sent them to camps in Germany.[112] About one third were released on various terms. Of the remainder, the officers and noncommissioned officers were kept in separate camps and did not work. The privates were sent out to work. About half of them worked in German agriculture, where food supplies were adequate and controls were lenient. The others work in factories or mines, where conditions were much harsher.[113]

Free French Forces (1940–45)

Free French Forces were created in 1940 as a rebel faction of the French Army, refusing both the armistice (they were called « *the fighting French* »)

Figure 52: *Free French welcomed on board Free Poles Navy destroyer ORP Piorun (G65), circa 1944.*

and Vichy's authority. Its allegiance was toward General de Gaulle and its HQ was in London; later moving to Algiers. Starting as a limited force made of volunteers from metropolitan France and French colonies but also from other countries (such as Belgium and Spain). It evolved to a full army after its merger with Giraud's Army of Africa, then with new recruits from the French Resistance (also called « *soldiers without uniform* »).

De Gaulle's appeals on the BBC (June 1940)

General Charles de Gaulle was a member of the French cabinet during the Battle of France, in 1940. As French defence forces were increasingly overwhelmed, de Gaulle found himself part of a group of politicians who argued against a negotiated armistice with Nazi Germany and Fascist Italy. These views being shared by the President of the Council, Paul Reynaud, de Gaulle was sent as an emissary to the United Kingdom, where he was when the French government collapsed.

On the 18 of June, de Gaulle spoke to the French people via BBC radio. He asked French soldiers, sailors and airmen to join in the fight against the Nazis. In France, De Gaulle's "Appeal of June 18" (*Appel du 18 juin*) was not widely heard, but subsequent discourse by de Gaulle could be heard nationwide. Some of the British Cabinet had attempted to block the speech, but were overruled

Figure 53: *Newly promoted brigadier general Charles de Gaulle (he was a colonel an armoured division commander during the Battle of France) reviews French navy sailors willing to pursue the fight as Free French Forces.*

by Winston Churchill. To this day, the Appeal of June 18 remains one of the most famous speeches in French history. Nevertheless, on 22 June, Petain's representative signed the armistice and he became leader of the new regime known as Vichy France. (Vichy is the French town where the government was based from July onwards.)

De Gaulle was tried *in absentia* in Vichy France and sentenced to death for treason and desertion; he, on the other hand, regarded himself as the last remaining member of the legitimate Reynaud government able to exercise power, seeing the rise to power of Pétain as an unconstitutional coup.

French SAS (1942–45)

On 15 September 1940, Free French Captain Georges Bergé created the airborne unit called *1re compagnie de l'air, 1re CIA* (1st Air Company) in Great Britain. This unit later known as *1re compagnie de chasseurs parachutistes, 1re CCP* (1st Parachute Light Infantry Company) joined the July 1941-created British Special Air Service airborne unit at David Stirling's demand to Charles de Gaulle in 1942 to become the SAS Brigade's French Squadron.

Figure 54: *The French SAS's motto is the translation of the British SAS's: He who dares, wins.*

The 3rd SAS (French) and 4th SAS (French) are also known as 1st Airborne Marine Infantry Regiment (1er RPIMa) and *2e régiment de chasseurs parachutistes* (2e RCP) respectively.

Composition (1940–1945)

Free French Forces (*Forces Françaises Libres, FFL*) comprised 1st Free French Division (*1re Division Française Libre, 1re DFL*), Free French Air Force (*Forces Aériennes Françaises Libres, FAFL*), Free French Naval Forces (*Forces Navales Françaises Libres, FNFL*), Free French Naval Air Service (*Aéronavale française libre, AFL*), Naval Commandos (*Commandos Marine*), the French Resistance branch called French Forces of the Interior (*Forces Françaises de l'Intérieur, FFI*), and the intelligence service Central Bureau of Intelligence and Operations (*Bureau Central de Renseignements et d'Action, BCRA*), all giving allegiance to General Charles de Gaulle, creator of the Free France (*France libre*).

French Expeditionary Corps (1943–1944)

It was close to Tripoli, Libya, where Leclerc's Free French Forces met Giraud's Army of Africa for the first time, in 1943.[114]

Free French Forces and Army of Africa merger (August 1, 1943)

In November 1943 the French forces received enough military equipment through Lend-Lease to re-equip eight divisions and allow the return of borrowed British equipment. At this point, the Free French forces and Army of Africa were merged to form the French Expeditionary Corps (*Corps Expéditionnaire Français, CEF*), under General Alphonse Juin, that would take part in the 1943 Italian Campaign and the August 1944 invasion in Southern France called Operation Dragoon.

By September 1944, the Free French forces stood at 560,000 (and the FFI at 300,000), which rose to 1 million by the end of 1944, and were fighting in Alsace, the Alps and Bretagne. By the end of the war in Europe (May 1945), the Free French forces comprised 1,250,000, including seven infantry and three armoured divisions fighting in Germany.

Other Free French units were directly attached to Allied forces including the British SAS, RAF and the Soviet air force.

Far East French Expeditionary Forces (1943–1945)

The *Forces Expéditionnaires Françaises d'Extrême-Orient* (FEFEO) was a French expeditionary corps created on 4 October 1943 to fight in the Asian theatre of World War II and liberate French Indochina which was still occupied by the Japanese since 1940. Recruiting posters of the FEFEO depicted a US-built M4 Sherman tank of general Leclerc's Free French 2nd Armoured Division, famous for its role in the 1944 liberation of Paris and Strasbourg, with the caption "Yesterday Strasbourg, tomorrow Saigon: Join the Far East French Expeditionary Forces".[115]

In 1945 after Japan surrendered and China was in charge in Indochina, the Provisional French Republic sent the French Far East Expeditionary Corps to Indochina to pacify the Vietnamese liberation movement and to restore French colonial rule.

Figure 55: *Brigadier Mike Calvert, Commandant SAS Brigade, at the ceremony marking the passing of 3 and 4 SAS (2 and 3 Regiment de Chasseurs Parachutistes) from the British to the French Army at Tarbes in southern France. 1945*

Gaurs & C.L.I. commandos (1943–1945)

Free French commando groups called *Corps Léger d'Intervention* (C.L.I.) were created by de Gaulle in November 1943 as part of the FEFEO and trained in French Algeria then in British India, after the British Chindits, to fight the Japanese forces in occupied French Indochina.

They served in French Indochina, under General Roger Blaizot, since 1944 and were dropped by the British Force 136's B-24 Liberator. The first C.L.I. commandos were rather known as "Gaurs", the gaur is an Indian bison.

Allied munitions (1942–1945)

British support

Free French aircrew formed squadrons under the operational control of the Royal Air Force with British or Lend-Lease equipment. British warships were lent to the Free French navy. Besides materiel, the British formed and trained some Free French pilots and airborne commandos such as the 3rd SAS (French) and 4th SAS (French) and the CLI: the latter were trained in Ceylon and created after the British Chindits.

US support

In 1941, while still neutral, the United States began providing Lend Lease munitions to Britain and China. Some went to the Free French in North Africa, starting in 1942. Among the large inventories of American equipment passed to Free French Forces were several versions of the M4 Sherman medium tank. French armored divisions were organized and equipped the same as U.S. Army armored divisions and were sizable offensive commands. In 1943, the French decided to raise a new army in North Africa, and had an agreement with the Americans to equip it with US modern weapons. The French 2nd Armored Division (French: *Division Blindée, DB*) entered the Battle of Normandy fully equipped with M4A2s. The 1st and 5th DB, which entered S. France as part of the First French Army were equipped with a mixture of M4A2 and M4A4 medium tanks. The 3rd DB, which served as a training and reserve organization for the three operational armored divisions was equipped with roughly 200 medium and light tanks. Of these, 120 were later turned in to the U.S. Army's Delta Base Section for reissue. Subsequent combat losses for the 1st, 2nd, and 5th Armored Divisions were replaced with standard-issue tanks from U.S. Army stocks.[116]

Beside tanks, the US Army supplied the Free French forces and Army of Africa with hundreds of US-built aircraft and materiel such as vehicles, artillery, helmets, uniforms and firearms, as well as fuel and rations, for many thousands of troops.

Units and commands on 8 May 1945

Armies

- French First Army
- Atlantic Army Detachment
- Alpine Army Detachment

Corps

- I Army Corps
- II Army Corps
- III Army Corps
- XIX Army Corps

Figure 56: *Arms of General Leclerc's 2nd Armoured Division involved in the battle for Paris.*

Divisions

- 1st Free French Division[117]
- 2nd Moroccan Infantry Division
- 3rd Algerian Infantry Division
- 4th Moroccan Mountain Division
- 9th Colonial Infantry Division
- 27th Alpine Infantry Division[118]
- 1st Armoured Division
- 2nd Armoured Division
- 3rd Armoured Division[119]
- 5th Armoured Division
- 1st Infantry Division
- 10th Infantry Division
- 14th Infantry Division
- 19th Infantry Division
- 23rd Infantry Division
- 25th Infantry Division
- 36th Infantry Division
- 1st Far East Colonial Division
- 2nd Far East Colonial Division

Figure 57: *Vichy French Légion des Volontaires (LVF) fighting with the Axis in the Russian front.*

- 3rd and 4th Free French S.A.S. (Special Air Service) Battalions

French State Army (1940–44)

The armistice army, which is the official name for the Vichy army, was headed by Marshal Pétain and had its headquarters in Vichy, capital of the French State with bases disseminated around the world as part of the French Colonial Empire. It was a limited force created in July 1940 following the occupation of metropolitan France by Germany. Northern part of the metropolitan territory was occupied from June 1940 to November 1942 as a consequence of the officially signed armistice, then, full metropolitan territory as a consequence of the Allied invasion of French North Africa (Operation Torch) and Allied allegiance of the colonial French Army of Africa. Beside its regular limited armistice army, the French State created irregular forces in order to fight the French Resistance and inner/outer communists; both considered enemies by Vichy and the German authorities.

Figure 58: *Military parade of the French Milice armed with machineguns in 1944.*

Legion of French Volunteers

French Legion of Fighters

The *Légion Française des Combattants* ("French Legion of Fighters") was the French State's first paramilitary force, created on 29 August 1940 by Xavier Vallat.

French Legion of Fighters and Volunteers of the National Revolution

On 19 November 1941, the force changed its name to *Légion française des combattants et des volontaires de la Révolution nationale* ("French Legion of Fighters and Volunteers of the National Revolution"). The National Revolution was the French State's official ideology.

Tricolore Legion (1941–1942)

The *Légion Tricolore* ("tricolore legion") was created by Pierre Laval and Jacques Benoist-Méchin in summer 1941 and was disbanded in autumn 1942.

Figure 59: *Secretary of State of the Vichy regime Fernand de Brinon (white coat) and other French and German officers visiting the graves of anticommunist Poles killed by the USSR's NKVD during the 1940 Katyn massacre, in 1943. This event was exploited by the anti-bolshevik Vichy French propaganda (watch the newsreel[120]).*

French Milice (1943–44)

The French Milice, ("militia") was a Vichy French paramilitary force created on 30 January 1943 by the French State for service as auxiliary of the German occupation army; hunting down the French Resistance maquisards. Its commander was Joseph Darnand a battle of France veteran and volunteer; he took an oath of loyalty to Adolf Hitler in October 1943 and received a rank of *Sturmbannführer* (Major) in the Waffen SS. By 1944, the French Milice had over 35,000 members.

Legionnaire Order Service (1940–43)

The French Milice originated as French Legion Volunteer's shock unit called *Service d'Ordre Légionnaire* (SOL).

Paramilitary forces (1940–44)

Just like the Vichy police agents, the national police forces collaborated with the German authorities, the French Youth Workings alumni had to claim allegiance to Marshal Pétain with a serment. The gesture was the Nazi salute while saying «*Je le jure !*» ("I swear it !") instead of cheering Hitler.

Figure 60: *German-Vichy French meeting at Marseille in 1943. SS-Sturmbannführer Bernhard Griese, Marcel Lemoine (regional préfet), Mühler (Commander of Marseille Sicherheitspolizei), -laughing- René Bousquet (General Secretary of the French National Police created in 1941) creator of the GMRs, -behind- Louis Darquier de Pellepoix (Commissioner for Jewish Affairs).*

French Youth Workings (1940–44)

The *Chantiers de la jeunesse française* ("French youth workings") were a paramilitary youth organization created on 30 July 1940 by ex-Scout Movement-Chief General Joseph de La Porte du Theil (42nd Infantry Division) as a substitute to the French army conscription (draft). Its members were under Vichy army officers and dressed with military uniforms[121] similar to those of the French Milice (béret included) and had to claim allegiance to Marshal Pétain with an arm salute.

The French Youth Workings were available in all French departments which it means they were also in those of French Algeria and apply to European settlers and Muslim locals.[122] However, Lieutenant-Colonel van Hecke advised La Porte du Theil to reject the young Jews, and so they were not anymore in the French Youth Workings by decree on 15 July 1942; twenty-four hours before the Vel' d'Hiv Roundup.

In November 1942, La Porte du Theil and van Hecke were both in French Algeria when the Allied invasion of Algiers and Oran took place. The first, loyal to Pétain, flew to metropolitan France, while the second sided on the Free French side and joined Henri Giraud's Army of Africa. Local French Youth

Workings became units of this military force, the most famous being the *7e régiment de chasseurs d'Afrique, 7e RCA* (7th Africa Chasers Regiment) created in 1943 and fighting the Italian, French and German Allied campaigns from 1944 to 1945 as hinted by its battle flag; *e.g.* the 1944 Battle of Monte Cassino (Garigliano), Operation Dragoon (Toulon) and the 1945 invasion of Germany (Württemberg). The famous battle song *Le Chant des Africains* version 1943 is dedicated to Lt.Col. van Hecke and his 7e RCA.

Reserve Mobile Group (1941–44)

The Reserve Mobile Group (*Groupe mobile de réserve, GMR*) was a paramilitary force of the French State created by Vichy French René Bousquet. It was a police version of the Mobile Gendarmerie that served as French Milice and German army auxiliary during battles against the French Resistance's *maquisards*. In December 1944, the GMRs were disbanded, with selected members joining the FFI, and replaced with the CRS Riot Police.

French Gestapo (1941–44)

Carlingue was the name of the French *Gestapo*, it was headed by Henri Lafont, Pierre Loutrel and Pierre Bonny. A famous Vichy French agent of the *Gestapo* was *Scharführer-SS* Pierre Paoli who served in central France, Cher department. Mould says, "It was staffed by the dregs of the French underworld."

French SS (1942–45)

8th Sturmbrigade SS Frankreich (1943–44)

The *8th Sturmbrigade SS Frankreich* ("French assault brigade") was created in 1943. Surviving troops were incorporated to the 286th Security Division in 1944.

33rd Waffen Grenadier Division of the SS Charlemagne (1943–45)

The French State's distinct forces L.V.F. and French Milice merged to become a full division of the German army. The division's name is a reference to the Frankish emperor Charlemagne who has common French and German roots.

The African Phalange (1942–43)

La Phalange africaine was created in November 1942 in French Tunisia to fight against the Allied, Free French and Army of Africa after Operation Torch. This unit was under Lieutenant-colonel Christian du Jonchay, Lieutenant-colonel Pierre Simon Cristofini and Captain André Dupuis, its nicknames alternative designations were *Französische Freiwilligen Legion* ("Legion of French Volunteers") or *Compagnie Frankonia* ("Frankonia company").

Figure 61: *French SS shows his suitcase bearing handscripted « Heil Hitler, Waffen SS Français » in Paris, October 1943*

North-African Legion (1944)

The *Légion nord-africaine*, *LNA*, or *Brigade nord-africaine*, *BNA* was a paramilitary force created by French Gestapo agent Henri Lafont and Muslim Algerian nationalist Mohamed el-Maadi. This unit was made of Parisians of Arab and Kabyle ancestry.

French Resistance (1940–1945)

Resistance groups (1940–1945)

The earlier French Resistance groups were created in June 1940 following Marshal Pétain's appeal to cease the fight on 17 June, and its subsequent signing of the French-German-Italian armistices in July 1940. There were a myriad of paramalitary groups from various size and political ideology which made difficult its latter unification under a single chain of command. Famous groups included communist *Francs-Tireurs et Partisans*, *FTP* ("Partisan irregular riflemen") and rebel police *Honneur de la police* ("Honour of the Police").

Figure 62: *Free Republic of Vercors flag used by the French Resistance during the Battle of Vercors. 1944*

Unification of the Resistance

The French Resistance gradually grew in strength. Charles de Gaulle set a plan to bring together the different groups under his leadership. He changed the name of his movement to *Forces Françaises Combattantes* (Fighting French Forces) and sent Jean Moulin back to France to unite the eight major French Resistance groups into one organisation. Moulin got their agreement to form the *Conseil National de la Résistance* (National Council of the Resistance). He was eventually captured, and died under torture.

French Colonial Empire (1940–1945)

Franco-French struggle for the colonies

During World War II (1939–1945), the French colonies were administered by the Minister of the Navy and Colonies. On 16 June 1940 Minister César Campinchi resigned and was replaced by Admiral François Darlan who became the colonies' authority.

On 21 June, Campinchi left metropolitan France, on board the *Massilia* ocean liner at Bordeaux, with other government members such as Interior Minister Georges Mandel and arrived in Casablanca, French Morocco, on 24 June. Mandel's idea was to leave Bordeaux to establish a government-in-exile in French North Africa, and from there continue the fight using the power of

Figure 63: *A Free French infantryman from Chad in 1942. Like Britain, France drew essential manpower from its colonial empire.*

the colonies. However, when the boat arrived in Casablanca, the politicians were arrested by French Morocco administrator, General Charles Noguès, under orders from General Maxime Weygand and Marshal Philippe Pétain; the latter had signed a French-German-Italian armistice on 22 June, and became the *de facto* chief of state. As a consequence of the Armistice, the French colonial world empire became Vichy French.

However, inspired by Mandel, General Charles de Gaulle eventually created a French government-in-exile in London and tried to rally the several colonies to his cause. He hoped to gain strategic bases and gather troops for forces sufficient to liberate metropolitan France. During 1940 a few colonies joined the Free French side, but others remained under Vichy control. General de Gaulle's reputation was then as a military man with no political experience or following. His charisma wasn't sufficient to gather the allegiance of senior colonial administrators or Generals. As a result, a battle was engaged between Free French colonies and Vichy French colonies, each one siding with the Axis or the Allies.

Figure 64: *Algiers, French Algeria. General Dwight D. Eisenhower, commander in chief of the Allied Armies in North Africa, and General Henri Honoré Giraud, commanding the French Forces, saluting the flags of both nations at Allied headquarters. circa 1943*

Army of Africa (1942–1943)

The Army of Africa is a historical colonial force created in 1830 as an expeditionary corps set to conquer the Regency of Algiers (proto-Algeria); mission fulfilled in 1847. It fought 1939–1940 as a force of the French Republic, then following the surrender of metropolitan France it became a Vichy force fighting the Allies (1940–1942) at the battle of Mers-el-Kebir and Operation Torch, then it evolved as a rebel faction of the Vichy forces in 1942. It eventually merged with the Free French Forces prior to the 1944 operations in mainland Europe.

It was headed by General Henri Giraud and made of mixed European settlers and indigenous colonial forces from the French North Africa, French West Africa and French Equatorial Africa. Unlike de Gaulle's Free French Forces, Giraud's Army of Africa was massively supplied by the United States through a lend-lease plan. This newly equipped force enjoying modern US-built material was nicknamed the « *Nouvelle armée française* » ("New French Army").

Giraud was the Commander of the French Forces in North Africa since he received this civil and military charge on 26 December 1942 as (*Commandement*

Figure 65: *Army of Africa French Forces leader General Henri Giraud shakes hands with Free French Forces leader General Charles de Gaulle at the Casablanca Conference in French Morocco, 14 January 1943.*

civil et militaire d'Alger) replacing murdered Vichy French admiral François Darlan.

Torch aftermath

During Operation Torch, the Allied invasion of Vichy-controlled French North Africa in November 1942, many Vichy troops surrendered and joined the Free French cause. Vichy coastal defences were captured by the French Resistance.

Following Operation Torch, Henri Giraud took the head of Army of Africa a third French force distinct from de Gaulle's Free French Forces and the Vichy French forces. The Army of Africa – (created in 1830) joined the Allied side as the French XIX Corps based in French Algeria.

Axis retaliations (1942–1943)

The Nazis suspected Vichy determination after *Torch* and they occupied the southern "free" part of metropolitan France known as Vichy France in November 1942, (*Case Anton*). Also, the Libya-based Luftwaffe performed several bombing attacks on Algiers's harbour and Eastern French Algeria cities (including Annaba and Jijel).

Figure 66: *Anti-aircraft fire during an air raid by the Nazis on Algiers, French Algeria. circa 1943*

Free French colonies

In the autumn of 1940, the French colonies of Cameroon, French India and French Equatorial Africa joined the Free French side. French colonies in New Caledonia, French Polynesia, Saint-Pierre and Miquelon and the New Hebrides joined later.

Vichy French colonies

French Indochina was under Vichy control and Japanese oversight 1940-44 and then under total Japanese rule. The colonies of Guadeloupe and Martinique in the West Indies remained under Vichy government control until 1942.[123]

Figure 67: *HMS Largs moored at Greenock. Formerly the Charles Plumier a French armed merchant cruiser, captured by the destroyer HMS Faulknor on 22 November 1940, off Gibraltar. 7 January 1942*

Allied Angary (1940)

From Operation Catapult to Lend-Lease

Starting with Operation Catapult on 3 July 1940, the British took pre-emptive actions to seize French vessels. Both combatants and merchant ships docked in British harbours of the English Channel (Plymouth), Mediterranean (Gibraltar) and Canada were suddenly taken captive by armed sailors and soldiers. The crews were interned and the ships were taken over and distributed to the British or Polish fleets.

Later, with the recognition of Charles de Gaulle as leader of the Free French government-in-exile, the interned personnel were set free and organized with new ships by the British. American aid supplied under Lend-Lease allowed expansion and reconstitution of a French navy as part of the Western allies.

Figure 68: *USS Lafayette (AP-53), US-captured French SS Normandie, on fire at New York harbour on 9 February 1942.*

British capture

French Navy ships in British ports were boarded by armed sailors, these included the *Surcouf* submarine under repair in Plymouth in July 1940 which resulted on four deaths (3 British, 1 French) and the capture of the merchant MV *Charles Plumier* at Gibraltar in November 1940, which became HMS *Largs* which was later used as a command ship in several amphibious landings.

Surcouf's repairs were completed and it was turned over to Free French forces by August 1940 and in 1941 was acting as escort to trans-Atlantic convoys.

Axis requisition (1940–1945)

German capture

As part of Case Anton, in operation Lila the Germans tried to seize the remaining French navy. In Toulon, the French ships were scuttled rather than let them be handed over. Seventy-seven vessels including three battleships, seven cruisers, and fifteen destroyers were deliberately sunk. Some submarines ignored their orders to scuttle and escaped to fight on the allied cause.

European Theatre of World War II

Phoney War (1939)

The invasion of Poland on 1 September 1939 was a resounding success for German forces. France declared war to Germany on 3 September 1939 and invaded its western territory, Saarland, with the Saar Offensive led by general Louis Faury. This attempt was led by France's military obligation to help Poland per the Franco-Polish Military Alliance, and was the following of the French Military Mission to Poland headed by the same commanding officer.

Although tactically successful, as the advance in German territory reached 8 km, the Saar operation was abandoned on 12 September when the Anglo French Supreme War Council decided that all offensive actions were to be halted immediately. This SWC was composed of Prime Minister Neville Chamberlain and Lord Chatfield as the British delegation while Prime Minister Édouard Daladier and General Maurice Gamelin formed the French delegation. As a result of the deliberations, General Gamelin ordered the French troops to withdraw to the Maginot Line in France, leaving Poland to its own fate facing the Germans and Soviets all alone; the latter entering Poland on 17 September. On 16 October, German general Erwin von Witzleben started a counter-offensive against France entering its territory a few kilometers and the last covering French forces left Germany the following day to defend their country.

Battle of Belgium (May 10–28, 1940)

The 1st, 7th and 9th armies moved into Belgium to counter a German attack similar to the Schlieffen Plan in the last world war, leaving them and the BEF open to later be out-flanked by the Ardennes thrust.

The unsuccessful defence of Belgium and the surrender of King Leopold III of Belgium on 28 May spurred the creation of the Free Belgian Forces.

Battle of the Netherlands (May 10–14, 1940)

The French 7th Army under General Henri Giraud fought the Germans in support to its allies of the Netherlands.

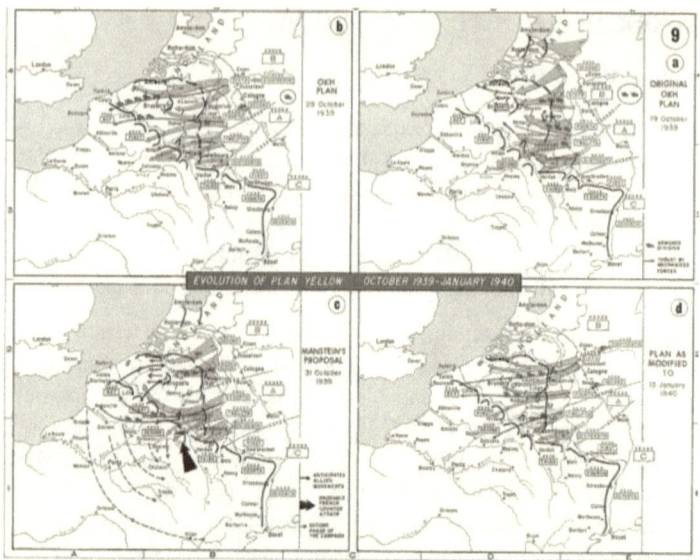

Figure 69: *The German plan was radically altered, catching the Allied army off guard.*

Battle of France (May 10 – June 25, 1940)

Prelude

Neither the French nor the British anticipated such a rapid defeat of Poland, and the quick German victory, relying on a new form of mobile warfare, disturbed some generals in London and Paris. However, the Allies still expected they would be able to contain the Germans, anticipating a war reasonably like the First World War, so they believed that even without an Eastern Front the Germans could be defeated by blockade, as in the previous conflict. This feeling was more widely shared in London than in Paris, which had suffered more severely during the First World War. The Prime Minister of France Édouard Daladier, also respected the large gap between France's human and economic resources as compared to those of Germany.

The commander of France's army, Maurice Gamelin, like the rest of the French government, was expecting a repeat of World War I. The Schlieffen Plan, Gamelin believed, would be repeated with a reasonably close degree of accuracy. Even though important parts of the French army in the 1930s had been designed to wage offensive warfare, the French only had the stomach for a defensive war, as the French military staff believed its country was not, for the moment, equipped militarily or economically to launch a decisive offensive. It would be better to wait until 1941 when the combined allied economic superiority over Germany could be fully exploited. To confront the expected German plan – which rested on a move into the Low Countries, outflanking the fortified Maginot Line – Gamelin intended to send the best units of the French army along with the British Expeditionary Force (BEF) north to halt the Germans in the area of the river Dyle, east of Brussels, until a decisive victory could be achieved with the support of the united British, Belgian, French and Dutch armies. The original German plan closely resembled Gamelin's expectations.

The crash in Belgium of a light plane carrying two German officers with a copy of the then-current invasion plan forced Hitler to scrap the plan and search for an alternative. The final plan for *Fall Gelb* (Case Yellow) had been suggested by General Erich von Manstein, then serving as Chief of Staff to Gerd von Rundstedt, but had been initially rejected by the German General Staff. It proposed a deep penetration further south of the original route which would take advantage of the speed of the unified Panzer divisions to separate and encircle the opposing forces. It had the virtue of being unlikely (from a defensive point of view), as the Ardennes was heavily wooded and implausible as a route for a mechanized invasion. It also had the considerable virtue of not having been intercepted by the Allies (for no copies were being carried about), and of being dramatic, which seems to have appealed to Hitler.

Manstein's aggressive plan was to break through the weak Allied centre with overwhelming force, trap the forces to the north in a pocket, and drive on to Paris. The plan would benefit from an Allied response close to how they would have responded in the original case; namely, that a large part of French and British strength would be drawn north to defend Belgium and Picardy. To help ensure this result, German Army Group B would still attack Belgium and the Netherlands in order to draw Allied forces eastward into the developing encirclement. The attack would also enable the Germans to secure bases for a later attack on Britain.

The Allied general staff and key statesmen, after capturing the original invasion plans, were initially jubilant that they had potentially won a key victory in the war before the campaign was even fought. Contrarily, General Gamelin and Lord Gort, the commander of the BEF, were shaken into realizing that whatever the Germans came up with instead would not be what they had initially expected. More and more Gamelin became convinced that the Germans would try to attempt a breakthrough by concentrating their mechanized forces. They could hardly hope to break the Maginot Line on his right flank or to overcome the allied concentration of forces on the left flank. That only left the centre. But most of the centre was covered by the river Meuse. Tanks were useless in defeating fortified river positions. However at Namur the river made a sharp turn to the east, creating a gap between itself and the river Dyle. This Gembloux Gap, ideal for mechanized warfare, was a very dangerous weak spot. Gamelin decided to concentrate half of his armoured reserves there. Of course the Germans might try to overcome the Meuse position by using infantry. But that could only be achieved by massive artillery support, the build-up of which would give Gamelin ample warning.

Campaign in the Low Countries and northern France

Germany launched its offensive, *Fall Gelb*, on the night prior to and principally on the morning of 10 May. During the night, German forces occupied Luxembourg and, in the morning, German Army Group B (Bock) launched a feint offensive into the Netherlands and Belgium. German Fallschirmjäger from the 7th Flieger and 22nd Air Landing divisions under Kurt Student executed surprise landings at The Hague, on the road to Rotterdam and against the Belgian Fort Eben-Emael on its opening day with the goal of facilitating Army Group B's advance.

The Allied command reacted immediately, sending forces north to combat a plan that, for all the Allies could expect, resembled the earlier Schlieffen plan. This move north committed their best forces, diminished their fighting power through loss of readiness and their mobility through loss of fuel. That evening French troops crossed the Dutch border.

The French and British air command was less effective than their generals had anticipated, and the Luftwaffe quickly obtained air superiority, depriving the Allies of key reconnaissance abilities and disrupting Allied communication and coordination.

While the German invaders secured all the strategically vital bridges in and toward Rotterdam, which penetrated "Fortress Holland" and bypassed the Water Line, an attempt to seize the Dutch seat of government, The Hague, ended in complete failure, which later led the Germans to skip paratrooper attacks. The airfields surrounding the city (Ypenburg, Ockenburg, and Valkenburg) were taken with heavy casualties on 10 May, only to be lost on the very same day to furious counterattacks launched by the two Dutch reserve infantry divisions.

The French marched north to establish a connection with the Dutch army, which came under attack from German paratroopers, but simply not understanding German intentions they failed to block German armoured reinforcements of the 9th Panzer Division from reaching Rotterdam on May 13. The Dutch, their poorly equipped army largely intact, surrendered on 14 May after the Germans bombed Rotterdam. However the Dutch troops in Zeeland and the colonies continued the fight while Queen Wilhelmina established a government-in-exile in Britain.

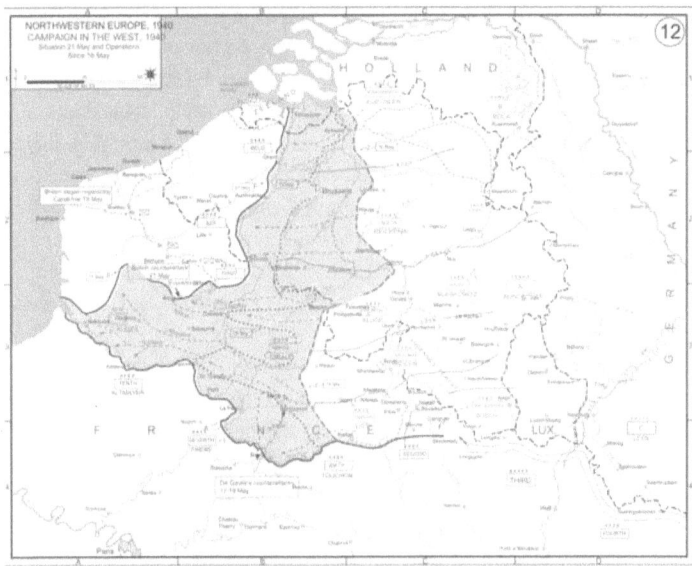

Figure 70: *The German Blitzkrieg offensive of mid-May, 1940.*

The centre of the Belgian defensive line, Fort Eben-Emael, had been seized by German paratroopers using gliders on May 10, allowing their forces to cross the bridges over the Albert Canal, although the arrival of the British Expeditionary Force managed to save the Belgians for a time. Gamelin's plan in the north was achieved when the British army reached the Dyle; then the expected major tank battle took place in the Gembloux Gap between the French 2nd and 3rd Divisions *Légères mécaniques*, (Mechanized Light Divisions), and the German 3rd and 4th Panzer divisions of Erich Hoepner's XVI Panzer Corps, costing both sides about 100 vehicles; the German offensive in Belgium seemed stalled for a moment. But this was a feint.

German breakthrough

In the centre German Army Group A smashed through the Belgian infantry regiments and French Light Divisions of the Cavalry (*Divisions Légères de cavalerie*) advancing into the Ardennes, and arrived at the Meuse River near Sedan the night of May 12/13. On May 13, the Germans forced three crossing near Sedan. Instead of slowly massing artillery as the French expected, the Germans replaced the need for traditional artillery by using the full might of their bomber force to punch a hole in a narrow sector of the French lines by carpet bombing (punctuated by dive bombing). Sedan was held by the 55th French Infantry Division (55e DI), a grade "B" reserve division. The forward elements of the 55e DI held their positions through most of the 13th, initially repulsing three of the six German crossing attempts; however, the German air attacks had disrupted the French supporting artillery batteries and created an impression among the troops of the 55e DI that they were isolated and abandoned. The combination of the psychological impact of the bombing, the generally slowly expanding German lodgements, deep penetrations by some small German infantry units and the lack of air or artillery support eventually broke down the 55e DI's resistance and much of the unit went into rout by the evening of May 13/14. The German aerial attack of May 13, with 1215 bomber sorties, the heaviest air bombardment the world had yet witnessed, is considered to have been very effective and key to the successful German river crossing. It was the most effective use of tactical air power yet demonstrated in warfare. The disorder begun at Sedan was spread down the French line by groups of haggard and retreating soldiers. During the night, some units in the last prepared defence line at Bulson panicked by the false rumour German tanks were already behind their positions. On May 14, two French tank battalions and supporting infantry from the 71st North African Infantry Division (71e NADI) counter-attacked the German bridgehead without success. The attack was partially repulsed by the first German armour and anti-tank units which had been rushed across the river as quickly as possible at 7:20 A.M. on pontoon bridges. On May 14, every available Allied light bomber was employed in an attempt to destroy the German pontoon bridges; but, despite incurring the highest single day action losses in the entire history of the British and French air forces, failed to destroy these targets.[124] Despite the failure of numerous quickly planned counterattacks to collapse the German bridgehead, the French Army was successful in re-establishing a continuous defensive position further south; on the west flank of the bridgehead, however, French resistance began to crumble.

The commander of the French Second Army, General Huntzinger, immediately took effective measures to prevent a further weakening of his position. An armoured division (3rd *Division Cuirassée de réserve*) and a motorized division blocked further German advances around his flank. However the commander of XIX Panzer Corps, Heinz Guderian, wasn't interested in Huntzinger's flank. Leaving for the moment 10th Panzer Division at the bridgehead to protect it from attacks by 3rd DCR, he moved his 1st and 2nd Panzer divisions sharply to the west on the 15th, undercutting the flank of the French Ninth Army by 40 km and forcing the 102nd Fortress Division to leave its positions that had blocked XVI Panzer Corps at Monthermé. While the French Second Army had been seriously mauled and had rendered itself impotent, now Ninth Army began to disintegrate completely, for in Belgium also its divisions, not having had the time to fortify, had been pushed back from the river by the unrelenting pressure of German infantry, allowing the impetuous

Erwin Rommel to break free with his 7th Panzer Division. A French armoured division (1st DCR) was sent to block him but advancing unexpectedly fast he surprised it while refuelling on the 15th and dispersed it, despite some losses caused by the heavy French tanks.

On the 16th, both Guderian and Rommel disobeyed their explicit direct orders to halt in an act of open insubordination against their superiors and moved their divisions many kilometres to the west, as fast as they could push them. Guderian reached Marle, 80 kilometres from Sedan, Rommel crossed the river Sambre at Le Cateau, a hundred kilometres from *his* bridgehead, Dinant. While nobody knew the whereabouts of Rommel (he had advanced so quickly that he was out of range for radio contact, earning his 7th Panzer Division the nickname *Gespenster-Division*, "Ghost Division"), an enraged von Kleist flew to Guderian on the morning of the 17 and after a heated argument relieved him of all duties. However, von Rundstedt would have none of it and refused to confirm the order.

Allied reaction

The Panzer Corps now slowed their advance considerably but had put themselves in a very vulnerable position. They were stretched out, exhausted and low on fuel; many tanks had broken down. There now was a dangerous gap between them and the infantry. A determined attack by a fresh large mechanized force could have cut them off and wiped them out.

The French high command, however, was reeling from the shock of the sudden offensive and was stung by a sense of defeatism. On the morning of May 15, French Prime Minister Paul Reynaud telephoned newly minted Prime Minister of the United Kingdom Winston Churchill and said "We have been defeated. We are beaten; we have lost the battle." Churchill, attempting to console Reynaud reminded the Prime Minister of the times the Germans had broken through allied lines in World War I only to be stopped. However, Reynaud was inconsolable.

Churchill flew to Paris on May 16. He immediately recognized the gravity of the situation when he observed that the French government was already burning its archives and preparing for an evacuation of the capital. In a sombre meeting with the French commanders, Churchill asked General Gamelin, "Where is the strategic reserve?" which had saved Paris in the First World War. "There is none", Gamelin replied. Later, Churchill described hearing this as the single most shocking moment in his life. Churchill asked Gamelin when and where the general proposed to launch a counterattack against the flanks of the German bulge. Gamelin simply replied "inferiority of numbers, inferiority of equipment, inferiority of methods".

Gamelin was right; most reserve divisions had by now been committed. The only armoured division still in reserve, 2nd DCR, attacked on the 16th. However the French armoured divisions of the Infantry, the *Divisions Cuirassées de Réserve*, were despite their name very specialized breakthrough units, optimized for attacking fortified positions. They could be quite useful for defence, if dug in, but had very limited utility for an encounter fight: they could not execute combined infantry-tank tactics as they simply had no important motorized infantry component; they had poor tactical mobility as the heavy Char B1 bis, their main tank in which half of the French tank budget had been invested, had to refuel twice a day. So 2nd DCR divided itself in a covering screen, the small subunits of which fought bravely – but without having any strategic effect.

Of course, some of the best units in the north had yet seen little fighting. Had they been kept in reserve they could have been used for a decisive counter strike. But now they had lost much fighting power simply by moving to the north; hurrying south again would cost them even more. The most powerful allied division, the 1st DLM (*Division Légère Mécanique*, "light" in this case meaning "mobile"), deployed near Dunkirk on the 10th, had moved its forward units 220 kilometres to the northeast, beyond the Dutch city of 's-Hertogenbosch, in 32 hours. Finding that the Dutch had already retreated to the north, it had withdrawn and was now moving to the south. When it would reach the Germans again, of its original 80 SOMUA S35 tanks only three would be operational, mostly as a result of break down.

Nevertheless, a radical decision to retreat to the south, avoiding contact, could probably have saved most of the mechanized and motorized divisions, including the BEF. However, that would have meant leaving about thirty infantry divisions to their fate. The loss of Belgium alone would be an enormous political blow. Besides, the Allies were uncertain about German intentions. They threatened in four directions: to the north, to attack the allied main force directly; to the west, to cut it off; to the south, to occupy Paris and even to the east, to move behind the Maginot Line. The French decided to create a new reserve, among which a reconstituted 7th Army, under General Robert Touchon, using every unit they could safely pull out of the Maginot Line to block the way to Paris.

Colonel Charles de Gaulle, in command of France's hastily formed 4th Armoured Division, attempted to launch an attack from the south and achieved a measure of success that would later accord him considerable fame and a promotion to Brigadier General. However, de Gaulle's attacks on the 17th and 19th did not significantly alter the overall situation.

Figure 71: *British and French soldiers taken prisoner in northern France.*

Channel attacks, battle of Dunkirk and the Weygand Plan (May 17–28)

While the Allies did little either to threaten them or escape from the danger they posed, the Panzer Corps used 17 and 18 May to refuel, eat, sleep and get some more tanks in working order. On 18 May, Rommel made the French give up Cambrai by merely feinting an armoured attack.

On 19 May, German High Command grew very confident. The Allies seemed incapable of coping with events. There appeared to be no serious threat from the south – indeed General Franz Halder, Chief of Army General Staff, toyed with the idea of attacking Paris immediately to knock France out of the war in one blow. The Allied troops in the north were retreating to the river Scheldt, their right flank giving way to the 3rd and 4th Panzer Divisions. It would be foolish to remain inactive any longer, allowing them to reorganize their defence or escape. Now it was time to bring them into even more serious trouble by cutting them off. The next day the Panzer Corps started moving again, smashed through the weak British 12th and 23rd Territorial divisions, occupied Amiens and secured the westernmost bridge over the river Somme at Abbeville isolating the British, French, Dutch and Belgian forces in the north. In the evening of 20 May, a reconnaissance unit from 2nd Panzer Division reached Noyelles, 100 kilometres (62 mi) to the west, where they could see the estuary of the Somme flowing into The Channel.

On May 20, French Prime Minister Paul Reynaud dismissed Maurice Gamelin for his failure to contain the German offensive and replaced him with Maxime Weygand, who immediately attempted to devise new tactics to contain the Germans. More pressing, however, was his strategic task: he formed the Weygand Plan, ordering to pinch off the German armoured spearhead by combined attacks from the north and the south. On the map, this seemed a feasible mission: the corridor through which von Kleist's two Panzer Corps had moved to the coast was a mere 40 kilometres (25 mi) wide. On paper, Weygand had sufficient forces to execute it: in the north, the three DLM and the BEF; in the south, de Gaulle's 4th DCR. These units had an organic strength of about 1,200 tanks and the Panzer divisions were very vulnerable again, the mechanical condition of their tanks rapidly deteriorating but the condition of the Allied divisions was far worse. Both in the south and the north they could in reality muster but a handful of tanks. Nevertheless, Weygand flew to Ypres on the 21st trying to convince the Belgians and the BEF of the soundness of his plan.

That same day, May 21, a detachment of the British Expeditionary Force under Major-General Harold Edward Franklyn had already attempted to at least delay the German offensive and, perhaps, to cut the leading edge of the German army off. The resulting Battle of Arras demonstrated the ability of the heavily armoured British Matilda tanks (the German 37 mm anti-tank guns proved ineffective against them) and the limited raid overran two German regiments. The panic that resulted (the German commander at Arras, Erwin Rommel, reported being attacked by 'hundreds' of tanks, though there were only 58 at the battle) temporarily delayed the German offensive. German reinforcements pressed the British back to Vimy Ridge the following day.

Although this attack wasn't part of any coordinated attempt to destroy the Panzer Corps, the German High Command panicked a lot more than Rommel. For a moment they feared to have been ambushed, that a thousand Allied tanks were about to smash their elite forces. But the next day they had regained confidence and ordered Guderian's XIX Panzer Corps to press north and push on to the Channel ports of Boulogne and Calais, in the back of the British and Allied forces to the north.

That same day, the 22nd, the French tried to attack south to the east of Arras, with some infantry and tanks, but by now the German infantry had begun to catch up and the attack was, with some difficulty, stopped by the 32nd Infantry Division.

Only on the 24th the first attack from the south could be launched when 7th DIC, supported by a handful of tanks, failed to retake Amiens. This was a rather weak effort; however, on May 27, part of the British 1st Armoured Division, hastily brought over from England, attacked Abbeville in force but was beaten back with crippling losses. The next day de Gaulle tried again with the same result. But by now even complete success couldn't have saved the forces in the north.

In the early hours of 23 May, Gort ordered a retreat from Arras. He had no faith in the Weygand plan nor in the proposal of the latter to at least try to hold a pocket on the Flemish coast, a *Réduit de Flandres*. The ports needed to supply such a foothold were already threatened. That day, the 2nd Panzer Division assaulted Boulogne and 10th Panzer assaulted Calais. The British garrison in Boulogne surrendered on 25 May although 4,368 troops were evacuated. Calais, though strengthened by the arrival of 3rd Royal Tank Regiment equipped with cruiser tanks and 30th Motor Brigade, fell to the Germans on 27 May.

While the 1st Panzer Division was ready to attack Dunkirk on the 25th, Hitler ordered it to halt on 24 May. This remains one of the most controversial decisions of the entire war. Hermann Göring had convinced Hitler the Luftwaffe could prevent an evacuation; Rundstedt had warned him that any further effort by the armoured divisions would lead to a much prolonged refitting period. Attacking cities wasn't part of the normal task for armoured units under any operational doctrine.

Allied evacuations (May 26 – June 25)

Encircled, the British, Belgian and French launched Operation Dynamo (May 26 – June 4) and later Operation Ariel (June 14–25), evacuating Allied forces from the northern pocket in Belgium and Pas-de-Calais, beginning on May 26. (see Battle of Dunkirk) The Allied position was complicated by King Léopold III of Belgium's surrender the following day, which was postponed until May 28.

Confusion still reigned however, as after the evacuation at Dunkirk and while Paris was enduring its short-lived siege, the First Canadian Division and a Scottish division were sent to Normandy and penetrated 200 miles inland toward Paris before they heard that Paris had fallen and France had capitulated. They retreated and re-embarked for England.

At the same time as the Canadian 1st division landed in Brest, the Canadian 242 Squadron of the RAF flew their Hawker Hurricanes to Nantes (100 miles south-east) and set up there to provide air cover.

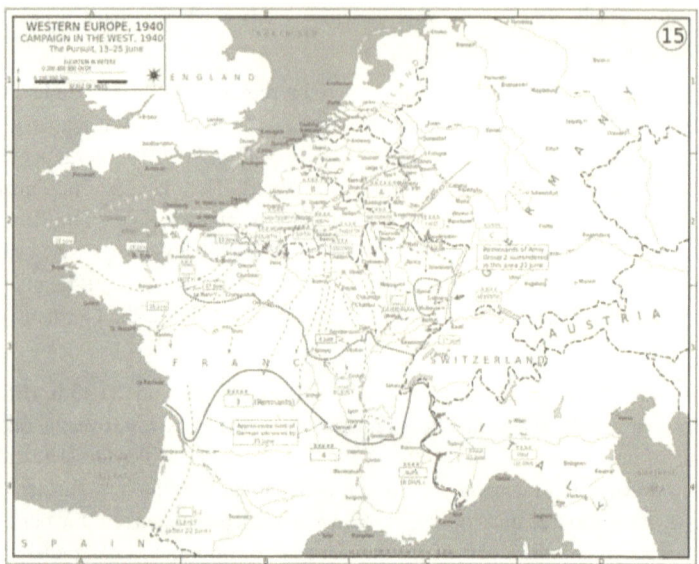

Figure 72: *The German offensive in June sealed the defeat of the Allies.*

British retreat, French defeat (June 5–10, 1940)

The best and most modern French armies had been sent north and lost in the resulting encirclement; the French had lost their best heavy weaponry and their best armoured formations. Weygand was faced with a haemorrhage in the front stretching from Sedan to the English Channel, and the French government had begun to lose heart that the Germans could still be defeated, particularly as the remaining British forces were retreating from the battlefield returning to Great Britain, a particularly symbolic event for French morale, intensified by the German anti-British propaganda slogan "The British will fight to the last Frenchman".

The Germans renewed their offensive on June 5 on the Somme. A panzer-led attack on Paris broke the scarce reserves that Weygand had put between the Germans and the capital, and on June 10 the French government fled to Bordeaux, declaring Paris an open city.

Italy's declaration of war, French-Italian air battles, UK ends French support (June 10–11, 1940)

On June 10, Italy declared war on France and Britain; Italian Royal Air Force (Regia Aeronautica) started its bomb raids over France. On June 13, French

Figure 73: *Barricades set in open city declared Paris, 1940.*

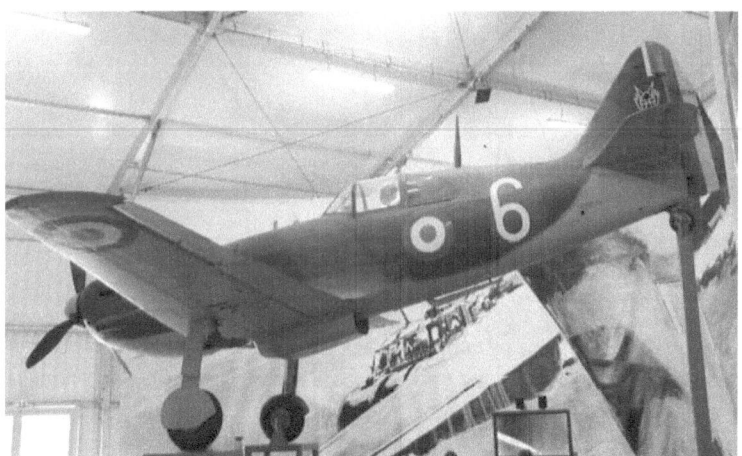

Figure 74: *French Republic air force Dewoitine D.520 similar to Pierre Le Gloan's.*

ace pilot Pierre Le Gloan shot down two Fiat BR.20 bombers with his Dewoitine D.520 fighter. On June 15, Le Gloan, along with another pilot, attacked a group of twelve Italian Fiat CR.42 fighters, and shot down three of them, while Cpt. Assolent shot down another. While returning to the airfield, Le Gloan shot down another CR.42 and another BR.20 bomber. For this achievement of destroying five aircraft in one flight, he was promoted to 2nd Lieutenant.

The following week, an Italian army crossed the Alps and fought with the French *Chasseurs Alpins* (Alpine Hunters), the Regia Aeronautica carried out 716 bombing missions in support of the invasion of France by the Italian Royal Army (Regio Esercito). Italian aircraft dropped a total of 276 tons of bombs.

Churchill returned to France on June 11, meeting the French War Council in Briare. The French, clearly in a panic, wanted Churchill to give every available fighter to the air battle over France; with only 25 squadrons remaining, Churchill refused to further help his ally, believing that the decisive battle would be fought over Britain (the Battle of Britain started on July 10). British support ended and France was left to its own fate facing the Germans and Italians all alone. Concerned about an upcoming German invasion of his own country, Churchill, at the meeting, obtained promises from French admiral François Darlan that the French Navy's fleet would not fall into German hands.

French-German negotiations, Pétain's appeal (June 16–17)

Paul Reynaud resigned because he believed a majority of his government favoured an armistice. He was succeeded by a patriarchal figure, 84-year-old World War I veteran *Maréchal* Philippe Pétain. On June 16, the new French President of the Council, Philippe Pétain (the President of the Republic office was vacant from July 11, 1940 until 16 January 1947), began negotiations with Axis officials. On June 17, 1940, Marshal Pétain delivered an infamous appeal to the French people via radio ordering them « *we must stop fighting* » (« *il faut cesser le combat* »).[125]

French-German and French-Italian armistices (June 22, 1940)

On June 21, Italian troops crossed the border in three places. Roughly thirty-two Italian divisions faced just four French divisions. Fighting continued in the east until General Pretelat, commanding the French Second Army group, was forced to surrender on June 22 by the armistice. France formally surrendered to the German armed forces on June 22 in the same railroad car at Compiègne in which Germany had been forced to surrender in 1918. This railway car was lost in allied air raids on the German capital of Berlin later in the war.

Figure 75: *Chief of collaborationist French State Marshal Pétain shaking hands with German Nazi leader Hitler at Montoire on October 24, 1940.*

German occupation, formation of Vichy France and Armistice army

Metropolitan France was divided into a German occupation zone in the north and west and an unoccupied zone in the south. Pétain set up a collaborationist government in the spa town of Vichy and the authoritarian regime French State, replacing the abolished French Republic, came to be known as Vichy France.

The formation of Free France and French Resistance

Charles de Gaulle, who had been made an Undersecretary of National Defense by Paul Reynaud, was in London at the time of the surrender: having made his Appeal of 18 June as an answer to Pétain's appeal of 17 June, he refused to recognize the Vichy government as legitimate – the President of France function was vacant – and began the task of organizing the Free French Forces. A number of French colonies like French Equatorial Africa joined de Gaulle's fight, while others like French Indochina were soon attacked by the Japanese or remained loyal to the Vichy government. Italy occupied a small area, essentially the Alpes-Maritimes, and Corsica.

Figure 76: *No.340 Free French RAF Squadron Spitfire bearing the Cross of Lorraine marking.*

Free French airmen in RAF (June 1940–1945)

The first Free French pilots flew from Bordeaux to rally de Gaulle in England on June 17, 1940. These individuals served in British squadrons until there were sufficient pilots to create All-Free French RAF flights.

Free French pilots in the battle of Britain (July 10 – October 31, 1940)

At least thirteen Free French pilots (from France) fought the battle of Britain against the German Luftwaffe. Among these men were Adjutant Émile Fayolle, son of an Admiral and grandson of French Marshal Marie Émile Fayolle. When the Armistice was signed on June 22, 1940 Fayolle was at the Fighter School at Oran, French Algeria. On June 30, he and a comrade flew to the British base at Gibraltar and from there sailed to Liverpool where they arrived on July 13 and joined the RAF. In November 1941 Fayolle went to Turnhouse to join 340 Squadron, the first all-French fighter unit. Another pilot with a similar course was Adjutant René Mouchotte, eleven Free French pilots were posted to No.1 School of Army Co-operation, Old Sarum on July 29. Mouchotte was posted to Turnhouse as Deputy 'A' Flight Commander with 340 Squadron on November 10. On January 18, 1943, Captain Mouchotte returned to Turnhouse to form and command the 341 Free French Squadron.

Figure 77: *Adjutant Emile Fayolle who fought the battle of Britain as RAF Free French and was shot down by AA (anti-aircraft) during the Battle of Dieppe on August 19, 1942.*

All-Free French RAF Squadrons (1941–1945)

In the summer of 1941, the British commander of the Fighter Command accepted the creation of the No.340 Free French (Fighter) Squadron (also known as *Groupe de chasse 2 "Île-de-France"*, a Free French unit attached to the No. 13 Group RAF, equipped with Spitfire aircraft and formed at Turnhouse, Scotland.[126] Other notable All-Free French RAF flights were the No. 327 Squadron RAF and No. 341 Squadron RAF.

French on the Eastern front (1941–1945)

Legion of French Volunteers Against Bolshevism (1941–1943)

The French State sent an expeditionary force, called *Légion des Volontaires Français Contre le Bolchevisme* (LVF), to fight the Red army along the German *Wehrmacht* on the Russian front. This volunteers unit, including old men and 15-year children as evidenced by Nazi propaganda archives, took part in the German invasion of Soviet Union called Operation Barbarossa.[127]

The L.V.F.'s German designation was *638.Infanterie-Regiment 638* ("638th Infantry Regiment") and it served under Field Marshal Günther von Kluge, commander of the Fourth Army.

Figure 78: *Field Marshal Günther von Kluge reviews the Vichy French LVF (638. Infanterie-Regiment) in Russia during Operation Barbarossa, November 1941.*

Battle of Diut'kovo (1941–1942)

The L.V.F. 638th Infantry Regiment fought the Battle of Diut'kovo (maybe Dyatkovo), which is part of the Battle of Moscow.

Battle of Berezina (1942–1943)

The L.V.F. 638th Infantry Regiment fought the Battle of Berezina as hinted by its flag.

Vichy French Sturmbataillon Charlemagne last defenders of Berlin (April–May 1945)

The Vichy French SS battalion Charlemagne (remains of the French SS Division Charlemagne) under *Hauptsturmführer* (Captain) Henri Fenet was among the last defenders of the Nazi German capital, fighting against Soviet forces during the Battle of Berlin in April–May 1945.

Free French Normandie-Niemen (1942–1945)

A fighter aviation group nicknamed Normandie-Niemen fought on the Russian front as part of the Soviet air force. These French volunteers were equipped with first-rate Yakovlev Soviet-built fighters.[128]

At de Gaulle's initiative, the Free French Air Force *Groupe de Chasse 3 "Normandie"* was formed on September 1, 1942, for service on the Eastern Front along the Soviet 1st Air Army. It served with distinction with Soviet aircraft and was awarded the supplementary title *Niemen* (from the Belaruss river) by Stalin. Its first commander was Jean Tulasne who was KIA[129]

The group Normandie-Niemen evolved from a single squadron called "Normandie" to a full regiment called Normandie-Niemen which included Squadron Caen, Squadron Le Havre and Squadron Rouen.

Their battle honors were Oryol 1943, Smolensk 1943, Orche 1944, Berezina 1944, Niemen 1944, Chernyakhovsk 1945 and Baltiysk 1945. By the end of World War II, the Free French unit counted 273 certified victories, 37 non-certified victories and 45 damaged aircraft with 869 fights and 42 dead.

On May 31, 1945, Normandie-Niemen squadrons were directed to Moscow by the Soviet authorities who decided to allow them to return in France with their aircraft as a reward. The 40 French pilots still active with the regiment flew back to France in Yak-3 fighter planes. They arrived at Elbląg, Poland on June 15, 1945, and in Paris Le Bourget, through Posen, Prague and Stuttgart, on June 21 (their arrival at Stuttgart and parade at Le Bourget were taped[130]).

Italian campaign (1943–1944)

Ist Army renamed French Expeditionary Force

During the Italian campaign of 1943, 130,000 Free French soldiers fought on the Allied side.

The 1st group, Ist Landing Corps (*1er groupement du Ier corps de débarquement*), later redesignated by as the French Expeditionary Corps (*Corps Expéditionnaire Français, CEF*) participated in the Italian Campaign with two divisions and two separate brigades from late 1943 to July 23, 1944.

Battle of Monte Cassino (17 January–18 May 1944)

In 1944, this corps was reinforced by two additional divisions and played an essential role in the Battle of Monte Cassino. After the Allied capture of Rome the Corps was gradually withdrawn from Italy and incorporated into the B Army (*Armée B*) for the invasion of Southern France.

Operation Diadem (May 1944)

Operation Diadem was a successful Allied assault, including the Free French Corps, on German Gustav Line defences in the Liri valley in Italy. Breaking through the German defensive lines, it relieved pressure on the Anzio beachhead.

Figure 79: *Free French Normandie-Niemen Yakovlev Yak-3 Soviet-built fighter.*

Operation Brassard (June 17–18, 1944)

This success was followed in June 1944 by the invasion of Elba in which the 9th Colonial Infantry Division (9 DIC) and *Choc* (special forces) battalions of I Corps assaulted and seized the heavily fortified island, defended by German fortress infantry and coastal artillery troops. Combat on the island was characterized by close-in fighting, use of flamethrowers, well-ranged German artillery, and the liberal use of mines.

France maquis warfare (January–July, 1944)

Battle of Vercors (January–July)

A force of 4,000 French Resistance (FFI) fighters proclaimed the Free Republic of Vercors opposing the German army and French Milice.

Battle of Mont Gargan (July 18–24)

FTP forces (*Francs-tireurs partisans*) under Georges Guingouin fought the *Wehrmacht* General Curt von Jesser's brigade.

Figure 80: *French colonial troops entering Portoferraio, Elba, in June 1944.*

Figure 81: *A truck of the FFI bearing the Free French Republic of Vercors emblem.*

Campaign of France (1944–1945)

By the time of the Normandy Invasion, the Free French forces numbered 500,000 regulars and more than 100,000 FFI. The Free French 2nd Armoured Division, under General Philippe Leclerc, landed at Utah Beach in Normandy on August 2 and eventually led the drive towards Paris later that month. The FFI (French Resistance) began to seriously harass the German forces, cutting roads, railways, making ambushes as well as fighting battles alongside their allies.

French SAS Brittany airborne landings (June 5–18, 1944)

Operation Dingson (June 5–18)

Free French airborne under Colonel Pierre-Louis Bourgoin dropped behind German lines in Brittany.

Free French contribution to the Normandy naval landings (June 1944)

French contribution on D-Day

Only a few French infantry were involved in the Allied landing operations on June 6, 1944. There were 209- 177 commandos and 32 airborne troopers. Additional personnel include a hundred French air force fighter and bomber pilots and hundreds of sailors from the French navy.

The first to touch the ground of France

Free French infantry fighting in the Normandy beaches on June 6 is limited to the 1er Bataillon de Fusiliers Marins Commandos (1er BFMC) under Free French Navy Major Philippe Kieffer.

The Free French Navy's 1er BFMC comprised 177 commandos and had been created at Achnacarry, Scotland after the British Commandos. This All-French unit, including many Bretons as Brittany was close to England, was attached to the British No. 4 Commando under Lieutenant-Colonel Dawson. It was the very first infantry unit to touch the sand of Ouistreham, (Normandy) in the landing full-scale operation *Operation Overlord*; preceding the 3rd British Infantry Division. This honor was a courtesy of 1st Special Service Brigade (S.S.B.) commander Scottish Brigadier Simon Fraser, 15th Lord Lovat who slowed down the British commandos landing crafts to let pass the French LCI 527 (Troop 1) and LCI 528 (Troop 8). The 1er BFMC's Normandy campaign lasted 83 days, casualty rate was high, from the 117 Kieffer commandos of June 6, only 24 survived.

Free French naval operations (June 3–16)

The Free French Navy under Admiral Ramsay took part in Operation Neptune which was the naval part of Operation Overlord, a series of missions were fulfilled on June 6:

- Juno Beach, French destroyer *La Combattante* under Commander André Patou shelled the German fortifications of Courseulles-sur-Mer while frigate *La Découverte* and corvette *Commandant-d'Estienne-d'Orves* escorted the Canadian infantry landing crafts.
- Gold Beach, the frigate *La Surprise* protected the British landing operation.
- Utah Beach, the corvettes *L'Aconit* and *La Renoncule* were in charge of patrolling against U-boats.
- Omaha Beach, in Vierville-sur-Mer, Saint-Laurent-sur-Mer and Colleville-sur-Mer sectors, the frigates *Escarmouche*, *Aventure* and the corvette *Roselys* escorted the US V Corps's landing crafts
- English Channel, eight fast patrol boats of the 23rd Flotilla patrolled for incoming German navy forces or seamines.

Another French mission from June 3 to 16, consisted in the shelling of Omaha Beach's defense by a fleet under Admiral Jaujard which comprised the 7,500 tons cruisers *Georges-Leygues* and *Montcalm*, with their 10,000 tons tanker, and the cruiser *Duquesne*. The three cruisers fired thousands of shells in four days.

Defense operations were also performed by the corvettes and frigates establishing a shuttle between English harbours and the French coast. They escorted the logistics maneuvers involving infantry landing crafts, medical evacuations from the battlefield and sought for any Kriegsmarine menace.

On June 9, the obsolete French cuirassé *Courbet* was disarmed and saborded – together with other ships – in the Hermanville-sur-Mer area to be used as artificial breakwaters.

All-Free French air force operations

Light bomber Boston equipped bomb group No. 342 Squadron RAF (GB 1/20 Lorraine), commanded by Michel Fouquet, supported the Omaha Beach invasion with a smoke screen campaign blinding and isolating the German defenders.

Heavy bombers of bomb groups GB 1/15 Touraine and No. 347 Squadron RAF (GB 1/25 Tunisie) and fighters of No. 329 Squadron RAF (GC 1/2 Cigognes), No. 345 Squadron RAF (GC 2/2 Berry), No. 341 Squadron RAF (GC 3/2 Alsace) and No. 340 Squadron RAF (GC 4/2 Île de France) serviced under Air Marshal Leigh-Mallory.

Figure 82: *2nd Armoured Division (2e DB) in Normandy during Operation Overlord.*

The Free French airmen were part of the first casualties of Day-D. These include the flying crew Boissieux-Canut-Henson from bomb group No. 342 Squadron RAF (GB 1/20 Lorraine) which left its base at dawn and was KIA when its Boston was shot down.

Leclerc's 2nd Armoured Division (August 1944 – January 1945)

The 2nd Division landed at Utah Beach (Normandy), on August 1, 1944, about two months after the D-Day landings, and served under General Patton's Third Army.

Battle for Normandy (July 1944)

The 2nd division played a critical role in Operation Cobra, the Allied breakthrough from Normandy, when it served as a link between American and Canadian armies and made rapid progress against German forces. They all but destroyed the 9th Panzer Division and defeated several other German units. During the Battle for Normandy, the 2nd Division lost 133 men killed, 648 wounded, and 85 missing. Division material losses included 76 armored vehicles, 7 cannons, 27 halftracks, and 133 other vehicles. In the same period, the 2nd Division inflicted losses on the Germans of 4,500 killed and 8,800 taken

Figure 83: *Crowds of French people line the Champs Élysées to view the French 2e DB tanks and half tracks pass before the Arc de Triomphe on 26 August 1944.*

prisoner, while the Germans' material losses in combat against the 2nd Division during the same period were 117 tanks, 79 cannons, and 750 wheeled vehicles.[131]

Liberation of Paris (August 24–25, 1944)

The most celebrated moment in the 2nd's history involved the Liberation of Paris. Allied strategy emphasized destroying German forces retreating towards the Rhine, but when the French Resistance under Colonel Rol-Tanguy staged an uprising in the city, Charles de Gaulle pleaded with Eisenhower to send help. Eisenhower agreed and Leclerc's forces headed for Paris. After hard fighting that cost the 2nd Division 35 tanks, 6 self-propelled guns, and 111 vehicles, von Choltitz, the military governor of Paris, surrendered the city at the Hôtel Meurice. Jubilant crowds greeted French forces, and de Gaulle conducted a famous parade through the city.

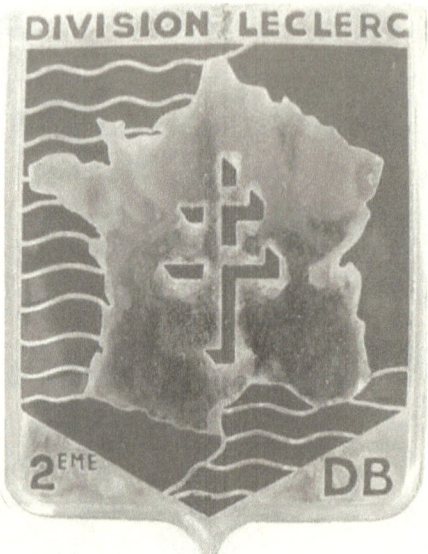

Figure 84: *Arms of the 2ème D.B., the Second Armoured Division commanded by Leclerc. The Division's emblem features the Cross of Lorraine.*

Lorraine Campaign, Liberation of Strasbourg (1944 – January 1945)

Subsequently, the 2nd Division campaigned with American forces in Lorraine, spearheading the U.S. Seventh Army drive through the northern Vosges Mountains and forcing the Saverne Gap. Eventually, after liberating Strasbourg in November 1944, defending against the German Nordwind counter-offensive in Alsace in January 1945, and conducting operations against the Royan Pocket on the Atlantic coast of France.

Liberation of southern France (June–August, 1944)

Operation Jedburgh (June)

Free French airborne commandos, called "Jedburgh", were dropped behind Nazi lines in Provence in order to support the upcoming Allied landing (Operation Dragoon) and prepare the French Resistance. This Allied operation was in conjunction with the Free French intelligence service Bureau Central de Renseignements et d'Action (BCRA); famous French Jedburghs are Jean Sassi and Paul Aussaresses.

Figure 85: *Free French armoured car "Joseph Camaret II" used during the Liberation of La Rochelle, Charente-Maritime (atlantic coast of France) in 1945.*

Figure 86: *Restored US-supplied French M10 tank destroyer of the 8e RCA (1st French Army) who fought the 1945 Colmar Pocket.*

Figure 87: *French Moroccan and African-American troops link up at Rouffach, Alsace during the 1945 Pocket of Colmar.*

Figure 88: *French Jedburgh commando Jean Sassi in 1944.*

Figure 89: *A French Army US-built Sherman tank lands on a Normandy beach from USS LST-517, 2 August 1944.*

Battle for Provence (August)

Operation Dragoon was the Allied invasion of southern France, on August 15, 1944, as part of World War II. The invasion took place between Toulon and Cannes. During the planning stages, the operation was known as *Anvil*, to complement *Operation Hammer*, which was at that time the codename for the invasion of Normandy. Subsequently, both plans were renamed, the latter becoming Operation Overlord, the former becoming Operation *Dragoon*; a name supposedly picked by Winston Churchill, who was opposed to the plan, and claimed to having been "dragooned" into accepting it.

The plan originally envisaged a mixture of Free French and American troops taking Toulon and later Marseille, with subsequent revisions encompassing Saint Tropez. The plan was revised throughout 1944, however, with conflict developing between British military staff — who were opposed to the landings, arguing that the troops and equipment should be either retained in Italy or sent there — and American military staff, who were in favour of the assault. This was part of a larger Anglo-American strategic disagreement.

The balance was tipped in favour of *Dragoon* by two events: the eventual fall of Rome in early June, plus the success of Operation Cobra, the breakout from

Figure 90: *Free French General Leclerc talks to his men from the 501° RCC (501st Tank Regiment).*

the Normandy pocket, at the end of the month. Operation *Dragoon's* D-Day was set for August 15, 1944. The final go-ahead was given at short notice.

The U.S. 6th Army Group, also known as the Southern Group of Armies, commanded by Lieutenant General Jacob L. Devers was created in Corsica and activated on August 1, 1944, to consolidate the combined French and American forces that were planning to invade southern France in Operation *Dragoon*. At first it was subordinate to AFHQ (Allied Forces Headquarters) under the command of Field Marshal Sir Henry Maitland Wilson who was the supreme commander of the Mediterranean Theater. One month after the invasion, command was handed over to SHAEF (Supreme Headquarters, Allied Expeditionary Forces) under U.S. General Dwight D. Eisenhower, the supreme commander of Allied forces on the Western Front.

The assault troops were formed of three American divisions of the VI Corps, reinforced by a French armoured division. The 3rd Infantry Division landed on the left at Alpha Beach (Cavalaire-sur-Mer), the 45th Infantry Division landed in the centre at Delta Beach (Saint-Tropez), and the 36th Infantry Division landed on the right at Camel Beach (Saint-Raphaël). These were supported by French commando groups landing on both flanks, and by Rugby Force, a parachute assault in the Le Muy-Le Luc area by the 1st Airborne Task

Figure 91: *US and French soldiers comparing their respective weapons in Couterne, Orne in 1944.*

Force: British 2nd Parachute Brigade, the U.S. 517th Parachute Regimental Combat Team, and a composite U.S. airborne glider regimental combat team formed from the 509th Parachute Infantry Battalion, the 550th Glider Infantry Battalion, and the 1st Battalion, 551st Parachute Infantry regiment. The 1st Special Service Force took two offshore islands to protect the beachhead.

Naval gunfire from Allied ships, including battleships *Lorraine*, HMS *Ramillies*, USS *Texas*, USS *Nevada* and USS *Arkansas* and a fleet of over 50 cruisers and destroyers supported the landings. Seven Allied escort carriers provided air cover.

Over ninety-four thousand troops and eleven thousand vehicles were landed on the first day. A number of German troops had been diverted to fight the Allied forces in Northern France after Operation Overlord and a major attack by French resistance fighters, coordinated by Captain Aaron Bank of the OSS, helped drive the remaining German forces back from the beachhead in advance of the landing. As a result, the Allied forces met little resistance as they moved inland. The quick success of this invasion, with a twenty-mile penetration in twenty-four hours, sparked a major uprising by resistance fighters in Paris.

Figure 92: *2e DB commander General Leclerc in a jeep.*

Follow-up formations included US VI Corps HQ, US Seventh Army HQ, French Army B (later redesignated the *French First Army*) and French I and II Corps.

The rapid retreat of the German Nineteenth Army resulted in swift gains for the Allied forces. The plans had envisaged greater resistance near the landing areas and underestimated transport needs. The consequent need for vehicle fuel outstripped supply, and this shortage proved to be a greater impediment to the advance than German resistance. As a result, several German formations escaped into the Vosges and Germany.

The *Dragoon* force met up with southern thrusts from Overlord in mid-September, near Dijon.

Operation *Dragoon* included a glider landing (Operation Dove) and a deception (Operation Span).

A planned benefit of *Dragoon* was the usefulness of the port of Marseille. The rapid Allied advance after Operation Cobra and *Dragoon* slowed almost to a halt in September 1944 due to a critical lack of supplies, as thousands of tons of supplies were shunted to NW France to compensate for the inadequacies of port facilities and land transport in northern Europe. Marseille and the southern French railways were brought back into service despite heavy damage to the Port of Marseille and its railroad trunk lines. They became a significant

Figure 93: *French military review in liberated Marseilles on August 29, 1944.*

supply route for the Allied advance into Germany, providing about a third of the Allied needs.

Operation Romeo (August 15, 1944)

French commandos assaulted German artillery position at Cap Nègre. 300 German soldiers were killed and 700 were taken prisoner. The French commandos suffered 11 men killed and 50 wounded.

Liberation of Toulon and Marseilles

The French First Army under Jean de Lattre de Tassigny performed spectacularly in the capture of Toulon and Marseilles. "The original plan intended to attack the two ports in succession. The accelerated landings of de Lattre's French forces, however, and the general situation allowed concurrent operations against both. De Lattre ordered Lt. Gen. Edgard de Larminat to move west against Toulon along the coast, with two infantry divisions supported by tanks and commandos. Simultaneously, a second force, under Maj. Gen. Goislard de Monsabert and consisting of one infantry division and similar supporting forces, would advance in a more northwesterly direction, encircling the naval port from the north and west and probing toward Marseille. De Lattre knew that the German garrisons at the ports were substantial: some 18,000 troops of all types at Toulon and another 13,000, mostly army, at Marseille.

Figure 94: *A jeep was mounted on rail in Normandy, on board French and British troops. 1944*

However, Resistance sources also told him that the defenders had not yet put much effort into protecting the landward approaches to the ports, and he was convinced that a quick strike by experienced combat troops might well crack their defenses before they had a chance to coalesce. Speed was essential.[132]

On the morning of August 20, with the German command in Toulon still in a state of confusion and the Nineteenth Army more concerned with Truscott's westward progress well north of the port, de Larminat attacked from the east while Monsabert circled around to the north, quickly outflanking Toulon's hasty defenses along the coast. By the 21st Monsabert had cut the Toulon-Marseille road, and several of his units had entered Toulon from the west, penetrating to within two miles of the main waterfront. Between 21 and 23 August, the French slowly squeezed the Germans back into the inner city in a series of almost continuous street fights. As the German defense lost coherence, isolated groups began to surrender, with the last organized resistance ending on the 26th and the formal German surrender occurring on 28 August. The battle cost de Lattre about 2,700 casualties, but the French claimed 17,000 prisoners, indicating that few Germans had followed the Fuehrer's "stand and die" order.

Even as French forces occupied Toulon, Monsabert began the attack on Marseille, generally screening German defenses along the coast and striking from the northeastern and northern approaches. Early gains on the 22d put French troops within five to eight miles of the city's center, while a major Resistance uprising within the port encouraged French soldiers to strike deeper.

Although de Lattre urged caution, concerned over the dispersion of his forces and the shortage of fuel for his tanks and trucks, Monsabert's infantry plunged into the heart of Marseille in the early hours of 23 August. Their initiative decided the issue, and the fighting soon became a matter of battling from street to street and from house to house, as in Toulon. On the evening of the 27th, the German commander parleyed with Monsabert to arrange terms and a formal surrender became effective on the 28th, the same day as the capitulation of Toulon. At Marseille, the French took over 1,800 casualties and acquired roughly 11,000 more prisoners. Equally important, both ports, although badly damaged by German demolitions, were in Allied hands many weeks ahead of schedule."

Liberation of north-eastern France (September 1944 – March 1945)

Moving north, the French First Army liberated Lyon on 2 September 1944[133] and moved into the southern Vosges Mountains, capturing Belfort and forcing the Belfort Gap at the close of November 1944.[134] Following the capture of the Belfort Gap, French operations in the area of Burnhaupt destroyed the German IV Luftwaffe Korps.[135] In February 1945, with the assistance of the U.S. XXI Corps, the First Army collapsed the Colmar Pocket and cleared the west bank of the Rhine River of Germans in the area south of Strasbourg.[136]

Western Allied invasion of Germany (1945)

First French Army in west Germany (March–April 1945)

In March 1945, the First Army fought through the Siegfried Line fortifications in the Bienwald Forest near Lauterbourg.[137] Subsequently, the First Army crossed the Rhine near Speyer and captured Karlsruhe and Stuttgart.[138] Operations by the First Army in April 1945 encircled and captured the German XVIII. S.S.-Armeekorps in the Black Forest[139] and cleared southwestern Germany.

Normandie-Niemen air raids over Königsberg (April 1945)

Free French *Normandie-Niemen* squadron's flag features Battle of Königsberg 1945 as battle honor and the unit was awarded the "Take of the Königsberg Fortress" medal.

Free French Division Leclerc at Berchtesgaden (May 4, 1945)

General Leclerc's 2nd Division finished its campaigning at the Nazi resort town of Berchtesgaden, in southeastern Germany, where Hitler's mountain residence, the Berghof, was located. Leclerc's armoured unit was along the U.S. 3rd Infantry Division.

French Army of Africa's 7e RCA at Württemberg (1945)

The (*7th Africa Chasers Regiment's*) battleflag hints this Army of Africa Free French unit fought at Württemberg during the Allied invasion of Germany in 1945.

Campaign of the Netherlands (1945)

French SAS Operation Amherst (April 7–8, 1945)

The operation began with the drop of 700 Special Air Service troopers of 3rd and 4th French SAS on the night of 7 April 1945. The teams spread out to capture and protect key facilities from the Germans. Advancing Canadian troops of the 8th Reconnaissance Regiment relieved the isolated French SAS.

Liberation of Belgium

Battle of the Bulge (1944–1945)

Two French Light Infantry Battalions (J. Lawton Collins's VII Corps (United States)) and six French Light Infantry Battalions from Metz region (Troy H. Middleton's VIII Corps (United States)) fought the Battle of the Bulge. The 3rd SAS French 1st Airborne Marine Infantry Regiment battle honor bears the Battle of Bulge ("*Ardennes Belges 1945*").

English Channel and North Sea theatre of World War II

"British treachery" over Free French navy (July 3 – August 31, 1940)

On 3 July 1940, Prime Minister Winston Churchill ordered the capture of French ships by the British as Operation Catapult. This included not only the enemy Vichy French ships in the Mediterranean (see Battle of Mers-el-Kebir) but also the allied Free French ships docked in Britain after the Dunkirk evacuation. The capture by force of docked ships led to fighting between Free French sailors and outnumbering British Marines, sailors and soldiers in the English harbours. A similar operation was executed in Canada. The British

Figure 95: *Members of the crew of Fantasque-class destroyer Le Triomphant in working rig, seated on gantries hanging over the ship's side, painting the ship's bow. Le Triomphant was one of the French naval ships that came to British ports after the fall of France and was crewed by Free French sailors, forming part of the Free French Navy. 1940*

assault on the then World's largest submarine *Surcouf* resulted in three dead British (2 Royal Navy officers and 1 British seaman) and one dead Free French (warrant officer mechanic Yves Daniel[140]).

Commandeered Free French vessels included *Fantasque*-class destroyer *Le Triomphant* which was captured by the British at Plymouth. Because of the complexity of her handling and of the need to support the Free France, *Le Triomphant* was handed to the FNFL, on 28 August 1940, and put under the command of captain Pierre Gilly. Her aft gun was replaced by a British model. *Chacal*-class destroyer *Léopard* was under repair at Portsmouth after the Dunkirk evacuation when she was captured by the British. She was handed over to the Free French Naval Forces on 31 August.[141] *Courbet*-class battleship *Paris* also under repair at Plymouth, along with her sister ship *Courbet*, eight torpedo boats, five submarines and a number of other ships of lesser importance. Britain planned to transfer her to the Polish Navy. The ceremony was to be held on 15 July 1940 and it was planned to rename the ship to OF *Paris* (OF – Okręt Francuski – "French ship") but due to lack of personnel the ship was never handed over to the Polish Navy and was used by the British as an accommodation ship in Devonport.

The commandeered *Bourrasque*-class destroyer *Ouragan* was not returned to the Free French but instead was transferred to the Free Polish Navy on 17 July 1940. Until 30 April 1941 she sailed under the Polish ensign with pennant number H16, but as OF *Ouragan* (OF – Okręt Francuski – "French ship"), instead of the usual ORP prefix. It was only after 287 days that *Ouragan* was returned to her owner, on 30 April 1941.

After the capture of Allied French ships, Britain tried to repatriate the captured Free French sailors. The British hospital ship that was carrying them back to metropolitan France was sunk by the Germans, and many of the French blamed the British for their deaths.

Operation Catapult was called «*treachery*» by both the Vichy and Free French. The French State exploited this series of events in its anti-British propaganda which has a long-running history back to the Perfidious Albion myth.

Atlantic theatre of World War II

Battle of the Atlantic

The French Navy took part in the naval Battle of the Atlantic from 1939 to 1940. After the armistice of June 1940, Free French Naval Forces, headed by admiral Émile Muselier, were created and pursued the war on the Allies side.

Last battle of the battleship Bismarck (May 26–27, 1941)

The Free French Navy's submarine *Minerve* was involved in the Allied battle against the Allied battle against the *Bismarck*.

Free French rescue of British Convoy HG-75 (October 24, 1941)

On 24 October 1941 the German submarine *U-564* attacked Allied Convoy HG-75, which was sailing from Almería, Spain, to Barrow-in-Furness, England. *U-564* fired five torpedoes, hitting and sinking three cargo ships: *Alhama*, *Ariosto* and *Carsbreck*. There were 18 survivors from *Carsbreck*, and all were rescued by the Free French *Elan*-class minesweeping aviso *Commandant Duboc* (F743).

Figure 96: *The French Browning Machine Gun being manned by two crew members wearing gas masks. They are on board the French minesweeping aviso FFS Commandant Duboc (F743) at Plymouth. The ship is crewed entirely by Free French. Note the pipe leading out of the jacket of the machine gun to circulate the liquid coolant. 28 August 1940.*

Laconia incident (12 September 1942)

Vichy French ships were involved with the Laconia incident.

Mediterranean theatre of World War II

Naval battle of the Mediterranean (1940–1945)

Both the Vichy French Navy and Free French Navy fought the Battle of the Mediterranean sea. A notable action took place in the Adriatic sea on 29 February 1944 known as the Battle off Ist when a German naval force of two corvettes and two torpedo boats escorting a freighter supported by three minesweepers were intercepted by the Free French Navy operated under British command as the 24th Destroyer flotilla. Under Captain Pierre Lancelot the *Super* or heavy Le Fantasque-class destroyers *Le Terrible* and *Le Malin* managed to destroy the German freighter and a corvette in return for no loss before withdrawing.

Figure 97: *Anti-aircraft guns at action stations during an alert on board a Free French Destroyer, part of the Free French Navy. circa 1940–1941*

Naval battle of Mers El Kébir (July 3, 1940)

The British began to doubt Admiral Darlan's promise to Churchill to not allow the French fleet at Toulon to fall into German hands by the wording of the armistice conditions. In the end, the British attacked French naval forces in Africa and Europe killing 1000 French soldiers at Mers El Kebir alone. This action led to feelings of animosity and mistrust between the Vichy French and their former British allies. During the course of the war, Vichy France forces lost 2,653 soldiers[142] and Free France lost 20,000.[143]

In German and Italian hands, the French fleet would have been a grave threat to Britain and the British Government was unable to take this risk. In order to neutralise the threat, Winston Churchill ordered that the French ships should rejoin the Allies, agree to be put out of use in a British, French or neutral port or, as a last resort, be destroyed by British attack (Operation Catapult). The Royal Navy attempted to persuade the French Navy to agree to these terms, but when that failed they attacked the French Navy at Mers El Kébir and Dakar (see), on July 3, 1940. This caused bitterness and division in France, particularly in the Navy, and discouraged many French soldiers from joining the Free French forces in Britain and elsewhere. Also, the attempt to persuade Vichy

French forces in Dakar to join De Gaulle failed. (See West African campaign and Operation Menace).

Sabotage operation in Greece (June 12–13, 1942)

In June 1942, British SAS C.O. David Stirling gave British captains George Jellicoe and Free French Georges Bergé a mission in the Greek island of Crete called Operation Heraklion. Bergé chose three Free French commandos Jacques Mouhot, Pierre Léostic and Jack Sibard, while Lieutenant Kostis Petrakis a local from Crete's special service joined them as civilian.

They managed to destroy 22 Junkers Ju 88 German bombers at the Candia-Heraklion airfield. However their retreat was betrayed and 17-year-old Pierre Léostic refused to surrender and was killed while the other three Free French were caught and transferred in Germany; the British and Cretian commandos escaped and were evacuated to Egypt.

Jacques Mouhot failed to escape three times, he eventually succeeded the fourth time. He subsequently crossed Germany, Belgium, France and Spain to arrive in London on August 22, 1943.

Scuttling of the French fleet in Toulon (November 27, 1942)

The Vichy French navy did sabotage on its docked fleet at Toulon in southern France. This act's purpose was to prevent the German *Kriegsmarine* to seize the Vichy French ships and to be able to use its firepower against the Allies and Free French.

Allied invasion of Sicily (July 9 – August 17, 1943)

Operation Husky involved infantry, air force and armored cavalry forces from the Army of Africa including 4th Moroccan Tabor (66th, 67th & 68th Goums landed on July 13 at Licata) from U.S. 7th Army, No. II/5 "LaFayette" French Squadron with Curtiss P-40s and No. II/7 "Nice" French Squadron with Spitfires (both from No. 242 Group RAF), II/33 Groupe "Savoie" with P-38 Lightning from the Northwest African Photographic Reconnaissance Wing and 131st RCC with Renault R35 tanks.

Liberation of Corsica (September–October 1943)

In September–October 1943, an ad hoc force (ca. 6,000 troops) of the French Ist Corps liberated Corsica, defended by the German 90th Panzergrenadier Division and the Sturmbrigade Reichsführer-SS (ca. 30,000 troops) (45,000 Italians were also present, but at least part of that force joined the Allies). Thereby Corsica became the first French metropolitan department liberated in World War II; the first liberated département was Algiers in November 1942.

Figure 98: *French II/33 Groupe "Savoie" P-38 Lightning were involved in Operation Husky. It was on board a F-5B-1-LO variant that Antoine de Saint-Exupéry (Le Petit Prince) was shot down in 1944.*

African theatre of World War II

West African campaign

Battle of Dakar (September 23–25, 1940)

The Battle of Dakar, also known as Operation Menace, was an unsuccessful attempt by the Allies to capture the strategic port of Dakar in French West Africa (modern-day Senegal), which was under Vichy French control, and to install the Free French under General Charles de Gaulle there.[144]

De Gaulle believed that he could persuade the Vichy French forces in Dakar to join the Allied cause. There were several advantages to this; not only the political consequences if another Vichy French colonies changed sides, but also more practical advantages, such as the fact that the gold reserves of the Banque de France and the Polish government in exile were stored in Dakar and, militarily, the better location of the port of Dakar for protecting the convoys sailing around Africa than Freetown, the base the Allies were using.

Figure 99: *British General Spears and French General de Gaulle en route to Dakar.*

Figure 100: *French cruiser Georges Leygues.*

It was decided to send a naval force of an aircraft carrier, two battleships (of World War I vintage), four cruisers and ten destroyers to Dakar. Several transports, would transport the 8,000 troops. Their orders were first to try and negotiate with the Vichy French governor, but if this was unsuccessful, to take the city by force.

The Vichy French forces present at Dakar were led by a battleship, the *Richelieu*, one of the most advanced in the French fleet. It had left Brest on the June 18 before the Germans reached it. *Richelieu* was then only about 95% complete. Before the establishment of the Vichy government, HMS *Hermes*, an aircraft carrier, had been operating with the French forces in Dakar. Once the Vichy regime was in power, *Hermes* left port but remained on watch, and was joined by the Australian heavy cruiser HMAS *Australia*. Planes from *Hermes* had attacked the *Richelieu*, and had struck it once with a torpedo. The French ship was immobilised but was able to function as a floating gun battery. Three Vichy submarines and several lighter ships were also at Dakar. A force of three cruisers (*Gloire*, *Georges Leygues*, and *Montcalm*) and three destroyers had left Toulon for Dakar just a few days earlier. The *Gloire* was slowed by mechanical troubles, and was intercepted by *Australia* and ordered to sail for Casablanca. The other two cruisers and the destroyers outran the pursuing Allied cruisers and had reached Dakar safely.

On September 23, the Fleet Air Arm dropped propaganda leaflets on the city. Free French aircraft flew off from *Ark Royal* and landed at the airport, but the crews were taken prisoner. A boat with representatives of de Gaulle entered the port but were fired upon. At 10:00, Vichy French ships trying to leave the port were given warning shots from *Australia*. The ships returned to port but the coastal forts opened fire on *Australia*. This led to an engagement between the battleships and cruisers and the forts. In the afternoon, *Australia* intercepted and fired on the Vichy destroyer *L'Audacieux*, setting it on fire and causing it to be beached.

In the afternoon, an attempt was made to set Free French troops ashore on a beach at Rufisque, to the north east of Dakar, but they came under heavy fire from strong points defending the beach. De Gaulle declared he did not want to "shed the blood of Frenchmen for Frenchmen" and the attack was called off.

During the next two days, the Allied fleet attacked the coastal defences, as the Vichy French tried to prevent them. Two Vichy French submarines were sunk, and a destroyer damaged. After the Allied fleet also took heavy damage (both battleships and two cruisers were damaged), they withdrew, leaving Dakar and French West Africa in Vichy French hands.

The effects of the Allied failure were mostly political. De Gaulle had believed that he would be able to persuade the Vichy French at Dakar to change sides, but this turned out not to be the case, which damaged his standing with the Allies.

Battle of Gabon (November 8–10, 1940)

The Battle of Gabon, in November 1940, was a successful attempt to rally the French African colony.

East African Campaign

Eithrea-Ethiopia campaign (1941)

Free French colonial forces from the Brigade of the East (*Brigade d'Orient*) under Colonel Monclar, including the 14th Battalion Légion Etrangère (13th Foreign Legion Demi-Brigade) and the 3rd Battalion de Marche (from Chad), fought Italian troops in their colonies of Ethiopia and Eritrea, and Vichy French Forces of French Somaliland.

Battle of Keren (February 3 – April 1, 1941)

The battle was fought from 5 February to 1 April 1941 between a mixed Italian army of regular and colonial troops and the attacking British, Commonwealth, and Free French forces.

North African campaign & Desert War

A large-scale Allied invasion of the French protectorate in Morocco and French departements of Algeria was set in November 1942, it is called Operation Torch. Naval and airbornes landings opposed American and British troops to Vichy French forces. The French Resistance interfered in the Allied side by setting a coup d'état against both Vichy French governors, one failed the other succeeded.

Operation Torch had an important aftermath on the French military rallying the Army of Africa to the Free French cause and in the same time infuriated Hitler who ordered the occupation of metropolitan France's southern, said free, zone as well as air raids against French Algeria cities by the Libya-based Luftwaffe.

North African Free French Air Force (July 1940–1945)

In July 1940, there were sufficient Free French pilots in African colonial bases to man several squadrons based in French North Africa. On July 8, 1940 were created the Free French Flight (FAFL) units based in Middle-Eastern French colonies. They were initially equipped with a mixture of British, French and American aircraft. From a strength of 500 in July 1940, the ranks of the *Forces Aériennes Françaises Libres* (FAFL) grew to 900 by 1941, including 200 fliers.

Besides the FAFL air force existed the Free French Naval Air Service. On August 3, 1943, de Gaulle's Free French forces merged with Giraud's Army of Africa.

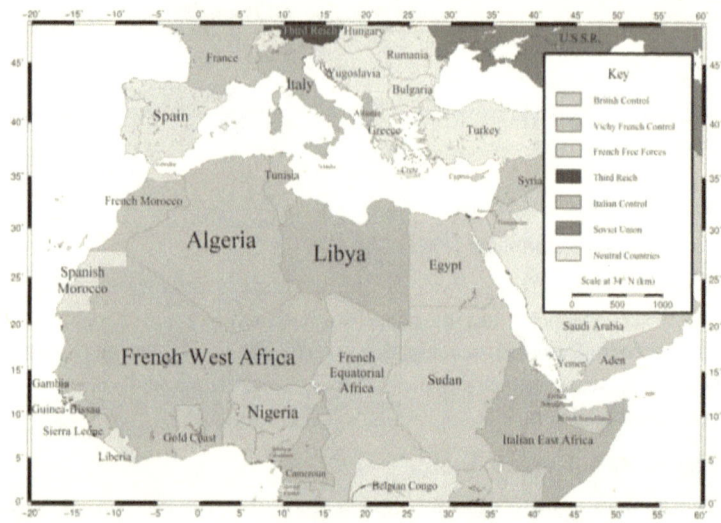

Figure 101: *African colonies after the 1940 Battle of France.*

Figure 102: *FAFL Free French GC II/5 "LaFayette" receiving ex-USAAF Curtiss P-40 fighters at Casablanca, French Morocco on 9 January 1943.*

Figure 103: *US-supplied Martin B-26 Marauder medium bomber of the GB II/20 Bretagne*

French Morocco-Algeria campaign (1942)

Coup of Casablanca (November 7)

On the night of 7 November – the eve of Operation Torch – pro-Allied French General Antoine Béthouart attempted a coup d'état against the Vichy French command in Morocco, so that he could surrender to the Allies the next day. His forces surrounded the villa of General Charles Noguès, the Vichy-loyal high commissioner. However, Noguès telephoned loyal forces, who stopped the coup. In addition, the coup attempt alerted Noguès to the impending Allied invasion, and he immediately bolstered French coastal defenses.

Coup of Algiers

As agreed at Cherchell, starting at midnight and continuing through the early hours of 8 November, as the invasion troops were approaching the shore, a group of 400 French resistance under the command of Henri d'Astier de la Vigerie and José Aboulker staged a coup in the city of Algiers. They seized key targets, including the telephone exchange, radio station, governor's house and the headquarters of 19th Corps.

Robert Murphy then drove to the residence of General Alphonse Juin, the senior French Army officer in North Africa, with some resistance fighters. While the resistance surrounded the house, making Juin effectively a prisoner, Murphy attempted to persuade him to side with the Allies. However, he was treated to a surprise: Admiral François Darlan, the commander of all French forces,

Figure 104: *Members of the 'French Squadron SAS' (1ere Compagnie de Chasseurs Parachutistes) during the link-up between advanced units of the 1st and 8th British armies in the Gabès–Tozeur area of Tunisia. Previously a company of Free French paratroopers, the French SAS squadron were the first of a range of units 'acquired' by Major Stirling as the SAS expanded.*

was in Algiers on a private visit. Juin insisted on contacting Darlan, and Murphy was unable to persuade either to side with the Allies. In the early morning, the Gendarmerie arrived and released Juin and Darlan.

French Tunisia campaign (1942–1943)

Giraud's Army of Africa fought in Tunisia (late North African Campaign) alongside de Gaulle's Free French Forces, the British 1st Army and the US II Corps for six months until April, 1943. Using antiquated equipment, they took heavy casualties – 16,000 – against modern armour of the German enemy.

Operation Pugilist (March 16–27, 1943)

The Operation Pugilist involves the Free French Flying Column (X Corps (United Kingdom), British Eighth Army under General Sir Bernard Montgomery) and Leclerc's Force (2nd Division (New Zealand)).

Libya campaign

Battle of Kufra (January 31 – March 1, 1941)

France had fallen, her empire in tatters, but her flag still flew from the isolated but strategically important ex-Italian fort of El Tag which dominated the Kufra oasis in Southern Libya. Free France had struck a blow, a beginning in the campaign to recapture France and defeat the Axis.

Colonel Leclerc and the intrepid Lt Col d'Ornano (commander of French Forces in Chad), on the orders of de Gaulle in London, were tasked with attacking Italian positions in Libya with the motley forces at their disposal in Chad which had declared for Free France. Kufra was the obvious target. The task of striking at the heavily defended oasis at Kufra was made all the more difficult by the use of inadequate transport to cross sand dunes and the rocky Fech Fech, considered to be impassable to vehicles.

Fortunately for the French, assistance was received from Major Clayton of the Long Range Desert Group (LRDG), who was keen to join with the Free French to test the Italians. Clayton had under his command G (Guards) and T (New Zealand) patrols, a total of seventy-six men in twenty-six vehicles.

In order to assist in the attack against Kufra, a raid was mounted against the airfield at the oasis of Murzuk, capital of the Fezzan region of Libya. Ten Free French (three officers, two sergeants and five native soldiers) under d'Ornano met with Clayton's LRDG patrols on January 6, 1941, at Kayouge. The combined force reached Murzuk on January 11. In a daring daylight raid, they surprised the sentries and swept through the oasis, devastating the base. The majority of the force attacked the main fort, while a troop from T patrol under Lieutenant Ballantyne engaged the airfield defences, destroying three Caproni aircraft and capturing a number of prisoners.

The success of the raid was tempered by the loss of a T patrol member and the intrepid d'Ornano. Another wounded French officer cauterised his leg wound with his own cigarette, much to the admiration of the LRDG. A diversionary raid by mounted Meharistes Colonial Cavalry failed after it was betrayed by local guides, prompting Leclerc to relegate these troops to recon duties only.

After the success of the Murzuk raid, Leclerc, who had assumed overall command, marshalled his forces to take on Kufra itself. Intelligence indicated that the Oasis was defended by two defensive lines based around the El Tag fort which included barbed wire, trenches, machine guns and light AA (anti-aircraft) defences. The garrison was thought to comprise a battalion of Askaris (Colonial Infantry) under Colonel Leo, plus supporting troops.

In addition to the static defences, the oasis was defended by La Compania Sahariana de Cufra, a specialist mobile force and the forerunner of the famous

"Sahariana" companies of the mid war period. The company was composed of desert veterans crewing various Fiat and Lancia trucks equipped with HMGs and 20 mm AA weapons, together with some armoured cars. The company also had the support of its own air arm to assist in long range reconnaissance and ground attack.

Leclerc could not pinpoint the Saharianas, so he tasked the LRDG with the job of hunting them down and robbing the defenders of their mobile reserve.

Unfortunately for the LRDG, a radio intercept unit at Kufra picked up their radio traffic and they were spotted from the air. The defenders had been on their guard since Murzuk.

G patrol had been kept in reserve and Major Clayton was leading T patrol, 30 men in 11 trucks.

The patrol was at Bishara on the morning of January 31 when an Italian aircraft appeared overhead.

The trucks scattered and made for some hills, and the plane flew away without attacking them. The patrol took cover among some rocks in a small wadi at Gebel Sherif and camouflaged the trucks, before preparing to have lunch. The plane returned and circled over the wadi, where it directed a patrol of the Auto-Saharan Company to intercept the Long Range Desert Group (LRDG).

During fierce fighting, the LRDG patrol came off second best to superior Italian firepower and constant air attack. After severe losses, the surviving seven trucks of the patrol were forced to withdraw, leaving behind their commanding officer, who was captured along with several others. Other survivors embarked on epic journeys to seek safety. After this reverse, the LRDG force was forced to withdraw and refit, leaving Leclerc the services of one LRDG vehicle from T patrol crucially equipped for desert navigation.

Leclerc pressed on with his attack, in spite of losing a copy of his plan to the enemy with the capture of Major Clayton. After conducting further reconnaissance, Leclerc reorganized his forces on February 16. He abandoned his two armoured cars and took with him the remaining serviceable artillery piece, a crucial decision.

On the 17th, Leclerc's forces brushed with the Saharianas and despite a disparity in firepower were able to drive them off, as the Kufra garrison failed to intervene.

Following this, El Tag was surrounded, despite a further attack from the Saharan's and harassment from the air, the French laid siege to the fort. The lone 75 mm gun was placed 3000 m from the fort, beyond range of the defences and accurately delivered 20 shells per day at regular intervals.

Figure 105: *Free French Foreign legionnaires charging an Axis stronghold during the Battle of Bir Hakeim (Libya, June 1942).*

Despite having superior numbers, Italian resolve faltered. Negotiations to surrender began on February 28 and finally on March 1, 1941, the Free French captured El Tag and with it, the oasis at Kufra.

Battle of Bir Hakeim (May 26 – June 11, 1942)

The Battle of Bir Hakeim was fought between the Afrika Korps and the Free French Brigade, with support from the British 7th Armoured Division. The German commander was Generaloberst Erwin Rommel and the French commander was General Marie Pierre Koenig. The outnumbered Free French Brigade heroically resisted for sixteen days. It allowed the Allied Forces to regroup and prepare for the battle of El Alamein.

The Germans attacked Bir Hakeim on May 26, 1942. Over the next two weeks, the Luftwaffe flew 1,400 sorties against the defences, whilst 4 German/Italian divisions attacked. On June 2, 3, and 5, the German forces requested that Koenig surrender, he refused and launched counterattacks with his Bren gun carriers. Despite the explosion of the defences ammunition dump, the French continued to fight using ammunition brought in by British armoured cars during the night. Meanwhile, the Royal Air Force dropped water and other supplies.

On June 9, the British Eighth Army authorized a retreat and during the night of June 10/June 11 the defenders of Bir Hakeim escaped.

Figure 106: *The fall of Damascus to the Allies, late June 1941. A car carrying the Free French commanders, General Georges Catroux and Major-General Paul Louis Le Gentilhomme, enters the city. They are escorted by Vichy French Circassian cavalry (Gardes Tcherkess).*

Subordinate units of the defending 1st Free French Brigade were:

- 2nd and 3rd battalions of the 13th half-brigade of the Foreign Legion
- 1st battalion of naval fusiliers
- 1st battalion of marine infantry
- the Pacific battalion
- 2nd march battalion of Oubangui-Chari
- 1st Artillery Regiment
- 22nd North African company (6 sections)
- 1st company (engineers)
- signals company
- 101st transport company (trains/automobiles)
- a light medical ambulance

Egypt campaign

Middle East theatre of World War II

French Syria–Lebanon Campaign (1941)

Free French forces faced Vichy Army of the Levant under General Henri Dentz during the Allied campaign set in French Mandate for Syria and the Lebanon.

Syrian Crisis (May-June 1945)

By 1945 continued French presence in the Levant saw nationalist demonstrations which the French tried to quell. With heavy civilian losses, Winston Churchill in June despite being rebuffed by Charles De Gaulle ordered British forces into Syria from Jordan with orders to impose a ceasefire. British forces then reached the Damascus following which the French were escorted and confined to their barracks. With political pressure added De Gaulle ordered a ceasefire and France withdrew from Syria the following year.

Indian Ocean theatre of World War II

Allied invasion of French Madagascar (May 5 – November 8, 1942)

Vichy French and Japanese miniature submarines defended the French colony of Madagascar during Allied Operation Ironclad. The Madagascar governor surrendered in November 1942.[145]

Free-Vichy French battle for La Réunion (November 22, 1942)

Réunion was under the authority of the Vichy Regime until 30 November 1942, when the island was liberated by the destroyer Léopard.

South-East Asian theatre of World War II

Vietnam-Laos-Cambodia campaign

Japanese invasion of French Indochina (September 1940)

Japan seized overall control of Indochina but the Vichy government ran local affairs until 1944.

Figure 107: *Defeated Japanese salute the Free French 6th Commando C.L.I. in French Indochina.*

Limited Allied support to French Indochina (1943–1945)

The FEFEO was created on paper by General de Gaulle in October 1943, however the actual composition of a full scale expeditionary force -the C.L.I./Gaur were small specialized units- dedicated to liberate French Indohina from the outnumbering Japanese forces was delayed as the European theatre of operations, and the liberation of metropolitan France, became a top priority for deployment of the limited French forces.

The United States Chief of Staff also formally restricted the Allied support to French Indochina, 14th USAAF Commander Claire Lee Chennault (a French-American) wrote in his memoirs the now famous statement: "I carried out my orders to the letter but I did not relish the idea of leaving Frenchmen to be slaughtered in the jungle while I was forced officially to ignore their plight."

In contrast, the British, who trained the first C.L.I./Gaurs supported French Indochina through its Force 136, flew aerial supply missions for the airborne commandos, delivering tommy guns, mortars and grenades from their Calcutta base.[146]

SOE's French Indo-China Section (1943–1945)

The FEFEO French expeditionary corps's C.L.I.s (or "gaurs") were dropped by the British Force 136 and fought the Japanese troops occupying the French colonies of Indochina (Vietnam, Laos, Cambodia). The Gaur *Polaire* ("polar") codename of Captain Ayrolles's commando unit dropped in the Traninh in order to prepare the arrival of the C.L.I., however they were taken by surprise by the Japanese *coup de force* of March 9, 1945, and Cpt. Ayrolles changed the original plan to a sabotage operation. The Gaur Polaire blew eight bridges on the RC 7 (*route coloniale 7*), assaulted Japanese detachments and convoys, blew airstrip holds and storages of the Khan Kai camp and also destroyed a fuel and vehicles storage. A Japanese battalion was sent after them, without success. The results of this operation was the Japanese entry in Luang Prabang was delayed for around three weeks.[147]

On March 17, 1945, Captain Cortadellas's Gaur K is dropped at Dien Bien Phu (area of the famous siege in the Indochina War (1946–1954)). At French Commander Marcel Alessandri's request, Gaur K, supported by 80 remaining legionnaires from the 3/5th REI (*Régiment Étranger d'Infanterie*), was sent to the *arrière-garde* of the Alessandri column retreating to China for hundreds kilometers of tracks in the high region. Battles ensued on April 11 at Houei Houn, April 15 at Muong Koua, April 21 at Boun Tai and April 22 at Muong Yo.

On October 9, 1945, Gaur Détachement C infiltrates Cambodia, restored French colonial administration and staged a discrete coup d'état to resume the King of Cambodia's rule.[148]

Gaurs roles were guerrilla warfare and the creation and training of Mèo and Thai local commandos. Following World War II, the GCMA French airborne commandos, servicing in the Indochina War, were created after the gaurs (C.L.I.) which were themselves created after the British Chindits special forces.

Another French special operations force secretly fought the Japanese in French Indochina. These were forty former French Jedburgh volunteers who embarked at Glasgow with layover at Port Said, Bombay and Colombo, and gathered in a camp at Ceylon in November 1944. Notable Force 136 members dropped in Laos during 1945 are French Colonels Jean Deuve (January 22), Jean Le Morillon (February 28) and Jean Sassi (June 4).

Local resistance was headed by General Eugène Mordant.[149]

Thailand campaign

Further reading

- Alexander, Martin S. *The Republic in Danger: General Maurice Gamelin and the Politics of French Defence, 1933-1940* (Cambridge University Press, 1992)
- Alexander, Martin S. "The fall of France, 1940." *Journal of Strategic Studies* (1990) 13#1 pp: 10-44.
- Bennett, G. H. "The RAF's Free French Fighter Squadrons: The Rebirth of French Airpower, 1940-44." *Global War Studies* (2010) 7#2 pp: 62-101.
- Brown, David, and Geoffrey Till. *The Road to Oran: Anglo-French Naval Relations, September 1939 – July 1940* (Routledge, 2004)
- Derrick, William Michael. *General Maurice Gamelin: scapegoat or guilty for the fall of France?* (Indiana University Press, 1994)
- Doughty, Robert A. *The Seeds of Disaster: The Development of French Army Doctrine, 1919–1939* (1986)
- Doughty, Robert A. *The Breaking Point: Sedan and the Fall of France, 1940* (1990)
- Funk, Arthur Layton. *Charles de Gaulle: The Crucial Years, 1943–1944* (1959) online edition[150]
- Gaunson, A. B. *The Anglo-French Clash in Lebanon and Syria, 1940-45* (1987)
- Gunsberg, Jeffrey. *Divided and Conquered: The French High Command and the Defeat of the West, 1940* (Greenwood Press, 1985)
- Higham, Robin. *Two Roads to War: The French and British Air Arms from Versailles to Dunkirk* (Naval Institute Press, 2012)
- Horne, Alistair. *To Lose A Battle: France 1940* (1999) excerpt and text search[151]
- Kersaudy, Francois. *Churchill and De Gaulle* (2nd ed 1990) 482pp
- Lacouture, Jean. *De Gaulle: The Rebel 1890–1944* (1984; English ed. 1991), 640pp; excerpt and text search[152]
- Laurent, Sebastien. "The Free French Secret Services: Intelligence and the Politics of Republican Legitimacy," *Intelligence & National Security* (2000) 15#4 pp 19–41
- Mangold, Peter. *Britain and the Defeated French: From Occupation to Liberation, 1940-1944* (IB Tauris, 2012)
- Porch, Douglas. "Military 'culture' and the fall of France in 1940: A review essay." *International Security* (2000) 24#4 pp: 157-180.
- Sharp, Lee, et al. *The French Army 1939–1945: Organisation, Order of Battle, Operational History* (5 vol Osprey 1998–2002); heavily illustrated
- Shepperd, Alan. *France 1940: Blitzkrieg in the West* (1990)

- Thomas, Martin. *The French Empire at War, 1940-1945* (Manchester University Press, 2007)
- Thomas, Martin. "Imperial backwater or strategic outpost? The British takeover of Vichy Madagascar, 1942," *Historical Journal* (1996) 39#4 pp 1049–75

Primary sources

- DeGaulle, Charles. *The Complete War Memoirs of Charles De Gaulle, 1940–1946* (3 vol 1984)
  - John C. Cairns, "General de Gaulle and the Salvation of France, 1944-46," *Journal of Modern History* (1960) 32#3 pp. 251–259 in JSTOR[153], review

Other sources

This article incorporates public domain material from the United States Army Center of Military History document "The U.S. Army Campaigns of World War II: Southern France"[154].

- **Chronology 1941–1945**, U.S. Army in World War II, Mary H. Williams (compiler), Washington: Government Printing Office, 1994.
- **Les Grandes Unités Françaises (GUF)**, Volume V, Part 2, Service Historique de l'Armée de Terre, Paris: Imprimerie Nationale, 1975.
- **Riviera to the Rhine**, U.S. Army in World War II, Jeffrey J. Clarke and Robert Ross Smith, United States Army Center of Military History, 1993.
- **The Last Offensive**, U.S. Army in World War II, Charles B. MacDonald, Washington: United States Army Center of Military History, 1993.

History of the French Navy

Motto: *Honneur, Patrie, Valeur, Discipline*

("Honour, Homeland, Valour, Discipline")

Command
Naval Ministers

Maritime Prefect

Components
Naval Action Force

Submarine Forces
- Strategic Oceanic Force (FOST)
- Squadron of Nuclear Attack Submarines (ESNA)

Naval Aviation

FORFUSCO (Marine Commandos, Naval Fusiliers)

Maritime Gendarmerie

Equipment
Current fleet

Current deployments

Personnel
Ranks in the French Navy

History
History of the French Navy

Future of the French Navy

Ensigns and pennants

Historic ships
- Battleships
- Cruisers
- Destroyers
- Submarines
- Ships of the line
- Sail frigates

Historic fleets

Awards

> Cross of War
> Military Medal
> Legion of Honour
> Ribbons

Although the **History of the French Navy** goes back to the Middle Ages, its history can be said to effectively begin with Richelieu under Louis XIII.

Since the establishment of her present territory, France had to face three major challenges on the naval level:

- Geographically France had two large sections of coastline separated by the Iberian Peninsula (Spain and Portugal), so she had to keep two naval forces and divide resources between the Mediterranean Sea and the Atlantic Ocean.
- Politically and strategically France's main threats came from central Europe which required a strong army rather than a strong navy.
- Inconsistent support for her navy. To be effective, navies require infrastructure, ports, dockyards, foundries which must be maintained in peacetime. Officers and crews need plenty of experience at sea. Shortage of resources and political misunderstanding repeatedly damaged the service, creating created a series of brilliant eras followed by disasters.

The History of the French Navy can be divided into the following eras:

- The creation of the first actual State Navy, under Louis XIII, thanks to the politics of Richelieu. This navy was largely ruined by the troubles of the Fronde.
- A rebuilt and brilliant era under Louis XIV, largely thanks to Jean-Baptiste Colbert. The effort was not pursued under the Régence of Philippe d'Orléans and the beginning of the reign of Louis XV; consequently, the Seven Years' War and the French and Indian War ended in disaster.
- A period of rebirth under the impulsion of Choiseul, which culminated under Louis XVI with de Grasse's victory over the British during the American Revolutionary War. In the same period, explorers like Bougainville expanded French geography, naval maps, and founded outposts. The downfall occurred during the French Revolution and the First Empire, leaving the British with a century of undisputed domination of the seas.

- Under Napoléon III, a modern navy was built, taking advantage of new technologies like steam and ship armour, which made elder fleets effectively obsolete. This force was an important instrument in the constitution and keeping of the French Empire. The fleet maintained a high standard, and between the two world wars (1925–1939), a significant effort was made counter the threat of the German and Italian navies. With the Fall of France, however, most of the Navy never got a chance to fight, and what survived Mers-el-Kebir was eventually annihilated in the scuttling of the French fleet in Toulon.

The French navy is affectionately known as *La Royale* ("the Royal"). The reason is not well known: it might be for its traditional attachment to the French monarchy; because, before being named "nationale", the Navy had been named "royale" (the navy did not sport the royal titles common with other European navies like the British Royal Navy); or simply because of the location of its headquarters, "rue Royale" in Paris.

Middle Ages

Medieval fleets, in France as elsewhere, were almost entirely composed of merchant ships enlisted into naval service in time of war. But the early beginning of the French Navy goes back to the Middle Ages, when it defeated the English Navy at the battle of Arnemuiden,[155] on 23 September 1338. The battle of Arnemuiden was also the first naval battle using artillery.[156]

Louis XIII and Richelieu

> "
> The tears of our sovereigns have the salted taste of the sea that they ignored.[157]
> "
>
> — Cardinal de Richelieu

During the reign of Henry IV, France was in an unstable state, and striving to guarantee her independence from Spanish and papal influences. This prompted both an emphasis on land forces, which drained resources, and an alliance with England, which would have unfavourably seen France challenging her naval supremacy.

When Richelieu became Minister of the Navy, he decided on a plan to rebuild a powerful navy, divided into two distinct forces.

The Mediterranean force was to be completely composed of galleys, to take advantage of the relatively calm sea. Initially, the plan called for 40 galleys,

Figure 108: *A warship, built in 1626 on orders of Louis XIII in a Dutch yard, arriving in a Dutch port under guidance of a Dutch ship, Jacob Gerritz. Loef.*

but was downsized to 24 of them, notably because of a lack of galley slaves — each galley was 400 or 500 slave strong.

The Oceanic force was to be composed of men-of-war. The designs were moderately large ships, for a lack of harbours fit for very large units, but very heavily armed with large calibre guns; these ships displaced between 300 and 2000 tonnes and bore up to 50 24-pound cannons, firing 150mm-round shots. The first ships were ordered from the Dutch, and French production started with the famous *Couronne*, a prestige ship typical of this era.

In 1627, the Navy was not ready to challenge the English fleet at the Siege of La Rochelle, which led to the construction of a seawall to establish a blockade. Fleets of this period were often largely composed of merchant vessels, hastily loaded with cannons, undercrewed and poorly handled.[158]

With newly built ships, designed as ships of war and crewed by sailors and trained gunners, fighting experience was gained in the Franco-Spanish War and the Thirty Years' War with notable victories at the Battle of Cádiz (1640) won by France's first Grand Admiral Jean Armand de Maillé-Brézé, son of Marshall Urbain de Maillé-Brézé and nephew of Cardinal Richelieu. The Navy built a French empire, conquering the "Nouvelle-Guyenne" (now Acadia), "Nouvelle France" (now Canada), Tortuga, Martinique, Guadeloupe, several other islands in the Caribbean, the Bahamas, and Madagascar.

Figure 109: *A ship of the line at the Battle of Martinique in 1780, flying the white ensign in use during the time of the House of Bourbon.*

Louis XIV and Colbert

Under the tutelage of the "Sun King," the French Navy was well financed and equipped, managing to score several early victories in the Nine Years War against the Royal Navy and the Dutch Navy. Financial troubles, however, forced the navy back to port and allowed the English and the Dutch to regain the initiative.

Under the impulsion of Jean-Baptiste Colbert's ambitious policy of ship building, the French navy began to gain a magnificence matching the symbolism of the Louis XIV era, as well as an actual military significance. The ship of the line *Soleil-Royal* is illustrative of the trend of the time. Colbert is credited with forging a good part of the naval tradition of France.

The French navy of this period was also in the forefront of the development of naval tactics. Paul Hoste (1652-1700) produced the first major work on naval tactics.[159]

Before the Nine Years War, in the Franco-Dutch War, the French navy managed to score a decisive victory over a combined Spanish-Dutch fleet at the Battle of Palermo (1676).

During the War of the Grand Alliance, Admiral Tourville won a decisive victory in the Battle of Beachy Head (1690, *Bataille de Bévezier*). France gained control of the English Channel. The event is regarded as one of the most glorious deeds of the French Navy, and Tourville earned a fame which lasts to present times (a number of ships were named *Bévezier* or *Tourville* to commemorate the battle).

The Battle of Barfleur in 1692 saw a French fleet attack and defeat the combined English and Dutch fleets, despite being heavily outnumbered. The French fought a magnificent fight against odds of more than two to one for twelve hours. They sunk one English ship and one Dutchman and had not lost a ship of their own, although all vessels on both sides were very battered.[160] However, once wind and tide changed, the French suffered heavily as they tried to get back to port for repairs. Some of the damaged French ships were forced to beach themselves at Cherbourg, where they were annihilated by English long boats and with fire ships. The crews were saved, but the lost fifteen ships-of-the-line were not replaced and France did not seriously challenge the combined English and Dutch fleet for decades.

France turned to commerce-raiding rather than large fleet actions with great success under such captains as Jean Bart, Claude de Forbin and René Duguay-Trouin.

Louis XV

Until what the British called the Annus Mirabilis of 1759, the French and British navies had a roughly even record of success in their many conflicts. This changed decisively in that year with a series of disasters for the French, who had begun the year planning an invasion of Britain. The British responded by blockading the French fleets at both Toulon and Brest; when the French emerged they were decisively defeated in the battles of Lagos and Quiberon Bay. The French navy was also unable to prevent the loss of the important colonies of New France (Quebec) and Guadeloupe. The year marked the beginning of the period of clear British dominance on the seas.

Following the disasters of the Seven Years' War, France was financially incapable of building up a fleet to challenge Britain's Royal Navy. However, efforts were made, and by the time of Louis XV's death in 1774, the *Marine Royale* was somewhat larger than it had been in 1763, and, crucially, had replaced numerous old vessels with more effective modern designs. Also worthy of note- in 1766, Bougainville led the first French circumnavigation of the world.

Figure 110: *Soleil-Royal (1749)*

Figure 111: *Héros (1752)*

History of the French Navy

Figure 112: *Le Foudroyant (1751)*

Figure 113: *Royal Louis (1759)*

Figure 115: *Etat de la Marine royale de France, 1785*

Figure 114: *Ville de Paris (1764)*

Louis XVI

King Louis XVI was keen on technical subjects and geography, and encouraged explorations including the commissioning of Jean-François de

Figure 116: *French Navy ships of the line in the Battle of Chesapeake.*

Galaup, comte de Lapérouse to undertake far reaching voyages of discovery. (L'expédition de Lapérouse, 1785–1788, réplique française au voyage de Cook[161]). Upon King Louis XVI's orders, Lapérouse departed Brest, France, in command of *L'Astrolabe* and *La Boussole* on 1 August 1785 on a scientific voyage of the Pacific inspired by the voyages of Cook. He never returned and his ships were later found wrecked at the island of Vanikoro, which is part of the isolated Santa Cruz group of islands in the South Pacific. Vessels designed by French engineer Jacques-Noël Sané started being constructed during the American Revolutionary War. He created what were to be, in effect, the ultimate designs of wind-powered fighting ship, with standard frigates carrying 18-pounder guns, and standard ships of the line of 64, 74, 80 and 118 guns ; his 74-gun ship of the line became the backbone of the French and English navies. The largest units, the 118-guns, were said to be "as manoeuvrable as a frigate" (the *Océan* class is a typical example).

During the American War of Independence the French Navy played a decisive role in supporting the American side. The French Navy was the only standing navy to fight the British, alongside the modest Continental and American state navies and American privateers.[162] In a very impressive effort, the French under de Grasse managed to defeat an English fleet at the Battle of the Chesapeake in 1781, thus ensuring that the Franco-American ground forces would win the ongoing Battle of Yorktown.

In India, Suffren managed impressive campaigns against the British (1770–1780), successfully contending for supremacy against Vice-Admiral Sir

Figure 117: *The Battle of the Basque Roads off Ile d'Aix, April 1809.*

Edward Hughes.

In 1789, the French navy counted 71 ships of the line, 64 frigates, 45 corvettes and 32 smaller units; 12 ships of the line and 10 frigates were under construction and expected to be launched within the year. The crews counted 75,000 sailors, 5,000 gunners, 2,000 officers and 14,000 *Fusiliers de Marine*. Ships were based mostly in Brest, Toulon and Rochefort, as well as in Lorient, Le Havre, Dunkerque, Bordeaux, Bayonne and Marseille.

French Revolution and the First Empire

The French Revolution, in eliminating numerous officers of noble lineage (among them, Charles d'Estaing), all but crippled the French Navy.

The National Convention dissolved the Fleet Gunners Corps, which effectively put a halt to the training in gunnery, abysmally degrading the rate of fire and precision of batteries;[163] in addition, the French doctrine was to fire at the rigging of enemy ships as to render them hapless; this doctrine could prove effective with highly trained crews, but was impractical with poorly trained gunners, and resulted in a number of instances where French ships did not manage to score a single hit on dangerously exposed English ships (as happened with the fight of the *Ça Ira*, or at the beginning of the Battle of Trafalgar). By contrast, the Royal Navy doctrine was to fire at the ship's hull in order to kill

Figure 118: *Battle of Veracruz (1838) : bombing of the Castle of San Juan de Ulúa, during the Pastry War.*

and maim the crew, and gradually degrade the firepower of their opponents — also much easier target for much better trained gunners.

Efforts to make it into a powerful force under Napoleon were dashed by the death of Latouche Tréville in 1804, and the Battle of Trafalgar in 1805, where the British all but annihilated a combined Franco-Spanish fleet. The disaster guaranteed British naval domination until the steam era.

From then on, the French navy was limited to frigate actions and privateers like Robert Surcouf. This started the French tendency to prefer large numbers of smaller but powerful and swift units, rather than large capital ships.

From the Bourbon Restoration to the Second Empire

In the nineteenth century, the navy recovered to become the second finest in the world after the Royal Navy.

During this period, explorer and naval officer Dumont d'Urville contributed to geography in Southern and Western Pacific, Australia, New Zealand, and Antarctica, and brought back previously unknown plants and animal species.

The French Navy also conducted a successful blockade of Mexico in the Pastry War of 1838 and obliterated the Chinese navy at the Battle of Foochow in 1884. It also served as an effective link between the growing parts of the French empire. Ever eager to challenge British naval supremacy, the French Navy took a leadership role in many areas of warship development, first with incremental improvements upon existing designs with the Commission de Paris, but also pioneering the introduction of several new technologies: steam propulsion, adoption of the screw propeller, adoption of armour plate protection, steel construction, and protected gun mounts.

- France led in the development of shell guns for the Navy, invented by Henri-Joseph Paixhans
- In 1850, *Napoléon* became the first purpose-built steam-powered battleship in history.
- *Gloire* became the first seagoing ironclad in history when she was launched in 1853.
- In 1863, the French Navy launched *Plongeur*, the world's first mechanically propelled submarine.
- In 1876, the *Redoutable* became the first steel-hulled warship ever.

Figure 119: *Napoléon (1850).*

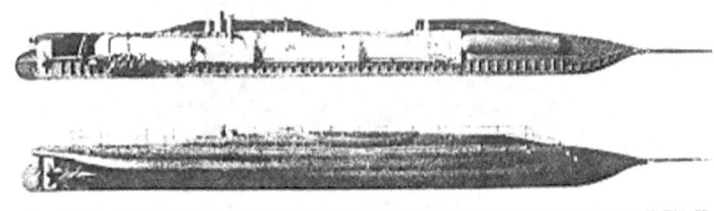

Figure 120: *Plongeur (1876).*

Figure 121: *Gloire (1863).*

Figure 122: *Redoutable (1876).*

Figure 123: *Jauréguiberry (1897).*

Global interventions

In a speech in 1852, Napoleon III famously proclaimed that "The Empire means peace" (*"L'Empire, c'est la paix"*), but actually he was thoroughly determined to follow a strong foreign policy to extend France's power and glory. The French Navy was involved in a multitude of actions around the world.

The Crimean War

Napoleon's challenge to Russia's claims to influence in the Ottoman Empire led to France's successful participation in the Crimean War (March 1854–March 1856). During this war Napoleon successfully established a French alliance with Britain, which continued after the war's close.

The French line-of-battle ship *Henri IV* and the *Pluton* ran aground after a storm that destroyed many Allied ships. The remains of Henri IV were used to construct a fortress. The Pluton was a total loss.

East Asia

Napoleon took the first steps to establishing a French colonial influence in Indochina. He approved the launching of a naval expedition in 1858 to punish the Vietnamese for their mistreatment of French Catholic missionaries and force the court to accept a French presence in the country. An important factor in his decision was the belief that France risked becoming a second-rate power by not expanding its influence in East Asia. Also, the idea that France had a civilising mission was spreading. This eventually led to a full-out invasion in 1861. By 1862 the war was over and Vietnam conceded three provinces in the south, called by the French Cochin-China, opened three ports to French trade, allowed free passage of French warships to Cambodia (which led to a French protectorate over Cambodia in 1867), allowed freedom of action for French missionaries and gave France a large indemnity for the cost of the war.

In China, France took part in the Second Opium War along with Great Britain, and in 1860 French troops entered Beijing. China was forced to concede more

Figure 124: *The French frigate La Guerrière commanded by Admiral Roze was the lead ship in the French Campaign against Korea, 1866. Here the ship is photographed in Nagasaki harbour, circa 1865.*

trading rights, allow freedom of navigation of the Yangzi river, give full civil rights and freedom of religion to Christians, and give France and Britain a huge indemnity. This combined with the intervention in Vietnam set the stage for further French influence in China leading up to a sphere of influence over parts of Southern China.

In 1866, French Navy troops made an attempt to colonize Korea, during the French Campaign against Korea. The French Navy also had a mild presence in Japan in 1867-1868, around the actions of French Military Mission to Japan, and the subsequent Boshin war.

Mexico

The French Navy was heavily involved in French intervention in Mexico (January 1862–March 1867). Napoleon, using as a pretext the Mexican Republic's refusal to pay its foreign debts, planned to establish a French sphere of influence in North America by creating a French-backed monarchy in Mexico, a project which was supported by Mexican conservatives tired of the anti-clerical Mexican republic.

Figure 125: *The ironclad Vauban (1882-1905), painting by Paul Jazet (1848-1918).*

Pre-dreadnought battleships

In the 1880s, the "Jeune École" doctrine had a more powerful influence within the French Navy than elsewhere. Derived from the traditions of privateer warfare, the Jeune École emphasised small, maneuverable craft such as torpedo boats and cruisers carrying shell guns, and prematurely deemed the battleship obsolete. However, in the early 1890s the pre-dreadnought battleship revived with surprising vigour and new protections against torpedoes and mines, and the torpedo boats proved to have inadequate nautical qualities for the open ocean.

French capital ships of this time were instantly identifiable by their small size (10,000 tons), huge spur rams, great height and pronounced tumble-home. Often carrying only half the main armament of their British contemporaries, French battleships had armoured masts with electric elevators inside, outsized funnels, and elaborate davit systems to swing out boats from the narrow upper decks.

France built a considerable fleet of these vessels, though seldom with such uniform class characteristics as seen in Britain and Germany. The *Bouvet*, *Masséna*, and *Jauréguiberry* were built as "sample battleships", as the design for a true class of battleships was fiddled with. It eventually materialised with the 3-ship *Charlemagne* class, which introduced armament nearly on a par with its British contemporaries.

France's conceptual and technological edge proved attractive to the newly industrialising Japan, when the French engineer Émile Bertin was invited for four years to design a new fleet for the Imperial Japanese Navy, which led to her success in the First Sino-Japanese War in 1894. French yards busily turned out warships for foreign customers, especially Imperial Russia, which copied French stylings in designing many of its cruisers and battleships. Despite her leads in some areas of technology (boilers, metallurgy), France did not have the productive capacity of her rival across the Channel, or her new nemesis, Germany.

Right at the turn of the century, French design absorbed influences from foreign practice. Her newer battleships featured two twin 300mm gun turrets as opposed to single mounts, less exaggerated tumble-home of the hull, and abandonment of the ram bow. This led to improved seakeeping characteristics, though the ships remained small.

In the *Liberté* class (completed 1907), French pre-dreadnought design finally caught up with U.S. and British standards; but 1907 also saw the debut of HMS *Dreadnought*, which made all the world's capital ships obsolete overnight. Through 1911, while rival navies were turning out new dreadnoughts, all France's available shipyards were dedicated to producing the 6-ship Danton class pre-dreadnoughts which, though they featured turbine/quad screw propulsion, still mounted only 4 heavy guns each, as against at least 10 for a dreadnought.

The first French dreadnoughts did not appear until 1914, and two classes totalling 7 ships, the *Courbet* and *Bretagne*-classes, were completed during the First World War. With the alliance with Britain, France's naval assets were concentrated in the Mediterranean, largely to face off the Austro-Hungarian fleet in the Adriatic Sea. Meanwhile, a large cruiser fleet was also built, seeing service in the Mediterranean, the Channel, and in France's imperial dominions in Indochina, Pacific Islands, West Africa, and the Caribbean.

French naval uniforms, 1884

Figure 126: *French sailor*

Figure 127: *'Going into battle'*

World Wars

The development of the French Navy slowed down in the beginning of the 20th century, and as a result, it was outnumbered by the German and US Navies. It was late to introduce new battleships - dreadnoughts and light cruisers and

Figure 128: *Seaplane carrier Foudre.*

it entered World War I with relatively few modern vessels: only one dreadnought in commission at war's start, though all four *Courbet*s by the end of 1914 and the 3 improved dreadnoughts by mid-1916. During the war, the main French effort was on land. While capital ships already on the ways were completed, few new warships were laid down. Despite its dated roster, the Marine Nationale performed well in World War I. The main operation of the French Navy was the Dardanelles Campaign. France's most significant losses during the war were four pre-dreadnought battleships, victims of mines and U-boat torpedoes.

A number of major ships of the French Navy at the outbreak / end of World War I[164]

- dreadnought battleships: 4/7
- pre-dreadnought battleships: 17/13
- armoured cruisers: 22/18
- protected cruisers: 13/12
- destroyers: 35/42 (capacity over 500 tons)
- torpedo boats: 180/164
- submarines: 50/61

The first proto-aircraft carrier

The invention of the seaplane in 1910 with the French Fabre Hydravion led to the earliest development of ships designed to carry airplanes, albeit equipped with floats. In 1911 appears the French Navy *Foudre*, the first seaplane carrier. She was commissioned as a seaplane tender, and carried float-equipped planes under hangars on the main deck, from where they were lowered on the sea with a crane. *Foudre* was further modified in November 1913 with a 10-metre flat deck to launch her seaplanes.[165]

Genesis of the flat-deck carrier

> "An airplane-carrying vessel is indispensable. These vessels will be constructed on a plan very different from what is currently used. First of all the deck will be cleared of all obstacles. It will be flat, as wide as possible without jeopardizing the nautical lines of the hull, and it will look like a landing field."
>
> Clément Ader, "L'Aviation Militaire", 1909

As heavier-than-air aircraft developed in the early 20th century various navies began to take an interest in their potential use as scouts for their big gun warships. In 1909 the French inventor Clément Ader published in his book "L'Aviation Militaire" the description of a ship to operate airplanes at sea, with a flat flight deck, an island superstructure, deck elevators and a hangar bay.[166] That year the US Naval Attaché in Paris sent a report on his observations[167] and the first experiments to test the concept were made in the United States from 1910.

Fleet Construction Between the World Wars

Every naval fleet consists of a variety of ships of different sizes, and no fleet has enough resources to make every vessel supreme in its class. Nonetheless, different countries strive to excel in particular classes. Between the world wars, the French fleet was remarkable in its building of small numbers of ships that were "over the top" with relation to their equivalents of other powers.

For example, the French chose to build "super-destroyers" which were deemed during the Second World War by the Allies as the equivalent of light cruisers. This was a way of bypassing the Treaty of Washington, which imposed restrictions on cruisers and battleships, but not on destroyers and smaller units. The *Fantasque* class of destroyer is still the world's fastest class of destroyer. The *Surcouf* submarine was the largest and most powerful of its day.

In 1933, the French Navy was considering building a super-battleship, the *Lyon* class, but the plans were canceled when the Germans came out with the so-called "pocket battleships" ; the French responded with a class of two ships of the *Dunkerque* type, a fast battleship class falling somewhere in between battlecruisers and battleships. The large battleship niche was filled with the *Richelieu* class.

Second World War

At the outset of the war, the French Navy participated in a number of operations against the Axis Powers, patrolling the Atlantic and bombarding Genoa. The French surrender and its armistice terms, however, completely changed the situation: the French fleet immediately withdrew from the fight.

Figure 129: *France's Fantasque class, the fastest destroyer class ever built.*

Destruction of the French Fleet and Vichy France

The British perceived the French fleet as a potentially lethal threat, should the French become formal enemies or, more likely, should Nazi Germany's *Kriegsmarine* gain control. It was essential that they should be put out of action. Some vessels were in British-controlled ports in Britain or Egypt and these were either persuaded to re-join the Allies as Free French ships or were boarded and disarmed.

An important part of the fleet, however, was in Dakar or Mers-el-Kebir. The Royal Navy delivered an ultimatum but, when agreement proved impossible, they opened fire and sunk or damaged much of the French fleet (Operation Catapult) on 3 July 1940. The action soured Anglo-French relations and inhibited further defections to the Allies. From this point on, the ships remaining in Vichyst hands spent the war trying to observe neutrality towards the Axis powers, while avoiding destructions or capture by the Allies and the Free French. They obtained anecdotical tactical successes which weighted for nought against the overall strategic disaster, like the Battle of Dakar or the Battle of Koh Chang.

In November, 1942, the Allies invaded French North Africa. In response, the Germans occupied (Case Anton) Vichy France, including the French naval port of Toulon, where the main part of the surviving French fleet lay. This was a major German objective and forces under SS command had been detailed

Figure 130: *FNFL ensign*

to capture them (Operation *Lila*). French naval authorities were divided on their response: Admiral Jean de Laborde, the commander of the Forces de Haute Mer (the High Seas Fleet) advocated sailing to attack the Allied invasion fleet while others, such as the Vichy Secretary of the Navy, Contre-Amiral Auphan favoured joining the Allies. On several warships, there were spontaneous demonstrations in favour of sailing with the Allies, chanting "*Vive de Gaulle! Appareillage!*".

The orders to French commanders to scuttle their ships in case of an attempted take-over had been reinforced, however, and, often despite the presence of German troops, this was done, in the Scuttling of the French fleet in Toulon. No capital ships and few others were taken in reparable condition. A few ships fled Toulon and joined the Allies, notably the submarine *Casabianca*.

The Free Naval French Forces

See also List of ships of the Forces navales françaises libres

In the wake of the Armistice and the Appeal of 18 June, Charles de Gaulle founded the Free French Forces, including a naval arm, the *Forces navales françaises libres* (FNFL, "Free Naval French Forces"). To distinguish the FNFL from the Vichist forces, vice-admiral Émile Muselier created the bow flag displaying the French colours with a red cross of Lorraine, and a cocarde also featuring the cross of Lorraine for aircraft.

The French fleet was widely dispersed. Some vessels were in port in France; others had escaped from France to British controlled ports, mainly in Britain itself or Alexandria in Egypt. At the first stage of Operation Catapult, the ships in the British ports of Plymouth and Portsmouth were simply boarded on the night of 3 July 1940. The then-largest submarine in the world, the *Surcouf*, which had sought refuge in Portsmouth in June 1940 following the German invasion of France, resisted the British operation. In capturing the submarine, two British officers and one French sailor were killed. Other ships were the two obsolete battleships *Paris* and *Courbet*, the destroyers *Le Triomphant* and the *Léopard*, 8 torpedo boats, 5 submarines and a number of other ships of lesser importance.

Most of these ships were surrendered to the FNFL (notably the submarine *Surcouf*), and other were leased by the British (like the corvette *Aconit*), constituting the embryo of a naval force.

When French Africa joined the Allies, important ships based in Dakar were obtained (notably the cruisers *Suffren*, *Gloire*, *Montcalm*, *Georges Leygues*, and the battleship *Richelieu*).

Beside warships, the FNFL developed special forces: Captain Philippe Kieffer took inspiration from the British commandos to train new units of "*Commandos Fusiliers-Marins*", which later would become the *Commandos Marine*. These commandos distinguished themselves during Battle of Normandy, climbing cliffs under fire to destroy German shore batteries. Captain d'Estienne d'Orves attempted to unite the French Resistance, became an inspiring symbol when he was arrested, tortured by the Gestapo and executed.

The FNFL also harboured technical innovators, like Captain Jacques-Yves Cousteau, who invented the modern aqua-lung, and Yves Rocard, who perfected the radar. The aqua-lung became a major improvement for commando operations.

French warships of the FNFL supported the landings in southern France (Operation Dragoon) and Normandy (Operation Neptune). These units also played their parts in the war in the Pacific. The *Richelieu* was present in Tokyo Bay during the signing of the Japanese Instrument of Surrender.

Modern navy

Currently, French naval doctrine calls for two aircraft carriers, but the French only have one, the *Charles de Gaulle*, due to restructuring.

The navy is in the midst of major technological and procurement changes. A naval version of the Rafale is replacing older aircraft. Newer strategic submarines of the SNLE-NG type have mostly replaced the elder SNLE, and a new

Figure 131: *The SNLE-NG Le Téméraire*

nuclear ballistic missile is under test, due for 2008. The experience acquired with the building of the SNLE-NG will also lead to a newer type of nuclear attack submarines, which are expected for 2017. Surface forces are upgrading in numbers and modernity, with two large destroyers and 11 frigates planned. More modern missiles are being issued, notably adding cruise missile capabilities.

Further reading

- Dull, Jonathan R. *The French Navy and the Seven Years' War* (Univ. of Nebraska Press, 2007), 445 pages
- Winfield, Rif, and Stephen S. Roberts. *French Warships in the Age of Sail 1626-1786: design, construction, careers and fates* (US Naval Institute Press, 2017), 464 pages

External links

- French naval leaders and the French navy in the American War for independence[168]
- fr:Administration et administrateurs de la Marine royale française (in French)

- Pictorial history of French navy vessels, 1850-1916, from BigBadBattleships.com[169]
- The French Navy during the napoleonic era[170]

French Army

French Army

French Army	
Armée de terre	

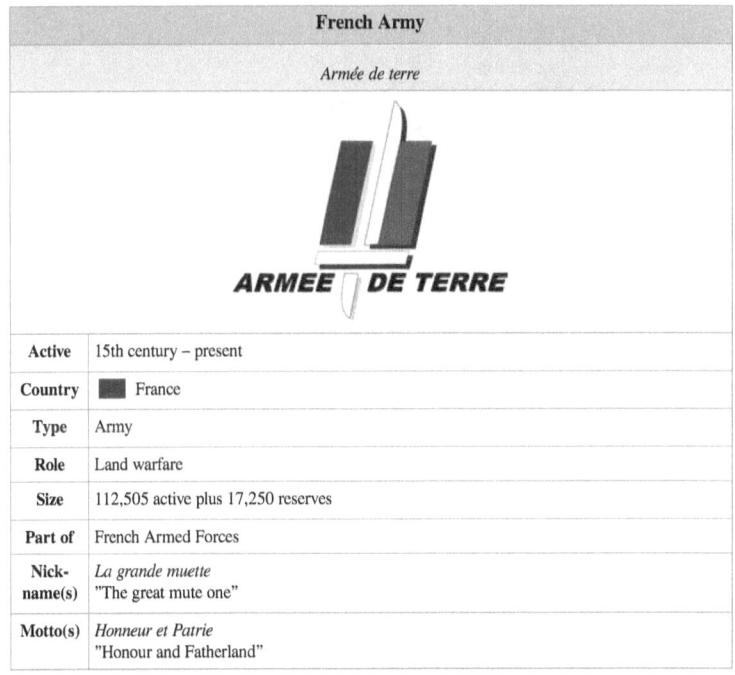

Active	15th century – present
Country	France
Type	Army
Role	Land warfare
Size	112,505 active plus 17,250 reserves
Part of	French Armed Forces
Nickname(s)	*La grande muette* "The great mute one"
Motto(s)	*Honneur et Patrie* "Honour and Fatherland"

Engage-
ments
	• Hundred Years' War (1337–1453)
	• Colonial Wars (1534–1980)
	• Italian Wars
	• Thirty Years' War
	• War of the League of Augsburg
	• War of the Spanish Succession
	• War of the Polish Succession
	• War of the Austrian Succession
	• Seven Years' War
	• American Revolutionary War
	• French Revolutionary Wars
	• Napoleonic Wars
	• French intervention in Spain
	• Greek War of Independence
	• Conquest of Algeria
	• Crimean War
	• Franco-Austrian War
	• Franco-Prussian War
	• Paris Commune
	• World War I
	• Levant Campaign
	• World War II
	   • Allied Forces
	   • Vichy French Forces
	      • Syria–Lebanon Campaign
	• Lebanese Civil War 1975–1990
	   • Multinational Force 1982–1984
	   • United Nations Interim Force in Lebanon (1978–present)[171]
	   • 1983 Beirut barracks bombing
	• Gulf War (1990–1991)
	• Kosovo War (1998–1999)
	• Global War on Terrorism (2001–present)
	   • War in Afghanistan (1978–present)
	      • Operation Enduring Freedom
	      • War in Afghanistan (2001–present)
	   • Northern Mali Conflict
	• Second Ivorian Civil War
	• Central African Republic conflict
	
	(List of wars involving France)

Website	www<wbr/>.defense<wbr/>.gouv<wbr/>.fr<wbr/>/terre[172]
Commanders	
Chef d'État-Major de l'Armée de Terre, CEMAT	Général d'armée Jean-Pierre Bosser
Major Général de l'Armée de Terre	French Army Deputy Chief

The **French Army**, officially the **Ground Army** (French: *Armée de terre* [aʀme də tɛʀ]) (to distinguish it from the French Air Force, Armée de L'air or Air Army) is the land-based and largest component of the French Armed Forces. It is responsible to the Government of France, along with the other four components of the Armed Forces. The current Chief of Staff of the French Army (CEMAT) is General Jean-Pierre Bosser, a direct subordinate of the Chief of the Defence Staff (CEMA). General Bosser is also responsible, in part, to the Ministry of the Armed Forces for organization, preparation, use of forces, as well as planning and programming, equipment and Army future acquisitions. For active service, Army units are placed under the authority of the Chief of the Defence Staff (CEMA), who is responsible to the President of France for planning for, and use, of forces.

All soldiers are considered professionals following the suspension of conscription, voted in parliament in 1997 and made effective in 2001.

As of 2017[173], the French Army employed 117,000 personnel (including the French Foreign Legion and the Paris Fire Brigade). In addition, the reserve element of the French Army consisted of 15,453 personnel of the Operational Reserve.

In 1999, the Army issued the *Code of the French Soldier*, which includes the injunctions:

> (...) Mastering his own strength, he respects his opponent and is careful to spare civilians. He obeys orders while respecting laws, customs of war and international conventions.(...) He is aware of global societies and respects their differences. (...)[174]

History

Early history

The first permanent army, paid with regular wages, instead of feudal levies, was established under Charles VII in the 1420–30s. The Kings of France needed reliable troops during and after the Hundred Years' War. These units of troops were raised by issuing *ordonnances* to govern their length of service, composition and payment. These Compagnies d'ordonnance formed the core of the Gendarme Cavalry into the sixteenth century. Stationed throughout France and summoned into larger armies as needed. There was also provision made for "Francs-archers" units of bowmen and foot soldiers raised from the non-noble classes but these units were disbanded once war ended.

The bulk of the infantry for warfare was still provided by urban or provincial militias, raised from an area or city to fight locally and named for their recruiting grounds. Gradually these units became more permanent, and in 1480s Swiss instructors were recruited and some of the 'Bandes' (Militia) were combined to form temporary 'Legions' of up to 9000 men. These men would be paid and contracted and receive training.

Figure 132: *The French Royal Army at the battle of Denain (1712)*

Henry II further regularised the French army by forming standing Infantry regiments to replace the Militia structure. The first of these—the Régiments de Picardie, Piémont, Navarre and Champagne—were called *Les Vieux Corps* (The Old Corps). It was normal policy to disband regiments after a war was over as a cost saving measure with the *Vieux Corps* and the King's own Household Troops the *Maison du Roi* being the only survivors.

Regiments could be raised directly by the King and so called after the region in which they were raised, or by the nobility and so called after the noble or his appointed colonel. When Louis XIII came to the throne he disbanded most of the regiments in existence leaving only the *Vieux* and a handful of others which became known as the *Petite Vieux* and also gained the privilege of not being disbanded after a war.

In 1684 there was a major reorganisation of the French infantry and again in 1701 to fit in with Louis XIV's plans and the War of the Spanish Succession. This reshuffle created many of the modern regiments of the French Army and standardised their equipment and tactics. The army of the Sun King tended to wear grey-white coats with coloured linings. There were exceptions and the foreign troops, recruited from outside France, wore red (Swiss, Irish...) or blue (Germans, Scots...) while the French Guards wore blue. In addition to these regiments of the line the *Maison du Roi* provided several elite units, the

Figure 133: *The Gardes françaises at the battle of Fontenoy (1745)*

Swiss Guards, French Guards and the Regiments of Musketeers being the most famous. The white/grey coated French Infantry of the line *Les Blancs* with their Charleville muskets were a feared foe on the battlefields of the seventeenth and eighteenth centuries, fighting in the Nine Years' War, the Wars of Spanish and Austrian Succession, the Seven Years' War and the American Revolution.

The revolution split the army with the main mass losing most of its officers to aristocratic flight or guillotine and becoming demoralised and ineffective. The French Guard joined the revolt and the Swiss Guards were massacred during the storming of the Tuileries palace. The remnants of the royal army were then joined to the revolutionary militias known as sans-culottes, and the "National Guard" a more middle class militia and police force, to form the French Revolutionary Army.

From 1792, the French Revolutionary Army fought against various combinations of European powers, initially reliant on large numbers and basic tactics, it was defeated bloodily but survived and drove its opponents first from French soil and then overran several countries creating client states.

Under Napoleon I, the French Army conquered most of Europe during the Napoleonic Wars. Professionalising again from the Revolutionary forces and using columns of attack with heavy artillery support and swarms of pursuit cavalry the French army under Napoleon and his marshals was able to outmanoeuvre and destroy the allied armies repeatedly until 1812. Napoleon introduced the concept of all arms Corps, each one a traditional army 'in miniature',

Figure 134: *The French Revolutionary Army at the battle of Jemappes (1792)*

permitting the field force to be split across several lines of march and rejoin or to operate independently. The *Grande Armée* operated by seeking a decisive battle with each enemy army and then destroying them in detail before rapidly occupying territory and forcing a peace.

In 1812 Napoleon marched on Moscow seeking to remove Russian influence from eastern Europe and secure the frontiers of his empire and client states. The campaign initially went well but the vast distances of the Russian Steppe and the cold winter forced his army into a shambling retreat preyed on by Russian raids and pursuit. The Grand Army of the 1812 Campaign could not be replaced and with the "ulcer" of the ongoing peninsular war against Britain and Portugal in Spain the French army was badly short of trained troops and French manpower was almost exhausted.

After Napoleon's abdication and return, halted by an Anglo-Dutch and Prussian alliance at Waterloo, the French army was placed back under the restored Bourbon Monarchy. The structure remained largely unchanged and many officers of the Empire retained their positions.

Figure 135: *After defeating Prussian forces at Jena, the Grande Armée entered Berlin on 27 October 1806*

The long 19th century and the second empire

The Bourbon restoration was a time of political instability with the country constantly on the verge of political violence.

The army was committed to a defense of the Spanish monarchy in 1824, achieving its aims in six months, but did not fully withdraw until 1828, in contrast to the earlier Napoleonic invasion this expedition was rapid and successful.

Taking advantage of the weakness of the bey of Algiers France invaded in 1830 and again rapidly overcame initial resistance, the French government formally annexed Algeria but it took nearly 45 years to fully pacify the country. This period of French history saw the creation of the *Armée d'Afrique*, which included the French Foreign Legion. The Army was now uniformed in dark blue coats and red trousers, which it would retain until the First World War.

The news of the fall of Algiers had barely reached Paris in 1830 when the Bourbon Monarchy was overthrown and replaced by the constitutional Orleans Monarchy, the mobs proved too much for the troops of the *Maison du Roi* and the main body of the French Army, sympathetic to the crowds, did not become heavily involved.

In 1848 a wave of revolutions swept Europe and brought an end to the Bourbon monarchy. The army was large uninvolved in the street fighting in Paris which

Figure 136: *Conquest of Algeria.*

Figure 137: *Battle of Magenta.*

overthew the King but later in the year troops were used in the suppression of the more radical elements of the new Republic which led to the election of Napoleon's nephew as president.

The Pope had been forced out of Rome as part of the Revolutions of 1848, and Louis Napoleon sent a 14,000 man expeditionary force of troops to the Papal State under General Nicolas Charles Victor Oudinot to restore him. In late April 1849, it was defeated and pushed back from Rome by Giuseppi Garibaldi's volunteer corps, but then recovered and recaptured Rome.

The French army was among the first in the world to be issued with Minié rifles, just in time for the Crimean War against Russia, allied with Britain. This invention gave line infantry a weapon with a much longer range and greater accuracy and would lead to new flexible tactics. The French army was more experienced at mass manoeuvre and war fighting than the British and the reputation of the French army was greatly enhanced.

A series of colonial expeditions followed and in 1856 France joined the Second Opium War on the British side against China; obtaining concessions. French troops were deployed into Italy against the Austrians, the first use of railways for mass movement.

The French army was now considered to be an example to others and military missions to Japan and the emulation of French Zouaves in other militaries added to this prestige. However an expedition to Mexico failed to create a stable puppet régime.

In 1870 France was humiliated by defeat in the Franco-Prussian war. The army had far superior infantry weapons in the form of the Chassepot and an early type of machine-gun but its tactics were inferior and by allowing the invading German force the initiative the army was rapidly bottled up into its fortress towns and defeated. The loss of prestige within the army lead to a great emphasis on aggression and close quarter tactics.

Early 20th century

In August 1914, the French Armed Forces numbered 1,300,000 soldiers. During the Great War the French Armed Forces reached a size of 8,300,000 soldiers, of which about 300,000 came from the colonies. During the war around 1,397,000 French soldiers were killed in action, mostly on the Western Front. It was the most deadly conflict in French history. The main generals were: Joseph Joffre, Ferdinand Foch, Charles Mangin, Philippe Pétain, Robert Nivelle, Franchet d'Esperey and Maurice Sarrail (See French Army in World War I). At the beginning of the war, the French Army was wearing the uniform of the Franco-Prussian War of 1870, but the uniform was unsuited to the trenches, and so in 1915 the French Army replaced the uniform, with the Adrian helmet replacing the képi. A uniform with a capote, of bleu-horizon colour adopted to the trenches, was adopted, and the uniform for colonial soldiers coloured khaki.

Figure 138: *French Poilus posing with their war torn flag in 1917, during World War I (1914–18)*

At the beginning of World War II the French Army deployed 2,240,000 combatants grouped into 94 divisions (of which 20 were active and 74 were reservists) from the Swiss border to the North Sea. These numbers did not include the Army of the Alps facing Italy and 600,000 men dispersed through the French colonial empire are not included in this figure. After defeat in 1940, the Vichy French regime was allowed to retain 100–120,000 personnel in unoccupied France, and larger forces in the French Empire: more than 220,000 in Africa (including 140,000 in French North Africa),[175] and forces in Mandate Syria and French Indochina.[176]

After 1945, despite enormous efforts in the First Indochina War of 1945–54 and the Algerian War of 1954–62, both lands eventually left French control. French units stayed in Germany after 1945, forming the French Forces in Germany. 5th Armored Division stayed on in Germany after 1945, while 1st and 3rd Armoured Divisions were established in Germany in 1951. However NATO-assigned formations were withdrawn to fight in Algeria; 5th Armoured Division was withdrawn in 1956. From 1948 to 1966, many French Army units fell under the integrated NATO Military Command Structure.[177] Commander-in-Chief Allied Forces Central Europe was a French Army officer, and many key NATO staff positions were filled by Frenchmen. While an upper limit of 14 French divisions committed to NATO had been set by

Figure 139: *Free French Foreign Legionnaires at the Battle of Bir Hakeim (1942)*

the Treaty of Paris, the total did not exceed six divisions during the Indochina War, and during the Algerian War the total fell as low as two divisions.

The Army created two parachute divisions in 1956, the 10th Parachute Division under the command of General Jacques Massu and the 25th Parachute Division under the command of General Sauvagnac.[178] After the Algiers putsch, the two divisions, with the 11th Infantry Division, were merged into a new light intervention division, the 11th Light Intervention Division, on 1 May 1961.[179]

Decolonisation

At the end of World War II France was immediately confronted with the beginnings of the decolonisation movement. The French army, which had employed indigenous North African spahis and tirailleurs in almost all of its campaigns since 1830, was the leading force in opposition to decolonization, which was perceived as a humiliation.[180] In Algeria the Army repressed an extensive rising in and around Sétif in May 1945 with heavy fire: figures for Algerian deaths vary between 45,000 as claimed by Radio Cairo at the time[181] and the official French figure of 1,020.

The Army saw maintaining control of Algeria as a high priority. By this time, one million French settlers had established themselves, alongside an indigenous

Figure 140: *Soldiers of the 4th zouaves regiment during the Algerian War*

population of nine million. When it decided that politicians were about to sell them out and give independence to Algeria, the Army engineered a military coup that toppled the civilian government and put General de Gaulle back in power in the May 1958 crisis. De Gaulle, however, recognized that Algeria was a dead weight and had to be cut free. Four retired generals then launched the Algiers putsch of 1961 against de Gaulle himself, but it failed. After 400,000 deaths, Algeria finally became independent. Hundreds of thousands of Harkis, Moslems loyal to Paris, went into exile in France, where they and their children and grandchildren remain in poorly assimilated "banlieue" suburbs.[182]

The Army repressed the Malagasy Uprising in Madagascar in 1947. French officials estimated the number of Malagasy killed from a low of 11,000 to a French Army estimate of 89,000.[183]

Cold War era

During the Cold War, the French Army, though not part of NATO's military command structure, planned for the defence of Western Europe.[184] In 1977 the French Army switched from multi-brigade divisions to smaller divisions of about four to five battalions/regiments each. From the early 1970s, 2nd Army Corps was stationed in South Germany, and effectively formed a reserve for NATO's Central Army Group. In the 1980s, 3rd Army Corps headquarters was moved to Lille and planning started for its use in support of NATO's

Figure 141: *Alignment of AMX-30 tanks during the Cold War. 1,258 were in service in 1989.*

Northern Army Group. The Rapid Action Force of five light divisions, including the new 4th Airmobile and 6th Light Armoured Divisions, was also intended as a NATO reinforcement force. In addition, the 152nd Infantry Division was maintained to guard the S3 intercontinental ballistic missile base on the Plateau d'Albion.

In the 1970s–1980s, two light armoured divisions were planned to be formed from school staffs (the 12th and 14th). The 12th Light Armoured Division (12 DLB) was to have its headquarters to be formed on the basis of the staff of the Armoured and Cavalry Branch Training School (French acronym EAABC) at Saumur.[185]

In the late 1970s an attempt was made to form 14 reserve light infantry divisions, but this plan, which included the recreation of the 109th Infantry Division, was too ambitious. The planned divisions included the 102nd, 104e, 107e, 108e, 109e, 110e, 111e, 112e, 114e, 115th, and 127th Infantry Divisions. From June 1984, the French Army reserve consisted of 22 military divisions, administering all reserve units in a certain area, seven *brigades de zone de defence*, 22 regiments interarmees divisionnaires, and the 152nd Infantry Division, defending the ICBM launch sites.[186] The plan was put into action from 1985, and *brigades de zone*, such as the 107th Brigade de Zone, were created. But with the putting-in-place of the "Réserves 2000" plan, the brigades de zone were finally disbanded by mid-1993.[187]

Post Cold War era

1st Army Corps was disbanded on 1 July 1990.

In February 1996 the President of the Republic decided on a transition to a professional service force, and as part of the resulting changes, ten regiments were dissolved in 1997.[188] The specialized support brigades were transferred

Figure 142: *An ERC 90 Sagaie of the 1st Parachute Hussar Regiment in Côte d'Ivoire in 2003*

on 1 July 1997 to Lunéville for the signals, Haguenau (the artillery brigade) and Strasbourg (engineers). The 2nd Armoured Division left Versailles on 1 September 1997 and was installed at Châlons-en-Champagne in place of the disbanding 10th Armoured Division. On 5 March 1998, in view of the ongoing structural adoptions of the French Army, the Minister of Defence decided to disband III Corps, and the dissolution became effective 1 July 1998. The headquarters transitioned to become Headquarters Commandement de la force d'action terrestre (CFAT) (the Land Forces Action Command).

During the late 1990s, during the professionalisation process, numbers dropped from the 236,000 (132,000 conscripts) in 1996 to around 140,000.[189] By June 1999, the Army's strength had dropped to 186,000, including around 70,000 conscripts. 38 of 129 regiments were planned to be stood down from 1997–99. The previous structure's nine 'small' divisions and sundry separate combat and combat support brigades were replaced by nine combat and four combat support brigades. The Rapid Action Force, a corps of five small rapid-intervention divisions formed in 1983, was also disbanded, though several of its divisions were re-subordinated.

War on Terror

Opération Sentinelle is a French military operation with 10,000 soldiers and 4,700 police and gendarmes deployed since the aftermath of the January 2015 Île-de-France attacks, with the objective of protecting sensitive "points" of the territory from terrorism. It was reinforced during the November 2015 Paris attacks, and is part of an ongoing state of emergency in France due to continued terror threats and attacks.

Structure and organisation

French Army
Components
Army Light Aviation
Armoured Cavalry
Troupes de marine
French Foreign Legion
Chasseurs alpins
List of current regiments
Structure of the French Army
Administration
Chief of Staff of the French Army
Equipment
Modern Equipment
History
Military history of France
Personnel
List of senior officers of the French Army

Ranks in the French Army
Awards
Croix de guerre
Médaille militaire
Légion d'honneur
Awards

The organisation of the army is fixed by Chapter 2 of Title II of Book II of the Third Part of the Code of Defense, notably resulting in the codification of Decree 2000-559 of 21 June 2000.

In terms of Article R.3222-3 of the Code of Defence,[190] the Army comprises:

- The Army Chief of Staff (Chef d'état-major de l'armée de terre (CEMAT)).
- The army staff (*l'état-major de l'Armée de terre* or EMAT), which gives general direction and management of all the components;
- The Army Inspectorate (*l'inspection de l'Armée de terre*);
- The Army Human Resources Directorate (*la direction des ressources humaines de l'Armée de terre* or DRHAT);
- The forces;
- A territorial organisation (seven regions, see below)
- The services;
- The personnel training and military higher training organisms.

The French Army was reorganized in 2016. The new organisation consists of two combined divisions (carrying the heritage of 1st Armored and 3rd Armored divisions) and given three combat brigades to supervise each. There is also the Franco-German Brigade. The 4th Airmobile Brigade was reformed to direct the three combat helicopter regiments. There are also several division-level (*niveau divisionnaire*) specialized commands including Intelligence, Information and communication systems, Maintenance, Logistics, Special Forces, Army Light Aviation, Foreign Legion, National Territory, Training.

Arms of the French Army

The Army is divided into arms (*armes*). They include the *Troupes de Marine*, the Armoured Cavalry Arm (*Arme Blindée Cavalerie*), the Artillery, the Engineering Arm (*l'arme du génie*); the Infantry, which includes the Chasseurs Alpins, specialist mountain infantry, Materiel *Matériel*; Logistics (*Train*); Signals (*Transmissions*). Parachute units are maintained by several of the *armes*.

The *Légion étrangère* (French Foreign Legion) was established in 1831 for foreign nationals willing to serve in the French Armed Forces. The Legion is commanded by French officers. It is an elite military unit numbering around 7,000 troops. The Legion has gained worldwide recognition for its service, most recently in Operation Enduring Freedom in Afghanistan since 2001. It is not strictly an *Arme* but a *commandement particulier*, whose regiments belong to several arms, notably the infantry and the engineering arm.

The Troupes de marine are the former Colonial Troops of the French army. They are the first choice units for overseas deployment and recruit on this basis. They are composed of Marine Infantry (*Infanterie de Marine*) (which includes parachute regiments such as 1er RPIMa and a tank unit, the RICM) and the Marine Artillery (*Artillerie de Marine*).

The *Aviation légère de l'Armée de terre* (ALAT, which translates as Army Light Aviation), was established on 22 November 1954 for observation, reconnaissance, assault and supply duties. It operates numerous helicopters in support of the French Army, its primary attack helicopter is the Eurocopter Tiger, of which 80 were ordered. It is an *Arme* with a *commandement particulier*.

Administrative services

On the administrative side, there are now no more than one **Direction** and two services.

The Army Human Resources Directorate (DRHAT) manages human resources (military and civilian) of the Army and training.

The two Services are the service of ground equipment, and the integrated structure of operational maintenance of terrestrial materials (SIMMT, former DCMAT). This joint oriented service is responsible for project management support for all land equipment of the French army. The holding-operational equipment the Army is headed by the Service de maintenance industrielle terrestre (SMITer).

Historically there were other services of the Army who were all grouped together with their counterparts in other components to form joint agencies serving the entire French Armed Forces.

After the health service and the service of species replaced respectively by the French Defence Health service and Military Fuel Service, other services have disappeared in recent years:

- In 2005, the Army historical service (SHAT) became the "Land" department of the Defence Historical Service (Service historique de la défense);

- In September 2005, the Central Engineering Directorate (Direction centrale du génie, DCG) was merged with its counterparts in the air force and the navy to form the Central Directorate of Defense Infrastructure (Direction centrale du service d'infrastructure de la défense);
- On 1 January 2006, the Central Directorate of Telecommunications and Informatics (DCTEI) was incorporated into the Central Directorate of the Joint Directorate of Infrastructure Networks and Information Systems (DIRISI);

The Army Commissariat was dissolved on 31 December 2009 and intégrated into the joint-service Service du commissariat des armées.

There is the Diocese of the French Armed Forces which provides pastoral care to Catholic members of the Army. It is headed by Luc Ravel and is headquartered in Les Invalides.

Military regions

For many years up to 19 military regions were active (see fr:Région militaire). The 10th Military Region (France) supervised French Algeria during the Algerian War.[191] However, by the 1980s the number had been reduced to six: the 1st Military Region (France) with its headquarters in Paris, the 2nd Military Region (France) at Lille, the 3rd Military Region (France) at Rennes, the 4th Military Region (France) at Bordeaux, the 5th and 6th at Lyons and Metz respectively.[192] Each supervised up to five *division militaire territoriale* – military administrative sub-divisions, in 1984 sometimes supervising up to three reserve regiments each. Today, under the latest thorough reform of the French security and defence sector, there are seven fr:Zone de défense et de sécurité each with a territorial ground army region: Paris (or Île-de-France, HQ in Paris), Nord (HQ in Lille), Ouest (HQ in Rennes), Sud-Ouest (HQ in Bordeaux), Sud (HQ in Marseille), Sud-Est (HQ in Lyon), Est (HQ in Strasbourg).[193]

Personnel

'Personnel strength of the French Army 2015	
Category	Strength
Commissioned officers	13,800
Non-commissioned officers	37,600
EVAT	57,300
VDAT	671
Civilian employees	8,100

Source:[194]

Soldiers

There are two types of enlistment for French army soldiers:

- *Volontaire de l'armée de terre (VDAT)* (Volunteer of the Army), one year-contract, renewable.
- *Engagé volontaire de l'armée de terre (EVAT)* (Armed Forces Volunteer), three- or five years contract, renewable.

Non-commissioned officers

NCOs serve on permanent contracts, or exceptionally on renewable five years-contracts. NCO candidates are either EVAT or direct entry civilians. High school diploma giving access to university is a requirement. *École Nationale des Sous-Officiers d'Active (ENSOA)*, Basic NCO school of 8 months, followed by combat school of 4 to 36 weeks depending on occupational specialty. A small number of NCO candidates are trained at the *Ecole Militaire de Haute Montagne (EMHM)* (High Mountain Military School). NCOs with the Advanced Army Technician Certificate (BSTAT) can serve as platoon leaders.

Officers

Career officers

Career officers serve on permanent contracts.

- Direct entry cadets with two years of Classe préparatoire aux grandes écoles or a bachelor's degree spend three years at École Spéciale Militaire de Saint-Cyr (ESM), and graduates as First Lieutenant.
- Direct entry cadets with a master's degree spend one year at ESM, and graduates as First Lieutenant.
- Non-commissioned officer with three years in the army, spend two years at École militaire interarmes, and graduates as First Lieutenant. 50% of the commissioned officers in the French Army are former NCOs.

Contract officers

Contract officers serves on renewable contracts for a maximum of 20 years service. A bachelor's degree is required. There are two different programs, combat officers and specialist officers. Officers in both programs graduates as Second Lieutenants and may reach Lieutenant Colonels rank. Combat officers spend six months at ESM, followed by one year at a combat school. Specialist officers spend three months at ESM, followed by a year of on the job-training within an area of specialization determined by the type of degree held.

Equipment

Figure 143: *The HK416F is the new service rifle of the French military.*

Figure 144: *Leclerc main battle tank*

Figure 145: *GCT 155mm self-propelled artillery*

Figure 146: *Eurocopter Tiger attack helicopter*

Uniform

In the 1970s, France adopted a light beige dress uniform which is worn with coloured kepis, sashes, fringed epaulettes, fourragères and other traditional items on appropriate occasions. The most commonly worn parade dress however consists of camouflage uniforms worn with the dress items noted above. The camouflage pattern, officially called Centre Europe (CE), draws heavily on the coloration incorporated into the US M81 woodland design, but with a thicker and heavier striping. A desert version called the Daguet has been worn since the First Gulf War which consist of large irregular areas of chestnut brown and light grey on a sand khaki base.

The legionnaires of the French Foreign Legion wear white kepis, blue sashes and green and red epaulettes as dress uniform, while the Troupes de marine wear blue and red kepis and yellow epaulettes. The pioneers of the French Foreign Legion wear the basic legionnaire uniform but with leather aprons and gloves. The Chasseurs Alpins wear a large beret, known as the "tarte" (the *pie*) with dark blue or white mountain outfits. The Spahis retain the long white cloak or "burnous" of the regiment's origin as North African cavalry.

Gendarmes of the Republican Guard retain their late 19th century dress uniforms, as do the military cadets of Saint-Cyr and the École Polytechnique. A dark blue/black evening dress is authorized for officers and individual branches or regiments may parade bands or "fanfares" in historic dress dating as far back as the Napoleonic period.

Further reading

- Anthony Clayton, 'France, Soldiers, and Africa', Brassey's Defence Publishers, 1988
- J A C Lewis, 'Going Pro: Special Report French Army,' Jane's Defence Weekly, 19 June 2002, 54–59
- Rupert Pengelley, 'French Army transforms to meet challenges of multi-role future,' Jane's International Defence Review, June 2006, 44–53
- Vernet, Jacques. Le réarmement et la réorganisation de l'Armée de terre française, 1943–1946. Service historique de l'armée de terre, 1980.

External links

Wikimedia Commons has media related to *French Army*.

- (in French) Official website[195]
- French Military Reform: Lessons for America's Army?[196], George A. Bloch (includes explanations of the structure of command)
- The French Army: Royal, Revolutionary and Imperial[197]

French Foreign Legion

	French Foreign Legion
	Légion étrangère
	 The Foreign Legion's grenade emblem and colours
Active	10 March 1831 – present
Country	France
Branch	French Army
Type	Foreign legion
Role	Foreign Infantry, Foreign airborne infantry, Foreign armoured cavalry, Foreign combat engineer, Foreign airborne engineer, Regimental Foreign military police
Size	c. 8,900 men in 11 regiments and one sub-unit (as Jan 2018)
Garrison/HQ	**Mainland France:**<ul><li>Foreign Legion Command</li><li>1st Foreign Regiment<ul><li>Foreign Legion Pionniers</li></ul></li><li>4th Foreign Regiment</li><li>Foreign Legion Recruiting Group</li><li>1st Foreign Cavalry Regiment</li><li>1st Foreign Engineer Regiment</li><li>2nd Foreign Infantry Regiment</li><li>2nd Foreign Engineer Regiment</li><li>13th Demi-Brigade of the Foreign Legion</li></ul>**Haute-Corse:**<ul><li>2nd Foreign Parachute Regiment</li></ul>**French Guiana:**<ul><li>3rd Foreign Infantry Regiment</li></ul>**Mayotte:**<ul><li>Foreign Legion Detachment in Mayotte</li></ul>
Nickname(s)	The Legion (English) *La Légion* (French)
Motto(s)	*Legio Patria Nostra* (The Legion is our Fatherland) *Honneur et Fidélité* (Honour and Fidelity) *Marche ou crève* (March or die, unofficial)

Branch colours Colour of Beret	Red and Green Green
March	Le Boudin
Anniversaries	Camerone Day (30 April)

Engagements	• French conquest of Algeria
	• First Carlist War
	• Crimean War
	• Second Italian War of Independence
	• French intervention in Mexico
	• French campaign against Korea
	• Franco-Prussian War
	• Sino-French War
	• Second Franco-Dahomean War
	• Second Madagascar expedition
	• Mandingo Wars
	• World War I
	• Levant Campaign
	• Rif War
	• World War II
	  • Syria–Lebanon Campaign
	• First Indochina War
	• Algerian War
	• Shaba II
	• Lebanese Civil War 1975–1990
	  • United Nations Interim Force in Lebanon (1978–present)
	  • Multinational Force in Lebanon 1982–1984
	• Gulf War
	• Global War on Terrorism (2001–present)
	  • War in Afghanistan (1978–present)
	  • Operation Enduring Freedom
	    • War in Afghanistan
	• First Ivorian Civil War
	• Second Ivorian Civil War
	• Northern Mali conflict
	• Central African Republic conflict (2012–present)

Website	www<wbr/>.legion-etrangere<wbr/>.com[198] (Official website) www<wbr/>.legion-recrute<wbr/>.com[199] (Official recruitment website)
Commanders	
Commandant	Major General Jean Maurin
Ceremonial chief	Wooden hand of Captain Jean Danjou carried by a selected officer or legionnaire from Foreign Legion Pionniers
Notable commanders	Paul-Frédéric Rollet
Insignia	

Identification symbol	
Legion flash	
Abbreviation	FFL (English) LE (French)

The **French Foreign Legion** (French: *Légion étrangère*) (**FFL**; French: *Légion étrangère* (French pronunciation: [leʒjɔ̃ etʁɑ̃ʒɛʁ]), *L.É.*) is a military service branch of the French Army established in 1831. **Legionnaires** are highly trained infantry soldiers and the Legion is unique in that it was, and continues to be, open to foreign recruits willing to serve in the French Armed Forces. However, when it was founded, the French Foreign Legion was not unique; other foreign formations existed at the time in France.

Commanded by French officers, it is open to French citizens, who amounted to 24% of the recruits in 2007.[200] The Foreign Legion is today known as a unit whose training focuses on traditional military skills and on its strong *esprit de corps*, as its men come from different countries with different cultures. This is a way to strengthen them enough to work as a team. Consequently, training is often described as not only physically challenging, but also very stressful psychologically. French citizenship may be applied for after three years' service. Although the Legion is part of the French military, it is the only unit of the military that does not swear allegiance to France, but to the Foreign Legion itself. Additionally, any soldier who becomes injured during a battle for France can immediately apply to be a French citizen under a provision known as *"Français par le sang versé"* ("French by spilled blood"). As of 2008, members come from 140 countries.

Since 1831, the Legion has suffered the loss of nearly 40,000 men on active service in France, Algeria, Morocco, Tunisia, Madagascar, West Africa, Mexico, Italy, the Crimea, Spain, Indo-China, Norway, Loyada, Syria, Chad, Zaïre, Lebanon, Central Africa, Gabon, Kuwait, Rwanda, Djibouti, former

Yugoslavia, Somalia, Republic of Congo, Ivory Coast, Afghanistan, Mali, Sahel and others.

The French Foreign Legion was primarily used to protect and expand the French colonial empire during the 19th century. The Foreign Legion was initially stationed only in Algeria, where it took part in the pacification and development of the colony. Subsequently, the Foreign Legion was deployed in a number of conflicts, including the First Carlist War in 1835, the Crimean War in 1854, the Second Italian War of Independence in 1859, the French intervention in Mexico in 1863, the Franco-Prussian War in 1870, the Tonkin Campaign and Sino-French War in 1883, supporting growth of the French colonial empire in Sub-Saharan Africa and pacifying Algeria, the Second Franco-Dahomean War in 1892, the Second Madagascar expedition in 1895, and the Mandingo Wars in 1894.

In World War I, the Foreign Legion fought in many critical battles on the Western Front. It played a smaller role in World War II than in World War I, though having a part in the Norwegian, Syrian and North African campaigns. During the First Indochina War (1946–1954), the Foreign Legion saw its numbers swell. The FFL lost a large number of men in the catastrophic Battle of Dien Bien Phu. During the Algerian War of Independence (1954–1962), the Foreign Legion came close to being disbanded after some officers, men, and the highly decorated 1st Foreign Parachute Regiment (1er REP) took part in the Generals' putsch. Notable operations during this period included the Suez Crisis, the Battle of Algiers and various offensives launched by General Maurice Challe including Operations Oranie and Jumelles.

In the 1960s and 1970s, Legion regiments had additional roles in sending units as a rapid deployment force to preserve French interests – in its former African colonies and in other nations as well; it also returned to its roots of being a unit always ready to be sent to conflict zones around the world. Some notable operations include: the Chadian–Libyan conflict in 1969–1972 (the first time that the Legion was sent in operations after the Algerian War), 1978–1979, and 1983–1987; Kolwezi in what is now the Democratic Republic of the Congo in May 1978. In 1981, the 1st Foreign Regiment and Foreign Legion regiments partook to the Multinational Force in Lebanon. In 1990, Foreign Legion regiments were sent to the Persian Gulf and took part in Opération Daguet, part of Division Daguet. Following the Gulf War in the 1990s, the Foreign Legion helped with the evacuation of French citizens and foreigners in Rwanda, Gabon and Zaire. The Foreign Legion was also deployed in Cambodia, Somalia, Sarajevo, Bosnia and Herzegovina. In the mid- to late-1990s, the Foreign Legion was deployed in the Central African Republic, Congo-Brazzaville and in Kosovo. The Foreign Legion also took part in operations in Rwanda in 1990–1994; and the Ivory Coast in 2002 to the present. In the 2000s, the

Foreign Legion was deployed in Operation Enduring Freedom in Afghanistan, Operation Licorne in Ivory Coast, the EUFOR Tchad/RCA in Chad, and Operation Serval in the Northern Mali conflict.

Other countries have tried to emulate the French Foreign Legion model. However, the contemporary French Foreign Legion relates the most to that of Spain, the Spanish Legion.

History

The French Foreign Legion was created by Louis Philippe,[201] the King of the French, on 10 March 1831 from the foreign regiments of the Kingdom of France. Recruits included soldiers from the recently disbanded Swiss and German foreign regiments of the Bourbon monarchy. The Royal Ordinance for the establishment of the new regiment specified that the foreigners recruited could only serve outside France. The French expeditionary force that had occupied Algiers in 1830 was in need of reinforcements and the Legion was accordingly transferred by sea in detachments from Toulon to Algeria.[202]

The Foreign Legion was primarily used, as part of the *Armée d'Afrique*, to protect and expand the French colonial empire during the 19th century, but it also fought in almost all French wars including the Franco-Prussian War, World War I and World War II. The Foreign Legion has remained an important part of the French Army and sea transport protected by the French Navy, surviving three Republics, the Second French Empire, two World Wars, the rise and fall of mass conscript armies, the dismantling of the French colonial empire, and the loss of the Foreign Legion's base, Algeria.

Conquest of Algeria 1830–1847

Created to fight "outside mainland France", the Foreign Legion was stationed in Algeria, where it took part in the pacification and development of the colony, notably by drying the marshes in the region of Algiers. The Foreign Legion was initially divided into six "national battalions" (Swiss, Poles, Germans, Italians, Spanish, and Dutch-Belgian). Smaller national groups, such as the ten Englishmen recorded in December 1832, appear to have been placed randomly.

In late 1831, the first legionnaires landed in Algeria, the country that would be the Foreign Legion's homeland for 130 years and shape its character. The early years in Algeria were hard on the legion because it was often sent to the worst postings and received the worst assignments, and its members were generally uninterested in the new colony of the French.[203] The Legion served alongside the Battalions of Light Infantry of Africa, formed in 1832, which was a penal military unit made up of men with prison records who still had to do their military service or soldiers with serious disciplinary problems.

The Foreign Legion's first service in Algeria came to an end after only four years, as it was needed elsewhere.

Carlist War 1835–1839

To support Isabella's claim to the Spanish throne against her uncle, the French government decided to send the Foreign Legion to Spain. On 28 June 1835, the unit was handed over to the Spanish government. The Foreign Legion landed via sea at Tarragona on 17 August with around 1,400 who were quickly dubbed *Los Algerinos* (the Algerians) by locals because of their previous posting.

The Foreign Legion's commander immediately dissolved the national battalions to improve the *esprit de corps*. Later, he also created three squadrons of lancers and an artillery battery from the existing force to increase independence and flexibility. The Foreign Legion was dissolved on 8 December 1838, when it had dropped to only 500 men. The survivors returned to France, many reenlisting in the new Foreign Legion along with many of their former Carlist enemies.

Crimean War

On 9 June 1854, the French ship *Jean Bart* embarked four battalions of the Foreign Legion for the Crimean Peninsula. A further battalion was stationed at Gallipoli as brigade depot. Eight companies drawn from both regiments of the Foreign Legion took part in the Battle of Alma (20 September 1854). Reinforcements by sea brought the Legion contingent up to brigade strength. As the "Foreign Brigade", it served in the Siege of Sevastopol, during the winter of 1854–1855.

The lack of equipment was particularly challenging and cholera hit the Allied expeditionary force. Nevertheless, the "leather bellies" (the nickname given to the legionnaires by the Russians because of the large cartridge pouches that they wore attached to their waist-belts), performed well. On 21 June 1855, the Third Battalion, left Corsica for the Crimea.

On 8 September the final assault was launched on Sevastopol. Two days later, the Second Foreign Regiment with flags and band playing ahead, marched through the streets of Sevastopol. Although initial reservations had been expressed about whether the Legion should be used outside Africa, the Crimean experience established its suitability for service in European warfare, as well as making a cohesive single entity of what had previously been two separate foreign regiments. Total Legion casualties in the Crimea were 1,703 killed and wounded.

Figure 147: *The Légion étrangère in 1852.*

Italian Campaign 1859

Like the rest of the "Army of Africa", the Foreign Legion provided detachments in the campaign of Italy. Two foreign regiments, grouped with the 2nd Regiment of Zouaves, were part of the Second Brigade of the Second Division of Mac Mahon's Corps. The Foreign Legion acquitted itself particularly well against the Austrians at the battle of Magenta (4 June 1859) and at the Battle of Solferino (24 June). Legion losses were significant and the 2nd Foreign Regiment lost Colonel Chabrière, its commanding officer. In gratitude, the city of Milan awarded, in 1909, the "commemorative medal of deliverance", which still adorns the regimental flags of the Second Regiment.[204]

Mexican Expedition 1863–1867

The 38,000 strong French expeditionary force dispatched to Mexico via sea between 1862 and 1863 included two battalions of the Foreign Legion, increased to six battalions by 1866. Small cavalry and artillery units were raised from legionnaires serving in Mexico. The original intention was that Foreign Legion units should remain in Mexico for up to six years to provide a core for the Imperial Mexican Army.[205] However the Legion was withdrawn with the other French forces during February–March 1867.

Figure 148: *Uniform of a legionnaire during the 1863 Mexican campaign*

It was in Mexico on 30 April 1863 that the Legion earned its legendary status. A company led by Captain Jean Danjou, numbering 62 Legionnaires and 3 Legion officers, was escorting a convoy to the besieged city of Puebla when it was attacked and besieged by three thousand Mexican loyalists, organised in two battalions of infantry and cavalry, numbering 2,200 and 800 respectively. The Legion detachment under Captain Jean Danjou, Sous-Lieutenant Jean Vilain, Sous-Lieutenant Clément Maudet made a stand in the *Hacienda de la Trinidad* – a farm near the village of *Camarón*. When only six survivors remained, out of ammunition, a bayonet assault was launched in which three of the six were killed. The remaining three wounded men were brought before the Mexican commander Colonel Milan, who allowed them to return to the French lines as an honor guard for the body of Captain Danjou. The captain had a wooden hand, which was later returned to the Legion and is now kept in a case in the Legion Museum at Aubagne, and paraded annually on Camerone Day. It is the Foreign Legion's most precious relic.

During the Mexican Campaign, 6,654 French died. Of these, 1,918 were from a single regiment of the Legion.

Figure 149: *Captain Danjou's prosthetic wooden hand.*

Franco-Prussian War 1870

According to French law, the Foreign Legion was not to be used within Metropolitan France except in the case of a national invasion,[206] and was consequently not a part of Napoleon III's Imperial Army that capitulated at Sedan. With the defeat of the Imperial Army, the Second French Empire fell and the Third Republic was created.

The new Third Republic was desperately short of trained soldiers following Sedan, so the Foreign Legion was ordered to provide a contingent. On 11 October 1870 two provisional battalions disembarked via sea at Toulon, the first time the Foreign Legion had been deployed in France itself. It attempted to lift the Siege of Paris by breaking through the German lines. It succeeded in retaking Orléans, but failed to break the siege. In January 1871, France capitulated but civil war soon broke out, which led to revolution and the short-lived Paris Commune. The Foreign Legion participated in the suppression of the Commune, which was crushed with great bloodshed.

Figure 150: *A Legionnaire sniper at Tuyên Quang.*

Tonkin Campaign and Sino-French War 1883–1888

The Foreign Legion's First Battalion (Lieutenant-Colonel Donnier) sailed to Tonkin in the autumn of 1883, during the period of undeclared hostilities that preceded the Sino-French War (August 1884 to April 1885), and formed part of the attack column that stormed the western gate of Sơn Tây on 16 December. The Second and Third Infantry Battalions (*chef de bataillon* Diguet and Lieutenant-Colonel Schoeffer) were also deployed to Tonkin shortly afterwards, and were present in all the major campaigns of the Sino-French War. Two Foreign Legion companies led the defence at the celebrated Siege of Tuyên Quang (24 November 1884 to 3 March 1885). In January 1885 the Foreign Legion's 4th Battalion (*chef de bataillon* Vitalis) was deployed to the French bridgehead at Keelung (Jilong) in Formosa (Taiwan), where it took part in the later battles of the Keelung Campaign. The battalion played an important role in Colonel Jacques Duchesne's offensive in March 1885 that captured the key Chinese positions of La Table and Fort Bamboo and disengaged Keelung.

In December 1883, during a review of the Second Legion Battalion on the eve of its departure for Tonkin to take part in the Bắc Ninh Campaign, General François de Négrier pronounced a famous *mot*: *Vous, légionnaires, vous êtes soldats pour mourir, et je vous envoie où l'on meurt!* ('You, Legionnaires, you are soldiers in order to die, and I'm sending you to where one dies!')

Figure 151: *Monument commemorating the soldiers of the Foreign Legion killed on duty during the South-Oranese campaign (1897–1902).*

Colonisation of Africa

As part of the Army of Africa, the Foreign Legion contributed to the growth of the French colonial empire in Sub-Saharan Africa. Simultaneously, the Legion took part to the pacification of Algeria, plagued by various tribal rebellions and razzias.

Second Franco-Dahomean War 1892–1894

In 1892, King Behanzin was threatening the French protectorate of Porto-Novo in modern-day Benin and France decided to intervene. A battalion, led by commandant Faurax, was formed from two companies of the First Foreign Regiment and two others from the second regiment. From Cotonou, the legionnaires marched to seize Abomey, the capital of the Kingdom of Dahomey. Two and a half months were needed to reach the city, at the cost of repeated battles against the Dahomean warriors, especially the Amazons of the King. King Behanzin surrendered and was captured by the legionnaires in January 1894.

Second Madagascar Expedition 1894–1895

In 1895, a battalion, formed by the First and Second Foreign Regiments, was sent to the Kingdom of Madagascar, as part of an expeditionary force whose mission was to conquer the island. The foreign battalion formed the backbone of the column launched on Antananarivo, the capital of Madagascar. After a few skirmishes, the Queen Ranavalona III promptly surrendered.[207] The Foreign Legion lost 226 men, of whom only a tenth died in actual fighting. Others, like much of the expeditionary force, died from tropical diseases. Despite the success of the expedition, the quelling of sporadic rebellions would take another eight years until 1905, when the island was completely pacified by the French under Joseph Gallieni. During that time, insurrections against the Malagasy Christians of the island, missionaries and foreigners were particularly terrible. Queen Ranavalona III was deposed in January 1897 and was exiled to Algiers in Algeria, where she died in 1917.[208]

Mandingo War 1898

From 1882 until his capture, Samori Ture, ruler of the Wassoulou Empire, fought the French colonial army, defeating them on several occasions, including a notable victory at Woyowayanko (2 April 1882), in the face of French heavy artillery. Nonetheless, Samori was forced to sign several treaties ceding territory to the French between 1886 and 1889. Samori began a steady retreat, but the fall of other resistance armies, particularly Babemba Traoré at Sikasso, permitted the colonial army to launch a concentrated assault against his forces. A battalion of two companies from the 2nd Foreign Regiment was created in early 1894 to pacify the Niger. The Legionnaires' victory at the fortress of Ouilla and police patrols in the region accelerated the submission of the tribes. On 29 September 1898, Samori Ture was captured by the French Commandant Gouraud and exiled to Gabon, marking the end of the Wassoulou Empire.

Marching Regiments of the Foreign Legion

World War I 1914–1918

The annexation of Alsace and Lorraine by Germany in 1871 led to numerous volunteers from the two regions enlisting in the Foreign Legion, which gave them the option of French citizenship at the end of their service

With the declaration of war on 29 July 1914, a call was made for foreigners residing in France to support their adopted country. While many would have preferred direct enlistment in the regular French Army, the only option immediately available was that of the Foreign Legion. On one day only (3 August 1914) a reported 8,000 volunteers applied to enlist in the Paris recruiting office of the Legion.

Figure 152: *Revue of the Marching Regiment of the Foreign Legion, R.M.L.E at the end of November 1918.*

Figure 153: *Americans in the Foreign Legion, 1916.*

Figure 154: *American poet Alan Seeger (1888–1916), in his Marching Regiment uniform.*

In World War I, the Foreign Legion fought in many critical battles on the Western Front, including Artois, Champagne, Somme, Aisne, and Verdun (in 1917), and also suffered heavy casualties during 1918. The Foreign Legion was also in the Dardanelles and Macedonian front, and was highly decorated for its efforts. Many young foreigners volunteered for the Foreign Legion when the war broke out in 1914. There were marked differences between the idealistic volunteers of 1914 and the hardened men of the old Legion, making assimilation difficult. Nevertheless, the old and the new men of the Foreign Legion fought and died in vicious battles on the Western front, including Belloy-en-Santerre during the Battle of the Somme, where the poet Alan Seeger, after being mortally wounded by machine-gun fire, cheered on the rest of his advancing battalion.[209]

Interwar Period 1918–1939

While suffering heavy casualties on the Western Front the Legion had emerged from World War I with an enhanced reputation and as one of the most highly decorated units in the French Army.[210] In 1919, the government of Spain raised the Spanish Foreign Legion and modeled it after the French Foreign Legion. General Jean Mordacq intended to rebuild the Foreign Legion as a larger

Figure 155: *Paul-Frédéric Rollet (1875–1941)
The Father of the Legion*

military formation, doing away with the legion's traditional role as a solely infantry formation. General Mordacq envisioned a Foreign Legion consisting not of regiments, but of divisions with cavalry, engineer, and artillery regiments in addition to the legion's infantry mainstay. In 1920, decrees ordained the establishment of regiments of cavalry and artillery. Immediately following the armistice the Foreign Legion experienced an increase of enlistments.[211] The Foreign Legion began the process of reorganizing and redeploying to Algeria.

The Legion played a major part in the Rif War of 1920–25. In 1932, the Foreign Legion consisted of 30,000 men, serving in 6 multi-battalion regiments including the 1st Foreign Infantry Regiment 1er REI – Algeria, Syria and Lebanon; 2nd Foreign Infantry Regiment 2ème REI, 3rd Foreign Infantry Regiment 3ème REI, and 4th Foreign Infantry Regiment 4ème REI – Morocco, Lebanon; 5th Foreign Infantry 5ème REI – Indochina; and 1st Foreign Cavalry Regiment 1er REC – Lebanon, Tunisia and Morocco. In 1931, Général Paul-Frédéric Rollet assumed the role of 1st Inspector of the Foreign Legion, a post created at his initiative. While Colonel Regimental Commander of the 1st Foreign Regiment 1er RE (1925–1931), Rollet had planned the centennial celebrations of the Legion's 100th year anniversary on Camaron day of April

Figure 156: *Legionnaires in Morocco, c. 1920.*

30, 1931. He was subsequently credited with creating much of the modern mystique of the Legion by restoring or creating many of its traditions.

World War II 1939–1945

The Foreign Legion played a smaller role in World War II in mainland Europe than in World War I, though there was involvement in many exterior theatres of operations, notably sea transport protection through to the Norwegian, Syria-Lebanon, and North African campaigns. The 13th Demi-Brigade, formed for service in Norway, found itself in the UK at the time of the French Armistice (June 1940), was deployed to the British 8th Army in North Africa and distinguished itself in the Battle of Bir Hakeim (1942). Reflecting the divisions of the time, part of the Foreign Legion joined the Free French movement while another part served the Vichy government. German legionnaires were incorporated into the Wehrmacht's 90th Light Infantry Division in North Africa.

The Syria–Lebanon Campaign of June 1941 saw legionnaire fighting legionnaire as the 13e D.B.L.E clashed with the 6th Foreign Infantry Regiment 6e REI at Damascus. Nevertheless, many legionnaires of the 6th Foreign Infantry Regiment 6e (dissolved on December 31, 1941) integrated the Marching Regiment of the Foreign Legion R.M.L.E in 1942. Later, a thousand of the rank-and-file of the Vichy Legion unit joined the 13e D.B.L.E. of the Free French forces which were also part as of September 1944 of Jean de Lattre de

French Foreign Legion

Figure 157: *Free French Foreign Legionnaires assaulting an Axis strong point at the battle of Bir Hakeim, 1942.*

Tassigny's successful Amalgam of the French Liberation Army (French: *Armée française de la Libération,*), the (400,000 men) amalgam consisted of the Armistice Army, the Free French Forces and the French Forces of the Interior which formed Army B and were later part of the French 1st Army with forces also issued from the French Resistance.

Alsace-Lorraine

Following World War II, many French-speaking German former soldiers joined the Foreign Legion to pursue a military career, an option no longer possible in Germany including French German soldiers of Malgré-nous. It would have been considered problematic if the men from Alsace-Lorraine didn't speak French. These French-speaking former German soldiers made up as much as 60 percent of the Legion during the war in Indochina. Contrary to popular belief however, French policy was to exclude former members of the Waffen-SS, and candidates for induction were refused if they exhibited the tell-tale blood type tattoo, or even a scar that might be masking it.

The high percentage of Germans was contrary to normal policy concerning a single dominant nationality however, and in more recent times Germans have made up a much smaller percentage of the Foreign Legion's composition.

Figure 158: *parachute company of the 3rd Foreign Infantry Regiment.*

First Indochina War 1946–1954

During the First Indochina War (1946–54) the Foreign Legion saw its numbers swell due to the incorporation of World War II veterans. Although the Foreign Legion distinguished itself in a territory where it had served since the 1880s, it also suffered a heavy toll during this war. Constantly being deployed in operations, units of the Legion suffered particularly heavy losses in the climactic Battle of Dien Bien Phu, before the fortified valley finally fell on May 7, 1954. No fewer than 72,833 served in Indochina during the eight-year war. The Legion suffered the loss of 10,283 of its own men in combat: 309 officers, 1082 sous-officiers and 9092 legionnaires .

While only one of several Legion units involved in Indochina, the 1st Foreign Parachute Battalion (1er BEP) particularly distinguished itself, while being annihilated twice. It was renamed the 1st Foreign Parachute Regiment (1er REP) after its third reformation.

The 1er BEP sailed to Indochina on November 12 and was then engaged in combat operations in Tonkin. On November 17, 1950 the battalion parachuted into That Khé and suffered heavy losses at Coc Xa. Reconstituted on March 1, 1951, the battalion participated in combat operations at Cho Ben, on the Black River and in Annam. On November 21, 1953 the reconstituted 1er BEP was parachuted into Dien Bien Phu. In this battle, the unit lost 575 killed and

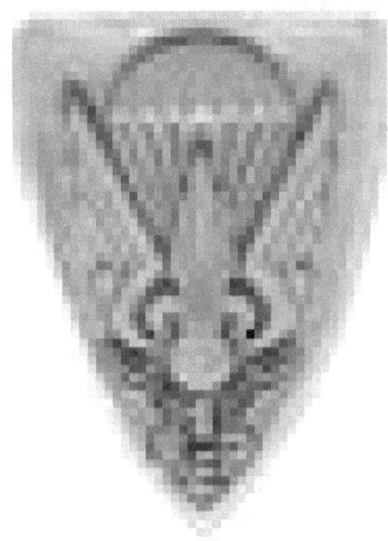

Figure 159: *1st Foreign Parachute Regiment formed and commanded by Legion Lieutenant Colonel Pierre Paul Jeanpierre (1912–1958).*

missing. Reconstituted for the third time on May 19, 1954, the battalion left Indochina on February 8, 1955. The 1er BEP received five citations and the fourragère of the colors of the Médaille militaire for its service in Indochina. The 1er BEP became the 1st Foreign Parachute Regiment (1er REP) in Algeria on September 1, 1955.

Dien Bien Phu fell on May 7, 1954 at 17:30. The couple of hectares comprising the battlefield today are corn fields surrounding a stele which commemorates the sacrifices of those who died there. While the garrison of Dien Bien Phu included French regular, North African, and locally recruited (Indochinese) units, the battle has become associated particularly with the paratroops of the Foreign Legion.

During the Indochina War, the Legion operated several Armored Trains which were an enduring *Rolling Symbol* during the chartered course duration of French Indochina. The Legion also operated various Passage Companies relative to the continental conflicts at hand.

Algerian War 1954–1962

Foreign Legion paratroops

The legion was heavily engaged in fighting against the National Liberation Front and the Armée de Libération Nationale (ALN). The main activity during the period 1954–1962 was as part of the operations of the 10th Parachute Division and 25th Parachute Division. The 1st Foreign Parachute Regiment, 1er REP, was under the command of the 10th Parachute Division (France), 10ème DP, and the 2nd Foreign Parachute Regiment, 2ème REP, was under the command of the 25th Parachute Division (France), 25ème DP. While both the 1st Foreign Parachute Regiment (1er REP), and the 2nd Foreign Parachute Regiment (2ème REP), were part of the operations of French parachute divisions (10ème DP and 25ème DP established in 1956), the Legion's 1st Foreign Parachute Regiment (1er REP), and the Legion's 2nd Foreign Parachute Regiment (2ème REP), are older than the French divisions. The 1er REP was the former thrice-reconstituted 1st Foreign Parachute Battalion (1er BEP) and the 2ème REP was the former 2nd Foreign Parachute Battalion (2ème BEP). Both battalions were renamed and their Legionnaires transferred from Indochina on August 1, 1954 to Algeria by November 1, 1954. Both traced their origins to the Parachute Company of the 3rd Foreign Infantry Regiment commanded by Legion Lieutenant Jacques Morin attached to the III/1er R.C.P.

With the start of the War in Algeria on November 1, 1954, the two foreign participating parachute battalions back from Indochina, the 1st Foreign Parachute Battalion (1er BEP, III Formation) and the 2nd Foreign Parachute Battalion (2ème BEP), were not part of any French parachute divisions yet and were not designated as regiments until September and December 1, 1955 respectively.

Main operations during the Algerian War included the Battle of Algiers and the Bataille of the Frontiers, fought by 60,000 soldiers including French and Foreign Legion paratroopers. For paratroopers of the Legion, the 1st Foreign Parachute Regiment (1er REP) and 2nd Foreign Parachute Regiment (2ème REP), were the only known foreign active parachute regiments, exclusively commanded by Pierre Paul Jeanpierre for the 1er REP and the paratrooper commanders of the 2ème REP. The remainder of French paratrooper units of the French Armed Forces were commanded by Jacques Massu, Buchond, Marcel Bigeard, Paul Aussaresses. Other Legion offensives in the mountains in 1959 included operations Jumelles, Cigales, and Ariège in the Aures and the last in Kabylie.

The image of the Legion as a professional and non-political force was tarnished when the elite 1st Foreign Parachute Regiment 1er REP, which was also part of the 10th Parachute Division played a leading role in the general's putsch of 1961 and was subsequently disbanded.

Figure 160: *Marche ou Crève and More Majorum for Legion Officers, Sous-Officiers and Legionnaires of the CEPs, BEPs and REPs of the Legion.*

Generals' Putsch 1961 and reduction of Foreign Legion

Coming out of a difficult Indochinese conflict, the French Foreign Legion, reinforced cohesion by extending the duration of basic training. Efforts exerted were successful during this transit; however, entering in December 1960 and the revolt the generals, a crisis hit the legion putting its faith at the corps of the Army.[212]

For having rallied to the generals putsch of April 1961, the 1st Foreign Parachute Regiment 1er REP of the 10th Parachute Division was dissolved on April 30, 1961 at Zeralda.

In 1961, at the issue of the putsch, the 1st Mounted Saharan Squadron of the Foreign Legion[213](French: *1er Escadron Saharien Porté de la Légion Etrangère, 1er ESPLE*) received the missions to assure surveillance and policing.

The independence of Algeria from the French in 1962 was traumatizing since it ended with the enforced abandonment of the barracks command center at Sidi Bel Abbès established in 1842. Upon being notified that the elite regiment was to be disbanded and that they were to be reassigned, legionnaires of the 1er REP burned the Chinese pavilion acquired following the Siege of Tuyên Quang in 1884. The relics from the Legion's history museum, including the wooden hand of Captain Jean Danjou, subsequently accompanied the Legion to

Figure 161: *Tenue of a Legionnaire of the Saharan Mounted Companies of the Foreign Legion (CSPLE). Often blue or red and worn by all the soldiers of the Army of Africa; the Legion however, officially adopted the Ceinture Bleue (blue sash) in 1882.*

France. Also removed from Sidi Bel Abbès were the symbolic Legion remains of General Paul-Frédéric Rollet (The Father of the Legion), Legion officer Prince Count Aage of Rosenborg, and Legionnaire Heinz Zimmermann (last fatal casualty in Algeria).

The Legion acquired its parade song "*Non, je ne regrette rien*" ("No, I regret nothing"), a 1960 Édith Piaf song sung by Sous-Officiers and legionnaires as they left their barracks for re-deployment following the Algiers putsch of 1961. The song has remained a part of Legion heritage since.

The 1st Foreign Parachute Regiment 1er REP was disbanded on April 30, 1961. However, the 2nd Foreign Parachute Regiment 2ème REP prevailed in existence, while most of the personnel of the Saharan Companies were integrated into the 1st Foreign Infantry Regiment, 2nd Foreign Infantry Regiment and 4th Foreign Infantry Regiment respectively.

Figure 162: *Legion Officer Lieutenant-colonel Prince Count Aage of Rosenborg (1887–1940).*

Post-colonial Africa

By the mid-1960s the Legion had lost its traditional and spiritual home in French Algeria and elite units had been dissolved. President de Gaulle considered disbanding it altogether but, being reminded of the Marching Regiments, and that the 13th Demi-Brigade was one of the first units to declare for him in 1940 and taking also into consideration the effective service of various Saharan units and performances of other Legions units, he chose instead to downsize the Legion from 40,000 to 8,000 men and relocate it to metropolitan France. With that however, other Legion units still remained on the respective continent.

1962–present

In the early 1960s, and besides ongoing global rapid deployments, the Legion also stationed forces on various continents while operating different function units.

From 1965 to 1967, the Legion operated several companies, including the 5th Heavy Weight Transport Company (CTGP), mainly in charge of evacuating the Sahara. The area of responsibility of some of these units extended from the confines of the in-between of the Sahara to the Mediterranean. Ongoing

Figure 163: *The 13th Demi-Brigade of the Foreign Legion parading through Roman ruins in Lambaesis, Algeria (circa 1958).*

interventions and rapid deployments two years later and the following years included in part:

- 1969–1971 : interventions in Chad
- 1978–present : Peacekeeping operations around the Mediterranean, including the United Nations Interim Force in Lebanon during the Global War on Terror
- 1978–1978 : Battle of Kolwezi (Zaïre)
- 1981–1984 : Peacekeeping operations in Lebanon at the corps of the United Nations Multinational Force during the Lebanese Civil War along with the 31ème Brigade which included the 1st Foreign Regiment 1er RE. Operation Épaulard I was spearheaded by Lieutenant-colonel Bernard Janvier. The Multinational Force also included the British Armed Forces 1st The Queen's Dragoon Guards, U.S. American contingents of United States Marine Corps and the United States Navy, the French Navy and 28 exclusive French Armed Forces regiments including French paratroopers regiments, companies, units of the 11th Parachute Brigade along with the 2nd Foreign Parachute Regiment 2^{e} REP. The multinational force also included the Irish Armed Forces and units of the French National Gendarmerie, Italian paratroopers from the Folgore Brigade, and infantry units from the Bersaglieri regiments and Marines of the San Marco Battalion.

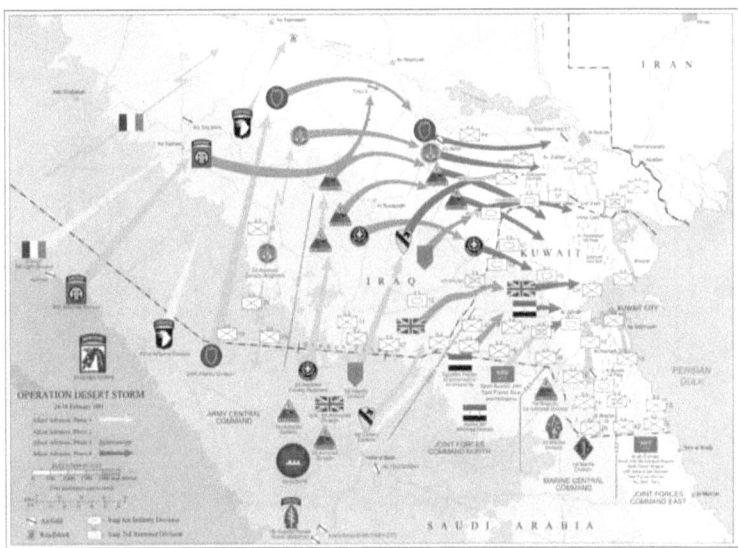

Figure 164: *The 6th Light Armoured Division 6ème D.L.B operating the left flank of the 34 nations coalition during the Gulf War.*

Gulf War 1990–1991

In September 1990, the 1st Foreign Regiment 1er RE, the 1st Foreign Cavalry Regiment 1er REC, the 2nd Foreign Parachute Regiment 2ème REP, the 2nd Foreign Infantry Regiment 2ème REI, and the 6th Foreign Engineer Regiment 6ème REG were sent to the Persian Gulf as a part of Opération Daguet along with the 1st Spahi Regiment, the 11th Marine Artillery Regiment, the 3rd Marine Infantry Regiment, the 21st Marine Infantry Regiment, the French Army Light Aviation, the Marine Infantry Tank Regiment, French paratroopers regiments including components of the 35th Parachute Artillery Regiment 35ème RAP, the 1st Parachute Hussard Regiment 1er RHP, the 17th Parachute Engineer Regiment 17ème RGP and other airborne contingents. Division Daguet was commanded by Général de brigade Bernard Janvier.

The Legion force, mainly comprising 27 different nationalities, was attached to the French 6th Light Armoured Division 6ème D.L.B, whose mission was to protect the Coalition's left flank while cover fired by the marine's artillery. During the Gulf War, DINOPS operated in support of the U.S. Army's 82nd Airborne Division, and provided the EOD services to the division. After the cease fire took hold they conducted a joint mine clearing operation alongside a Royal Australian Navy Clearance Diver Team Unit.

Figure 165: *A Legion honour guard of the 2nd Foreign Infantry Regiment stands at attention as they await the arrival of Norman Schwarzkopf, Jr. and Lt. Gen. Khalid bin Sultan bin Abdul Aziz, commander of Joint Forces in Saudi Arabia, during Operation Desert Shield.*

After the four-week air campaign, coalition forces launched the ground offensive. They quickly penetrated deep into Iraq, with the Legion taking the As-Salman Airport, meeting little resistance. The war ended after a hundred hours of fighting on the ground, which resulted in very light casualties for the Legion.

Post 1991

- 1991: Evacuation of French citizens and foreigners in Rwanda, Gabon and Zaire.
- 1992: Cambodia and Somalia
- 1993: Sarajevo, Bosnia and Herzegovina
- 1995: Rwanda
- 1996: Central African Republic
- 1997: Congo-Brazzaville
- Since 1999: KFOR in Kosovo and Macedonia

Global War on Terror 2001–present

- 2001–present: Operation Enduring Freedom in Afghanistan
- 2002–2003: Operation Licorne in Ivory Coast
- 2008–2008: EUFOR Tchad/RCA in Chad
- 2013–2014: Operation Serval in the Northern Mali conflict

Composition and organization

Prior to the end of the Algerian War the legion had not been stationed in mainland France except in wartime. Until 1962, the Foreign Legion headquarters, garrison quartier Vienot of Sidi Bel Abbès was in French Algeria. Today, some units of the Légion are in Corsica or overseas possessions (mainly in French Guiana, guarding Guiana Space Centre), while the rest are in the south of mainland France. Current headquarters, garrison quartier Vienot of Aubagne is in France, just outside Marseille. As a result of a recruiting drive in the wake of the November 2015 Paris attacks, the Legion will be 8,900 men strong in 2018.[214]

- Mainland France
  - 1st Foreign Regiment (1er RE), based in Aubagne, France (HQ, selection and administration, other specific missions)
    - Pionniers Sections of Tradition
  - 1st Foreign Cavalry Regiment (1er REC), based in Camp de Carpiagne (Bouches-du-Rhône), France (armoured troops)
  - 1st Foreign Engineer Regiment (1er REG) former 6th Foreign Engineer Regiment (6ème REG), based in Laudun, France
    - Pionniers Groups
  - 2nd Foreign Infantry Regiment (2ème REI), based in Nîmes, France
  - 2nd Foreign Engineer Regiment (2ème REG), based in St Christol, France
    - Pionniers Groups
  - 2nd Foreign Parachute Regiment (2ème REP), based in Calvi, Corsica
  - 4th Foreign Regiment (4^{ème}RE), based in Castelnaudary (training), France
    - Pionniers Groups
  - Foreign Legion Recruiting Group (G.R.L.E), based at Fort de Nogent (military recruiting and other), France
  - 13th Demi-Brigade of the Foreign Legion (13ème DBLE) stationed in Djibouti until 2011, then the United Arab Emirates until 2016. As of January 2016, the 13e DBLE is progressively based at Camp Larzac to integrate the 6e BLB
- French Overseas Territories and Overseas Collectives, France

- 3rd Foreign Infantry Regiment (3ème REI), based in French Guiana
  - Pionniers Groups
- Foreign Legion Detachment in Mayotte (DLEM)

Current deployments

These are the following deployments:

Note: English names for countries or territories are in parentheses.

- *Opérations extérieures* (other than at home bases or on standard duties)
  - Guyane (French Guiana) Mission de presence sur l'Oyapok – **Protection** – 3ème REI Protection CSG ; 2ème REP / CEA; 2ème REI / 4ème compagnie
  - Afghanistan **Intervention** 1er REC / 3° escadron (1 peloton); 2ème REI / 4° compagnie OMLT; 2ème REG / 1ère compagnie
  - Mayotte (Departmental Collectivity of Mayotte) **Prevention** DLEM Mission de souveraineté
  - Gabon **Prevention** 2ème REP / 3ème compagnie – 4ème compagnie

Units

Acronym	French Name	English Meaning
CEA	Compagnie d'éclairage et d'appuis	Reconnaissance and Support Company
CAC	Compagnie anti-char	Anti-Tank Company
UCL	Unité de commandement et de logistique	Unit of Command and Logistics
EMT	État-major tactique	Tactical Command Post
NEDEX	Neutralisation des explosifs	Neutralisation and Destruction of Explosives
OMLT	Operational Mentoring and Liaison Team *(The official name for this branch is in English)*	

Figure 166: *Legionnaires in Paris on Vigipirate, France's counter-terrorism security alert system, in November 2010*

Figure 167: *ERC 90 light tank of the 13th Demi-Brigade of the Foreign Legion (13ème DBLE) in Djibouti*

Figure 168: *Paratroopers of 2ème REP in Djibouti*

Figure 169: *Snipers of the 2nd Foreign Infantry Regiment (2ème REI) using a PGM Hécate and a FR-F2 in Afghanistan in 2005*

Figure 170: *Legionnaire of 2ème REI with an M2 heavy machine gun*

Figure 171: *Legionnaire using an FR F2 in Afghanistan (2007)*

DINOPS, PCG and Commandos

- 2ème REP Commando Parachute Group (GCP); Pathfinders qualified in Direct Actions, Special Recco and IMEX.
- 1st Foreign Engineer Regiment 1er REG; Parachute Underwater Demolition P.C.G Teams (Combat Engineer Divers, French: *Plongeurs du Combat du Génie*), former DINOPS Teams of Nautical Subaquatic Intervention Operational Detachment (French: *Détachement d'Intervention Nautique Operationnelle Subaquatique*).
- 2nd Foreign Engineer Regiment 2ème REG; Parachute Underwater Demolition P.C.G Teams (Combat Engineer Divers, French: *Plongeurs du Combat du Génie*), former DINOPS Teams of Nautical Subaquatic Intervention Operational Detachment (French: *Détachement d'Intervention Nautique Operationnelle Subaquatique*) and Mountain Commando Group (GCM) in some cases as double specialties.

Recruitment process

Arrival	1 to 3 days in a Foreign Legion Information Center. Reception, information, and terms of contract. Afterwards transferred to Paris, Foreign Legion Recruitment Center.
Pre-selection	1 to 4 days in a Foreign Legion Recruitment Center (Paris). Confirmation of motivation, initial medical check-up, finalising enlistment papers and signing of 5-year service contract.
Selection	7 to 14 days in the Recruitment and Selection Center in Aubagne. Psychological and personality tests, logic tests (no education requirements), medical exam, physical condition tests, motivation and security interviews. Confirmation or denial of selection.
Passed Selection	Signing and handing-over of the five-year service contract. Incorporation into the Foreign Legion as a trainee.

Basic training

The majority of French Officers of the Legion are seconded from the French Army and are referred to as Legion Officers (French: *Officiers de Légion*). Similarly, Majors, Adjudant-chefs (Legion Chief Warrant Officers), Adjudants (Legion Warrant Officers), and a limited number of both French and non-French Officers (French: *Officier du Rang de La Légion*) are seconded from the ranks of the Legionnaires. These Foreign Legion Officers serving at Foreign Titles represented in 2016, 10% of the Officer Corps of the Legion [215]

Basic training for the Foreign Legion is conducted in the 4th Foreign Regiment. This is an operational combat regiment which provides a training course of 15–17 weeks, before recruits are assigned to their operational units:

Figure 172: *Légionnaires training in French Guiana*

- Initial training of 4–6 weeks at The Farm La Ferme – introduction to military lifestyle; outdoor and field activities.
- March Marche Képi Blanc – a 31-mile (50 km) 2 day march (25 km per day) in full kit, followed by the Kepi Blanc ceremony on the 3rd day.
- Technical and practical training (alternating with barracks and field training) – 3 weeks.
- Mountain training (Chalet at Formiguière in the French Pyrenees) – 1 week.
- Technical and practical training (alternating barracks and field training) – 3 weeks.
- Examinations and obtaining of the elementary technical certificate (CTE) – 1 week.
- March Raid Marche – a 75-mile (120 km) final march, which must be completed in 3 days.
- Light vehicle drivers education (drivers license) – 1 week.
- Return to Aubagne before reporting to the assigned operational regiment – 1 week.

Education in the French language (reading, writing and pronunciation), is taught on a daily basis, throughout all of basic training.

Figure 173: *Legionnaires roping from a Puma over Calvi.*

Figure 174: *Legionnaires at Mayotte.*

Figure 175: *Legionnaires HALO jump from a C-160.*

Figure 176: *Legionnaires parachute from a C-160 while training at Camp Raffalli in Corsica.*

Traditions

As the Foreign Legion is composed of soldiers of different nationalities and backgrounds, it needed to develop an intense *esprit de corps*, which is achieved through the development of camaraderie, specific traditions, the loyalty of its legionnaires, the quality of their training, and the pride of being a soldier in an élite unit.

Code of honour

The "Legionnaire's Code of Honour" is the Legion's creed, recited in French only.[216,217]

	Code d'honneur du légionnaire	Legionnaire's Code of Honour
Art. 1	Légionnaire, tu es un volontaire, servant la France avec honneur et fidélité.	Legionnaire, you are a volunteer serving France with honour and fidelity.
Art. 2	Chaque légionnaire est ton frère d'armes, quelle que soit sa nationalité, sa race ou sa religion. Tu lui manifestes toujours la solidarité étroite qui doit unir les membres d'une même famille.	Each legionnaire is your brother in arms whatever his nationality, his race or his religion might be. You show him the same close solidarity that links the members of the same family.
Art. 3	Respectueux des traditions, attaché à tes chefs, la discipline et la camaraderie sont ta force, le courage et la loyauté tes vertus.	Respect for traditions, devotion to your leaders, discipline and comradeship are your strengths, courage and loyalty your virtues.
Art. 4	Fier de ton état de légionnaire, tu le montres dans ta tenue toujours élégante, ton comportement toujours digne mais modeste, ton casernement toujours net.	Proud of your status as legionnaire, you display this in your always impeccable uniform, your always dignified but modest behaviour, and your clean living quarters.
Art. 5	Soldat d'élite, tu t'entraînes avec rigueur, tu entretiens ton arme comme ton bien le plus précieux, tu as le souci constant de ta forme physique.	An elite soldier, you train rigorously, you maintain your weapon as your most precious possession, and you take constant care of your physical form.
Art. 6	La mission est sacrée, tu l'exécutes jusqu'au bout et si besoin, en opérations, au péril de ta vie.	The mission is sacred, you carry it out until the end and, if necessary in the field, at the risk of your life.
Art. 7	Au combat, tu agis sans passion et sans haine, tu respectes les ennemis vaincus, tu n'abandonnes jamais ni tes morts, ni tes blessés, ni tes armes.	In combat, you act without passion and without hate, you respect defeated enemies, and you never abandon your dead, your wounded, or your arms.

Mottos

Honneur et Fidélité

In contrast to all other French Army units, the motto embroidered on the Foreign Legion's regimental flags is not *Honneur et Patrie* (Honour and Fatherland) but *Honneur et Fidélité* (Honour and Fidelity).

Legio Patria Nostra

Legio Patria Nostra (in French *La Légion est notre Patrie*, in English *The Legion is our Fatherland*) is the Latin motto of the Foreign Legion. The adoption of the Foreign Legion as a new "fatherland" does not imply the repudiation by the legionnaire of his original nationality. The Foreign Legion is required to obtain the agreement of any legionnaire before he is placed in any situation where he might have to serve against his country of birth.

Figure 177: *Commemoration of the Battle of Camarón by the 1st Foreign Cavalry Regiment at the Roman Theatre of Orange.*

Figure 178: *Regimental flags of the 1st Foreign Regiment and 2nd Regiments in Paris, 2003.*

Regimental mottos

Eleven colonels with 11 regimental mottos

- 1er R.E: Honneur et Fidélité
- G.R.L.E: Honneur et Fidélité
- 1er REC: Honneur et Fidélité & **Nec Pluribus Impar** (*No other equal*)
- 2e REP: Honneur et Fidélité & **More Majorum**[218] (*in the manner, ways and traditions of our veterans*[219] *foreign regiments*)
- 2e REI: Honneur et Fidélité & **Être prêt** (*Be ready*)
- 2e REG: Honneur et Fidélité & **Rien n'empêche** (*Nothing prevents*)
- 3e REI: Honneur et Fidélité & **Legio Patria Nostra** (*The Legion our Fatherland*)
- 4e R.E: Honneur et Fidélité & **Creuset de la Légion et Régiment des fortes têtes** (*The crucible of the Legion and the strong right minded regiment*)
- 6e R.E.G then 1e REG: Honneur et Fidélité & **Ad Unum** (*All to one end – for the regiment until the last one*)
- 13e DBLE: Honneur et Fidélité & **More Majorum** (*in the manner, ways and traditions of our veterans foreign regiments*)
- DLEM: Honneur et Fidélité & **Pericula Ludus** (*Dangers game* – for the regiment *To Danger is my pleasure* of the 2nd Foreign Cavalry Regiment)

Insignia

Regiment	Colors	Insignia	Beret Insignia	Tenure	Notable Commandants
Le Commandement de la Légion étrangère (C.O.M.L.E)				1931–present	général Paul-Frédéric Rollet général Raoul Magrin-Vernerey général Jean-Claude Coullon

French Foreign Legion

Regiment				Dates	Notable Figures
1st Foreign Regiment (1er R.E.)				1841–Present	François Achille Bazaine Colonel Raphaël Vienot Pierre Joseph Jeanningros Captain Jean Danjou Peter I of Serbia Herbert Kitchener, 1st Earl Kitchener Paul-Frédéric Rollet Commandant Pierre Segrétain Lieutenant Colonel Pierre Paul Jeanpierre
4th Foreign Regiment (4ème R.E.)	*			1920–1940 1941–1943 1948–1963 1976 –Present	
Foreign Legion Recruiting Group (G.R.L.E)	*			2007-Present	
Legion Pionniers (Pionniers de La Légion Etrangère) 1st Foreign Regiment Pionniers Sections of Tradition 1st Foreign Engineer Regiment Pionniers Groups 2nd Foreign Engineer Regiment Pionniers Groups 3rd Foreign Infantry Regiment Pionniers Groups 4th Foreign Regiment Pionniers Groups Foreign Legion Detachment in Mayotte Pionniers Groups			1e RE 1e REG 2e REG 3e RE 4e RE D.L.E.M	1831–Present	
Communal Depot of the Foreign Regiments (D.C.R.E)			*	1933–1955 1955-Present	Colonel Louis-Antoine Gaultier
1st Foreign Infantry Regiment (1er R.E.I)				(1950–1955)	

1st Foreign Cavalry Regiment (1er R.E.C)		Nec Pluribus Impar	1921–Present	
Foreign Air Supply Company (C.E.R.A)	*		1951	
Parachute Company of the 3rd Foreign Infantry Regiment (Para Co. du 3ème R.E.I)	*		1948–1949 1st Foreign Parachute Battalion 1er BEP (1948–1955)	Lieutenant Jacques Morin (Company Commander) Lieutenant Paul Arnaud de Foïard (Section-Platoon, Commander)
1st Foreign Parachute Battalion (1er B.E.P)	*		1948–1955	Commandant Pierre Segrétain (1er BEP, I formation) Lieutenant Colonel Pierre Jeanpierre (1er BEP, I, II and III formations) Captain Pierre Sergent
1st Foreign Parachute Regiment (1er R.E.P)	*	Marche ou Creve	1955–1961	Lieutenant Colonel Pierre Jeanpierre Commandant Hélie de Saint Marc Captain Pierre Sergent Guy Rubin de Cervens
1st Foreign Parachute Heavy Mortar Company (1ère C.E.P.M.L)	*		1953–1954	Lieutenant Jacques Molinier Lieutenant Paul Turcy Lieutenant Erwan Bergot Lieutenant Jean Singland
1st Foreign Engineer Regiment (1er R.E.G)		Ad Unum	1999–Present	

French Foreign Legion 243

Unit				Dates	Commanders
2nd Foreign Engineer Regiment (2ème R.E.G)		*Rien n'empêche*		1999- Present	
2nd Foreign Cavalry Regiment (2ème R.E.C)	*			1939–1940 1945–1962	
2nd Foreign Infantry Regiment (2ème R.E.I)		*Être Prêt*		3 Apr 1841 – 1 Apr 1943 1 Aug 1945 – 1 Jan 1968 1 Sept 1972 – Present	Patrice de MacMahon, Duke of Magenta François Certain Canrobert Jean-Luc Carbuccia Colonel de Chabrières Pierre Joseph Jeanningros Captain Jean Danjou Commandant Pierre Segrétain Lieutenant Colonel Pierre Paul Jeanpierre
2nd Foreign Parachute Battalion (2ème B.E.P)	*			1948–1955	Commandant Barthélémy Rémy Raffali Captain Georges Hamacek
2nd Foreign Parachute Regiment (2ème R.E.P)		*More Majorum*		1955- Present	Lieutenant Colonel Paul Arnaud de Foïard

Regiment		Image		Dates	Notable
2nd Marching Regiment of the 1st Foreign Regiment- 2èmeRM.1er RE – (1914–1915) 3rd Marching Regiment of the 1st Foreign Regiment- 3èmeRM.1erRE – (1914–1915) 4th Marching Regiment of the 1st Foreign Regiment- 4èmeRM.1erRE – (1914–1915) 2nd Marching Regiment of the 2nd Foreign Regiment- 2èmeRM.2èmeRE – (1914–1915) Marching Regiment of the Foreign Legion (R.M.L.E)	*			1915–1920 1942–1945 3rd Foreign Infantry Regiment-present	Colonel Paul-Frédéric Rollet Lieutenant-Colonel Peppino Garibaldi Colonel Alphonse Van Hecke Eugene Bullard American poet Alan Seeger Swiss poet, French naturalized Blaise Cendrars Lieutenant Colonel Prince Count Aage of Rosenborg Italian writer, Curzio Malaparte Lazare Ponticelli
3rd Foreign Infantry Regiment (3ème R.E.I)	*	*Legio Patria Nostra*		11 November 1915 – Present	
Marching Regiments of Foreign Volunteers (R.M.V.E) 21st Marching Regiment of Foreign Volunteers- 21e RMVE – (1939–1940) 22nd Marching Regiment of Foreign Volunteers- 22e R.M.V.E – (1939–1940) 23rd Marching Regiment of Foreign Volunteers- 23e R.M.V.E – (1940)	*			1939–1940	
3rd Foreign Parachute Battalion (3ème B.E.P)	*			1948–1955	Captain Darmuzai[220]
3rd Foreign Parachute Regiment (3ème R.E.P)	*			1955–1955	Captain Darmuzai
5th Foreign Infantry Regiment (5ème R.E.I)				1930–2000	

French Foreign Legion

Unit		Badge	Dates	Commander
6th Foreign Infantry Regiment (6ème R.E.I)	▌▌	Ad Unum	1939–1940; 1949–1955	Commadant Pierre Segrétain Lieutenant Colonel Pierre Jeanpierre
6th Foreign Engineer Regiment (6ème R.E.G)	▌▌	Ad Unum	1984–1999 1999 – 1e REG	
11th Foreign Infantry Regiment (11ème R.E.I)	*		1939–1940	
12th Foreign Infantry Regiment (12ème R.E.I)	*		1939–1940	
13th Demi-Brigade of the Foreign Legion (13ème D.B.L.E)	▌▌	More Majorum	1940-Present	
Foreign Legion Detachment in Mayotte (D.L.E.M)	*	Pericula Ludus	1973-Present	

Marching songs

Le Boudin

"*Le Boudin*" is the marching song of the Foreign Legion.

Other songs

- "*Non, Je Ne Regrette Rien*", 1st Foreign Parachute Regiment
- "*Sous Le Ciel de Paris*", *The Choir of the French Foreign Legion*
- "*Anne Marie du 3e*" REI (in German)
- "*Adieu, adieu*"
- "*Aux légionnaires*"

Figure 179: *The chapeau chinois (literally "Chinese hat" in French) is the French name of an old Ottoman music instrument that was popular in the eighteenth century, but was progressively abandoned by most European military bands in the nineteenth century, except by the Foreign Legion and the Spahis.*

- "*Anne Marie du 2e REI*"
- "*Adieu vieille Europe*"
- "*Chant de l'Oignon*"
- "*Chant du quatrième escadron*"
- "*Chez nous au 3e*"
- "*C'est le 4*"
- "*Connaissez-vous ces hommes*"
- "*Contre les Viêts*" (song of the 13th Demi-Brigade of the Foreign Legion after having been the marching song adopted by the 1st Foreign Parachute Regiment)
- "*Cravate verte et Képi blanc*"
- "*Dans la brume, la rocaille*"
- "*Défilé du 3e REI*"
- "*C'était un Edelweiss*"
- "*Écho*"
- "*En Afrique*"
- "*En Algérie*" (1er RE)
- "*Es steht eine Mühle*" (in German)

- *"Eugénie"*
- *"Les Képis Blancs"* (1e RE)
- *"Honneur, Fidélité"*
- *"Ich hatt' einen Kameraden"* (in German)
- *"Il est un moulin"*
- *"J'avais un camarade"*
- *"Kameraden (in German)"*
- *"La colonne"* (1er REC)
- *"La Légion marche"* (2e REP)
- *"La lune est claire"*
- *"Le Caïd"*
- *"Il y a des cailloux sur toutes les routes"*
- *"Le fanion de la Légion"*
- *"Le Soleil brille"*
- *"Le front haut et l'âme fière"* (5e RE)
- *"Légionnaire de l'Afrique"*
- *"Massari Marie"*
- *"Monica"*
- *"Sous le Soleil brûlant d'Afrique"* (13e DBLE)
- *"Nous sommes tous des volontaires"* (1er RE)
- *"Nous sommes de la Légion"*
- *"La petite piste"*
- *"Pour faire un vrai légionnaire"*
- *"Premier chant du 1er REC"*
- *"Quand on an une fille dans l'cuir"*
- *"Rien n'empêche"* (2er REG)
- *"Sapeur, mineurs et bâtisseurs"* (6e REG)
- *"Soldats de la Légion étrangère"*
- *"Souvenirs qui passe"*
- *"Suzanna"*
- *"The Windmill"*
- *"Venu volontaire"*
- *"Véronica"*

Ranks

All volunteers in the French Foreign Legion begin their careers as basic legionnaires with one in four eventually becoming a *sous-officier* (non-commissioned officer). On joining, a new recruit receives a monthly salary of €1,200 in addition to food and lodgings. He is also given his own new rifle, which according to the lore of the *Legion* must never be left on a battlefield. Promotion is concurrent with the ranks in the French Army.

Foreign Legion rank	Equivalent rank	NATO Code	Period of service	Insignia
Engagé Volontaire	Recruit	–	15 weeks basic training.	None
Legionnaire 2e Classe	Private / 2nd Class Legionnaire	OR-1	On completion of training and *Marche képi blanc* (March of the White Kepi).	None
Legionnaire 1e Classe	Private / 1st Class Legionnaire	OR-2	After 10 months of service.	▬◄
Caporal	Corporal	OR-3	Possible after 1-year of service, known as the *Fonctionnaire Caporal* (or Caporal "Fut Fut") course. Recruits selected for this course need to show good leadership skills during basic training.	▬◄◄
Caporal Chef	Senior Corporal	OR-4	After 6 years of service.	▬◄◄◄

Table note: Command insignia in the Foreign Legion use gold lace or braid indicating foot troops in the French Army. But the *Légion étrangère* service color is green (for the now-defunct colonial *Armée d'Afrique*) instead of red (regular infantry).

Figure 180: *A Caporal-chef, with 3 chevrons of seniority, bugling during the Bastille Day Military Parade. UNIQ-ref-0-b93c926f6ef2bd57-QINU*

Figure 181: *A Caporal-chef Pionniers de la Légion of the 1st Foreign Regiment. The pionniers insigna depicts 2 crossed axes, instead of a grenade for the regular infantry.*

Non-Commissioned and Warrant Officers

The insignia for a *Sous-officier* contains three components. In this case, three upward gold chevrons indicates a *Sergent-chef*. The diamond-shaped regimental patch (or *Écusson*) is created from three green borders indicating a Colonial unit; rather than one for "Regulars" or two for "Reserves". The grenade has seven flames rather than the usual five. Two downward chevrons of seniority attests to at least 10 years service. Some *Caporal-Chef*'s have as much as 6 "chevrons of seniority" attesting to 30 years (plus) of service.

Sous-officiers (NCOs) including warrant officers account for 25% of the current Foreign Legion's total manpower.

Foreign Legion rank	Equivalent rank	NATO Code	Period of service	Insignia
Sergent	Sergeant	OR-5	After 3 years of service as Caporal.	
Sergent Chef	Senior Sergeant	OR-6	After 3 years as *Sergent* and between 7 and 14 years of service.	

Adjudant	Warrant Officer	OR-8	After 3 years as *Sergent Chef*.	
Adjudant Chef[221] </ref>	Chief Warrant Officer	OR-9	After 4 years as *Adjudant* and at least 14 years service.	
Major[222]	Major[223]	OR-9	Appointment by either: (i) passing an examination or (ii) promotion after a minimum of 14 years service (without an examination).	

Commissioned Officers

Most officers are seconded from the French Army though roughly 10% are former non-commissioned officers promoted from the ranks.

Foreign Legion rank	Equivalent rank	NATO Code	Command responsibility	Insignia
Sous-Lieutenant	Second lieutenant	OF-1	Junior *section* leader	
Lieutenant	First lieutenant	OF-1	A *platoon*.	
Capitaine	Captain	OF-2	A *company*.	
Commandant	Major	OF-3	A *battalion*.	
Lieutenant-Colonel	Lieutenant colonel	OF-4	Junior *régiment* or *demi-brigade* leader.	
Colonel	Colonel	OF-5	A *régiment* or *demi-brigade*.	
Général de brigade	Brigadier General	OF-6	Brigade comprising *régiments* or *demi-brigades*.	
Le Commandement de la Légion étrangère (*Général de division*)	Général de division	OF-7	Entire division or Army Corps of the French Foreign Legion	

Chevrons of seniority

The Foreign Legion still uses chevrons to indicate seniority (*chevrons d'ancienneté*). Each gold chevron, which are only worn by ordinary legionnaires and non-commissioned officers, denotes five years service in the Legion. They are worn beneath the rank insignia.

Figure 182: *An insignia for a Sous-officier*

Honorary ranks

The French Army had awarded honorary ranks to individuals credited with exceptional acts of courage since 1796.

In the Foreign Legion, General Paul-Frédéric Rollet introduced the practice of awarding of honorary Legion ranks to distinguished individuals, both civilian and military; men and women in the early 20th century. Recipients of these honorary appointments had participated in an exemplary manner on active service with units of the Legion, or had rendered exceptional service to the Legion in non-combat situations.[224]

More than 1,200 individuals have been granted honorary ranks in the Legion *pour services éminent*. The majority of these awards have been made to military personnel in wartime, earning titles such as *Legionnaire d'Honneur* or *Sergent-Chef de Légion d'honneur*. But other recipients have included nurses, journalists, painters, and ministers who have rendered meritorious service to the Foreign Legion.

Figure 183: *Pioneers of the 1st Foreign Regiment.*

Pioneers

The *Pionniers* (pioneers) are the combat engineers and a traditional unit of the Foreign Legion. The sapper traditionally sport large beards, wear leather aprons and gloves and hold axes. The sappers were very common in European armies during the Napoleonic Era but progressively disappeared during the 19th century. The French Army, including the Legion disbanded its regimental sapper platoons in 1870. However, in 1931 one of a number of traditions restored to mark the hundredth anniversary of the Legion's founding was the reestablishment of its bearded *Pionniers*.[225]

In the French Army, since the 18th century, every infantry regiment included a small detachment of pioneers. In addition to undertaking road building and entrenchment work, such units were tasked with using their axes and shovels to clear obstacles under enemy fire opening the way for the rest of the infantry. The danger of such missions was recognised by allowing certain privileges, such as being authorised to wear beards.

The current pioneer platoon of the Foreign Legion is provided by the Legion depot and headquarters regiment for public ceremonies. The unit has reintroduced the symbols of the Napoleonic sappers: the beard, the axe, the leather apron, the crossed-axes insignia and the leather gloves. When parades of the Foreign Legion are opened by this unit, it is to commemorate the traditional role of the sappers "opening the way" for the troops.

Figure 184: *The French Foreign Legion has its own military band.*

Cadences and marching steps

Also notable is the marching pace of the Foreign Legion. In comparison to the 116-step-per-minute pace of other French units, the Foreign Legion has an 88-step-per-minute marching speed. It is also referred to by Legionnaires as the "crawl". This can be seen at ceremonial parades and public displays attended by the Foreign Legion, particularly while parading in Paris on 14 July (Bastille Day Military Parade). Because of the impressively slow pace, the Foreign Legion is always the last unit marching in any parade. The Foreign Legion is normally accompanied by its own band, which traditionally plays the march of any one of the regiments comprising the Foreign Legion, except that of the unit actually on parade. The regimental song of each unit and "Le Boudin" is sung by legionnaires standing at attention. Also, because the Foreign Legion must always stay together, it does not break formation into two when approaching the presidential grandstand, as other French military units do, in order to preserve the unity of the legion.

Contrary to popular belief, the adoption of the Foreign Legion's slow marching speed was not due to a need to preserve energy and fluids during long marches under the hot Algerian sun. Its exact origins are somewhat unclear, but the official explanation is that although the pace regulation does not seem to have been instituted before 1945, it hails back to the slow marching pace of the Ancien Régime, and its reintroduction was a "return to traditional roots".[226] This

Figure 185: *Because of its slower pace, the Foreign Legion is always the last unit marching in any parade (Parade in Rome, June 2007).*

was in fact, the march step of the Foreign Legion's ancestor units – the *Régiments Étrangers* or Foreign Regiments of the *Ancien Régime* French Army, the *Grande Armée*'s foreign units, and the pre-1831 foreign regiments.

Uniform

From its foundation until World War I the Foreign Legion normally wore the uniform of the French line infantry for parade with a few special distinctions.[227] Essentially this consisted of a dark blue coat (later tunic) worn with red trousers. The field uniform was often modified under the influence of the extremes of climate and terrain in which the Foreign Legion served. Shakos were soon replaced by the light cloth kepi, which was far more suitable for North African conditions. The practice of wearing heavy *capotes* (greatcoats) on the march and *vestes* (short hip-length jackets) as working dress in barracks was followed by the Foreign Legion from its establishment. One short lived aberration was the wearing of green uniforms in 1856 by Foreign Legion units recruited in Switzerland for service in the Crimean War. In the Crimea itself (1854–59) a hooded coat and red or blue waist sashes were adopted for winter dress, while during the Mexican Intervention (1863–65) straw hats or sombreros were sometimes substituted for the kepi.[228] When the latter was

Figure 186: *Légionnaires in modern dress uniform. Note the green and red epaulettes, the distinctive white kepi and the blue sash. They carry France's standard assault rifle, the FAMAS.*

worn it was usually covered with a white "havelock" – the predecessor of the white kepi that was to become a symbol of the Foreign Legion. Foreign Legion units serving in France during the Franco-Prussian War of 1870–71 were distinguishable only by minor details of insignia from the bulk of the French infantry. However subsequent colonial campaigns saw an increasing use of special garments for hot weather wear such as collarless *keo* blouses in Tonkin 1884–85, khaki drill jackets in Dahomey (1892) and drab covered topees worn with all-white fatigue dress in Madagascar[229] (1895).

In the early 20th century the legionnaire wore a red kepi with blue band and piping, dark blue tunic with red collar, red cuff patches, and red trousers.[230] Distinctive features were the green epaulettes (replacing the red of the line) worn with red woollen fringes;[231] plus the embroidered Legion badge of a red flaming grenade, worn on the kepi front instead of a regimental number. In the field a light khaki cover was worn over the kepi, sometimes with a protective neck curtain attached. The standard medium-blue double breasted greatcoat (*capote*) of the French infantry was worn, usually buttoned back to free the legs for marching. From the 1830s the legionnaires had worn a broad blue woollen sash around the waist, like other European units of the French Army of Africa (such as the Zouaves or the Chasseurs d'Afrique), while indigenous

Figure 187: *A drawing showing French Foreign Legion troops in action against tribesmen in Morocco in 1908. The legionnaires are incorrectly shown wearing the red sashes of native regiments and not the medium blue of the Legion*

units of the Army of Africa (spahis and tirailleurs) wore red sashes. White linen trousers tucked into short leather leggings were substituted for red serge in hot weather. This was the origin of the "Beau Geste" image.

In barracks a white bleached kepi cover was often worn together with a short dark blue jacket ("veste") or white blouse plus white trousers. The original kepi cover was khaki and due to constant washing turned white quickly. The white or khaki kepi cover was not unique to the Foreign Legion at this stage but was commonly seen amongst other French units in North Africa. It later became particularly identified with the Foreign Legion as the unit most likely to serve at remote frontier posts (other than locally recruited tirailleurs who wore fezzes or turbans). The variances of climate in North Africa led the French Army to the sensible expedient of letting local commanders decide on the appropriate "tenue de jour" (uniform of the day) according to circumstances. Thus a legionnaire might parade or walk out in blue tunic and white trousers in hot weather, blue tunic and red trousers in normal temperatures or wear the blue greatcoat with red trousers under colder conditions. The sash could be worn with greatcoat, blouse or veste but not with the tunic. Epaulettes were a detachable dress item worn only with tunic or greatcoat for parade or off duty wear.[232]

Officers wore the same dark blue (almost black) tunics as those of their colleagues in the French line regiments, except that black replaced red as a facing colour on collar and cuffs.[233] Gold fringed epaulettes were worn for full dress and rank was shown by the number of gold rings on both kepi and cuffs. Trousers were red with black stripes or white according to occasion or conditions. All-white or light khaki uniforms (from as early as the 1890s) were often worn in the field or for ordinary duties in barracks.[234] Non-commissioned officers were distinguished by red or gold diagonal stripes on the lower sleeves of tunics, vestes and greatcoats.[235] Small detachable stripes were buttoned on to the front of the white shirt-like blouse.

Prior to 1914 units in Indo-China wore white or khaki Colonial Infantry uniforms with Foreign Legion insignia, to overcome supply difficulties. This dress included a white sun helmet of a model that was also worn by Foreign Legion units serving in the outposts of Southern Algeria, though never popular with its wearers. During the initial months of World War I, Foreign Legion units serving in France wore the standard blue greatcoat and red trousers of the French line infantry, distinguished only by collar patches of the same blue as the capote, instead of red. After a short period in sky-blue the Foreign Legion adopted khaki with steel helmets, from early 1916. A mustard shade of khaki drill had been worn on active service in Morocco from 1909, replacing the classic blue and white. The latter continued to be worn in the relatively peaceful conditions of Algeria throughout World War I, although increasingly replaced by khaki drill. The pre-1914 blue and red uniforms could still be occasionally seen as garrison dress in Algeria until stocks were used up about 1919.

During the early 1920s plain khaki drill uniforms of a standard pattern became universal issue for the Foreign Legion with only the red and blue kepi (with or without a cover) and green collar braiding to distinguish the Legionnaire from other French soldiers serving in North African and Indo-China. The neck curtain ceased to be worn from about 1915, although it survived in the newly raised Foreign Legion Cavalry Regiment into the 1920s. The white blouse (*bourgeron*) and trousers dating from 1882 were retained for fatigue wear until the 1930s.

At the time of the Foreign Legion's centennial in 1931, a number of traditional features were reintroduced at the initiative of the then commander Colonel Rollet. These included the blue sash and green/red epaulettes. In 1939 the white covered kepi won recognition as the official headdress of the Foreign Legion to be worn on most occasions, rather than simply as a means of reflecting heat and protecting the blue and red material underneath. The Third Foreign Infantry Regiment adopted white tunics and trousers for walking-out dress during the

1930s and all Foreign Legion officers were required to obtain full dress uniforms in the pre-war colours of black and red from 1932 to 1939.

During World War II the Foreign Legion wore a wide range of uniform styles depending on supply sources. These ranged from the heavy capotes and Adrian helmets of 1940 through to British battledress and American field uniforms from 1943 to 1945. The white kepi was stubbornly retained whenever possible.

From 1940 until 1963 the Foreign Legion maintained four Saharan Companies (*Compagnies Sahariennes*) as part of the French forces used to patrol and police the desert regions to the south of Morocco and Algeria. Special uniforms were developed for these units, modeled on those of the French officered Camel Corps (*Méharistes*) having prime responsibility for the Sahara. In full dress these included black or white zouave style trousers, worn with white tunics and long flowing cloaks. The Legion companies maintained their separate identity by retaining their distinctive kepis, sashes and fringed epaulettes.

The white kepis, together with the sash and epaulettes survive in the Foreign Legion's modern parade dress. Since the 1990s the modern kepi has been made wholly of white material rather than simply worn with a white cover. Officers and senior noncommissioned officers still wear their kepis in the pre-1939 colours of dark blue and red. A green tie and (for officers) a green waistcoat recall the traditional branch colour of the Foreign Legion. From 1959 a green beret (previously worn only by the legion's paratroopers) became the universal ordinary duty headdress, with the kepi reserved for parade and off duty wear.[236,237] Other items of currently worn dress are the standard issue of the French Army.

Equipment

The Foreign Legion is basically equipped with the same equipment as similar units elsewhere in the French Army. These include:

- The FAMAS assault rifle, a French-made automatic bullpup-style rifle, chambered in the 5.56×45mm NATO round. In bullpup-style firearms, the action and magazine insert is behind the trigger section. This layout shortens the length of the weapon, while retaining the barrel length.
- The SPECTRA is a ballistic helmet, designed by the French military, fitted with real-time positioning and information system, and with light amplifiers for night vision.
- The FÉLIN suit, an infantry combat system that combines ample pouches, reinforced body protections and a portable electronic platform.

Commandement de la Légion Étrangère Tenure (1931–present)

Commandement de la Légion Étrangère (1931–1984)

Inspector Tenure

Inspection de la Légion étrangère (I.L.E)

Name	Portrait	Rank	Tenure	Note
Paul-Frédéric Rollet		Général	1931–1935	
Raoul Magrin-Vernerey		Général	1948–1950	

Autonomous Group Tenure

Groupement autonome de la Légion étrangère (G.A.L.E)

Name	Portrait	Rank	Tenure	Note
Jean Olié		Général	1950	
Paul Gardy	–	Général	1951	

Command Tenure

Commandement de la Légion étrangère (C.O.L.E)

Name	Portrait	Rank	Tenure	Note
René Lennuyeux	–	Général	1955	colonel then Général

Technical Inspection Tenure

Inspection technique de la Légion étrangère (I.T.L.E)

Name	Portrait	Rank	Tenure	Note
René Lennuyeux	–	Général	1957	
Paul Gardy	–	Général	1958	
René Morel (Légion étrangère)	–	Général	1960	
Jacques Lefort	–	Général	1962	

Groupment Tenure

Groupement de la Légion étrangère (G.L.E)

Name	Portrait	Rank	Tenure	Note
Marcel Letestu	–	Général	1972	
Gustave Fourreau	–	Général	1973	
Bernard Goupil	–	Général	1976	
Paul Lardry	–	Général	1980	
Jean-Claude Coullon	–	Général	1982	

Commandement de la Légion Étrangère (1984–present)

Command Tenure

Commandement de la Légion étrangère (C.O.M.L.E)

#	Name	Portrait	Rank	Tenure	Note
1	Jean-Claude Coullon	–	Général	1984	
2	Jean Louis Roué	–	Général	1985	
3	Raymond Le Corre	–	Général	1988	
4	Bernard Colcomb	–	Général	1992	
5	Christian Piquemal	–	Général	1994	
6	Bernard Grail	–	Général	1999	
7	Jean-Louis Franceschi	–	Général	2002	
8	Bruno Dary		Général	2004	

9	Louis Pichot de Champfleury	–	Général	2006	
10	Alain Bouquin	–	Général	2009	
11	Christophe de Saint-Chamas	–	Général	2011	
12	Jean Maurin	–	Général	2014	

Gallery

Figure 188: *This monument to the Legionnaires at Aubagne originally stood at the Legion's headquarters in Sidi Bel Abbès but was moved to France when Algeria gained independence in 1962. The gold parts on the globe mark countries where the legions been deployed. It is inscribed La Legion A Ses Morts (The Legion to its dead)*

Figure 189: *Le Commandement de la Légion étrangère (1931–present)*

Figure 190: *French Foreign Legion headquarters in Aubagne.*

Figure 191: *White kepi (Képi blanc) of the French Foreign Legion*

Figure 192: *The FAMAS F1 is the standard issue rifle of the French Foreign Legion*

Figure 193: *Green beret (Béret vert) of the French Foreign Legion*

Figure 194: *First pattern beret cap badge*

Figure 195: *Second pattern beret cap badge, worn until 1990*

Composition

The Foreign Legion is the only unit of the French Army open to people of any nationality. Most legionnaires still come from European countries but a growing percentage comes from Latin America. Most of the Foreign Legion's commissioned officers are French with approximately 10 percent being Legionnaires who have risen through the ranks.[238]

Legionnaires were, in the past, forced to enlist under a pseudonym ("declared identity"). This policy existed in order to allow recruits who wanted to restart their lives to enlist. The Legion held the belief that it was fairer to make all new recruits use declared identities. French citizens can enlist under a declared, fictitious, foreign citizenship (generally, a francophone one, often that of Belgium, Canada, or Switzerland).Wikipedia:Citation needed As of 20 September 2010, new recruits may enlist under their real identities or under declared identities. Recruits who do enlist with declared identities may, after one year's service, regularise their situations under their true identities.[239] After serving in the Foreign Legion for three years, a legionnaire may apply for French citizenship. He must be serving under his real name, must have no problems with the authorities, and must have served with "honour and fidelity". A soldier who becomes injured during a battle for France can immediately apply for French citizenship under a provision known as "Français par le sang versé" ("French by spilled blood").

While the Foreign Legion historically did not accept women in its ranks, there was one official female member, Susan Travers, an Englishwoman who joined Free French Forces during World War II and became a member of the Foreign Legion after the war, serving in Vietnam during the First Indochina War.

Women were barred from service until 2000, which then-French Defence Minister Alain Richard had stated that he wanted to take the level of female recruitment in the Legion to 20 percent by 2020.

Membership by country

As of 2008, legionnaires came from 140 countries. The majority of enlisted men originate from outside France, while the majority of the officer corps consists of Frenchmen. Many recruits originate from Eastern Europe and Latin America. Neil Tweedie of *The Daily Telegraph* said that Germany traditionally provided many recruits, "somewhat ironically given the Legion's bloody role in two world wars." He added that "Brits, too, have played their part, but there was embarrassment recently when it emerged that many British applicants were failing selection due to endemic unfitness."

Alsace-Lorraine

Original nationalities of the Foreign Legion reflect the events in history at the time they join. Many former Wehrmacht personnel joined in the wake of World War II[240] as many soldiers returning to civilian life found it hard to find reliable employment. Jean-Denis Lepage reports that "The Foreign Legion discreetly recruited from German P.O.W. camps", but adds that the number of these recruits has been subsequently exaggerated. Bernard B. Fall, who was a supporter of the French government, writing in the context of the First Indochina War, questioned the notion that the Foreign Legion was mainly German at that time, calling it:

> [a] canard...with the sub-variant that all those Germans were at least SS generals and other much wanted war criminals. As a rule, and in order to prevent any particular nation from making the Foreign Legion into a Praetorian Guard, any particular national component is kept at about 25 percent of the total. Even supposing (and this was the case, of course) that the French recruiters, in the eagerness for candidates would sign up Germans enlisting as Swiss, Austrian, Scandinavian and other nationalities of related ethnic background, it is unlikely that the number of Germans in the Foreign Legion ever exceeded 35 percent. Thus, without making an allowance for losses, rotation, discharges, etc., the maximum number of Germans fighting in Indochina at any one time reached perhaps 7,000 out of 278,000. As to the ex-Nazis, the early arrivals contained a number of them, none of whom were known to be war criminals. French intelligence saw to that.
>
> Since, in view of the rugged Indochinese climate, older men without previous tropical experience constituted more a liability than an asset, the average age of the Foreign Legion enlistees was about 23. At the time of

the battle of Dien Bien Phu, any legionnaire of that age group was at the worst, in his "Hitler Youth" shorts when the [Third] Reich collapsed.

The Foreign Legion accepts people enlisting under a nationality that is not their own. A proportion of the Swiss and Belgians are actually likely to be Frenchmen who wish to avoid detection.[241] In addition many Alsatians are said to have joined the Foreign Legion when Alsace was part of the German Empire, and may have been recorded as German while considering themselves French.

Regarding recruitment conditions within the Foreign Legion, see the official page (in English) dedicated to the subject: With regard to age limits, recruits can be accepted from ages ranging from 17 ½ (with parental consent) to 39.5 years old.

Countries that allow post-Foreign Legion contract

In the Commonwealth Realms, its collective provisions provide for nationals to commute between armies in training or other purposes. Moreover, this 'blanket provision' between member-states cannot exclude others for it would seem inappropriate to single out individual countries, that is, France in relation to the Legion. For example, Australia and New Zealand may allow post-Legion enlistment providing the national has commonwealth citizenship. Britain allows post-Legion enlistment. Canada allows post-Legion enlistment in its ranks with a completed five-year contract.Wikipedia:Citation needed

In the European Union framework, post Legion enlistment is less clear. Denmark, Norway, Germany and Portugal allow post-Legion enlistment while The Netherlands has constitutional articles that forbid it. [Rijkswet op het Nederlanderschap, Artikel 15, lid 1e, (In Dutch:)] (that is: one can lose his Dutch nationality by accepting a foreign nationality or can lose his Dutch nationality by serving in the army of a foreign state that is engaged in a conflict against the Dutch Kingdom or one of its allies[242]). The European Union twin threads seem to be recognized dual nationality status or restricting constitutional article.

The United States allows post-FFL enlistment in its National Guard, and career soldiers, up to the rank of captain only and to Green Card holders.

Israel allows post-Legion enlistment.

One of the biggest national groups in the Legion are Poles. Polish law basically allows service in a foreign army, but only after written permission from the Ministry of National Defense.

Emulation by other countries

Chinese Ever Victorious Army

The Ever Victorious Army was the name given to a Chinese imperial army in the late 19th century. The new force originally comprised about 200 mostly European mercenaries, recruited in the Shanghai area from sailors, deserters and adventurers. Many were dismissed in the summer of 1861, but the remainder became the officers of the Chinese soldiers recruited mainly in and around Sungkiang (Songjiang). The Chinese troops were increased to 3,000 by May 1862, all equipped with Western firearms and equipment by the British authorities in Shanghai. Throughout its four-year existence the Ever Victorious Army was mainly to operate within a thirty-mile radius of Shanghai. It was disbanded in May 1864 with 104 foreign officers and 2,288 Chinese soldiers being paid off. The bulk of the artillery and some infantry transferred to the Chinese Imperial forces. It was the first Chinese army trained in European techniques, tactics, and strategy.

Israeli Mahal

In Israel, Mahal (Hebrew: מח"ל, an acronym for *Mitnadvei Ḥutz LaAretz*, which means *Volunteers from outside the Land [of Israel]*) is a term designating non-Israelis serving in the Israeli military. The term originates with the approximately 4,000 both Jewish and non-Jewish volunteers who went to Israel to fight in the 1948 Arab–Israeli War including Aliyah Bet.[243] The original Mahalniks were mostly World War II veterans from American and British armed forces.

Today, there is a program, Garin Tzabar, within the Israeli Ministry of Defense that administers the enlistment of non-Israeli citizens in the country's armed forces. Programs enable foreigners to join the Israel Defense Forces if they are of Jewish descent (which is defined as at least one grandparent).

Netherlands KNIL Army

Though not named "Foreign Legion", the Dutch Koninklijk Nederlandsch-Indische Leger (KNIL), or Royal Netherlands-Indian Army (in reference to the Dutch East Indies, now Indonesia), was created in 1830, a year before the French Foreign Legion, and is therefore not an emulation but an entirely original idea and had a similar recruitment policy. It stopped being an army of foreigners around 1900 when recruitment was restricted to Dutch citizens and to the indigenous peoples of the Dutch East Indies. The KNIL was finally disbanded on 26 July 1950, seven months after the Netherlands formally recognised Indonesia as a sovereign state, and almost five years after Indonesia declared its independence.Wikipedia:Citation needed

Rhodesian Light Infantry and 7 Independent Company

During the Rhodesian Bush War of the 1960s and 1970s, the Rhodesian Security Forces enlisted volunteers from overseas on the same pay and conditions of service as locally based regulars. The vast majority of the Rhodesian Army's foreigners joined the Rhodesian Light Infantry (RLI), a heliborne commando regiment with a glamorous international reputation; this unit became colloquially known as the "Rhodesian foreign legion" as a result, even though foreigners never made up more than about a third of its men. According to Chris Cocks, an RLI veteran, "the RLI was a mirror of the French Foreign Legion, in that recruiters paid little heed as to a man's past and asked no questions. ... And like the Foreign Legion, once in the ranks, a man's past was irrelevant." Just as French Foreign Legionnaires must speak French, the Rhodesian Army required its foreigners to be anglophone. Many of them were professional soldiers, attracted by the regiment's reputation—mostly former British soldiers, or Vietnam veterans from the United States, Australian and New Zealand forces—and these became a key part of the unit. Others, with no military experience, were often motivated to join the Rhodesian Army by anti-communism, or a desire for adventure or to escape the past.

After the Rhodesians' overseas recruiting campaign for English-speakers, started in 1974, proved successful, they began recruiting French-speakers as well, in 1977. These francophone recruits were placed in their own unit, 7 Independent Company, Rhodesia Regiment, which was commanded by French-speaking officers and operated entirely in French. The experiment was not generally considered a success by the Rhodesian commanders, however, and the company was disbanded in early 1978.

Russian "Foreign Legion"

In 2010 the service conditions of the Russian Military have been changed. The actual term "Russian Foreign Legion" is a colloquial expression without any official recognition. Under the plan, foreigners without dual citizenship are able to sign up for five-year contracts and will be eligible for Russian citizenship after serving three years. Experts say the change opens the way for Commonwealth of Independent States citizens to get fast-track Russian citizenship, and counter the effects of Russia's demographic crisis on its army recruitment.

Spanish Foreign Legion

The Spanish Foreign Legion was created in 1920, in emulation of the French one, and had a significant role in Spain's colonial wars in Morocco and in the Spanish Civil War on the Nationalist side. The Spanish Foreign Legion recruited foreigners until 1986 but unlike its French model, the number of non-Spanish recruits never exceeded 25%, most of these from Latin America. It is now called the *Spanish Legion* and only recruits Spanish nationals.Wikipedia:Citation needed

References in popular culture

Beyond its reputation as an elite unit often engaged in serious fighting, the recruitment practices of the French Foreign Legion have also led to a somewhat romanticised view of it being a place for disgraced or "wronged" men looking to leave behind their old lives and start new ones. This view of the legion is common in literature, and has been used for dramatic effect in many films, not the least of which are the several versions of *Beau Geste*.

Further reading

<templatestyles src="Template:Refbegin/styles.css" />

- MR Tony Geraghty (1987). *March Or Die: A New History of the French Foreign Legion*. ISBN 978-0-8160-1794-2.
- Evan McGorman (1 January 2002). *Life in the French Foreign Legion: How to Join and What to Expect When You Get There*. Hellgate Press. ISBN 978-1-55571-633-2.
- Douglas Porch (23 June 1992). *The French Foreign Legion: Complete History of The Legendary Fighting Force*. Harper Perennial. ISBN 978-0-06-092308-2.
- Roger Rousseau, *The French Foreign Legion in Kolwezi*, 2006. ISBN 978-2-9526927-1-7
- Tibor Szecsko (1991). *Le grand livre des insignes de la Légion étrangère*. ISBN 978-2-9505938-0-1.

External links

 Wikimedia Commons has media related to *French Foreign Legion*.

- Official Website[244] (in French)
- Official Website[245] (in English)
- Le Musée de la Légion étrangère (Foreign Legion museum)[246]
- Website about the French Daguet Division (First Gulf War 1990–1991)[247]
- Foreign Legion Information[248] – unofficial website about the French Foreign Legion (in English)

Books

- In the Foreign Legion (1910)[249] – by Erwin Rosen (b. 1876)
- Books on Legion from 1905 to Present[250]

Coordinates: 43.2925°N 5.5534°E[251]

Modern Military

Modern equipment of the French Army

French Army
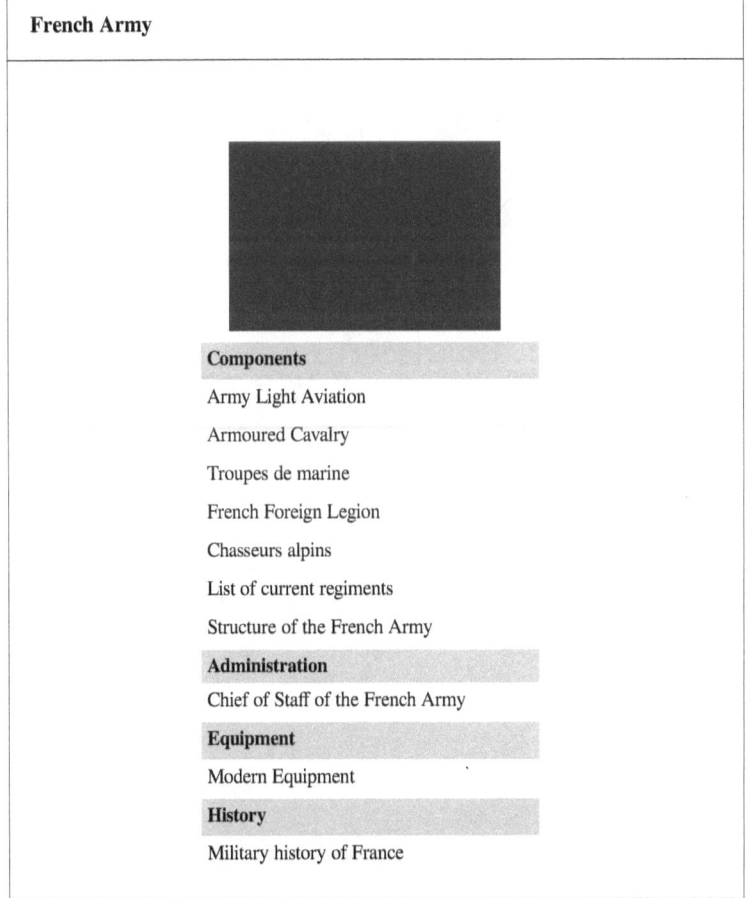 **Components** Army Light Aviation Armoured Cavalry Troupes de marine French Foreign Legion Chasseurs alpins List of current regiments Structure of the French Army **Administration** Chief of Staff of the French Army **Equipment** Modern Equipment **History** Military history of France

Personnel
List of senior officers of the French Army
Ranks in the French Army
Awards
Croix de guerre
Médaille militaire
Légion d'honneur
Awards

Modern equipment of the French Army is a list of equipment currently in service with the French Army. Figures are provided by the French Ministry of Defense for July 1, 2017.

Infantry equipment

Pistols

Name	Origin	Type	Cartridge	Photo	Notes
MAC 50	France	Semi-automatic pistol	9 mm		In service since 1953. Being replaced.
PAMAS G1	France Italy	Semi-automatic pistol	9 mm		Entered into operational service in 1989 with the national gendarmerie, in 1992 with the Air Force, and in 1999 for the Army and Navy. 97,502 weapons in 2002.
Glock 17	Austria	Semi-automatic pistol	9 mm		
HK USP.SD	Germany	Semi-automatic pistol	9 mm		Used by French Army's special forces.

Submachine Guns

Name	Origin	Type	Cartridge	Photo	Notes
HK MP5 A5 HK MP5 SD3	Germany	Submachine gun	9mm		Used by French Army's special forces.
FN P90	Belgium	Submachine gun	5.7x28mm		Used by French Army's special forces.

Assault, battle rifles

Name	Origin	Type	Cartridge	Photo	Notes
FAMAS F1	France	Assault rifle	5.56mm		The FAMAS was the standard-issue service rifle of the French military, with over 700,000 in total delivered. Scheduled to be phased out of service in the mid 2020s.
HK416 A5 HK416 D14.5RS HK416 F	Germany	Assault rifle	5.56mm		The HK416F will replace the FAMAS as the standard-issue assault rifle beginning in 2017. 102,000 weapons have been ordered.
FN SCAR-L	Belgium	Assault rifle	5.56mm		Used by French Army's special forces.
M16 A2 M203 M16 723 M203	United States	Assault rifle	5.56mm		Used by French Army's special forces.

Shotguns

Name	Origin	Type	Cartridge	Photo	Notes
Benelli M3T Super 90	Italy	Semi-automatic shotgun	12-Gauge		Used by French army's special forces.
Mossberg 500	United States	Pump-action shotgun	12-Gauge		Used by French army's special forces and units in French Guiana.

Sniper and Anti-materiel rifles

Name	Origin	Type	Cartridge	Photo	Notes
FR-F2	France	Sniper rifle	7.62 mm		In service since 1986.
PGM Ultima Ratio	France	Sniper rifle	7.62 mm		
HK MSG90	Germany	Sniper rifle	7.62 mm		
HK 417	Germany	Sniper rifle	7.62 mm		
PGM Hécate II	France	Anti-materiel rifle	12.7 mm		

Machine Guns

Name	Origin	Type	Cartridge	Photo	Notes
FN Minimi	Belgium	Light machine gun	5.56mm		10.881 ordered in 2011
ANF1	France	General purpose machine gun	7.62 mm		
FN MAG	Belgium	General purpose machine gun	7.62 mm		
M2 Browning	United States	Heavy machine gun	.50 cal		

Portable Anti-Materiel Weapons

Name	Origin	Type	Caliber	Photo	Notes
AT4 CS	Sweden	Anti-tank weapon	84mm		
MILAN	France Germany	Anti-tank guided missile	115mm		528
FGM-148 Javelin	United States	Fire-and-forget anti-tank missile	127mm		76
ERYX	France	Anti-tank guided missile	136mm		678
MMP	France	Fire-and-forget anti-tank missile	140mm		Successor of MILAN. To de deployed in 2018.

Grenade-Based Weapons

Name	Origin	Type	Caliber	Photo	Notes
LGI Mle F1 (Lance-grenade individuel Mle F1)	France	Grenade launcher	51mm		
Heckler & Koch AG36	Germany	Grenade launcher	40mm		Service in limited numbers since at least 2014. 10,767 ordered in September 2016.
M203 grenade launcher	United States	Grenade launcher	40mm		

Equipment

- SPECTRA helmet
- FÉLIN – infantry combat system (18,552)

Vehicles

Armored Vehicles

Name	Origin	Variant	Number	Photo	Notes
Tanks					
AMX Leclerc	France	Main battle tank	241		206 in storage (406 in total)
Armoured Recce					
AMX-10 RC	France	Armoured recce	248		Will be replaced by EBRC Jaguar from 2020.
ERC 90 Sagaie	France	Armoured recce	80		Will be replaced by EBRC Jaguar from 2020.
Armoured personnel carriers					
VBCI	France	• VCI: Infantry fighting vehicle • VPC: Armoured command vehicle • VTT: Armoured personnel carrier	629		110 of the vehicles are the armoured command variant.

Name	Origin	Variant	Number	Photo	Notes
VAB	France	• VAB VTT: Armoured personnel carrier • VAB MILAN: ATGM vehicle • VCAC Mephisto: ATGM vehicle • VAB ERYX: APC/ATGM • VOA: Artillery observation vehicle • VAB Reco: NBC reconnaissance	2,661		Will be replaced by VBMR Griffon from 2018. Vehicle numbers include some: 100 VAB MILAN, 175 VAB ERYX, 25 VAB Reco, 30 VCAC Mephisto and 89 VOA.
VHM VHM Armoured	Sweden United Kingdom	Armoured personnel carrier	53		Order split between Bv206S and BvS10
VBL	France	Armoured car	1,462		
PVP	France	Armoured car	1,179		
Armoured recovery					
Leclerc DCL	France	Armoured recovery vehicle	18		
AMX-30D	France	Armoured recovery vehicle	30		

Engineering

Name	Origin	Variant	Number	Photo	Notes
Armoured engineering vehicles					
Nexter Aravis	France	Mine-resistant ambush protected	14		
Buffalo	United States	Mine-resistant ambush protected	4		
Engin Blindé du Génie	France	Armoured engineering vehicle	40		Used with 14 SDPMAC (Mine Clearance Explosives) Systems.
MINOTAUR	France	Anti-tank Mines Dispersion Vehicle			
unarmoured engineering vehicles					
ECA COBRA MK2	France	Multi-function Military Robot	30		Used for Mine Clearing, Chemical detection, Reconnaissance 30 delivered in 2012
iRobot Packbot 510	United States	Mine Clearing Robot	15		Ordered in 2009

Name	Origin	Variant	Number	Photo	Notes
ECA UGV IGUANA	France	Mine Clearing Robot	15		15 to be delivered in 2018 and 43 until 2024
EFA	France	Ferry/Mobile bridge	30 (2013)		
PFM	France	Mobile bridge	70 (2013)		
SPRAT	France	Modular assault bridge	10		
TNA	France	Airborne leveling tractor	6		
MFRD	France	Rapid Destruction Drilling Truck	122		
Liebherr LTM 1050-3.1	Germany	Mobile crane	50		
EGAME	France	Bulldozer	35		
SOUVIM	South Africa	Interim Vehicle Mounted Mine Detector	8		
MPG	France	Bulldozer	?		
Caterpillar D6	United States	Bulldozer	40		
EGRAP	United Kingdom	Backhoe loader	92		
UNAC 20TRR	France	Road–rail Excavator	2		
Scania P340	Sweden	Dump truck	161		

Unarmored Vehicles

Name	Origin	Variant	Number	Photo	Notes
Unarmoured Vehicles					
VLRA	France	Truck			
VMA	France	Airport crash tender			Used by French Army Light Aviation.
Peugeot P4	France	Light Utility Vehicle	2,500		13,500 delivered between 1982 and 1992, 600 withdrawn from service every year.
Land Rover Defender	United Kingdom	Light Utility Vehicle	550		
VPS	France	Light Utility Vehicle	51		Used by special forces.

Polaris	United States	All-terrain vehicle	300		Also used by French special forces.
Renault Trafic III	France	Minibus	60		Used by counter terrorist forces.
Ford Ranger	Argentina	Light Utility Vehicle	3700		Used by Sentinelle forces.
Renault Master II	France	Van			
Renault Kangoo	France	Light Utility Vehicle	460		Used by counter terrorist forces.

Artillery and air-defence

Name	Origin	Variant	Number	Photo	Notes
	Self-propelled artillery					
AMX 30 AuF1	France	155 mm self-propelled howitzer	32		
CAESAR	France	155 mm wheeled self-propelled howitzer	77		
M270 MLRS	United States	227mm self-propelled multiple rocket launcher	13		
	Towed artillery					
TRF1	France	155 mm towed howitzer	12		
	Mortars					
RTF1	France	120 mm mortar	140		
Mo 81 LLR F1	France	81 mm mortar			
	Anti-aircraft artillery					
Mistral	France	very short-range surface-to-air missile system	221		

Logistics

Name	Origin	Variant	Number	Photo	Notes
Porteur polyvalent terrestre (PPT)	France Italy	• PPLOG : Logistic vehicle • PPLD : Recovery vehicle	485		1600 on order
TRM 10000	France	Truck	~1,000		
TRM 700-100	France	Truck	119		
TRM 2000	France	Truck			
Renault GBC 180	France	Truck	5,500		
Vehicule porte conteneurs maritimes (VPCM)	France United Kingdom	8x8 Container carrier	12		
Camion citerne polyvalent (CCP10)	France Sweden	6x6 Tank transporter	461		
Camion lourd de depannage routier (CLDR)	France	8x4 recovery vehicle	?		

Aircraft

Aircraft	Origin	Type	Quantity	Photo	Notes
Fixed-wing aircraft					
Pilatus PC-6	Switzerland	Transport & Parachuting	5		
SOCATA TBM	France	VIP transport & Utility	8		
Helicopters					
Eurocopter Tiger HAP/-HAD	Europe	Attack helicopter	62		9 more on order. 40 HAP and 18 HAD. (All HAP will be upgraded to HAD standard)
NHIndustries NH90	Europe	Transport helicopter	23		2 batches of 34 ordered in May 2013. Six more helicopters were ordered in January 2016, bringing the total number of aircraft on order to 74.
Aérospatiale Puma	France	Transport helicopter	68		

Eurocopter Caracal	France	Transport helicopter	8		Transferred to the Air Force by 2021.
Eurocopter Cougar	France	Transport helicopter	26		
Aérospatiale Gazelle	France	Reconnaissance helicopter	99		One lost on 11 January 2013.
Eurocopter Fennec	France	Training helicopter	18		
Eurocopter Calliope	Europe	Training helicopter	36		
UAVs					
Sperwer	France	Reconnaissance	25		In service since 2005. Will be replaced from 2018 by the SAGEM Patroller.
EADS DRAC	France	Reconnaissance	60		
Thales Spy'Ranger	France	Reconnaissance			105 to be delivered in 2018 and 105 in 2019
ECA IT180 DroGen	France	Reconnaissance	5		

External links

- Official website of the French Ministry of Defense (in French)[[Category:Articles with French-language external links[252]]]
- *Les hélicoptères de l'armée de terre : situation et perspectives* – Report from the French Senate (in French)[[Category:Articles with French-language external links[253]]]
- *Le rôle des drones dans les armées* – Report from the French Senate (in French)[[Category:Articles with French-language external links[254]]]
- *Projet de loi de finances pour 2003 : Forces terrestres* – Report from the French Senate (in French)[[Category:Articles with French-language external links[255]]]
- *Projet de loi de finances pour 2007 : Défense – Forces terrestres* – Report from the French Senate (in French)[[Category:Articles with French-language external links[256]]]

France and weapons of mass destruction

France	
First nuclear weapon test	February 13, 1960
First fusion weapon test	August 23, 1968
Last nuclear test	January 27, 1996
Largest yield test	**2.6 Mt** (August 24, 1968)
Total tests	210
Peak stockpile	540 (in 1992)
Current stockpile (usable and not)	300 warheads (2016)
Current strategic arsenal	**290** usable warheads (2016) (methods of delivery include Bombers, and SLBMs)
Cumulative strategic arsenal in megatonnage	$\sim 51.6^{257}$
Maximum missile range	>10,000 km/6,000 mi (M51 SLBM)
NPT party	**Yes** (1992, one of five recognized powers)

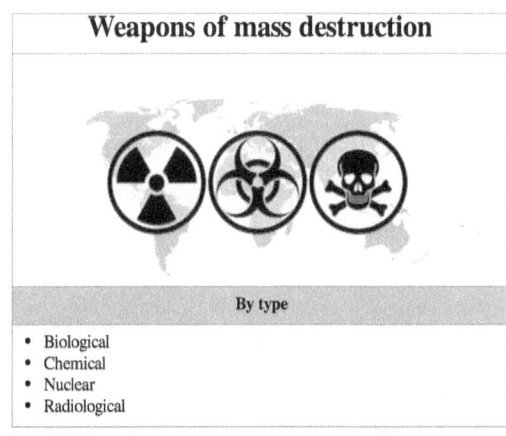

Weapons of mass destruction

By type
- Biological
- Chemical
- Nuclear
- Radiological

By country
- Albania
- Algeria
- Argentina
- Australia
- Brazil
- Bulgaria
- Canada
- China
- Egypt
- France
- Germany
- India
- Iran
- Iraq
- Israel
- Italy
- Japan
- Libya
- Mexico
- Myanmar
- Netherlands
- North Korea
- Pakistan
- Philippines
- Poland
- Romania
- Russia
- Saudi Arabia
- South Africa
- South Korea
- Sweden
- Switzerland
- Syria
- Taiwan
- Ukraine
- United Kingdom
- United States
Proliferation
- Chemical - Nuclear - Missiles

Treaties
- List of treaties
- 📖 Book - 📂 Category
- v - t - e²⁵⁸

Nuclear weapons

Background

- History
- Warfare
- Design
- Testing
- Delivery
- Yield
- Effects and estimated megadeaths of explosions
- Winter
- Workers
- Ethics
- Arsenals
- Arms race
- Espionage
- Proliferation
- Disarmament
- Terrorism
- Opposition

Nuclear-armed states

NPT recognized
United States
Russia
United Kingdom
France
China
Others
India
Israel (undeclared)
Pakistan
North Korea
Former
South Africa
Belarus
Kazakhstan
Ukraine

- v
- t
- e[259]

France is one of the five "Nuclear Weapons States" under the Treaty on the Non-Proliferation of Nuclear Weapons, but is not known to possess or develop any chemical or biological weapons. France was the fourth country to test an independently developed nuclear weapon in 1960, under the government of Charles de Gaulle. The French military is currently thought to retain a weapons stockpile of around 300 operational nuclear warheads, making it the third-largest in the world, speaking in terms of warheads, not megatons.[260] The weapons are part of the national *Force de frappe*, developed in the late 1950s and 1960s to give France the ability to distance itself from NATO while having a means of nuclear deterrence under sovereign control.

France did not sign the Partial Nuclear Test Ban Treaty, which gave it the option to conduct further nuclear tests until it signed and ratified the Comprehensive Nuclear-Test-Ban Treaty in 1996 and 1998 respectively. France denies currently having chemical weapons, ratified the Chemical Weapons Convention (CWC) in 1995, and acceded to the Biological Weapons Convention (BWC) in 1984. France had also ratified the Geneva Protocol in 1926.

History

France was one of the nuclear pioneers, going back to the work of Marie Skłodowska Curie. Curie's last assistant Bertrand Goldschmidt became the father of the French BombWikipedia:Please clarify. French Professor Frédéric Joliot-Curie, High Commissioner for Atomic Energy, told the *New York Herald Tribune* that the 1945 "Report on atomic Energy for Military Purposes" wrongfully omitted the contributions of French scientists.

After World War II France's former position of leadership suffered greatly because of the instability of the Fourth Republic, and the lack of finance available. During the Second World War Goldschmidt invented the now-standard method for extracting plutonium while working as part of the British/Canadian team participating in the Manhattan Project. But after the Liberation in 1945, France had to start its own program almost from scratch. Nevertheless, the first French reactor went critical in 1948 and small amounts of plutonium were extracted in 1949. There was no formal commitment to a nuclear weapons program at that time, although plans were made to build reactors for the large scale production of plutonium.[261] Francis Perrin, French High-Commissioner for Atomic Energy from 1951 to 1970, stated that from 1949 Israeli scientists were invited to the Saclay Nuclear Research Centre, this cooperation leading to a joint effort including sharing of knowledge between French and Israeli scientists especially those with knowledge from the Manhattan Project,[262,263] the French believed that cooperation with Israel could give them access to international Jewish nuclear scientists.[264] According to Lieutenant Colonel Warner D. Farr in a report to the USAF Counterproliferation Center while France was previously a leader in nuclear research "Israel and France were at a similar level of expertise after the war, and Israeli scientists could make significant contributions to the French effort. Progress in nuclear science and technology in France and Israel remained closely linked throughout the early fifties. Farr reported that Israeli scientists probably helped construct the G-1 plutonium production reactor and UP-1 reprocessing plant at Marcoule."[265]

However, in the 1950s a civilian nuclear research program was started, a byproduct of which would be plutonium. In 1956 a secret Committee for the Military Applications of Atomic Energy was formed and a development program for delivery vehicles was started. The intervention of the United States in the Suez Crisis that year is credited with convincing France that it needed to accelerate its own nuclear weapons program to remain a global power.[266] As part their military alliance during the Suez Crisis in 1956 the French agreed to secretly build the Dimona nuclear reactor in Israel and soon after agreed to construct a reprocessing plant for the extraction of plutonium at the site. In 1957, soon after Suez and the resulting diplomatic tension with both the USSR and the United States, French president René Coty decided on the creation of the C.S.E.M. in the then French Sahara, a new nuclear testing facility replacing the CIEES.

In 1957 Euratom was created, and under cover of the peaceful use of nuclear power the French signed deals with Germany and Italy to work together on nuclear weapons development.[267] The West German Chancellor Konrad Adenauer told his cabinet that he "wanted to achieve, through EURATOM, as quickly as possible, the chance of producing our own nuclear weapons".[268]

The idea was short-lived. In 1958 de Gaulle became President and Germany and Italy were excluded.Wikipedia:Citation needed

With the return of Charles de Gaulle to the presidency of France in the midst of the May 1958 crisis, the final decisions to build an atomic bomb were taken, and a successful test took place in 1960 with Israeli scientists as observers at the tests and unlimited access to the scientific data.[269] Following tests de Gaulle moved quickly to distance the French program from involvement with that of Israel.[270] Since then France has developed and maintained its own nuclear deterrent, one intended to defend France even if the United States refused to risk its own cities by assisting Western Europe in a nuclear war.

The United States began providing technical assistance to the French program in the early 1970s through the 1980s. The aid was secret, unlike the relationship with the British nuclear program. The Nixon administration, unlike previous presidencies, did not oppose its allies' possession of atomic weapons and believed that the Soviets would find having multiple nuclear-armed Western opponents more difficult. Because the Atomic Energy Act of 1946 prohibited sharing information on nuclear weapon design, a method known as "negative guidance" or "Twenty Questions" was used; French scientists described to their American counterparts their research, and were told whether they were correct. Areas in which the French received help included MIRV, radiation hardening, missile design, intelligence on Soviet anti-missile defences, and advanced computer technology. Because the French program attracted "the best brains" of the nation, the Americans benefited from French research as well. The relationship also improved the two nations' military ties; despite its departure from NATO's command structure in 1966, France developed two separate nuclear targeting plans, one "national" for the Force de Frappe's role as a solely French deterrent, and one coordinated with NATO.

France is understood to have tested neutron or enhanced radiation bombs in the past, apparently leading the field with an early test of the technology in 1967[271] and an "actual" neutron bomb in 1980.[272]

Testing

There were 210 French nuclear tests from 1960 through 1995. Seventeen of them were done in the Algerian Sahara between 1960 and 1966, starting in the middle of the Algerian War. One-hundred ninety-three were carried out in French Polynesia.[273,274]

A summary table of French nuclear testing by years can be found here: France's nuclear testing series.

Saharan experiments centres (1960–66)

After studying Réunion, New Caledonia, and Clipperton Island, General Charles Ailleret, head of the Special Weapons Section, proposed two possible nuclear test sites for France in a January 1957 report: French Algeria in the Sahara Desert, and French Polynesia. Although he recommended against Polynesia because of its distance from France and lack of a large airport, Ailleret stated that Algeria should be chosen "provisionally", likely due in part to the Algerian War.

A series of atmospheric nuclear tests was conducted by the *Centre Saharien d'Expérimentations Militaires* ("Saharan Military Experiments Centre") from February 1960 until April 1961. The first, called *Gerboise Bleue* ("Blue jerboa") took place on 13 February 1960 in Algeria. The explosion took place at 40 km from the military base at Hammoudia near Reggane, which is the last town on the Tanezrouft Track heading south across the Sahara to Mali, and 700 km/435 mi. south of Béchar.[275] The device had a 70 kiloton yield. Although Algeria became independent in 1962, France was able to continue with underground nuclear tests in Algeria through 1966. The General Pierre Marie Gallois was named *le père de la bombe A* ("Father of the A-bomb").

Three further atmospheric tests were carried out from 1 April 1960 to 25 April 1961 at Hammoudia. Military, workers and the nomadic Touareg population of the region were present at the test sites, without any significant protection. At most, some took a shower after each test according to *L'Humanité*.[276] Gerboise Rouge (5kt), the third atomic bomb, half as powerful as Hiroshima, exploded on 27 December 1960, provoking protests from Japan, USSR, Egypt, Morocco, Nigeria and Ghana.[277]

After the independence of Algeria on 5 July 1962, following the 19 March 1962 Evian agreements, the French military moved the test site to another location in the Algerian Sahara, around 150 km north of Tamnarasset, near the village of In Eker. Underground nuclear explosion testing was performed in drifts in the Taourirt Tan Afella mountain, one of the granite Hoggar Mountains. The Evian agreements included a secret article which stated that "Algeria concede[s]... to France the use of certain air bases, terrains, sites and military installations which are necessary to it [France]" during five years.

The C.S.E.M. was therefore replaced by the *Centre d'Expérimentations Militaires des Oasis* ("Military Experiments Center of the Oasis") underground nuclear testing facility. A total of 13 underground nuclear tests were carried out at the In Eker site from 7 November 1961 to 16 February 1966. By July 1, 1967, all French facilities were evacuated.

An accident happened on May 1, 1962, during the "Béryl" test, four times more powerful than Hiroshima and designed as an underground shaft test.[278]

Due to improper sealing of the shaft, radioactive rock and dust were released into the atmosphere. Nine soldiers of the 621st Groupe d'Armes Spéciales unit were heavily contaminated by radiation.[279] The soldiers were exposed to as much as 600 mSv. The Minister of Armed Forces, Pierre Messmer, and the Minister of Research, Gaston Palewski, were present. As many as 100 additional personnel, including officials, soldiers and Algerian workers were exposed to lower levels of radiation, estimated at about 50 mSv, when the radioactive cloud produced by the blast passed over the command post, due to an unexpected change in wind direction. They escaped as they could, often without wearing any protection. Palewski died in 1984 of leukemia, which he always attributed to the Beryl incident. In 2006, Bruno Barillot, specialist of nuclear tests, measured on the site 93 microsieverts by hour of gamma ray, equivalent to 1% of the official admissible yearly dose. The incident was documented in the 2006 docudrama *"Vive La Bombe!*.[280]

Saharan facilities

- CIEES (*Centre Interarmées d'Essais d'Engins Spéciaux*, "Joint Special Vehicle Testing Center" in English): Hammaguir, 12 kilometres (7.5 mi) southwest of Colomb-Béchar, Algeria:

  used for launching rockets from 1947 to 1967.[281]

- C.S.E.M. (*Centre Saharien d'Expérimentations Militaires*): Reggane, west of In-Salah, Tanezrouft, Algeria:

  used for atmospheric tests from 1960 to 1961.

- C.E.M.O. (*Centre d'Expérimentations Militaires des Oasis*): In Ekker, in the Hoggar, 150 km/93 mi from Tamanrasset, Tan Afella, Algeria:

  used for underground tests from 1961 to 1967.

Pacific experiments centre (1966–1996)

Despite its initial choice of Algeria for nuclear tests, the French government decided to build Faa'a International Airport in Tahiti, spending much more money and resources than would be justified by the official explanation of tourism. By 1958, two years before the first Sahara test, France began again its search for new testing sites due to potential political problems with Algeria and the possibility of a ban on above-ground tests. Many overseas France islands were studied, as well as performing underground tests in the Alps, Pyrenees, or Corsica; however, engineers found problems with most of the possible sites in metropolitan France.

By 1962 France hoped in its negotiations with the Algerian independence movement to retain the Sahara as a test site until 1968, but decided that it

Figure 196: *The French nuclear-powered aircraft carrier Charles de Gaulle and the American nuclear-powered carrier USS Enterprise (left), each of which carry nuclear-capable fighter aircraft*

needed to be able to also perform above-ground tests of hydrogen bombs, which could not be done in Algeria. Mururoa and Fangataufa in French Polynesia were chosen that year. President Charles de Gaulle announced the choice on 3 January 1963, describing it as a benefit to Polynesia's weak economy. The Polynesian people and leaders broadly supported the choice, although the tests became controversial after they began, especially among Polynesian separatists.

A total of 193 nuclear tests were carried out in Polynesia from 1966 to 1996. On 24 August 1968 France detonated its first thermonuclear weapon—codenamed Canopus—over Fangataufa. A fission device ignited a lithium-6 deuteride secondary inside a jacket of highly enriched uranium to create a 2.6 megaton blast.

Simulation programme (1996–2012)

More recently, France has used supercomputers to simulate and study nuclear explosions.

Current nuclear doctrine and strategy

French law requires at least one out of four nuclear submarines to be on patrol in the Atlantic Ocean at any given time, like the UK's policy.[282]

Figure 197: *Protests in Australia in 1996 against French nuclear tests in Pacific*

In 2006, French President Jacques Chirac noted that France would be willing to use nuclear weapons against a state attacking France by terrorism. He noted that the French nuclear forces had been configured for this option.[283]

On 21 March 2008, President Nicolas Sarkozy announced that France will reduce its aircraft deliverable nuclear weapon stockpile (which currently consists of 60 TN 81 warheads) by a third (20 warheads) and bring the total French nuclear arsenal to fewer than 300 warheads.[284,285]

Anti–nuclear tests protests

- In July 1959, after France announced that they would begin testing nuclear bombs in the Sahara, protests were held in Nigeria and Ghana, with the Liberian and Moroccan governments also denouncing the decision. On November 20th, 1959 the United Nations General Assembly passed a resolution supported by 26 Afro-Asian countries expressing concern and requesting "France to refrain from such tests."[286]
- By 1968 only France and China were detonating nuclear weapons in the open air and the contamination caused by the H-bomb blast led to a global protest movement against further French atmospheric tests.
- From the early 1960s New Zealand peace groups CND and the Peace Media had been organising nationwide anti nuclear campaigns in protest of atmospheric testing in French Polynesia. These included two large national petitions presented to the New Zealand government which led to a joint New Zealand and Australian Government action to take France to the International Court of Justice (1972).
- In 1972, Greenpeace and an amalgam of New Zealand peace groups managed to delay nuclear tests by several weeks by trespassing with a ship in the testing zone. During the time, the skipper, David McTaggart, was beaten and severely injured by members of the French military.

- In 1973 the New Zealand Peace Media organised an international flotilla of protest yachts including the Fri, Spirit of Peace, Boy Roel, Magic Island and the Tanmure to sail into the test exclusion zone.
- In 1973, New Zealand Prime Minister Norman Kirk as a symbolic act of protest sent two navy frigates, HMNZS *Canterbury* and HMNZS *Otago*, to Moruroa. They were accompanied by HMAS *Supply*, a fleet oiler of the Royal Australian Navy.
- In 1985 the Greenpeace ship *Rainbow Warrior* was bombed and sunk by the French DGSE in Auckland, New Zealand, as it prepared for another protest of nuclear testing in French military zones. One crew member, Fernando Pereira of Portugal, photographer, drowned on the sinking ship while attempting to recover his photographic equipment. Two members of DGSE were captured and sentenced, but eventually repatriated to France in a controversial affair.
- French president Jacques Chirac's decision to run a nuclear test series at Mururoa in 1995, just one year before the Comprehensive Test Ban Treaty was to be signed, caused worldwide protest, including an embargo of French wine. These tests were meant to provide the nation with enough data to improve further nuclear technology without needing additional series of tests.[287]
- The French Military conducted almost 200 nuclear tests at Mururoa and Fangataufa atolls over a thirty-year period ending in 1996, 46 of them atmospheric, of which five were without significant nuclear yield. In August 2006, an official French government report by INSERM confirmed the link between an increase in the cases of thyroid cancer and France's atmospheric nuclear tests in the territory since 1966.

Veterans' associations and symposium

An association gathering veterans of nuclear tests (AVEN, "*Association des vétérans des essais nucléaires*") was created in 2001.[288] Along with the Polynesian NGO Moruroa e tatou, the AVEN announced on 27 November 2002 that it would depose a complaint against X (unknown) for involuntary homicide and putting someone's life in danger. On 7 June 2003, for the first time, the military court of Tours granted an invalidity pension to a veteran of the Sahara tests. According to a poll made by the AVEN with its members, only 12% have declared being in good health. An international symposium on the consequences of test carried out in Algeria took place on 13 and 14 February 2007, under the official oversight of President Abdelaziz Bouteflika.

One hundred fifty thousand civilians, without taking into account the local population, are estimated to have been on the location of nuclear tests, in Algeria or in French Polynesia. One French veteran of the 1960s nuclear tests in Algeria described being given no protective clothing or masks, while being ordered to witness the tests at so close a range that the flash penetrated through the arm he used to cover his eyes.[289] One of several veteran's groups claiming to organise those suffering ill effects, AVEN had 4500 members in early 2009.

Test victims compensation

In both Algeria and French Polynesia there have been long standing demands for compensation from those who claim injury from France's nuclear testing program. The government of France had consistently denied, since the late 1960s, that injury to military personnel and civilians had been caused by their nuclear testing.[290] Several French veterans and African and Polynesian campaign groups have waged court cases and public relations struggles demanding government reparations. In May 2009, a group of twelve French veterans, in the campaign group "Truth and Justice", who claim to have suffered health effects from nuclear testing in the 1960s had their claims denied by the government Commission for the Indemnification of Victims of Penal Infraction (CIVI), and again by a Paris appeals court, citing laws which set a statute of limitations for damages to 1976.[291] Following this rejection, the government announced it would create a 10m Euro compensation fund for military and civilian victims of its testing programme; both those carried out in the 1960s and the Polynesian tests of 1990–1996. Defence Minister Hervé Morin said the government would create a board of physicians, overseen by a French judge magistrate, to determine if individual cases were caused by French testing, and if individuals were suffering from illnesses on a United Nations Scientific Committee on the Effects of Atomic Radiation list of eighteen disorders linked to exposure to testing.[292] Pressure groups, including the Veterans group "Truth and Justice" criticised the programme as too restrictive in illnesses covered and too bureaucratic. Polynesian groups said the bill would also unduly restrict applicants to those who had been in small areas near the test zones, not taking into account the pervasive pollution and radiation.[293] Algerian groups had also complained that these restrictions would deny compensation to many victims. One Algerian group estimated there were 27,000 still living victims of ill effects from the 1960–66 testing there, while the French government had given an estimate of just 500.[294]

Non-nuclear WMD

France states that it does not currently possess chemical weapons. The country ratified the Chemical Weapons Convention (CWC) in 1995, and acceded to the Biological and Toxin Weapons Convention (BWC) in 1984. France also ratified the Geneva Protocol in 1926.

During World War I, France, not Germany as commonly believed, was actually the first nation to use chemical weapons though this was only a nonlethal tear gas attack (xylyl bromide) carried out in August 1914. Once the war generated into trench warfare and new methods to attain an advantage were sought, the German Army initiated a chlorine gas attack against the French Army at Ypres on 15 April 1915, initiating a new method of warfare but failing that day to exploit the break in the French line. In time, the more potent phosgene replaced chlorine in use by armies on the Western Front, including France, leading to massive casualties on both sides of the conflict however the effects were mitigated by development of protective clothing and masks as the war progressed.

At the outbreak of World War II, France maintained large stockpiles of mustard gas and phosgene but did not utilize them against the invading Axis troops, and no chemical weapons were used by the Axis invaders. During the invasion, German forces captured a French biological research facility and purportedly found plans to use potato beetles against Germany. Immediately after the end of the war, the French military began testing captured German stores in Algeria, then a French colony, notably Tabun, an extremely toxic nerve agent. By the latter part of the 1940s, testing of Tabun-filled ordnance had become routine, often using livestock to test their effects. The testing of chemical weapons occurred at B2-Namous, Algeria, an uninhabited desert proving ground located 100 kilometers (62 mi) east of the Moroccan border, but other sites existed.[295,296]

In 1985, France was estimated to have 435 tonnes of chemical weapons in its stockpile, the second largest in NATO following the United States. At a conference in Paris in 1989, France declared that it was no longer in possession of chemical weaponry, despite maintaining the manufacturing capacity to readily produce them if needed.

Bibliography

- (in French) Jean-Hugues Oppel, *Réveillez le président*, Éditions Payot et rivages, 2007 (ISBN 978-2-7436-1630-4). The book is a fiction about the nuclear weapons of France; the book also contains about ten chapters on true historical incidents involving nuclear weapons and strategy (during the second half of the twentieth century).

External links

- In-depth background of the Development of the French Program[297]
- Video archive of French Nuclear Testing[298] at sonicbomb.com[299]
- A Change in the French Nuclear Doctrine?[300], Rault, Charles - *ISRIA*, 25 January 2006.
- Country overview: France[301] (from the Nuclear Threat Initiative)
- Bulletin of the Atomic Scientists[302]
  - *Nuclear Notebook: French nuclear forces, 2008*[303], September/October 2008.
  - *Nuclear policy: France stands alone*[304] July/August 2004
  - *The French atomic energy program*[305] September 1962
- Greenpeace movie[306] (on the French bombing of the *Rainbow Warrior*, a ship about to protest French nuclear tests)
- Nuclear Files.org[307] (current information on nuclear stockpiles in France)
- (in French) Archives sur le Centre d'Expérimentations Nucléaires du Pacifique (C.E.P.) à Moruroa, Hao et Fangataufa[308]
- Annotated bibliography for the French nuclear weapons program from the Alsos Digital Library for Nuclear Issues[309]
- The Woodrow Wilson Center's Nuclear Proliferation International History Project[310] The Wilson Center's Nuclear Proliferation International History Project has primary source documents on US-French nuclear relations.

White Paper

2008 French White Paper on Defence and National Security

The **2008 French White Paper on Defence and National Security** was a defence reform of the French Armed Forces. On 31 July 2007, president Nicolas Sarkozy ordered M. Jean-Claude Mallet, a member of the Council of State, to head up a 35-member commission charged with a wide-ranging review of French defence. The commission issued its white paper (French: *livre blanc*) in early 2008.[311] Acting upon its recommendations, Sarkozy began making radical changes in French defence policy and structures starting in the summer of 2008. The proposed force structure was to be complete by 2014-15.[312]

Summary

- As part of the white paper Sarkozy declared that France "will now participate fully in NATO."
- Total cuts of 54,000 personnel.
- The French Armed Forces will retain the ability to deploy up to 30,000 troops in a single overseas deployment.
- For the first time, cyber security (both defensive and offensive) was also listed as a key priority for the French state.

French Army

- A reduction in personnel to 131,000 regular and civilian personnel. Of which the 'operational force' of the army will consist of 88,000 troops.
- A reduction of over 150 Leclerc main battle tanks to an operational fleet of 250.
- A strength of 80 attack helicopters and 130 support helicopters.
- Orders for 25,000 FELIN-type infantry combat suits.

French Navy

- A reduction in personnel to 44,000 regular and civilian personnel.
- Possibility of a new aircraft carrier to complement the existing Charles de Gaulle (R91). Final decision to be made in 2012.
- Possibility of a 4th Mistral-class amphibious assault ship.
- The 5 La Fayette-class light frigates to be re-classified as "1st rank frigates".
- A total strength of 18 "1st rank frigates" (including the less powerful La Fayette-class).
- Expected order of FREMM multipurpose frigates reduced from 17 to 11. Units 10 and 11 to be built in the air-defence role (FREDA derivative).
- 6 light surveillance frigates to remain in service (the Floréal-class).
- The construction of 6 Barracuda-class submarines.

French Air Force

- A reduction in personnel to around 50,000 regular and civilian personnel.
- Operational command of French Air Force and French Navy fast-jet combat aircraft will be **combined** under the Chief of the Defence Staff.
- The air force and navy will operate no more than 300 fast-jet combat aircraft consisting of; Dassault Rafale multi-role fighters and modernised Mirage 2000-D strike aircraft.
- Ability to deploy up to 70 fast-jet combat aircraft over seas.
- 4 air force and 3 navy AEW&C systems.
- A fleet of refueling tanker and transports aircraft comprising; 14 Airbus A330 refueling tankers and 70 tactical transport aircraft.

2013 French White Paper on Defence and National Security

The **2013 French White Paper on Defense and National Security** is the most recent defence reform of the French Armed Forces and the fourth ever defence white paper in French history. It was released on the 29 April 2013. The white paper reaffirmed France's commitment to NATO, the security of the European Union as well as its enhanced defence-relationship with the United Kingdom after the 2010 Lancaster House treaties on defence and security co-operation.

Figure 198: *Leclerc Main Battle Tank.*

Summary

- Additional cuts of 24,000 personnel on top of the 54,000 already cut in the 2008 French White Paper on Defence and National Security.
- Core defence budget frozen at 31.4 billion euros and reduced to 1.5% of GDP. However, the defence budget will continue to remain the third largest in NATO after the United States and United Kingdom.
- A "Joint Reaction Force" of 2,300 personnel maintained a high readiness and the ability to deploy up-to 15,000 troops in a single overseas deployment.
- Particular emphasis on developing intelligence gathering capabilities, cyber warfare, the strengthening of special forces and the purchase of unmanned aerial vehicles (UAVs).
- Number of ships, helicopters, transport aircraft and tanks to be reduced.[313]

French Army

- Reduction in personnel to the "operational force" of the army from 88,000 troops to 66,000.
- The French Army will restructure to 7 Brigades; 2 heavy, 3 medium and 2 light role.
- A reduction of 50 Leclerc main battle tanks to an operational fleet of 200.
- 80 attack helicopters, 115 support helicopters, 40 reconnaissance helicopters.

- Purchase of 30 "tactical" UAVs, most likely the British Watchkeeper WK450.

French Navy

- The possibility of a new aircraft carrier has been officially abandoned.
- The possibility of a 4th Mistral-class amphibious assault ship has been officially abandoned.
- The 5 La Fayette-class light frigates which were re-classified as "1st rank frigates" in the 2008 white paper will be upgraded with a sonar.
- A reduction in the number of "1st rank frigates" from 18 to 15. The figure of 15 includes "less powerful combatants" such as the La Fayette-class.
- Expected deliveries of FREMM multipurpose frigates to the French Navy reduced from 11 to 8.
- The two Horizon-class frigates will be the two primary air-defence frigates in service with the Navy when the ageing Cassard-class are decommissioned. However, the possibility remains that out of the 8 FREMM destined for the French Navy, 2 could be configured with enhanced air-defence capabilities (i.e. the FREDA derivative).
- 6 light surveillance frigates to remain in service (the Floréal-class).
- A total of 15 offshore patrol vessels.
- The construction of 6 Barracuda-class submarines.
- The last of the Foudre-class landing platform docks (L9012 *Siroco*) to be decommissioned.
- The white paper asserted that a naval task group would require "collaboration" with the Royal Navy to sustain operations. Bringing the Lancaster House treaties into practice.

French Air Force

- The air force and navy will operate no more than 225 fast-jet combat aircraft (reduced from 300) consisting of; Dassault Rafale multi-role fighters and modernised Mirage 2000-D strike aircraft.
- The Mirage 2000-N nuclear strike force will remain.
- The number of expected Dassault Rafale orders will be reduced.
- Ability to deploy up to 40 fast-jet combat aircraft in an over seas conflict.
- 4 air force and 3 navy AEW&C systems.
- A fleet of refueling tanker and transports aircraft comprising; 12 Airbus A330 refueling tankers (reduced from 14) and 50 tactical transport aircraft (reduced from 70).

External links

- Défense : les cinq éléments marquants du livre blanc[314]
- Hollande sanctuarise la dissuasion[315]

French Air Force

History of the Armée de l'Air (1909–1942)

History of the *Armée de l'Air*[316]
History of the Armée de l'Air (1909–1942)
Free French Air Force
Vichy French Air Force
History of the Armée de l'Air in the colonies (1939–62)

The *Armée de l'Air* (literally, "army of the air") is the name used for the French Air Force in its native language since it was made independent of the Army in 1933. This article deals exclusively with the history of the French air force from its earliest beginnings until its destruction after the occupation of France. French naval aviation, the *Aéronautique Navale* is covered elsewhere.[317]

Military aviation to 1914

During the first decade of the 20th century France was at the forefront of aviation progress, with pioneers such as Louis Blériot, Henri Farman, Gabriel Voisin, Édouard Nieuport and Louis Béchereau and this led to early interest in aircraft by the military. The French defeat during the Franco-Prussian War of 1870–1871 was still very fresh, and France expected to face Germany again. From December 1909, the French Department of War began to send individuals from all branches of the army, especially engineering and artillery, to undergo flying training at civilian schools as "pupil-pilots" (*élèves-pilotes*) such as at Reims and Bron. In March 1910, the *Établissement Militaire d'Aviation* (EMA) was created to conduct experiments with aircraft and on 22 October 1910 the *Aéronautique Militaire* was formed as a branch of the Army[318] under the command of General Pierre Roques Although they would have to wait until

Figure 199: *The French roundel gave rise to similar roundels for other air forces.*

Figure 200: *Restored Blériot XI in Aéronautique Militaire markings.*

mid-1911 the first military aviation brevets to be awarded to army pilots and 29 March 1912 for the law officially establishing the *Aéronautique Militaire* to be passed.

Training of military pilots was the same as civilian pilots until 1910 when the General Staff introduced the military pilot license. Military pilot badge N°1 was issued to Lieutenant Charles de Tricornot de Rose following training at the Blériot Flying School in Pau, in southwest of France, where the Wright Brothers had established the first aviation school the year before.

Shortly after the *Aéronautique Militaire* became be the world's first "air force" using aircraft, the German army began training airmen in 4 July 1910Wikipedia:Citation needed but didn't create an official formation until 1 April 1911 when it formed the *Fliegertruppen des deutschen Kaiserreiches*.Wikipedia:Citation needed The British Air Battalion Royal Engineers (a precursor to the Royal Flying Corps), was formed on 1 April 1911.Wikipedia:Citation needed The *Armée de l'Air* was renamed in August 1933 when it gained operational independence from the Army, much later than for Germany, or the United Kingdom although before that of the United States.

First World War

At the start of the First World War (*La Première Guerre mondiale* in French), France led the world in aircraft design and by mid-1912 the *Aéronautique Militaire* had five squadrons (*escadrilles*). This had grown to 132 machines and 21 *escadrilles* by 1914, the same year when, on 21 February, it formally received a budget under the Ministry of War (*Ministère de la Guerre*). On 3 August, Germany declared war against France.

At the beginning of what eventually became known as First World War, the *Aéronautique Militaire* concentrated on reconnaissance with aircraft like the Blériot XI. On 8 October, though, the commander-in-chief, General Barès, proposed a massive expansion to 65 escadrilles. Furthermore, he proposed that four types of aircraft could be used for four different tasks: Morane-Saulnier Ls would be used as scouts, Voisin IIIs as bombers, Farman MF.11s as reconnaissance aircraft, and Caudron G.IIIs as artillery spotters.[319,320]

On October 5, 1914, *Sergent* Joseph Franz and his mechanic *Caporal* Louis Quénault became the first to shoot down another aircraft when they downed a German Aviatik. However, air fighting was revolutionized when a reconnaissance pilot, Roland Garros, mounted a Hotchkiss machine gun on the cowling of his Morane-Saulnier L with a mechanical interrupter mechanism. The inconsistent firing rate of the Hotchkiss prevented the mechanism from working

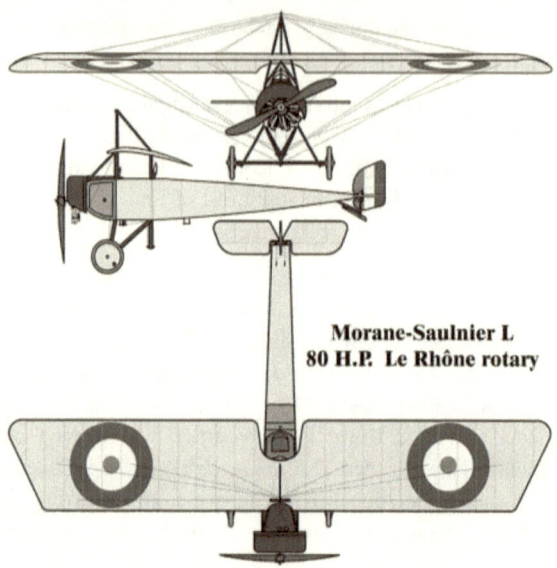

Figure 201: *1914 Morane-Saulnier L reconnaissance monoplane*

Figure 202: *1915 Voisin V bomber*

Figure 203: *1916 Nieuport 23*

Figure 204: *SPAD S.XIII, the most numerically important French fighter*

Figure 205: *1918 Breguet 14 reconnaissance bomber*

properly and he added deflector wedges to the rear of the propeller blades, so that the wooden propeller would not be shot to pieces whenever he opened fire on German aircraft. With this setup, Garros became the world's first fighter pilot, but he was captured shortly afterwards when his engine failed.

Independently, Anthony Fokker succeeded when he fitted a Fokker M.5K *Eindecker* (monoplane) with a Parabellum MG14 machine gun equipped with a gun synchronizer, thus changing the way in which the air war was fought, as German and Allied fighter aircraft fought each other in the air, producing "ace" pilots. Three prominent French "aces" were René Fonck, who became the top-scoring Allied pilot of World War I with 75 enemy aircraft shot down, Georges Guynemer who was killed after 54 victories, and Charles Nungesser, who achieved 43 victories and survived the war, and Georges Madon who had 41 victories.

Prior to 1916, escadrilles operated a variety of different types of aircraft together to accomplish specific assigned tasks with the first fighters being distributed piecemeal to each escadrille. This type of organization was common at the time. In 1916, as a result of their failure to achieve aerial supremacy over the Battle of Verdun and the inability of the reconnaissance aircraft to track German movements, Charles de Tricornot de Rose grouped the new Nieuport 11 fighters into dedicated fighter units, so that so could operate together more effectively. This so revolutionized air combat that the Germans were forced to follow suit shortly thereafter.

During this period the Lafayette Escadrille (designated N.124) was formed around a group of mainly American volunteers while their parent country remained neutral. Initially operating a mixture of Nieuport 11s, 16s and 17s, when the SPAD S.XIII entered service, they would be redesignated S.124.

Figure 206: *Nieuport-Delage NiD.29 C.1 fighter used in the early post-WW1 period.*

The entry of the United States into the war resulted in most of their surviving personnel would be transferred to the U.S. Army Air Service (USAAS) in February 1918. The unit's leading "ace" was French-born American Raoul Lufbery, who shot down 16 enemy aircraft (all but one with the Escadrille) prior to his death in action on 19 May 1918. Other American volunteer pilots, including the first black fighter pilot, Eugene Bullard, flew with regular French *Aéronautique Militaire escadrilles*.

By April 1917, the *Aéronautique Militaire* had 2,870 aircraft with 60 fighter and 20 bomber squadrons and 400 observation aircraft, yet, by October, an even more radical expansion to over 300 squadrons was proposed. By May 1918, over 600 fighters and bombers came under the command of the *Division Aérienne*. Two months later, long-range reconnaissance squadrons had been formed. At the armistice, the *Aéronautique Militaire* had some 3,222 front-line combat aircraft on the Western Front, making it the world's largest air force. During the war the *Aéronautique Militaire* claimed 2,049 enemy aircraft and 357 balloons destroyed, for some 3,500 killed in action, 3,000 wounded/missing and 2,000 killed in accidents.[321] Some 182 pilots of the *Aéronautique Militaire* were deemed flying aces for having scored five or more air-to-air victories.[322]

Figure 207: *Nieuport-Delage NiD.62 C.1 fighter, mainstay of the Armée de l'Air in the late 20s and early 30s.*

1918–1939

The end of war may have brought peace to France, yet the country itself and its infrastructure had been ravaged by four years of warfare, and the scars left behind were not just physical. As a result, it took some time for industry to recover. Not unexpectedly, orders for military aeroplanes dropped after the Armistice, resulting in reductions being made to squadron strengths.

France had an Colonial empire extending around the globe, and it needed to be defended. Anti-Government elements in French Morocco were clamouring to expel the French. On 27 April 1925, therefore, alongside tactical and logistical support, air operations in Morocco were begun owing to the Rif War and they were to continue until December 1934.

In the 1930s, the French aeronautical industry was primarily composed of small companies such as Latécoère, Morane-Saulnier, Nieuport-Delage and Amiot, each only producing small numbers of aircraft. As a result, the French aeronautical industry proved itself incapable of delivering the aircraft that the annual fiscal budgets had called for which had been greatly increased as a result of Hitler coming to power in January 1933 and his remilitarization of Germany in defiance of the Allies and the Treaty of Versailles that ended the First World War.

Pierre Cot, the secretary of the French Air Force, decreed that national security was too important for the production of warplanes to be left in the hands of the private enterprises that were thus far failing to meet production goals.

Figure 208: *Dewoitine D.510 monoplane fighters from the mid-1930s*

In July 1936 the French government began nationalizing many of the larger aircraft companies, creating six state-owned companies, which encompassed the majority of aeronautical production, and regrouping those companies to their geographical regions. Bloch was nationalized in January 1937. However, the aircraft engine industry, even as it proved incapable of providing the badly needed powerful engines, escaped nationalization.

By 1937, it was clear that more modern aircraft were needed, since the air force was still flying relatively antiquated aircraft like the Dewoitine D.500 and orders to construct more than 2,500 modern machines, among them the Bloch MB.170 bomber and the Dewoitine D.520 fighter resulted. The inadequacy of the French aeronautical programs, as well as indecision in high command resulted in the French Air Force being in a position of weakness, confronting a modern and well organized *Luftwaffe*, which had just helped the Fascist dictator Francisco Franco win the Spanish Civil War in March 1939 against the democratically elected Spanish government.

France attempted to respond to the likelihood of another European war via an intensive re-equipment and modernization program in 1938–39, as did other countries desperately in need of new aircraft including Poland whose 1939 orders of 160 MS-406 fighters from France still hadn't been delivered by the German invasion of Poland. Germany production outstripped that of its neighbours, so it was a question of "too little, too late" as far as the French – as well as the whole continent of Europe – were concerned.

Figure 209: *Morane-Saulnier MS.406 fighters*

September 1939 – June 1940

A re-organisation of the air force took place during September 1939. Prior to the reshuffle, the basic unit structure consisted of two Escadrilles (Squadron) forming a Groupe, extending to multiple Groupe's (normally two or more), forming an Escadre. Following the re-organisation an 'Escadre' became a 'Groupement' Groupement de Bombardement No.6 formed a part of the Bomber contingent of Zone D'Opérations Aériennes Nord or *ZOAN* [lit. trans. 'Air Operations North']. ZOAN was one of four geographically distinct areas of command. The others, comprising; Zone D'Opérations Aériennes Sud *ZOAS*, Zone D'Opérations Aériennes Est *ZOAE* and Zone D'Opérations Aériennes Alps *ZOAA*, were responsible for the Southern, Eastern and Alpine regions of the French mainland respectively. The national divisions these areas represented were drawn up to correspond to the boundaries of defence responsibility for French army groups. Zone D'Opérations Aériennes Nord was responsible for the air cover and protection of the most Northern regions of France. Two units of bomber squadrons fell within the command of Groupement de Bombardement No.6; Groupe de Bombardement I/12 and Groupe de Bombardement II/12. The Officer Commanding Groupement de Bombardement No.6 was Colonel Lefort. Headquarters were at Soissons in the Picardy

Figure 210: *Dewoitine D.520 fighter*

Figure 211: *Bloch MB.200 bomber*

Figure 212: *Obsolete Amiot 143M bombers still in use during the Invasion of France.*

Region of north-east France. The existence of the entire revised *Armée de L'Air* organisational structure was short-lived.

When the war began the *Armée de l'Air* suffered from disorganisation in government, armed forces and industry which had led to only 826 fighters and 250 bombers to be anything like combat-ready. Many more aircraft were not ready because of shortages of equipment and components, machine-guns had not been calibrated and some bombers lacked bomb-sights when they were delivered to squadrons. The French had no comparable organisation to the Air Transport Auxiliary (ATA) and front-line pilots in France became responsible for ferrying new aircraft from factories to the squadrons, temporarily depleting front-line strength.

On 10 May 1940, the Germans had more aircraft and many aircrews were veterans of the war in Spain. French inter-service rivalry led a Potez reconnaissance aircraft crew, which had spotted a huge concentration of *Panzers* and supporting infantry units concealed in the Ardennes forests two days after the start of the invasion, not being believed by the army commanders who refused to act on what they called air force scaremongering.

The Armée de l'Air was beset by obsolete strategy, tactics, aircraft, weapons and even in communications, and the lack of equipment owing to "technical problems." Both became apparent when the Germans advanced swiftly through France and Belgium. On 11 May, nearly 20 French bombers and over 30 British fighter escorts were shot down attacking German crossings over the Meuse river. French fighter and bomber strength was rapidly depleted in May as *Luftwaffe* fighters and *Flak* shot down aircraft, which attacked the advancing Germans. Squadrons were often out of contact with any French army units that they were supposedly supporting, partly to the poor coordination of communication between the army and the air force and partly to the outdated, unreliable army communications equipment being used.

As it became clear that the war was lost for France, the high command ordered what remained of the *Armée de l'Air* to French colonies in North Africa to continue the fight, such that *Armée de l'Air* units were stationed at places like Alger-Maison-Blanche and Oran in Algeria and Meknes and Rayack in Morocco. The Vichy government ordered the dissolution of many of the air force squadrons, including the fighter unit designated GC II/4, nicknamed *Les Petits Poucets*. GC II/4 had been formed at Rheims in May 1939, then moved to Xaffévilliers by the start of the war. It flew US-built Curtiss H-75A Hawk fighters, with which the unit claimed the first two French air victories on 8 September 1939, two Bf 109s of I/JG 53. Just 17 days later, it lost its commanding officer, Captain Claude, in combat, yet the pilots were especially shocked to discover that his body had been discovered with two bullets in the head, suggesting that a German pilot may have murdered him after bailing out of his aeroplane.

At dawn on 10 May 1940, the day of the German invasion, *Luftwaffe* aircraft attacked the air base at Xaffévilliers, destroying six Hawks. By 15 May, GC II/4 was down to seven operational aircraft, which shot down a Heinkel He 111 bomber, four Bf 109s and possibly a Henschel Hs 126 observation aircraft for no loss. The good luck continued for GC II/4 when four enemy aircraft were destroyed the next day for no loss. Unfortunately, the aforementioned state of chaos with regard to preparing France for war was still evident when some GC II/4 pilots were shocked to discover that new Curtiss H-75A-3s being prepared at Châteaudun had vital equipment missing – including radios.

On 16 June, GC II/4 lost its second commanding officer in nine months when Commandant (Major) Borne took off on a reconnaissance sortie near Châtillon-sur-Seine and was shot down by three Bf 109s. The next day, nine unserviceable Curtisses were set on fire by ground crews at Dun-sur-Auron before 23 remaining were flown to Meknès in Morocco. GC II/4 was disbanded on 25 August 1940, having been credited with 14 aircraft shot down during the *Drôle de guerre* and another 37 after the invasion, for the loss of eight pilots killed, seven wounded and one taken prisoner.

Figures for aircraft losses during the Battle of France are still debated, although it is reasonable to suggest that the French did inflict considerable losses on the Germans. General Albert Kesselring, reflected that *Luftwaffe* effectiveness had been reduced to almost 30 percent of what it had been before the invasion of France. The armistice of 22 June 1940 did not necessarily mean the end of the war for French pilots, those who escaped from France fought on in the Free French Forces (*Forces Françaises Libres*) and those who remained flew for the French Armistice Air Force on behalf of the Vichy government.

Vichy: June 1940 – December 1942

In a parallel of what had happened to Germany after World War I, the French government, now with its seat moved to Vichy, was forced by the Germans to accept its terms for a reduced army and navy, both of which would be only strong enough to maintain order in France and in its colonies. (It is of interest to note that France was allowed to keep her colonies, whereas Germany had been forced to cede all of hers under the terms of the Treaty of Versailles, signed in June 1919.) Germany ordered that, with regard to the warplanes that had survived the Battle of France, including those now stationed in Tunisia, Algeria and Morocco, they were to be surrendered, either in whole or else already disassembled, if not destroyed altogether – again a parallel of what had happened to Germany's air force in 1919.

However, Vichy's air force was spared (for the moment) from non-existence owing to the consequences of an event, which would damage, if not completely change, the relationship between occupied France and free Britain. Winston Churchill had no intention of allowing the French Navy's capital ships to remain intact so long as there was any chance of them essentially becoming adjuncts of the *Kriegsmarine* (German navy). The last thing he wanted was for the Kriegsmarine to bolstered enough to attempt an invasion of Britain.

He implemented the plan – codenamed "Operation Catapult" – for a British fleet, coded "Force H" and based in Gibraltar, to sail to the harbour of Mers-el-Kébir, near Oran in Algeria, where four capital ships and other vessels were stationed, in order to persuade Admiral Marcel-Bruno Gensoul to disobey orders from Vichy and have his vessels sail either to British waters or else to those of French colonies in the Far East or even to the (still neutral) USA with a view to preventing them from being used against the Allies. The overture was soundly rejected, so Royal Navy Admiral James Somerville gave the orders to destroy the French vessels. More than 2,000 sailors allegedly died in the attack, carried out on 3 July 1940, which saw one battleship sunk and two others severely damaged. The incident predictably stunned the French and gave the Germans a golden propaganda tool to discredit the British as France's real enemies.

Vichy and Berlin agreed, if reluctantly, that the ***Armée de l'Air de Vichy*** (as it is termed) was still needed in case French interests were to be attacked by the British once again – and, of course, for attacking the British themselves. Goering ordered that all *Armée de l'Air* aircraft would now be identified by special markings on the fuselage and tailplane of each one. Initially, the rear fuselage and tailplane (excluding the rudder) were painted a bright yellow, yet the markings were later changed so that they consisted of horizontally-oriented red and yellow stripes. In all cases, French national markings (roundel on the fuselage and tricolor on the tailplane) were retained as before.

Nearly three months afterwards, on 23 September 1940, the Vichy air force saw action again when the British tried to take Dakar, the capital of Senegal, after a failed attempt (as at Mers-el-Kébir) to persuade the French to join the Allied cause against the Axis. This time, however, the French managed to repulse the British torpedo-bomber attacks launched from the carrier HMS *Ark Royal* during several days of fighting with only light casualties on their side.

Syrian-based Vichy air force units saw action against the British from April 1941, when a *coup d'état* in Iraq briefly installed the nationalist Rashid Ali Al-Gaylani as prime minister of in order to secure the vital oil supplies at Kirkuk (under British control since 1934) in northeastern Iraq for the pro-Axis nationalists who wanted the British to be expelled from the country. However, the RAF base at Habbaniya withstood the nationalists, and in May the British, Indian and Commonwealth "Iraqforce" invaded Iraq *via* Basra. The ensuing Anglo-Iraqi War ended with Iraqforce defeating the nationalists at the end of May and restoring a pro-Allied government in Iraq.

Allied operations during the Anglo-Iraqi War included attacks on Vichy air force bases in Lebanon and Syria, which served as staging posts for *Regia Aeronautica* and *Luftwaffe* units flying to Mosul to support the Iraqi nationalist *coup*. Then in June 1941 British, Commonwealth, Empire and Free French forces invaded Syria and Lebanon. Vichy French air units, some of which were equipped with Dewoitine D.520 fighters and US-built Martin Maryland bombers had initial air superiority, but the Allied invaders inflicted heavy casualties on Vichy air and ground forces. By mid-July the Allied invasion was victorious and put Syria and Lebanon under Free French control.

Operation Torch: November 8–10, 1942

The last major battles against the Allied forces, in which the Vichy French air force took part, took place during Operation Torch, launched on 8 November 1942 as the Allied invasion of North Africa. Facing the U.S. Navy task force headed for Morocco, consisting of the carriers *Ranger*, *Sangamon*, *Santee* and *Suwannee*, were, in part, Vichy squadrons based at Marrakech, Meknès, Agadir, Casablanca and Rabat, which between them could muster some 86 fighters and 78 bombers. Overall, the aircraft may have been old compared to the Grumman F4F Wildcats of the U.S. Navy, yet they were still dangerous and capable in the hands of combat veterans who had seen action against both the Germans and the British since the start of the war.

Wildcats attacked the airfield at Rabat-Salé around 07.30 on the 8th and destroyed nine LeO 451 bombers of GB I/22, while a transport unit's full complement of various types was almost entirely wiped out. At Casablanca, Douglas SBD Dauntless dive-bombers succeeded in damaging the French battleship *Jean Bart*, and Wildcats strafed the bombers of GB I/32 at Camp Cazes airfield, some of which exploded as they were ready for take-off with bombs already on board, thus ensuring their mission never went ahead. The U.S. Navy did not have it all their own way, though, as several Wildcat pilots were shot down and taken prisoner.

The day's victory tally of enemy aircraft shot down by the French fighter pilots totaled seven confirmed and three probable, yet their losses were considered heavy – five pilots killed, four wounded and 13 aircraft destroyed either in combat or on the ground – when one considers that GC II/5, based in Casablanca, had lost only two pilots killed during the whole of the six-week campaign in France two years before. In the meantime, Wildcats of U.S. Navy Fighter Squadron VF-41 from *Ranger* strafed and destroyed three U.S.-built Douglas DB-7 bombers of GB I/32, which were being refueled and rearmed at Casablanca, leaving three others undamaged.

Nevertheless, having been reinforced by two other bombers, GB I/32 carried out a bombing mission against the beaches at Safi, where more U.S. soldiers were landing, the next morning. One of the bombers was damaged and attempted to make a forced landing, only it exploded upon contact with the ground, killing the entire crew. Fighter unit GC I/5 lost four pilots in combat that day (9 November) and it was on that same day that *Adjudant* (Warrant Officer) Bressieux had the distinction of becoming the last pilot in the Vichy French air force to claim a combat victory, in this case a Wildcat of VF-9. Shortly afterwards, 13 Wildcats attacked the airfield at Médiouna and destroyed a total of 11 French aircraft, including six from GC II/5.

On the morning of 10 November 1942, the Vichy French air force units in Morocco had a mere 37 combat-ready fighters and 40 bombers left to face the might of the U.S. Navy Wildcats. Médiouna was attacked once again and several of the fighters were left burning, while two reconnaissance Potez were shot down, one by an F4F Wildcat and the other by an SBD Dauntless over the airfield at Chichaoua, where three Wildcats would later destroy four more Potez in a strafing attack.

Ultimately, the presence of Vichy France in North Africa as an ally of the Germans came to an end on Armistice Day, 11 November 1942, when General Noguès, the commander-in-chief of the Vichy armed forces, requested a ceasefire; that did not stop a unit of U.S. Navy aircraft from attacking the airfield at Marrakech and destroying several French aircraft, apparently on the initiative of the unit's commander. Once the ceasefire request was accepted, the war between the Allies and the Vichy French came to an end, after two and a half years of what was termed "fratricidal" fighting.

"Torch" had resulted in a victory for the Allies, even though it was fair to say that the French had no choice but to engage the Americans, otherwise the Americans would (and did) engage them since they were technically enemies. As a result, 12 air force and 11 navy pilots lost their lives in the final four days of combat between (Vichy) France and the Allies during World War II. Barely two weeks later, the Germans invaded the then-unoccupied zone of metropolitan France and ordered the complete dissolution of the Vichy French armed forces on 1 December 1942. Those units then not under Vichy control would then be free to join with their Free French colleagues to fight the common enemy: Nazi Germany.

Further reading

- Alexander, Martin S. *The Republic in danger: General Maurice Gamelin and the politics of French defence, 1933–1940* (Cambridge University Press, 2003)
- Ballarini, Phillippe (2001), "Where is the French Air Force?", article translated by Mike Leveillard and posted on Aerostories website[323]
- Cain, Anthony C. *Forgotten Air Force: French Air Doctrine in the 1930s* (Smithsonian History of Aviation and Spaceflight Series, 2002)
  - Cain, Anthony C. "Neither Decadent, Nor Traitorous, Nor Stupid: The French Air Force and Air Doctrine in the 1930s" (PhD dissertation, Ohio State University 2000) online[324]; Bibliography pp 231-
- Christienne, Charles. *French Military Aviation: A Bibliographical Guide*. New York: Garland, 1989.
- Doughty, Robert A. *The Seeds of Disaster: The Development of French Army Doctrine, 1919–39* (Stackpole Books, 2014)
- Doughty, Robert A. *The Breaking Point: Sedan and the Fall of France, 1940* (Stackpole Books, 2014)
- Duroselle, Jean-Baptiste. *France and the Nazi Threat: The Collapse of French Diplomacy 1932–1939* (2013); translation of his *La Décadence, 1932–1939* (1979) 508pp
- Gunsburg, Jeffery A. *Divided and conquered: the French high command and the defeat of the West, 1940* (Greenwood, 1979)

- Haight, John McVickar. *American aid to France, 1938–1940* (1970)
- Higham, Robin. *Two Roads to War: The French and British Air Arms from Versailles to Dunkirk* (Naval Institute Press, 2012)
- Jackson, Julian. *The Fall of France: The Nazi Invasion of 1940* (2003)
- Kiesling, Eugenia C. *Arming against Hitler: France and the limits of military planning* (University Press of Kansas, 1996)
- Kirkland, Faris R. "The French Air Force in 1940: Was it defeated by the Luftwaffe or by Politics?." *Air University Review* 36 (1985): 101–17
- Kirkland, Faris R. "French Air Strength in May 1940," *Air Power History* (1993) 40#1 pp 22–34.
- Porch, Douglas. "Military "culture" and the fall of France in 1940: A review essay." *International Security* 24#4 (2000): 157–180.
- Van Haute, Andre. *Pictorial History of the French Air Force: 1909–40*; *Pictorial History of the French Air Force: 1941–74* (2 vol. 1975)
- Vennesson, Pascal. "Institution and airpower: The making of the French air force." *Journal of Strategic Studies* 18#1 (1995): 36–67.
- Young, Robert J. *In Command of France: French Foreign Policy and Military Planning, 1933–1940* (Harvard Univ Pr, 1978)

In French

- Ehrengardt, Christian-Jacques (2000), *La chasse française: le GC II/4*, in *Aéro-Journal* magazine, edition #16 (December 2000 – January 2001), *Aéro-Editions SARL*, Fleurance, pp. 60–63 (print edition in French)
- Ehrengardt, Christian-Jacques (2004), *Casablanca: 8 novembre 1942: les Américains débarquent*, in *Aéro-Journal* magazine, edition #35 (February–March 2004), *Aéro-Editions SARL*, Fleurance, pp. 4–31 (print edition in French)
- Olivier, Jean-Marc, (ed.), *Histoire de l'armée de l'air et des forces aériennes françaises du XVIIIe siècle à nos jours* [History of the French Air Force since the 18th century to the present], Toulouse, Privat, 2014, 552 p.
- Osché, Philippe (2000), *"Mécano aux Cigognes"*, in *Aéro-Journal* magazine, edition #13 (June–July 2000), *Aéro-Editions SARL*, Fleurance, pp. 51–56 (print edition in French)

External links

- Acepilots.com article on the Lafayette Escadrille[325]
- Acepilots.com article on Raoul Lufbery[326]
- City of Rheims web site[327] A comprehensive history of aviation as pertains to the city of Rheims (in French)

- Official Government of France Defense Department[328] Website pages detailing the history of the Armée de l'Air to 1914 (in French)
- Official Government of France Defense Department[329] Website pages detailing the history of the Armée de l'Air from 1914 to 1918 (in French)
- Official Government of France Defense Department[330] Website pages detailing the history of the Armée de l'Air from 1918 to 1939 (in French)
- SLHADA (Société Lyonnaise d'Histoire et de Documentation Aéronautique) website[331] SLHADA is a Lyons-based society dealing with the history of the city and its aviation roots in particular (in French)
- Spartacus (UK-based) – a web site for schools[332]
- WWI Aircraft Profile Gallery: France[333] *An Illustrated History of World War I*

History of the Armée de l'Air in the colonies (1939–62)

History of the *Armée de l'Air*[334]
History of the Armée de l'Air (1909–1942)
Free French Air Force
Vichy French Air Force
History of the Armée de l'Air in the colonies (1939–62)

Indochina (1939–1940)

The outbreak of the war in Europe in September 1939 did not immediately affect the status of the Armée de l'Air in French Indochina because it had the task of defending a wide area of Southeast Asia, including the future Laos, Cambodia and Vietnam. And yet its array of airplanes seemed inadequate to perform any kind of real defense against any incursion by an enemy, because there were less than 100 airplanes available to it, all obsolescent or obsolete. In September 1931, Japan invaded and occupied Manchuria. This was an area of northeast China, which encompassed the provinces of Jilin, Liaoning and Heilongjiang. Nearly six whole years later, in July 1937, the Second Sino-Japanese War had begun. As yet, the French colonial authorities were hoping that the Japanese would not be brazen enough to take on the might of a European power. However, it became increasingly likely after the German invasion of Poland in September 1939, since Japan was part of the Axis alliance and thus Germany's ally.

On September 26, 1940, Japanese troops landed in Haiphong, violating a cease-fire which had been signed only the previous day. From the middle of the following month, the French became heavily involved in repelling Japanese army assaults.

The French-Thai War (1940–1941)

Following the Fall of France in 1940, Thais perceived a chance to regain the territories they had lost years earlier. The collapse of Metropolitan France made the French hold on Indochina tenuous. After the Japanese invasion of French Indochina in September 1940, the French were forced to allow the Japanese to set up military bases. This seemingly subservient behavior convinced the Thai regime that Vichy France would not seriously resist a confrontation with Thailand.

French forces in Indochina consisted of an army of approximately fifty thousand men, The most obvious deficiency of the French army lay in its shortage of armor; however, the Armée de l'Air had in its inventory approximately a hundred aircraft, of which around sixty could be considered first line. These consisted of thirty Potez 25 TOEs, four Farman 221s, six Potez 542s, nine Morane M.S.406s, and eight Loire 130 flying boats.[335]

The Thai Army was a relatively well-equipped force. Consisting of some sixty thousand men, with artillery and tanks. The Royal Thai Navy—consisting of several vessels, including two coastal defence ships, twelve torpedo boats and four submarines—was inferior to the French naval forces, but the Royal Thai Air Force held both a quantitative and qualitative edge over l'Armee de l'Air.[336] Among the 140 aircraft that composed the air force's first-line strength were twenty-four Mitsubishi Ki-30 light bombers, nine Mitsubishi Ki-21 and six Martin B-10 twin-engine bombers, seventy Vought Corsair dive bombers, and twenty-five Curtiss Hawk 75 fighters.[337]

While nationalistic demonstrations and anti-French rallies were held in Bangkok, border skirmishes erupted along the Mekong frontier. The superior Royal Thai Air Force conducted daytime bombing runs over Vientiane, Sisophon, and Battambang with impunity. The French retaliated with their own planes, but the damage caused was less than equal. The activities of the Thai air force, particularly in the field of dive-bombing,[338] was such that Admiral Jean Decoux, the governor of French Indochina, grudgingly remarked that the Thai planes seemed to have been flown by men with plenty of war experience.[339]

In early January 1941, the Thai Burapha and Isan Armies launched their offensive on Laos and Cambodia. French resistance was instantaneous, but many units were simply swept along by the better-equipped Thai forces. The Thais swiftly took Laos, but Cambodia proved a much harder nut to crack.

On January 16, 1941 the French launched a large counterattack on the Thai-held villages of Yang Dang Khum and Phum Preav, initiating the fiercest battle of the war. Because of over-complicated orders and nonexistent intelligence, the French counterattacks were cut to pieces and fighting ended with a French withdrawal from the area. The Thais were unable to pursue the retreating French, as their forward tanks were kept in check by the gunnery of French Foreign Legion artillerists.

On January 24, the final air battle took place when Thai bombers raided the French airfield at Angkor near Siem Reap. The last Thai mission commenced at 0710 hours on January 28, when the Martins of the 50th Bomber Squadron set out on a raid on Sisophon, escorted by three Hawk 75Ns of the 60th Fighter Squadron.[340,341]

The Japanese mediated the conflict, and a general armistice was arranged to go into effect on January 28. On May 9 a peace treaty was signed in Tokyo,[342,343] with the French being coerced by the Japanese into relinquishing their hold on the disputed territories.

About 30% of the French aircraft were rendered unserviceable by the end of the war, some as a result of minor damage sustained in air raids that remained unrepaired.[344] The Armée de l'Air admitted the loss of one Farman F221 and two Morane M.S.406s destroyed on the ground, but in reality its losses were greater.[345]

In the course of its first experience of combat, the Royal Thai Air Force claimed to have shot down five French aircraft and destroyed seventeen on the ground, for the loss of three of its own in the air and another five to ten destroyed in French air raids on Thai airfields.

Post Pearl Harbor 1941–1945

The month of December 1941 was a watershed in the war in the Pacific, yet the French aircraft were more or less left to deteriorate on the ground from that time on as Japan began, firstly, to impose what would today be termed "no-fly" zones over the conquered territory and, subsequently, to demand that airfields in French control be surrendered. Cut off from (Nazi-occupied) Europe, the Armée de l'Air in Indochina became an air force virtually in name only, as lack of fuel and spares kept aircraft grounded, forcing the authorities to strike them off charge progressively as the war progressed.

In March 1945, Japan decided to neutralize altogether the token French presence in Indochina, initially by capturing the high-ranking French service chiefs

Figure 213: *A French A-26C in Indochina.*

at their headquarters in the capital, Saigon. Despite having less than 30 antiquated aircraft remaining in serviceable condition, though, the *Armée de l'Air* responded to this aggression and inflicted heavy casualties Wikipedia:Citation needed on Japanese troops, who were pursuing French forces withdrawing towards China,Wikipedia:Citation needed where they did benefit from being re-armed with U.S.-built hardware.

The last years of French colonialism in Indochina (1945–1954)

Japan, even though a defeated power by the summer of 1945, exploited long-standing Vietnamese resentment of French colonialism. The first signs of the beginning of the end of the French empire in Indochina came when Vietnamese insurgents attacked and killed French residents in Saigon, prompting the French to send in a combat command (light brigade) of Leclerc's old 2nd Armored Division, among other troops, to help restore order. The *Armée de l'Air* reinforced the army units in the guise of the so-called *Groupe marchant de l'extrême-orient* (the Far East Forward Group), which included U.S.-built aircraft such as the ubiquitous Douglas C-47 Skytrain, totaling eighteen in number after reinforcements had been brought in. In November 1945, the personnel of the 1st Fighter Wing (consisting of GC I/7 and II/7) arrived in

Saigon, but without airplanes. Later on, those units received the F.VIII and F.IX variants of the British Supermarine Spitfire. However, the complement was completed with seized Japanese aircraft, mostly ones dedicated to liaison duties. Although the C-47s were not bombers, a lot of them were jury-rigged in order to fulfill bombing missions over the nine years which remained to the French empire in Indochina. By March 1946, the *Armée de l'Air* consisted of four units, two of which were fighter units equipped with the Spitfire F.IX, a transport/bombing unit equipped with the C-47 and a further one consisting of examples of the Junkers Ju 52/3m. Indeed, the only French-built aircraft available were Morane-Saulnier MS.500 and Nord NC.702 liaison aircraft, which would be used for observation and evacuation duties as well. (The MS.500 was actually a copy of the German Fieseler Fi 156 "*Storch*" (Stork) aircraft.). By March 1947, the "*Cigognes*" and "*Alsace*" fighter groups had come to Indochina, and they had been joined by the "*Corse*" group, equipped with the de Havilland Mosquito. However, just as their RAF counterparts had experienced when stationed in Burma during World War II, the aircraft, dubbed the "Wooden Wonder" by the British, began to deteriorate as a result of their exposure to a climate that they were not designed to operate in at all. That same month, the Nam-Dinh garrison was encircled, so the transport groups were called upon to drop over 350 airborne troops in order to relieve the besieged troops and thus break the enemy's encirclement. Little by little, the insurgents, fighting the French as a guerrilla army, began to perfect the art and science of guerrilla warfare.

The future capitals of North and South Vietnam would witness the presence of *Armée de l'Air* fighter units during the summer and autumn of 1949, as the situation began to deteriorate. Units were relocated from North Africa to Indochina, including I/5 "*Vendée*" and II/5 "*Ile de France*" which were equipped with the Bell P-63 and would remain in theater until January 1951. Firstly, they were stationed at Saigon's main military airbase at Tan Son Nhut before being relocated to the future North Vietnamese capital, where II/6, better known as the famous and highly decorated "*Normandie-Niemen*" fighter regiment from their stint in the Soviet Union between 1942 and 1945, joined them. They were certainly needed, as they participated in counterattacks against Viet Minh guerrillas encircling French army positions in the Tonkin region.

Fresh from establishing the People's Republic, the new Maoist government of mainland China began to provide logistical support to the insurgents short of actually supplying troops, something that China would do during the war in Korea, which would start in late June 1950. Communist expansion into what remained of "free" South-East Asia (apart from Japan, which was still under U.S. occupation at the time) seemed inevitable, and so the U.S. government under Harry S. Truman began to revise their position. In March, General Hartmann, who commanded the *Armée de l'Air* in Indochina until his death in an

Figure 214: *Frenchs Grumman F8F Bearcat in Đà Nẵng, 1954.*

air crash in April 1951, wanted to create a "Battle Air Corps" composed of four fighter, two bomber and four transport groups. Jets were in service with the U.S. Air Force and the U.S. Navy at this time, yet Hartmann believed that they were actually not up to the task of dealing with insurgents as opposed to fighting conventional armies on the ground.

As a result, piston-engined fighters, such as the F8F Bearcat, an aircraft from the Grumman stable with one of the most powerful piston engines ever developed for a single-engined aircraft, the Pratt & Whitney P&W R-2800 radial engine, would be used to combat the insurgents. With this powerful engine (2100 hp), the Bearcat was probably the fastest propeller-driven aircraft with a maximum speed of over 450 mph. (The Americans would follow their lead in their war against the Viet Minh by using the Douglas A-1 Skyraider piston-engined aircraft during the 1960s.) For the task of dropping large "hardware" on guerrilla groups, the twin-engined bomber Douglas B-26 Invader would also be chosen. A revised command structure for the *Armée de l'Air* in Indochina was also put in effect with the creation of three *Groupes aériens tactiques* (Gatac) ("Aerial Tactical Groups"): Gatac North in Hanoi, Gatac Center in Hué and Gatac South in Saigon/Tan Son Nhut. Renewed fighting between the French and the insurgents (in the guise of the 308th and 312th Divisions, commanded by Vo Nguyen Giap) broke out in January 1951 at Vinh Yen, located in the Tonkin region. Air cover for the French army's "mobile groups" led by de Lattre was provided by two fighter groups, namely III/6 *"Roussillon"* and I/9 *"Limousin,"* which were able to muster about forty P-63s, and these were reinforced by eight F6Fs lent from II/6 "Normandie Niemen" and I/6 *"Corse*." During the month, more than 1,700 fighter sorties were flown by 114 out of the 147 aircraft, mostly from Gatac North, then in service protecting Hanoi, while the *"Normandie-Niemen"* fighter group was charged with the protection of the southern sector. French bombing capability was very much enhanced with the operational missions flown by dedicated B-26 bombers, assigned to GB I/19 *"Gascogne,"* during the battle for Mao-Khe (which was the center of the coal mine region in northern Vietnam, and its loss would hurt the French) to protect Haiphong. Giap himself was partly to blame for the fact that the Viet Minh had been trounced, since air power, which had seen Vinh Yen remain in French hands, and naval power, which had seen Mao Khe remain in French hands, were beyond his experience, and he had thus not planned for them. The *Armée de l'Air*, now under the command of Chassin, Hartmann's successor, managed to support the French army in repelling a new insurgency from late May to early June 1951, having at its disposal some 48 F8Fs and 23 P-63s in the fighter groups, yet its bomber arm was down to a mere eight B-26s. In support were a combined total of 40 C-47s and Ju-52s. Several months later, after about 6,000 French troops had been killed by Viet Minh insurgents, General Jean de Lattre de Tassigny became commander-in-chief of all the then-190,000-strong French Expeditionary Corps in Indochina (having previously been the commander-in-chief of the Free French forces during the Second World War). He decided to reverse the trend and have the French armed forces adopt an offensive stance as opposed to a defensive one. De lattre won crushing victories at Vinh yen, Mao khé and on the Day. The viet minh never attacked again hanoï after this. But he was the nrapatrieted to France without have destroyed the viet minh. He would die of cancer in January 1952 after being promoted—almost posthumously—to the rank of Marshal of France. Despite Chassin's call for substantial reinforcements for the *Armée de l'Air*, whose personnel in theater had been subject to the punishing pace of conducting operations for months, it was ignored. Gatac-Laos, grouping fighters and bombers aircraft which had been requisitioned from various units, was created as a reaction to a Viet Minh offensive in Laos, launched in April 1953. Three months later, 56 F8Fs and ten B-26s, as well as MS.500s and helicopters, participated in *Operation Hirondelle* ("Swallow"), whose objective was to destroy the *matériel* provided to the insurgents by Maoist China, yet the Viet Minh did not suffer significantly as a result. The arms were being transported along what became famous as the so-called "Ho Chi Minh trail", and, in November 1953, to counter this, the French military decided to choose a site near the border with Laos, from which missions could be launched to strike against both Giap's insurgent army in order to eliminate it altogether. Its name was Dien Bien Phu, and it became operational on the 24th of the month, four days after General Henri Navarre launched Operation "Castor".

Dien Bien Phu: the last gasp in Indochina (January–May 1954)

By the beginning of 1954, Dien Bien Phu alone required 20 C-119s and 50 C-47s, so, on January 2, Navarre's second-in-command asked for additional aircraft and crews under the so-called "Navarre Plan." U.S. President Eisenhower, fearing both domestic and international backlashes if he were to send in U.S. troops, sent an American mission to Indochina to determine the extent of help that the French needed. Following a personal letter from the French prime minister, Joseph Laniel, Eisenhower authorized the loan of aircraft with French markings painted on them and flown by crews from Civil Air Transport (CAT), a commercial airline, which had been started in 1946 by then-retired Major General Chennault, the famous commander of the American Volunteer Group (AVG), better known as the "Flying Tigers", in China during World War II, and then purchased by the CIA in the year war broke out in Korea. He further authorized the dispatch of American "specialists" to Indochina, that is, mechanics from the Far East Air Force (FEAF) of the USAF. Once sworn to secrecy owing to the political ramifications of their presence, they would go to work on B-26s at Da Nang (then called Tourane) in the south and on C-47s at Do Son, located south of Haiphong, in the north, respectively. (In fact, Eisenhower was so concerned about their presence, which itself caused the Chinese government to label the American mechanics as "combatants", that he told U.S. Secretary of State John Foster Dulles that he wanted them withdrawn by the end of June 1954 no matter what the situation in Indochina was at that time.)

The first Viet Minh artillery attacks against the base came on March 16, 1954, as a result of which six French F8Fs, five MS.500s and two helicopters were destroyed. The French response could only come from bases located in the northern sector. The Armée de l'Air mustered two fighter groups with F8Fs, two bomber groups with B-26s, while the *Aéronavale* (naval aviation) could muster F6F Hellcats, SB2C Helldivers, F4AU-1 and four-engined PB4Y Privateers (navalized versions of the B-24 Liberator heavy bomber). The transport groups provided approximately 100 C-47s, but there were also the twelve Fairchild C-119Cs "Boxcars" crewed by 24 CAT personnel, to air-drop to the French garrison personnel, food, ammunition, and artillery pieces, as well as tons of barbed wire and other supplies. There was some initial friction between the French and the Americans, as the French commander at the base lodged complaints that the CAT crews were not actually following instructions directly, though this was more to do with a language barrier, as few, if any, of the CAT crews had any Francophone linguistic skills that could allow them to communicate well with the French air traffic controllers. Fortunately, the French garrison included British-born Legionnaires, so they were used as interpreters. As a result, the 37 CAT pilots excelled at their duties, flying a total of 682 missions over Dien Bien Phu and earning the respect of the French. (This respect was finally recognized half a century later when seven of the surviving CAT pilots were created *Chevaliers de la Légion d'Honneur* at a special ceremony at the French embassy in Washington, D.C., on February 24, 2005.)

At the same time, however, the insurgents were equipped with Soviet-made weaponry, including 37-mm antiaircraft guns, which were to take a toll of the U.S. and French aircraft trying to attack their forces, including with napalm, in an effort to repel them and thus relieve the besieged garrison, which eventually capitulated to Giap's troops on May 7, 1954. In total, the French lost sixty-two aircraft destroyed or severely damaged in the last major battle fought in French Indochina, which, as a colony, was consigned to history with the signing of an agreement in Geneva in July to carve up Vietnam into two countries along the 17th parallel. France, though, was permitted to maintain a small military presence in the new Republic of Vietnam, known to the West as South Vietnam, and the Americans still present were also permitted to remain, servicing the *Armée de l'Air's* contingent of B-26s and C-47s, plus the C-119s. They even packed parachutes for French airborne troops. The Americans left Vietnam eventually on September 6, 1954, albeit five days after the original leaving date promised by the French. Other *Armée de l'Air* units were meanwhile dedicating itself to the training of Vietnamese Air Force (VNAF) technical and flight personnel at Nha-Trang.

Algeria: the last days of empire in North Africa (1954–1962)

After the fall of the French empire in Indochina, the French Empire was crumbling, as more and more countries vied for independence from Paris. Yet the post-1945 era was one of massive decolonization, and France was having to deal with the realities that went with being a colonial power.

France still maintained a sizable presence in North Africa with countries such as Algeria, Morocco and Tunisia as colonies. Yet uprisings were on the rise in the 1950s, undoubtedly inspired by the Viet Minh victory over French expeditionary forces, as it showed that a "mighty" European power could be dislodged from "conquered" territory.

To meet this threat, the French expanded their presence in North Africa. For the *Armée de l'Air* in particular, it meant being equipped primarily with U.S.-built aircraft, as had been the case in Indochina. One bomber type in the French armory was the B-26 Invader, equipped with two Pratt & Whitney R-2800 engines. The B-26 began to equip two bombardment wings from the autumn of 1956 onwards based in Algeria, starting with GB 1/91 *Gascogne*, based at Oran la Senia, followed three months later by GB 2/91 *Guyenne* based at Bône in eastern Algeria. The B-26 was used in four versions. The B-26B, with a solid nose equipped with 6 to 8 12,7 mm machines-guns and B-26C glass nosed aircraft were used as bombers and for close air support with rockets, bombs and napalm. The famous Norden bombsight fitted to B-26C's could help bombardiers to aim bombs (up to two tons) on targets accurately, even in bad weather. The RB-26 photo-reconnaissance version was used by ERP.1/32 *Armagnac*. In terms of organizational practice, four RB-26s were grouped alongside 16 B-26s. All these aircraft were designated to perform combat duties at a maximum range of some 600 kilometers from base with a maximum duration of 20 minutes over the target, or else up to 800 kilometers from base with a very short duration over the target. The final version was unofficially called the B-26N, a B-26C converted into a night fighter to interdict planes smuggling weapons from Tunisia. The glass nose was re-designed and equipped with British AI Mk.X radar taken from Meteor NF.11's. The B-26N was armed with two underwing gun pods with two 12,7 mm machine guns each and two rocket pods for air-to-air rockets.

The armor on the B-26 made it a particularly useful and versatile aircraft for both bombing and counter-insurgency operations. On March 15, 1957, for example, in the Nord-Constantanois area, a force of no less than 12 B-26s was sent to destroy insurgents hiding in the Movis forest. However, one mission flown on July 15, 1959, witnessed the use of napalm. French army paratroopers had been brought to a standstill by a rebel group near Rafaa, allowing the rebels to control a significant amount of terrain. A B-26 from GB 2/91 took off from Oran, armed with four containers of napalm under the wings. Contact with the army paratroopers proved to be difficult initially, and bad visibility—because it was already dark—did not help when the B-26 flew so low that it clipped some trees only meters away from the paratroopers themselves. Worse was the fact that the radio became temporarily inoperable. It was up to the pilot himself to release the napalm on his target even if he was flying at high speed and at (very) low altitude. Probably through blind luck, he managed to drop his load without endangering the lives of the paratroopers.

References

- Armée de l'Air[346]—Marcel Paquelier's website on his experiences in the Armée de l'Air also includes a history of the involvement of this air force in Indochina
- Embassy of France in Washington, D.C.[347]—Article about the honor ceremony for the seven CAT pilots who participated in the Dien Bien Phu battle
- Vietnam Veterans of America (VVA) website[348]—Article called "Mechanics at the Edge of War: U.S. Ground Forces in Vietnam, 1953-1954", written by John Prados
- The History Net website[349]—Article called "Setting the Stage in Vietnam" by David T. Zabecki
- On War website[350]—"A timeline of events, 1800-1999: French Indochina War, 1946-1954"
- Aerostories: Algeria 1954-1962[351]—Patrick-Charles Renaud's article about the role in Algeria of the French army air corps (ALAT), entitled Bananes a l'assaut des djebels.
- Aerostories: Algeria 1954-1962[352]—Patrick-Charles Renaud's article about the B-26 bomber in Algeria.
- B-26.com[353]—Site dedicated to enthusiasts of the B-26 Marauder bomber.

French Air Force

	French Air Force
	Armée de l'Air
	Logo of the Armée de l'Air since 24 March 2010
Active	Part of the French Army in 1909 – An independent service arm in 1934 2 July 1934 (official)
Country	France
Type	Air force
Role	Aerial warfare
Size	41,160 personnel (2017)[354] 687 aircraft, of which 226 are combat aircraft.
Part of	French Armed Forces
Motto(s)	« Faire face » (French) (also motto of the École de l'air) « *Face honestly, truthfully & correctly*[355] *straight forward* » (Eng)
Engagements	World War I World War II Indochina War Algerian War Chadian–Libyan conflict Gulf War Kosovo War War in Afghanistan (2001–2014) Opération Harmattan Military intervention against ISIL
Website	www<wbr/>.defense<wbr/>.gouv<wbr/>.fr<wbr/>/air[356]
Commanders	
Chief of Staff of the French Air Force	Général d'armée aérienne André Lanata, since September 21, 2015
Insignia	
Identification symbol	
Aircraft flown	
Electronic warfare	Boeing E-3 Sentry

French Air Force

Fighter	Rafale, Mirage 2000.
Helicopter	Eurocopter AS532 Cougar, Eurocopter Fennec, Eurocopter EC725,
Trainer	Alpha jet, Pilatus PC-21, Socata TB 30 Epsilon, SAN Jodel D.140 Mousquetaire, SOCATA TBM, Extra EA-300
Transport	C-130, Airbus 310, Airbus 340, Airbus A400, Dassault Falcon 7X, Dassault Falcon 900, Dassault Falcon 2000, Transall C-160 C-135FR

The **French Air Force** (French: *Armée de l'Air Française*) [aʀme də lɛʀ], literally *Aerial Army*) is the air force of the French Armed Forces. It was formed in 1909 as the *Service Aéronautique*, a service arm of the French Army, then was made an independent military arm in 1934. The number of aircraft in service with the French Air Force varies depending on source, however sources from the French Ministry of Defence give a figure of 658 aircraft in 2014.[357,358] The French Air Force has 247 combat aircraft in service, with the majority being 137 Dassault Mirage 2000 and 110 Dassault Rafale. As of early 2017, the French Air Force employs a total of 41,160 regular personnel. The reserve element of the air force consisted of 5,187 personnel of the Operational Reserve.[359]

The Chief of Staff of the French Air Force (CEMAA) is a direct subordinate of the Chief of the Defence Staff (CEMA).

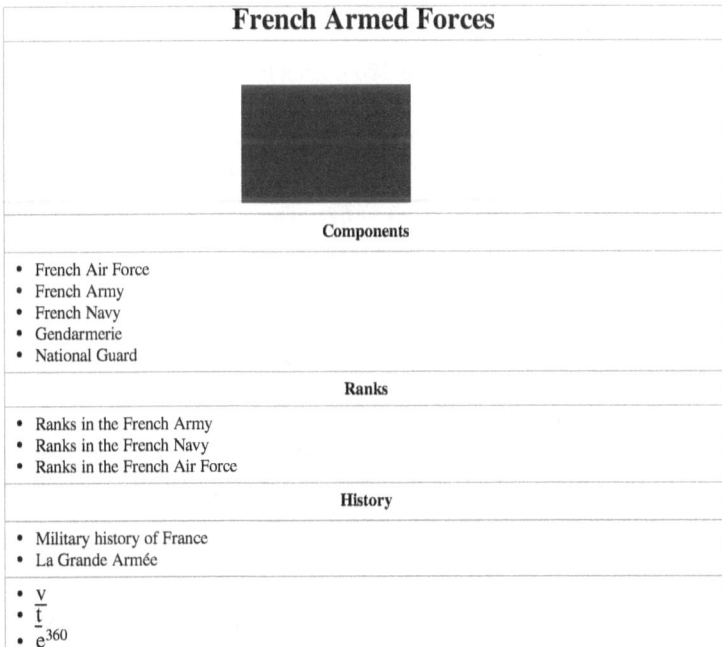

French Armed Forces

Components

- French Air Force
- French Army
- French Navy
- Gendarmerie
- National Guard

Ranks

- Ranks in the French Army
- Ranks in the French Navy
- Ranks in the French Air Force

History

- Military history of France
- La Grande Armée

- v
- t
- e[360]

Figure 215: *French aircraft during World War I, flying over German held territory, 1915.*

History

French military aviation was born in 1909. After the approval of the law by the French National Assembly on March 29, 1912,[361] French Military Aeronautics became officially part of the French Army, alongside the four traditional branches of the French Army, the infantry, cavalry, artillery and engineers.

France was one of the first states to start building aircraft. At the beginning of First World War, France had a total of 148 planes (8 from French Naval Aviation (Aéronautique navale) and 15 Airships. By the time of the armistice in November 1918, 3608 planes were in service.[362] 5,500 pilots and observers were killed from the 17,300 engaged in the conflict, amounting then to 31% of endured losses[363]

Military Aeronautics was established as a "special arm" by the law of December 8, 1922.[364] however, the later remained under the auspicious of the French Army. It wasn't until July 2, 1934, that the "special arm" became an independent service and was totally independent.

Figure 216: *A North American T-28 Trojan, used against guerrillas during the Algerian War.*

Interwar period

The initial air arm was also the cradle of French military parachuting, responsible for the first formation of the « Air Infantry Groups » Groupements de l'Infanterie de l'Air in the 1930s, out of which the Air Parachute Commandos (French: *commandos parachutistes de l'air*) descended.

The French Air Force maintained a continuous presence across the French colonial empire particularly from the 1920s to 1943.

World War II

The French Air Force played an important role, most notable during the Battle of France of 1940. The engagement of the Free French Air Forces from 1940 to 1943, then the engagement of the aviators of the French Liberation Army, were equally marking episodes of the History of the French Air Force. The sacrifices of Commandant René Mouchotte and Lieutenant Marcel Beau illustrated their devotion.

The Vichy French Air Force had a significant presence in the French Levant.

Figure 217: *Mirage IIIC of EC 2/10 "Seine" pictured in 1980 armed with a Matra R.530.*

1945–present

After 1945, France rebuilt its aircraft industry. The French Air Force participated in several colonial wars during the Empire such as French Indochina after the Second World War. Since 1945, the French Air Force was notably engaged in Indochina (1945–1954).

The French Air Force was also active in Algeria from 1952 until 1962 and Suez (1956), then later Mauritania and Chad, the Persian Gulf (1990–1991), ex-Yugoslavia and more recently in Afghanistan, Mali and Iraq.

From 1964 until 1971 the French Air Force had the unique responsibility for the French nuclear arm via Dassault Mirage IV or ballistic missiles of Air Base 200 Apt-Saint-Christol on the Plateau d'Albion.

Accordingly, from 1962, the French political leadership reprioritized its military emphasis on nuclear deterrence, implementing a complete reorganisation of the Air Force, with the creation of four air regions and seven major specialised commands, among which were the Strategic Air Forces Command, COTAM, the Air Command of Aerial Defense Forces (French: *Commandement Air des Forces de Défense Aérienne*, CAFDA), and the *Force aérienne tactique* (FATac).[365] In 1964 the Second Tactical Air Command was created at Nancy to take command of air units stationed in France but not assigned to NATO. The Military Air Transport Command had previously been

Figure 218: *A 1986 view of a Mirage F1 of Escadron de Chasse 2/30 Normandie-Niemen and another Mirage of Escadron de Chasse 3/30 Lorraine, armed with Matra R530. Both respective squadron insignias are visible on the aircraft.*

formed in February 1962 from the *Groupement d'Unités Aériennes Spécialisées*. Also created in 1964 was the *Escadron des Fusiliers Commandos de l'Air* (EFCA), seemingly grouping all FCA units. The Dassault Mirage IV, the principal French strategic bomber, was designed to strike Soviet positions as part of the French nuclear triad.

In 1985, the Air Force had four major flying commands, the Strategic Air Forces Command, the Tactical Air Forces Command, the Military Air Transport Command, and CAFDA (air defence).

CFAS had two squadrons of S2 and S-3 IRBMs at the Plateau d'Albion, six squadrons of Mirage IVAs (at Mont de Marsan, Cazaux, Orange, Istres, St Dizier, and EB 3/94 at Luxeuil), and three squadrons of C-135F, as well as a training/reconnaissance unit, CIFAS 328, at Bordeaux. The tactical air command included wings EC 3, EC 4, EC 7, EC 11, EC 13, and ER 33, with a total of 19 squadrons of Mirage III, Jaguars, two squadrons flying the Mirage 5F (EC 2/13 and EC 3/13, both at Colmar), and a squadron flying the Mirage F.1CR. CoTAM counted 28 squadrons, of which ten were fixed-wing transport squadrons, and the remainder helicopter and liaison squadrons, at least five of which were overseas. CAFDA numbered 14 squadrons mostly flying the Mirage F.1C. Two other commands had flying units, the Air Force Training

Command, and the Air Force Transmissions Command, with four squadrons and three trials units.

Dassault Aviation led the way mainly with delta-wing designs, which formed the basis for the Dassault Mirage III series of fighter jets. The Mirage demonstrated its abilities in the Six-Day War, Yom Kippur War, the Falklands War, and the Gulf War, becoming one of the most popular jet fighters of its day, selling very widely.

In 1994 the Commandment of the Fusiliers Commandos de l'Air was reestablished under a different form.

The French Air Force is expanding and replacing its aircraft inventory. The Air Force is awaiting the Airbus A400M military transport aircraft, which is still in development. As of late November 2016, 11 A400M aircraft had been delivered to ET00.061 at Orleans-Bricy, and integration of the new Dassault Rafale multi-role jet fighter was underway, whose first squadron of 20 aircraft became operational in 2006 at Saint-Dizier.

In 2009 France rejoined the NATO Military Command Structure, having been absent since 1966.[366] France was also a lead nation, alongside the United States, Great Britain and Italy in implementing the UN sponsored no-fly zone in Libya (NATO Operation Unified Protector), deploying 20 fighter aircraft to Benghazi in defense of rebel held positions and the civilian population.[367]

The last remaining squadron of Dassault Mirage F1s were retired in July 2014 and replaced by the Dassault Rafale.

Structure

The Chief of Staff of the French Air Force (CEMAA) determines French Air Force doctrines application and advises the Chief of the Defence Staff (CEMA) on the deployment, manner, and use of the Air Force. He is responsible for the preparation and logistic support of the French Air Force. The CEMAA is assisted by a Deputy Chief, the *Major Général de de l'Armée de l'Air*. Finally, the CEMAA is assisted by the Inspectorate of the French Air Force (IAA) and by the French Air Force Health Service Inspection (ISSAA).

The Air Force is organized in conformity to Chapter 4/ Title II/ Book II of the Third Part of the Defense Code (French: *code de la Défense*), which replaced decree n° 91-672 of July 14, 1991.

Under the authority of the Chief of Staff of the French Air Force (CEMAA) in Paris, the Air Force includes:

Figure 219: *Général d'armée aérienne André Lanata, chief of staff of the Armée de l'Air.*

- Chief of Staff of the French Air Force, heading the *Etat-major de l'Armee de l'air* (EMAA) ;
- Forces;
- Air Bases;
- Directorate of Human Resources of the French Air Force;
- Services.[368]

Air Force headquarters is co-located, alongside the Chief of the Defence Staff's offices (EMA) as well with Army and Navy headquarters at the Ballard site, more commonly known as the « French Pentagon » or « Balardgone ». It numbers 150 aviators. The new site succeeds the former Paris Air Base (BA 117), the air staff headquarters buildings, dissolved on June 25, 2015.

Commands

The French Air Force has three commands: two grand operational commands (CDAOA and CFAS) and one organic command (CFA)).

- Air Defense and Air Operations Command (French: *Commandement de la Défense Aérienne et des Opérations Aériennes* (CDAOA)), is responsible for surveillance of French airspace, as well as all aerial operations in progress. This command does not possess aircraft. Instead it exercises operational control over units of the Air Forces Command.

- Strategic Air Forces Command (CFAS)), is responsible for the air force's nuclear strike units (Mirage 2000 N and Dassault Rafale armed with ASMP-A missiles), as well as the tanker / strategic transport aircraft (C-135FR, Boeing KC-135 Stratotanker).
- Air Forces Command (CFA)), Bordeaux-Mérignac Air Base, as an organic command, prepares units to fulfill operational missions. From September 2013, the former organic commands CFA and CSFA were merged into CFA. CFA is organized in six brigades:
  - Fighter Brigade – (French: *Brigade Aérienne de l'Aviation de Chasse* (BAAC)), is responsible for all air defense, air-to-ground and reconnaissance aircraft (including Dassault Rafale, Mirage 2000-5F, Mirage 2000B/C/D, Transall C-160 Gabriel). In February 2016 it was commanded by Brigadier General (Air) Philippe Lavigne.
  - Projection and Support Air Force Brigade (French: *Brigade Aérienne d'Appui et de Projection* (BAAP)), is responsible for all tactical transport and liaison aircraft (aircraft and helicopters: Transall, C-160, Hercules C-130, A310/319, Dassault Falcon 50/900, Aérospatiale SA 330 Puma, Eurocopter Fennec, Eurocopter AS332 Super Puma, SOCATA TBM);
  - Airspace Control Brigade (French: *Brigade Aérienne de Contrôle de l'Espace* (BACE)), is responsible for (Airborne early warning and control aircraft, and ground radar, ground-based air defense systems and missile defence, communication networks) airspace surveillance, constituting the Système de Commandement et de Conduite des Opérations Aérospatiales). Since 2007 the command, control and information systems network of the air force have been is integrated into the Joint Directorate of Infrastructure Networks and Information Systems (DIRISI)).
  - Air Force Security and Intervention Forces Brigade (French: *Brigade Aérienne des Forces de Sécurité et d'Intervention* (BAFSI)), is responsible for units of the French Air Force's commando riflemen (Fusiliers Commandos de l'Air, tasked with special operations, CSAR and target acquisition), amongst which the most elite is the Air Force Parachute Commando n° 10, C.P.A 10 (, unit of the French Special Forces. The BAFSI also includes the security units of the air bases (34 squadrons (of company strength) and detachments (of platoon strength)) and the rescue and firefighting personnel (called *incident technicians* and grouped into *squadrons* of company size);
  - **Air Force Aerial Weapon Systems Brigade** (French: *Brigade Aérienne des Systèmes d'Armes Aériens* (BASAA)) provides the maintenance and repair of aerial weapons and target systems.
  - **Air Force Maneuver Support Brigade** (French: *Brigade Aérienne*

d'Appui à la Manœuvre Aérienne (BAAMA)) provides the ground-based engineer and logistics personnel (including expeditionary) needed for the sustainment of air operations.

These last two brigades belonged until 2013 to the Air Force Support Command (CSFA), which maintained the arms systems, equipment, information and communication systems (SIC) as well as infrastructure; the CSFA supported the human element, the military logistics (supply and transport), wherever forces of the French Air Force operated or trained; these two brigades are now subordinated to the CFA.

All air regions were disestablished on 1 January 2008. In the 1960s, there were five air regions (RA). The number was then reduced to four by a decree of June 30, 1962 with the disestablishment of the 5th Aerial Region (French North Africa). The decree of July 14, 1991 reduced the air regions to three: « RA Atlantic », « RA Mediterranean » and « RA North-East ». On July 1, 2000 was placed into effect an organization consisting of « RA North » (RAN) and « RA South » (RAS). The territorial division was abolished by decree n°2007-601 of April 26, 2007[369] . [370]

From 2008–2010 the French Air Force underwent the "Air 2010" streamlining process. The main targets of this project were to simplify the command structure, to regroup all military and civil air force functions and to rationalise and optimise all air force units. Five major commands, were formed, instead of the former 13, and several commands and units were disbanded.[371]

The Air Force directs the Joint Space Command.

Support services

The Directorate of Human Resources of the Air Force (DRH-AA) recruits, forms, manages administers and converts personnel of the French Air Force. Since January 2008, the DRH-AA groups the former directorate of military personnel of the French Air Force (DPMMA) and some tasks of the former Air Force Training Command. The directorate is responsible for Air Force recruitment via the recruiting bureau.

French joint defence service organisations, supporting the air force, include:

- The Integrated Structure of Maintaining Operational Conditioning of Aeronautical Defense Materials (French: *Structure Intégrée de Maintien en Condition Opérationnelle des Matériels Aéronautiques de la Défense*) (SIMMAD).
- The Aeronautical Industrial Service (French: *Service Industriel de l'Aéronautique*) (SIAE).

- The « Air Commissariat » (French: *« Commissariat de l'Air »*) between 1947 and 2007, then « Financial and General Administration Service » (French: *« Service de l'Administration Générale et des Finances » (SAGF)*) from 2008 until 2009, and finally the « Commissariat Service of the Armed Forces » (SCA) (French: *Service du Commissariat des Armées*) since 2010, have successively been designated as administrative services of the French Air Force. The Commissioners as well as Civilians of this service carry out : operations support, individual legal rights, judicial, internal control accountability, financial and purchase executions, and support and protection of the combatant.[372]

Wings

Commanded by a Lieutenant-colonel or Colonel, the Escadre is a formation that assembles various units and personnel dedicated to the same mission. The designation of « Escadre » was replaced with that of regiment in 1932 and was designated until 1994, a unit grouping :

- units (escadrons or groups) generally equipped with the same type of aircraft or at least assuring the same type of mission
- units of maintenance and support.

Escadres (wings) were dissolved from 1993 as part of the *Armées 2000* reorganisation, were reestablished in 2014.[373] The problems caused by having the aircraft maintenance units not responsible to the flying squadrons they supported eventually forced the change.

Four Escadres were reformed in the first phase:

- **31e Escadre Aérienne de Ravitaillement et de Transport Stratégiques at Istres-Le Tubé Air Base on 27 August 2014;**
- **36e Escadre de Commandement et de Conduite Aéroportée** at Avord Air Base on 5 September 2014;
- **Escadre Sol-Air de Défense Aérienne – 1er Régiment d'Artillerie de l'Air** (ESADA – 1er RAA) at Avord Air Base (3 September 2014) ;
- the **3e Escadre de Chasse** at Nancy-Ochey Air Base (5 September 2014)

In the second phase, the French Air Force announced in August 2015 the creation of six additional wings:

- the **8e Escadre de Chasse at Cazaux Air Base (25 August 2015) ;**
- the **4e Escadre de Chasse** at Saint-Dizier (26 August 2015)
- the **64e Escadre de Transport** at Évreux-Fauville Air Base (27 August 2015) ;
- the **2e Escadre de Chasse** at Luxeuil Air Base (3 September 2015) ;

- the **61e Escadre de Transport** (French: *fr:61e escadre de transport*) at Orléans – Bricy Air Base (1 September 2015) ;
- the **30e Escadre de Chasse at Mont-de-Marsan Air Base (3 September 2015).**

Also established was the **Escadre Aérienne de Commandement et de Conduite Projetable** (French: *Escadre Aérienne de Commandement et de Conduite Projetable*) at Évreux-Fauville Air Base on 27 August 2015.

The French Air Force also announced in August 2015 that unit numbering, moves of affected aircraft, and the transfer of historic material (flags, traditions and names) would be completed in 2016.

Squadrons and flights

Commanded by a lieutenant-colonel, the Escadron is the basic operational unit. This term replaced that of Group as of 1949 with the aim to standardize usage with the allies of NATO who were using the term 'squadron'. However, the term Group did not entirely disappear: the term was retained for the Aerial Group 56 Mix Vaucluse, specialized in Special Operations or Group – Groupe de Ravitaillement en Vol 02.091 Bretagne (French: *Groupe de Ravitaillement en Vol 02.091 Bretagne*) which is still carrying the same designation since 2004.

A fighter squadron (escadron) can number some twenty machines, spread in general in three Escadrilles. A Transport Escadron (French: *Escadron de Transport*) can theoretically count a dozen Transall C-160, however, numbers are usually much less for heavier aircraft (three Airbus A310-300 and two Airbus A340-200 for the Transport Escadron 3/60 Estérel (French: *Escadron de Transport 3/60 Estérel*)).

The squadrons have retained the designations of the former Escadres disbanded during in the 1990s. For instance: Transport Escadron 1/64 Béarn (French: *escadron de transport 1/64 Béarn*) (more specifically Transport Escadron 01.064 Béarn), which belonged to the 64th Transport Escadre (French: *64e Escadre de Transport*) during the dissolution of the later (recreated on August 2015). Not all escadrons (Squadrons) are necessarily attached to an Escadre.

The Escadrille (flight) has both an administrative and operational function, even of the essential operational control is done at the level of the Esacdron. A pilot is assigned to the Escadrille, however the equipment and material devices, on the other hand, are assigned to the Escadron. Since the putting into effect of the ESTA (Aeronautic Technical Support Escadrons), material devices and the mechanics are assigned directly to the base then put at disposition of the based Escadrons.

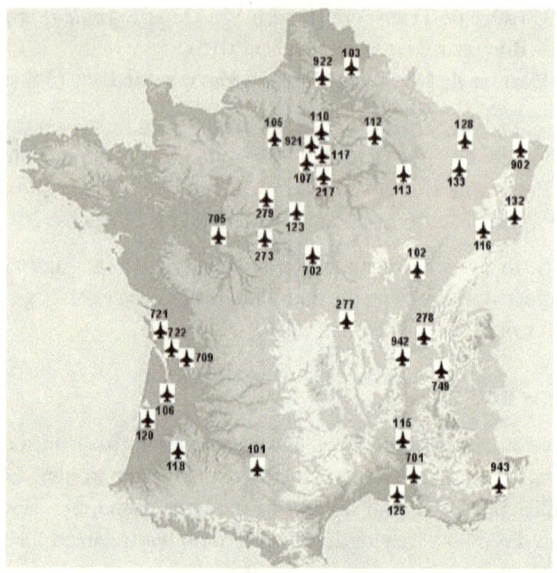

Figure 220: *Air bases in Metropolitan France.*

The Escadrilles adopted the traditions of the prestigious units out of which most (SPA and SAL),[374] are those traditions of the First World War.

Fusiliers Commandos de l'Air

The Fusiliers Commandos de l'Air comprise:[375]

- Protection squadrons (French: *escadron de protection*) (EP);
- Commando Parachutiste de l'Air 10 (CPA 10),
- Air Parachute Commando 20,
- Air Parachute Commando 30 (CPA 30)

Protection Squadrons protect airbases inside and outside the national territory, and in exterior operations as well.

The CPAs carry out common missions, as well as specialized tasks; including intervention and reinforcement of protection at the profit of sensible points « air » inside and outside the national territory.

Figure 221: *Crotale missile-launchers of the Air Defense Ground-to-Air Squadron of the French Air Force.*

Airbases

AirFlying activity in France is carried out by a network of bases, platforms and French air defence radar systems. It is supported by bases, which are supervised and maintained by staff, centres of operations, warehouses, workshops, and schools. Both in France and abroad, bases have similar infrastructure to provide standardised support.

The French Air Force has, as of August 1, 2014:

- Within the metropolitan territory of France, 27 airbases, out of the which 18 aeronautical platform with perceived runways and 5 Bases non platform, two schools, 3 air detachments and « one attached air element » (EAR).
- Beyond the metropole/Europe, 7 Aerial Bases or permanent detachments in overseas or country.

Some French air bases house radar units (e.g. Lyon, Mont-Verdun, Drachenbronn, Cinq-Mars-la-Pile, Nice, Mont-Agel) to carry out air defence radar surveillance and air traffic control. Others house material warehouses or command posts. Temporary and semi-permanent foreign deployments include transport aircraft at Dushanbe (Tajikistan, Operation Héraclès), and fighter aircraft in N'Djamena (Tchad, Opération Épervier), for instance.

Figure 222: *CABA 117 Paris, air force headquarters until 2015.*

As swift as the French Air Force operates, the closure of Aerial Bases is more constant and immediate, having known a strong acceleration since the 1950s. An airbase commander has authority over all units stationed on his base. Depending on the units tasks this means that he is responsible for approximately 600 to 2500 personnel.

On average, a base, made up of about 1500 personnel (nearly 3500 people including family), provides a yearly economic boost to its area of about 60 million euros. Consequently, determining the sites for air bases constitutes a major part of regional planning.[376]

- BA 105 Évreux-Fauville Air Base. Command, operational and logistic support. Air transport units with 27× CASA CN-235M, 21× Transall C-160 NG and 4× Mirage 2000-5F to defend a Paris.
- Vélizy – Villacoublay Air Base (BA 107). Helicopter and heavy air transport units.
- Saint-Dizier – Robinson Air Base (BA 113) 4e Escadre de Chasse, Escadron de Chasse 01-007 "Provence" with the new Dassault Rafale C, and EC 1/4 "Gascogne", a conventional/nuclear strike squadron with Dassault Rafale B.
- Luxeuil Air Base (BA 116). Air defence fighter base with 24× Mirage 2000-5F.
- Orléans – Bricy Air Base (BA 123). Air transport units with 14× A400M Atlas and 15× C-130 Hercules. CFPSAA operational command.
- Nancy - Ochey Air Base (BA 133). Three strike fighter squadrons units with 68× Mirage 2000D, SAM sqns.

- Châteaudun Air Base (BA 279). Airplane maintenance, repair and storage airbase.
- Avord Air Base (BA 702). CFAS nuclear strike stockpile. AWACS 4× E-3F Sentry unit. Inflight refueling C-135FR unit.
- BA 705 Tours airbase. Fighter pilot training school equipped with Alpha Jet.
- DA 273 Romorantin air detachment. Logistic unit.
- Air Base 106 Bordeaux-Mérignac Airport. Transport support base for the air staff.
- Air Base 115 Orange-Caritat. Air defence escadron de chasse 02.005 Île-de-France equipped with 10× Mirage 2000C and transition squadron equipped with six Dassault Mirage 2000B.
- Air Base 118 Mont-de-Marsan Air Base. The base is home to two squadrons Rafale B and Rafale C. Home of CEAM, the Air Force military experimentation and trials organisation, Air defence radar command reporting centre, instruction centre for air defence control.
- Air Base 120 Cazaux, situated South-west of the port city of Bordeaux. Fighter pilot training squadron equipped with Alpha Jet. Air force airplane stockpile.
- Air Base 125 Istres. Conventional/nuclear strike squadron, EC02.004 Lafayette equipped with 21× Mirage 2000N – will be transition to Rafale B by September 2018. Two Transall C-160 G strategic communication flight. Inflight refueling unit with 14× C-135FR. CEAM – the Air Force military test centre.
- Air Base 126 Solenzara. Fighter gunnery range. SAR unit.
- Varennes-sur-Allier (DA 277) Air Force supply depot. DA 277 was dissolved on June 30, 2015.
- Air Base 278 Ambérieu. Logistic support base.
- BA 701 Salon de Provence. Officer instruction school. Enlisted instruction school.
- Air Base 709 Cognac-Châteaubernard. Basic flight training school equipped with 33× Socata TB-30 Epsilon.
- Air Base 721 Rochefort. Home of the NCO school, the École de formation des sous-officiers de l'armée de l'air.
- Air Base 942 Lyon-Mont Verdun. Air defence radar command reporting centre. National Air Operations Command (CNOA) location.
- EAR 943 Nice Mont-Agel. Air defence radar GM 406.
- DA 204 Bordeaux-Beauséjour air detachment. Logistic unit.
- EETAA 722 Saintes. Air force electronic, technical instruction also as Military basic Bootcamp.
- EPA 749 Grenoble. Air force child support school.

Figure 223: *A E-3F flanked by 5 Mirage 2000 during the military parade of July 14, 2006.*

Overseas

- BA 160 Dakar, Senegal. Mixed units.
- Escadron de transport 50, fr:Détachement air 181 La Réunion, Réunion, Indian Ocean.
- BA 188 Djibouti, Africa. Mixed units.
- Air elements Libreville/Gabon.
- Air elements N'Djamena/Chad. Mixed units.
- BA 190 French Polynesia (*Overseas collectivity*). Mixed unit.
- BA 365 Martinique (*French department*), West Indies. Mixed unit.
- BA 367 French Guiana (*French department*), South America. Mixed units.
- BA 376 fr:Base aérienne 186 Nouméa, New Caledonia (*special collectivity of France*)
- BA 104 Abu Dhabi

More than ten bases have been closed since 2009. Doullens Air Base (BA 922) was a former command and reporting centre; Toulouse - Francazal Air Base (BA 101), was closed on Sept. 1, 2009; Colmar-Meyenheim Air Base (BA 132) was closed on June 16, 2010; Metz-Frescaty Air Base (BA 128) was closed on June 30, 2011; Brétigny-sur-Orge Air Base (BA 217), closed June

26, 2012; Cambrai - Épinoy Air Base, was closed on June 28, 2012; Reims – Champagne Air Base (June 2012); Drachenbronn Air Base (BA 901) closed on July 17, 2015; Dijon Air Base (BA 102), was vacated on June 30, 2016;[377] Creil Air Base (BA 110) vacated on August 31, 2016; and Taverny Air Base (DA 921), the former Strategic Air Forces Command headquarters.

Aircraft inventory

Aircraft of the French Air Force include:

Type	Origin	Class	Role	Introduced	In service	Total	Notes
Mirage 2000B	France	Jet	Trainer	2000	6		
Mirage 2000C	France	Jet	Fighter	1983	32		
Mirage 2000-5F	France	Jet	Fighter	1997	28		
Mirage 2000D	France	Jet	Attack	1995	71		2000N variant was retired 21 June 2018.[378]
Rafale B/C	France	Jet	Omni-role	2006	110[379] (+ 42 Rafale M in naval aviation)		[380]
Aérospatiale SA330 Puma	France	Rotorcraft	Transport	1968	26		
Airbus A310	EU	Jet	Transport	1993	3	3	
Airbus A340	EU	Jet	Transport	2006	2	2	[381]
Airbus A400M Atlas	EU	Propeller	Transport	2014	14	14	36 more on order.
Boeing E-3F Sentry	USA	Jet	AEW&C	1990	4	4	
Boeing C-135FR	USA	Jet	Tanker	1964	14	14	
CASA CN235M-200/300	Spain	Propeller	Transport	2012	27	27	
Alpha Jet	France/Germany	Jet	Trainer	1978	84	92	
Dassault Falcon 7X	France	Jet	Transport		2	2	
Dassault Falcon 900	France	Jet	Transport		2	2	

Dassault Falcon 2000	France	Jet	Transport		2	2	
DHC-6 Twin Otter	Canada	Propeller	Transport	1976	5		
Diamond HK36 Super Dimona	Austria	Propeller	Trainer		5	5	
Embraer EMB 121 Xingu	Brazil	Propeller	Trainer		23		
Eurocopter AS532 Cougar	EU	Rotorcraft	Utility		10		
Eurocopter AS555 Fennec	EU	Rotorcraft	Trainer		40		
Eurocopter EC725 Caracal	EU	Rotorcraft	SAR		11		
Extra EA-300	Germany	Propeller	Utility		3	3	
General Atomics MQ-9 Reaper	USA	UAV	ISR	2013	6	6	10 more on order
Jodel D.140 Mousquetaire	France	Propeller	Trainer	1966	17		
Lockheed C-130 Hercules	USA	Propeller	Transport	1972	14	14	
Lockheed C-130J Super Hercules	USA	Propeller	Tanker & Transport	2018-2019	2		4 on order (2 KC-130J and 2 C-130J) to support Special Forces Operations
Pilatus PC-21	Switzerland	Propeller	Trainer	2018	.	.	17 on order
Socata TB 30 Epsilon	France	Propeller	Trainer	1984	33		
Socata TBM 700	France	Propeller	Transport	1990	15		
Transall C-160	France/-Germany	Propeller	Transport/-ELINT	1968	23		
Beechcraft Super King Air 350	USA	Propeller	ISR	2018	3		382

Figure 224: *Fusiliers Commandos de l'Air at the opening of a war memorial.*

Personnel

Since the end of the Algerian War, the percentage of formations of the French Air Force in the comparison with the ensemble of the Armies corresponded to 17 to 19%.[383] In 1990, at the end of the Cold War, numbers reached 56,400 military personnel under contract, out of which 36,300 were part of conscription and 5,400 civilians.[384]

In 2008, forecasts for personnel of the French Air Force were expected to number 50,000 out of which 44,000 aviators on the horizon in 2014.

In 2010, the number personnel of the French Air Force was reduced to 51,100 men and women (20%) out of which: 13% officers; 55% sous-officier; 29% air military technicians (MTA); 3% volunteers of national service and aspirant volunteers; 6,500 civilians (14%). They form several functions:

Non-Flying Personnel

Non-navigating personnel of the French Air Force include and are not limited to : Systems Aerial Mechanics (French: *mécanicien système aéronautique*), Aerial Controllers (French: *contrôleur aérien*), Meteorologists (French: *météorologue*), Administrative Personnel, Air Parachute Commandos (French: *Commandos parachutistes de l'air*), in Informatics, in Infrastructures, in Intelligence, Commissioner of the Armies (French: *Commissaire*) (Administrator Task).

Figure 225: *Students of the École de l'air (Air School) during the military parade of July 14th in 2007 on the Champs-Élysées.*

Flying Personnel

Pilots, Mechanical Navigating Officer (French: *Mécanicien Navigant*), Navigating Arms Systems Officer (French: *Navigateur Officier Système d'Armes*) (NOSA), Combat Air Medic (French: *Convoyeur de l'Air*) (CVA).

Training of personnel

Officers, within their recruitment and future specialty, are trained at:

- École de l'air (French: *École de l'air*) (Air School) de Provence;
- École Militaire de l'Air (French: *École militaire de l'air*) (Military Air School);
- École des commissaires des armées (French: *École des commissaires des armées*) (Commissioners Armies School);
- École de pilotage de l'Armée de l'air (French: *École de pilotage de l'Armée de l'air*) (Piloting School of the French Air Force);
- École de l'aviation de transport (French: *École de l'aviation de transport*) (Aviation Transport School);
- École de l'aviation de chasse (French: *École de l'aviation de chasse*) (Aviation Hunter Fighter Pilot School);
- École de transition opérationnelle (French: *École de transition opérationnelle*) (Operational Transition School).

Officers of the French Air Force are spread in three corps:

- Air Officer (French: *Officiers de l'air*);
- Officer Mechanics (French: *Officiers Mécaniciens*);
- Aerial Base Officer (French: *officiers des bases de l'air*), amongst which, officers of the Air Parachute Commandos (French: *Commandos parachutistes de l'air*) are featured.

Sous-Officiers are formed at:

- École de formation des sous-officiers de l'Armée de l'air (French: *École de formation des sous-officiers de l'Armée de l'air*) (EFSOAA) de Rochefort;
- École interarmées (French: *École interarmées*) (Inter-arm School) for administrative specialists;
- Escadron de formation des commandos de l'air (French: *Escadron de formation des commandos de l'air*) (EFCA) of Aerial Base 115 Orange-Caritat (French: *Orange-Caritat*) for concerned specialists;

Military Air Technicians (French: *militaires techniciens de l'air*) having been trained until July 1, 2015 at the Center of Elementary Military Formation (French: « *Centre de formation militaire élémentaire* ») of the Technical Instruction School of the French Air Force (French: *École d'enseignement technique de l'Armée de l'air*) of Saintes. Since July 1, 2015, training has taken place at Orange-Caritat Air Base (BA 115), within the « Operational Combatant Preparation Center of the Air Force » (French: *Centre de préparation opérationnelle du combattant de l'Armée de l'air*).

Air traffic controllers are trained at the Center of Control Instruction and Aerial Defense (French: *Centre d'Instruction du Contrôle et de la Défense Aérienne*).

Ranks

Officers

NATO code	OF-10	OF-9	OF-8	OF-7	OF-6	OF-5	OF-4	OF-3	OF-2	OF-1		OF(D)	Student officer
France (Edit)	*No equivalent*												
		Général d'armée aérienne	Général de corps aérien	Général de division aérienne	Général de brigade aérienne	Colonel	Lieutenant-Colonel	Commandant	Capitaine	Lieutenant	Sous-Lieutenant	Aspirant	Élève-officier

Student

Aspirant élève de l'École de l'air (EA)
(Officer candidate, air force academy)

Aspirant élève de l'École militaire de l'air (EMA)
(Officer candidate, military flight school)

Élève officier de l'École de l'air (EA)
(Officer cadet, air force academy)

Elève officier du personnel navigant (EOPN)
(Navigation officer cadet)

Enlisted

NATO Code	OR-9	OR-8	OR-7	OR-6	OR-5	OR-4	OR-3	OR-2	OR-1
■ France (Edit)			No equivalent						
	Major	Adjudant-chef	Adjudant		Sergent-chef	Sergent	Caporal-chef	Caporal	Aviateur 1e classe	Aviateur 2e classe

References

Further reading

- Olivier, Jean-Marc, (ed.), *Histoire de l'armée de l'air et des forces aériennes françaises du XVIIIe siècle à nos jours"* [History of the Air Force and French aerial forces since the 18th century to the present], Toulouse, Privat, 2014, 552 p.
- Pither, Tony (1998). *The Boeing 707 720 and C-135*. England: Air-Britain (Historians) Ltd. ISBN 978-0-85130-236-2.
- Diego Ruiz Palmer, "France's Military Command Structures in the 1990s," in Thomas-Durell Young, Command in NATO After the Cold War: Alliance, National and Multinational Considerations, U.S. Army Strategic Studies Institute, June 1997

External links

 Wikimedia Commons has media related to *Air force of France*.

- (in French) Official website[356]
- (in English) Official website[385]
- (in French) List of air bases[386], appendix of the budget bill for 2006, French Senate

French Navy

French Navy

French Navy	
Marine Nationale	
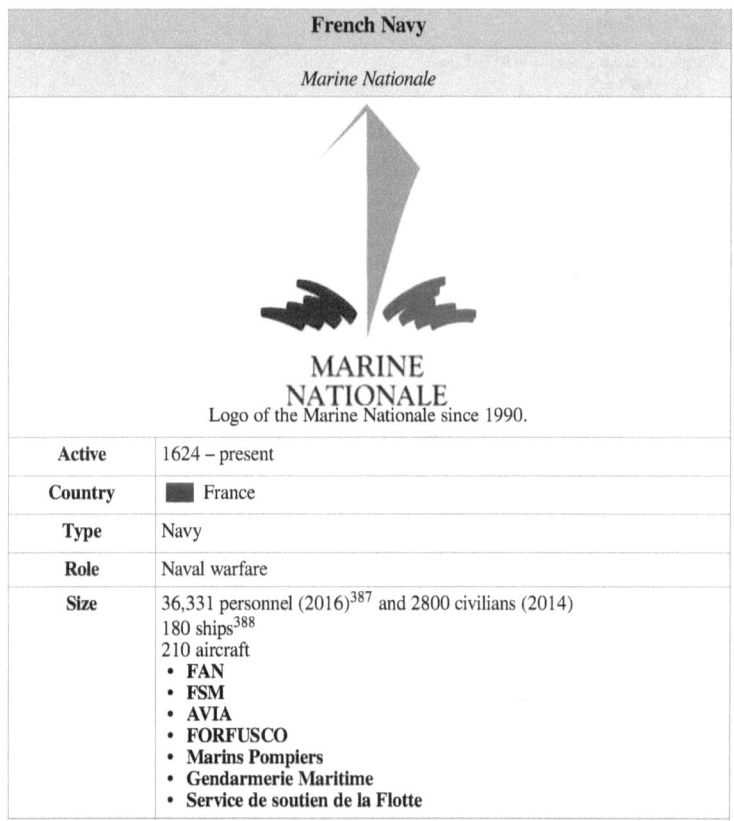 Logo of the Marine Nationale since 1990.	
Active	1624 – present
Country	France
Type	Navy
Role	Naval warfare
Size	36,331 personnel (2016)[387] and 2800 civilians (2014) 180 ships[388] 210 aircraft • **FAN** • **FSM** • **AVIA** • **FORFUSCO** • **Marins Pompiers** • **Gendarmerie Maritime** • **Service de soutien de la Flotte**

Garrison/HQ	**Main**: Brest, Île Longue, Toulon **Secondary**: Cherbourg, Lorient **French overseas territories**: Fort de France, Degrad des Cannes, Port des Galets, Dzaoudzi, Nouméa, Papeete **Overseas**: Dakar, Djibouti, Abu Dhabi
Nickname(s)	La Royale
Motto(s)	Honneur, patrie, valeur, discipline ("Honour, homeland, valour, discipline")
Colours	Blue, white, red
Ships	Current Fleet
Engagements	
Website	www<wbr/>.etremarin<wbr/>.fr[389]
Commanders	
Chef d'État-Major de La Marine, CEMM	Amiral Christophe Prazuck
Major Général de La Marine	Amiral Denis Béraud
Insignia	
Insignia	Ranks in the French Navy
Naval Ensign	
Aircraft flown	
Attack	Rafale M
Electronic warfare	Hawkeye
Fighter	Rafale M
Helicopter	NH90, Eurocopter Lynx, Panther, Dauphin
Utility helicopter	Alouette III
Patrol	Atlantique 2, Falcon 50, Falcon 200
Trainer	Mudry CAP 10, MS-88 Rallye, Falcon 10, Xingu

The **French Navy** (French: *Marine Nationale*), informally *"La Royale"*, is the maritime arm of the French Armed Forces. Dating back to 1624, the French Navy is one of the world's oldest naval forces. It has participated in conflicts around the globe and played a key part in establishing the French colonial empire.

The French Navy consists of six main branches and various services: the Force d'Action Navale, the Forces Sous-marines (FOST, ESNA), the Maritime Force of Naval Aeronautics, the Fusiliers Marins (including Commandos Marine), the Marins Pompiers, and the Gendarmerie Maritime.

As of June 2014, the French Navy employed a total of 36,776 personnel along with 2,800 civilians. Its reserve element consisted of 4,827 personnel of the Operational Reserve. As a blue-water navy, it operates a wide range of fighting vessels, which include nuclear-powered aircraft carrier with various aeronaval capabilities, attack submarines and ballistic missile submarines, frigates, patrol boats and support ships.

Origins

The history of French naval power dates back to the Middle Ages, and had three loci of evolution:

- The Mediterranean Sea, where the *Ordre de Saint-Jean de Jérusalem* had its own navy, the Levant Fleet, whose principal ports were Fréjus, Marseille, and Toulon. The *Ordre*, which was both a religious and military order, recruited knights from the families of French nobility. Members who had fulfilled their service at sea were granted the rank of Knights Hospitaller, elites who served as the officer corps. The *Ordre* was one of the ancestors of modern French naval schools including the French Naval Academy.
- The Manche along Normandy which, since William the Conqueror, always tendered capable marines and sailors from its numerous active seaports;
- The Atlantic Ocean, where the navy of the Duchy of Brittany eventually constituted the nucleus of the royal Flotte du Ponant.

Names and symbols

The first true French Royal Navy (French: *la Marine Royale*) was established in 1624 by Cardinal Richelieu, chief minister to King Louis XIII. During the French Revolution, *la Marine Royale* was formally renamed *la Marine Nationale*. Under the First French Empire and the Second French Empire, the navy was designated as the Imperial French Navy (*la Marine Française Impériale*). Institutionally, however, the navy has never lost its short familiar nickname, *la Royale*.

The symbol of the French Navy was since its origin a golden anchor, which, beginning in 1830, was interlaced by a sailing rope. This symbol was featured on all naval vessels, arms, and uniforms.[390] Although anchor symbols are still used on uniforms, a new naval logo was introduced in 1990. Authorized by Naval Chief of Staff Bernard Louzeau, the modern design incorporates the tricolour by flanking the bow section of a white warship with two ascending red and blue spray foams, and the inscription *"Marine nationale"*.

History

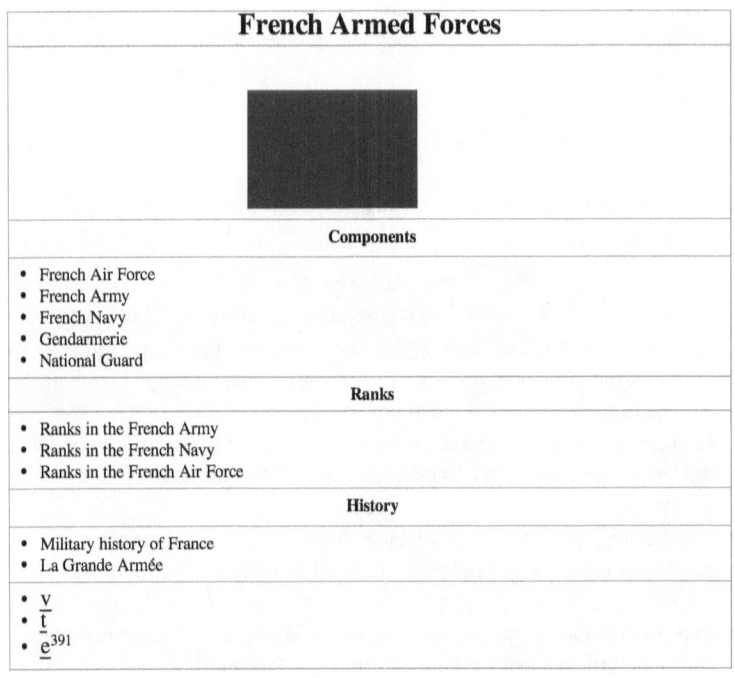

17th century

Cardinal Richelieu personally supervised the Navy until his death in 1643. He was succeeded by his protégé, Jean Baptiste Colbert, who introduced the first code of regulations of the French Navy, and established the original naval dockyards in Brest and Toulon. Colbert and his son, the Marquis de Seignelay, between them administered the Navy for twenty-nine years.

During this century, the Navy cut its teeth in the Anglo-French War (1627–1629), the Franco-Spanish War (1635–59), the Second Anglo-Dutch War, the Franco-Dutch War, and the Nine Years' War. Major battles in these years include the Battle of Beachy Head, the Battles of Barfleur and La Hougue, the Battle of Lagos, and the Battle of Texel.

Figure 226: *The historic "Golden Anchor" symbol*

18th century

The 1700s opened with the War of the Spanish Succession, over a decade long, followed by the War of the Austrian Succession in the 1740s. Principal engagements of these wars include the Battle of Vigo Bay and two separate Battles of Cape Finisterre in 1747. The most grueling conflict for the Navy, however, was the Seven Years' War, in which it was virtually destroyed. Significant actions include the Battle of Cap-Français, the Battle of Quiberon Bay, and another Battle of Cape Finisterre.

The Navy regrouped and rebuilt, and within 15 years it was eager to join the fray when France intervened in the American Revolutionary War. Though outnumbered everywhere, the French fleets held the British at bay for years until victory. After this conflict and the concomitant Anglo-French War (1778–1783), the Navy emerged at a new height in its history. Major battles in these years include the Battle of the Chesapeake, the Battle of Cape Henry, the Battle of Grenada, the invasion of Dominica, and three separate Battles of Ushant.

Within less than a decade, however, the Navy was decimated by the French Revolution when large numbers of veteran officers were dismissed or executed for their noble lineage. Nonetheless, the Navy fought vigorously through the

French Revolutionary Wars as well as the Quasi-War. Significant actions include a fourth Battle of Ushant (known in English as the Glorious First of June), the Battle of Groix, the Atlantic campaign of May 1794, the French expedition to Ireland, the Battle of Tory Island, and the Battle of the Nile.

19th century

Other engagements of the Revolutionary Wars ensued in the early 1800s, including the Battle of the Malta Convoy and the Algeciras Campaign. The Quasi-War wound down with single-ship actions including USS *Constellation* vs *La Vengeance* and USS *Enterprise* vs *Flambeau*.

When Napoleon was crowned Emperor in 1804, he attempted to restore the Navy to a position that would enable his plan for an invasion of England. His dreams were dashed by the Battle of Trafalgar in 1805, where the British all but annihilated a combined Franco-Spanish fleet, a disaster that guaranteed British naval superiority throughout the Napoleonic Wars. Still, the Navy did not shrink from action: among the engagements of this time were the Battle of the Basque Roads, the Battle of Grand Port, the Mauritius campaign of 1809–11, and the Battle of Lissa,

After Napoleon's fall in 1815, the long era of Anglo-French rivalry on the seas began to close, and the Navy became more of an instrument for expanding the French colonial empire. Under King Charles X, the two nations' fleets fought side by side in the Battle of Navarino, and throughout the rest of the century they generally behaved in a manner that paved the way for the Entente Cordiale.

Charles X sent a large fleet to execute the invasion of Algiers in 1830. The next year, his successor, Louis Philippe I, made a show of force against Portugal at the Battle of the Tagus, and in 1838 conducted another display of gunboat diplomacy, this time in Mexico at the Battle of Veracruz. Beginning in 1845, a five-year Anglo-French blockade of the Río de la Plata was imposed on Argentina over trade rights.

The Emperor Napoleon III was determined to follow an even stronger foreign policy than his predecessors, and the Navy was involved in a multitude of actions around the world. He joined in the Crimean War in 1854; major actions for the Navy include the siege of Petropavlovsk and the Battle of Kinburn. The Navy was heavily involved in the Cochinchina Campaign in 1858, the Second Opium War in China, and the French intervention in Mexico. It took part in the French campaign against Korea, and fought Japan in the bombardment of Shimonoseki. In the Franco-Prussian War in 1870, the Navy imposed an effective blockade of Germany, but events on land proceeded at such a rapid pace that it was superfluous. Isolated engagements between French and German ships took place in other theaters, but the war was over in a matter of weeks.[392,393]

The Navy continued to protect colonial safety and expansion under the French Third Republic. The Sino-French War saw considerable naval action including the Battle of Fuzhou, the Battle of Shipu, and the Pescadores Campaign. In Vietnam, the Navy helped wage the Tonkin Campaign which included the Battle of Thuận An, and it later participated in the Franco-Siamese War of 1893.

The 19th century French Navy brought forth numerous new technologies. It led the development of naval artillery with its invention of the highly effective Paixhans gun. In 1850, *Napoléon* became the first steam-powered battleship in history, and *Gloire* became the first seagoing ironclad warship nine years later. In 1863, the Navy launched *Plongeur*, the first submarine in the world to be propelled by mechanical power. In 1876, *Redoutable* became the first steel-hulled warship ever. In 1887, *Dupuy de Lôme* became the world's first armoured cruiser.

20th century

The first seaplane, the French Fabre Hydravion, was flown in 1910, and the first seaplane carrier, *Foudre*, was christened in the following year.[394] Despite that innovation, the general development of the French Navy slowed down in the beginning of the 20th century as the naval arms race between Germany and Great Britain grew in intensity. It entered World War I with relatively few modern vessels, and during the war few warships were built because the main French effort was on land. While the British held control of the North Sea, the French held the Mediterranean, where they mostly kept watch on the Austro-Hungarian Navy. The largest operations of the Navy were conducted during the Dardanelles Campaign. In December 1916, French warships bombarded Athens, forcing the pro-German government of Greece to change its policies. The French Navy also played an important role in countering Germany's U-boat campaign by regularly patrolling the seas and escorting convoys.

Between the World Wars, the Navy modernized and expanded significantly, even in the face of limitations set by the 1922 Washington Naval Treaty. New additions included the heavy and fast *Fantasque* class "super-destroyers", the massive *Richelieu*-class battleships, and the submarine *Surcouf* which was the largest and most powerful of its day.

From the start of World War II, the Navy was involved in a number of operations, participating in the Battle of the Atlantic, the Norwegian Campaign,

Figure 227: *Battleship Richelieu*

the Dunkirk evacuation and, briefly, the Battle of the Mediterranean. However, after the fall of France in June 1940, the Navy was obligated to remain neutral under the terms of the armistice that created the truncated state of Vichy France. Worldwide, some 100 naval vessels and their crews heeded General Charles de Gaulle's call to joined forces with the British, but the bulk of the fleet, including all its capital ships, transferred loyalty to Vichy. Concerned that the German Navy might somehow gain control of the ships, the British mounted an attack on Mers-el-Kébir, the Algerian city where many of them were harbored. The incident poisoned Anglo-French relations, leading to Vichy reprisals and a full-scale naval battle at Casablanca in 1942 when the Allies invaded French North Africa. But the confrontations were set aside once the Germans occupied Vichy France. The capital ships were a primary goal of the occupation, but before they could be seized they were scuttled by their own crews. A few small ships and submarines managed to escape in time, and these joined de Gaulle's Free French Naval Forces, an arm of Free France that fought as an adjunct of the Royal Navy until the end of the war. In the Pacific theatre as well, Free French vessels operated until the Japanese capitulation; *Richelieu* was present at the Japanese Instrument of Surrender.

The Navy later provided fire support and troop transport in the Indochina War, the Algerian War, the Gulf War, and the Kosovo War.

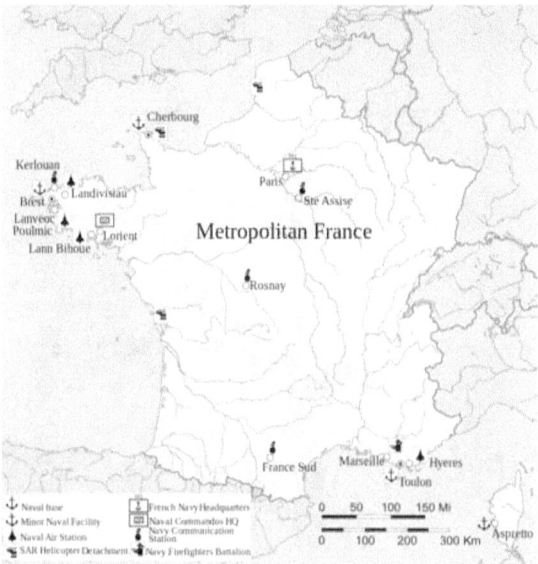

Figure 228: *French navy facilities in metropolitan France (status 2015)*

21st century

Since 2000, the Navy has given logistical support to the War in Afghanistan (2001–2014) as well as the global War on Terror. In 2011, it assisted Opération Harmattan in Libya.

Organisation

The chief of the naval staff is Vice-amiral d'escadre Arnaud de Tarlé, and as of 2014 the Navy has an active strength of 36,776 military personnel and 2,909 civilian staff. The Navy is organised into four main operational branches:

- The Force d'Action Navale (Naval Action Force) – The surface fleet.
- The Forces Sous-marines (Submarine forces) – Nuclear-powered ballistic missile submarines and fleet submarines.
- The Aviation Navale (Naval air force) – Ground and sea-based aircraft.
- The Fusiliers Marins (Naval riflemen) – Protection force and infantry including the Navy special forces (Commandos Marine).

In addition, the National Gendarmerie of France maintain a maritime force of patrol boats that falls under the operational command of the French Navy:

- The Gendarmerie maritime – The coast guard of France.

Figure 229: *Horizon-class frigate*

During most of the Cold War, the Navy was organised in two squadrons based in Brest and Toulon, commanded by ALESCLANT (*Amiral commandant l'escadre de l'Atlantique*) and ALESCMED (*Amiral commandant l'escadre de la Méditerranée*) respectively. Since the post-Cold War restructuring process named Optimar '95, the two components have been divided into the Naval Action Force (commanded by ALFAN) and the Antisubmarine Group (commanded by ALGASM).[395]

Main naval bases

As of 2014, the largest French naval base is the military port of Toulon. Other major bases in metropolitan France are the Brest Arsenal and Ile Longue on the Atlantic, and Cherbourg Naval Base on the English Channel. Overseas French bases include Fort de France and Degrad des Cannes in the Americas; Port des Galets and Dzaoudzi in the Indian Ocean; and Nouméa and Papeete in the Pacific. In addition, the navy shares or leases bases in foreign locales such as Abu Dhabi, Dakar and Djibouti.

Figure 230: *Dassault Rafale*

Equipment

Ships and submarines

Although French naval doctrine calls for two aircraft carriers, as of 2015 the French only have one, *Charles de Gaulle*. Originally a planned order for French aircraft carrier PA2 was based on the design of the British *Queen Elizabeth*-class aircraft carrier recently constructed and launched for the British Royal Navy. However the French programme had been delayed several times for budgetary reasons and the result was priority being given to the more exportable FREMM project. In April 2013 it was confirmed that the second aircraft carrier project would be abandoned due to defence cuts announced in the 2013 French White Paper on Defence and National Security.

The French Navy operates three amphibious assault ships, one amphibious transport dock, two air defence frigates, seven anti-submarine frigates, five general purpose frigates and six fleet submarines (SSNs). This constitutes the French Navy's main oceangoing war-fighting forces. In addition the French Navy operates six light surveillance frigates and nine avisos (light corvettes). They undertake the navy's offshore patrol combat duties, the protection of French Naval bases and territorial waters, and can also provide low-end escort capabilities to any oceangoing task force. The four ballistic missile submarines (SSBN) of the navy's Strategic Oceanic Force provide the backbone of the French nuclear deterrent.

Aircraft

The French Naval Aviation is officially known as the *Aéronautique navale* and was created on the 19 June 1998 with the merging of Naval patrol aircraft and aircraft carrier squadrons. It has a strength of around 6,800 civilian and military personnel operating from four airbases in Metropolitan France. The Aéronavale is currently in the process of modernisation with a total order of 40 Rafale light fighters on order. Forty have so far been delivered and operate from the aircraft carrier *Charles de Gaulle*.

Personnel

Personnel strength of the French Navy 2015	
Category	**Strength**
Commissioned officers	4,500
Petty officers	23,600
Seamen	6,600
Volunteers	767
Civilian employees	2,800
Source:[396]	

Application requirement

Seamen

Seamen must be at least 17 but no more than 24 years old, with a minimum level of schooling.

Petty Officers

Petty officers must be at least 17 but no more than 24 years old, with at least a high school diploma giving access to university studies. Petty Officer Candidate begin training with five months at the Petty Officer School at Brest.

Contract officers

Contract officers serve on an initial eight-year contract, renewable up to 20 years.

- Operational officers must be 21 to 26 years old, with at least a bachelor of science degree, or having passed a classe préparatoire aux grandes écoles in engineering or business.
- Staff officers have to be 21 to 29 years old, with an honors degree or master's degree in a field corresponding to the military occupational specialty.

Career officers

- Less than 22 years old, having passed a *classe préparatoire* in science. After four years at the École Navale (naval academy) a cadet will graduate as Lieutenant junior grade with an engineering degree.
- Less than 25 years old, having an honors degree in science. After three years at the naval academy a cadet will graduate as Lieutenant Jg. with an engineering degree.
- Less than 27 years old, having a master's degree. After two years at the naval academy a cadet will graduate as Lieutenant Jg.

Customs and traditions

Ranks

The rank insignia of the French Navy are worn on shoulder straps of shirts and white jackets, and on sleeves for navy jackets and mantels. Until 2005, only commissioned officers had an anchor on their insignia, but enlisted personnel are now receiving them as well. Commanding officers have titles of *capitaine*, but are called *commandant* (in the army, both *capitaine* and *commandant* are ranks, which tends to stir some confusion among the public). The two highest ranks, *vice-amiral d'escadre* and *amiral* (admiral), are functions, rather than ranks. They are assumed by officers ranking *vice-amiral* (vice admiral). The only *amiral de la flotte* (Admiral of the Fleet) was François Darlan after he was refused the dignity of *amiral de France* (Admiral of France). Equivalent to the dignity of Marshal of France, the rank of *amiral de France* remains theoretical in the Fifth Republic; it was last granted in 1869, during the Second Empire, but retained during the Third Republic until the death of its bearer in 1873. The title of *amiral de la flotte* was created so that Darlan would not have an inferior rank than his counterpart in the British Royal Navy, who had the rank of Admiral of the Fleet.

Addressing officers

Unlike in the French army and air force, one does not prepend *mon* to the name of the rank when addressing an officer (that is, not *mon capitaine,* but simply *capitaine*).[397] Addressing a French Navy *lieutenant de vaisseau* (for instance) with a "*mon capitaine*" will attract the traditional answer "*Dans la Marine il y a Mon Dieu et mon cul, pas mon capitaine!*" ("In the Navy there are My God and my arse, no 'my captain'!").

Uniforms

Figure 231: *Winter Uniform (22)*

Figure 232: *Summer Uniform (26)*

Figure 233: *Overseas (25)*

Figure 234: *Light Duty Firefighter Suit*

Figure 235: *FREMM multipurpose frigate at Lorient*

Future

France's financial problems have affected all branches of her military. The 2013 French White Paper on Defence and National Security cancelled the long-planned new aircraft carrier and a possible fourth *Mistral*-class amphibious assault ship, and conceded that British help would be needed to sustain an enduring presence. The backbone of the fleet will be the *Aquitaine*-class FREMM anti-submarine frigates, replacing the *Georges Leygues* class, but plans to buy a possible seventeen FREMMs were cut back to eleven and then to eight. The cancellation of the third and fourth Horizon destroyers mean that the last two FREMM hulls in 2021/2 will be fitted out as FREDA air-defence ships to replace the *Cassard* class.[398] DCNS has shown a FREMM-ER concept to meet this requirement, emphasising ballistic missile defence with the Thales Sea Fire 500 AESA radar. Industrial considerations mean that the funds for FREMMs 9-11 will now be spent on five more exportable *frégates de taille intermédiaire* (*FTI*, "intermediate size frigates") from 2023 to replace the *La Fayette* class which in the meantime will be upgraded with new sonars.

On 9 January 2014 it was announced that the two remaining Batrals in French service would be replaced in 2016/17 by three 1500-tonne (empty) Bâtiments Multimission (B2M) at a cost of ~€100m (US$136m), later increased to four. DCNS has funded the construction of the Gowind-class corvette *L'Adroit* and loaned her to the MN for fishery patrols to support an overseas marketing campaign for the design. At Euronaval 2010 DCNS showed a 30,000t concept

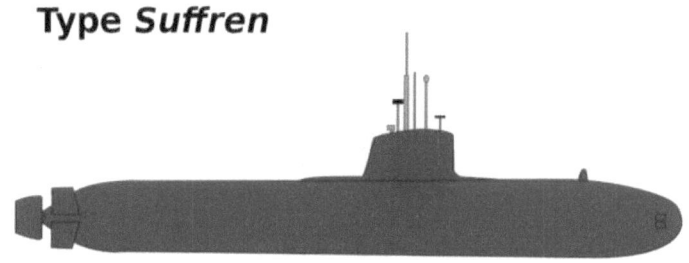

Figure 236: *Barracuda-class submarine*

Figure 237: *EDA-R landing craft on the beach*

called the BRAVE-class replenishment and support ship to replace the *Durance* class, three Flotlog replenishment ships are planned along with four BSAH offshore support vessels. Construction has started on the first of six Barracuda-class nuclear attack submarines; commissioning of *Suffren* is planned for 2018. The first MM40 Exocet Block 3 missile was test-fired in 2010 to be produced. Naval versions of the *SCALP EG* land-attack cruise missile are under development, along with a planned Aster Block 1NT with greater capabilities against ballistic missiles.

Notable French naval officers

Corsairs

- Vice-admiral (*lieutenant-général*) du Casse
- Vice-admiral (*lieutenant-général*) Duguay-Trouin
- Rear admiral (*chef d'escadre*) Jean Bart
- Rear admiral Pierre Bouvet
- Captain Cassard
- Captain Surcouf
- Captain Thurot

Heroes of the First Republic

- Vice-admiral de Latouche-Tréville
- Vice-admiral de Villaret-Joyeuse
- Vice-admiral Bruix
- Rear Admiral du Chayla
- Captain du Petit Thouars
- Captain Casabianca

Explorers

- Vice-Admiral Bougainville
- Rear-Admiral d'Entrecasteaux
- Rear-Admiral Dumont d'Urville
- Commodore Lapérouse
- Captain Samuel de Champlain
- Captain d'Iberville
- Captain Nicolas Baudin
- Captain Louis de Freycinet
- Commander Doudart de Lagrée
- Lieutenant de St Aloüarn
- Lieutenant Francis Garnier
- Lieutenant Savorgnan de Brazza

Other important French naval officers

- Admiral Florent de Varennes—first admiral of France
- Admiral Jean de Vienne—admiral of the French fleet during the Hundred Years' War
- Admiral d'Estaing—admiral of the French fleet which helped the United States secure independence
- Admiral de Grasse—commander of the French fleet at Chesapeake Bay during the American Revolutionary War.
- Admiral Courbet
- Vice-Admiral Tourville—commander of the French fleet at the Battle of Beachy Head
- Vice-Admiral Villeneuve—commander of the French and Spanish fleets at the Battle of Trafalgar
- Vice-Admiral Duquesne—commander of the French fleet at the Battle of Agosta
- Lieutenant commander Paul Teste, pioneer of the modern aeronaval operations.

Notable people who served in the French Navy

- Marcel Cerdan, world boxing champion during the 1940s
- Jean Cocteau, poet, novelist, dramatist, designer, playwright, artist and filmmaker
- Jacques-Yves Cousteau
- Philippe de Gaulle, the son of the general Charles de Gaulle
- Alain Delon, actor, served as a fusilier marin in the First Indochina War
- Bob Denard, a mercenary notorious for coup attempts and wars in Africa
- Jean Gabin, another major French actor, he joined the free French naval force during the Second World War
- Paul Gauguin, painter, sculptor, print-maker, ceramist, and writer
- Bernard Giraudeau, actor, film director, scriptwriter, producer and writer
- André Marty, a leading figure in the French Communist Party (PCF) from 1923 to 1955
- Albert II, Prince of Monaco, reserve Lieutenant Commander
- Pierre Loti, mostly known for his literary works
- Michel Serres, philosopher and author
- Eric Tabarly, a famous yachtsman
- Victor Segalen, ethnographer, archeologist, writer, poet, explorer, art-theorist, linguist and literary critic
- Eugène Sue, a famous 19th-century novelist
- Paul Emile Victor, an ethnologist and polar explorer

Further reading

- Jenkins, E H (1973). *A History of the French Navy from its Beginnings to the Present Day*. London: Macdonald and Jane's. ISBN 0356-04196-4.
- Randier, Jean (2006). *La Royale: L'histoire illustrée de la Marine nationale française*. ISBN 978-2-35261-022-9.
- Winfield, Rif and Roberts, Stephen S., *French Warships in the Age of Sail, 1626-1786: Design, Constructions, Careers and Fates* (Seaforth Publishing, 2017) ISBN 978-1-4738-9351-1; *French Warships in the Age of Sail, 1786-1861: Design, Constructions, Careers and Fates* (Seaforth Publishing, 2015) ISBN 978-1-84832-204-2.

External links

 Wikimedia Commons has media related to *Navy of France*.

- (in French) Marine nationale[399]—Official site
- (in English) French Navy 2011[400]—Guide Book
- (in English) French Navy 2011[401]—Information File
- (in English) Net-Marine[402]—A well documented database on French navy.
- (in French) Mer & Marine[403]—Main website on French maritime affairs (only in French)
- (in English) French Fleet Air Arm[404], about French naval aviation.
- (in English) French Navy in World War 1, including warship losses[405]

National Gendarmerie

National Gendarmerie

National Gendarmerie	
Gendarmerie nationale	
Active	1791–present
Country	France
Type	Gendarmerie (Military provost), Government agency
Role	Law enforcement
Size	c. 100,000 members (2014)[406] 25,000 reserve
Garrison/HQ	Paris
Motto(s)	*Une force humaine* (A humane force)
Other informations	Annual budget: €7.7 billion Size area: 674,843 km² Population: 67 million
Website	gendarmerie.interieur.gouv.fr[407]
Commanders	
Directeur-Général	Général d'Armée Richard Lizurey

The **National Gendarmerie** (French: *Gendarmerie nationale* [ʒɑ̃daʁməʁi nasjɔnal]) is one of two national police forces of France, along with the National Police. It is a branch of the French Armed Forces placed under the jurisdiction of the Ministry of the Interior—with additional duties to the Ministry of Defense. Its area of responsibility includes smaller towns, rural and suburban areas, while the *Police Nationale*—a civilian force—is in charge of cities and downtowns. Due to its military status, the Gendarmerie also fulfills a range of military and defense missions. The Gendarmes also have a

Figure 238: *Gendarmes on patrol*

Figure 239: *Garde républicaine cavalry*

cybercrime division. It has a strength of more than 100,000 personnel as of 2014.

The Gendarmerie is heir to the *Maréchaussée* (Marshalcy—see below), the oldest police force in France, dating back to the Middle Ages. It has influenced the culture and traditions of gendarmerie forces all around the world—and especially in the former French colonial empire.

History

Early history of the institution

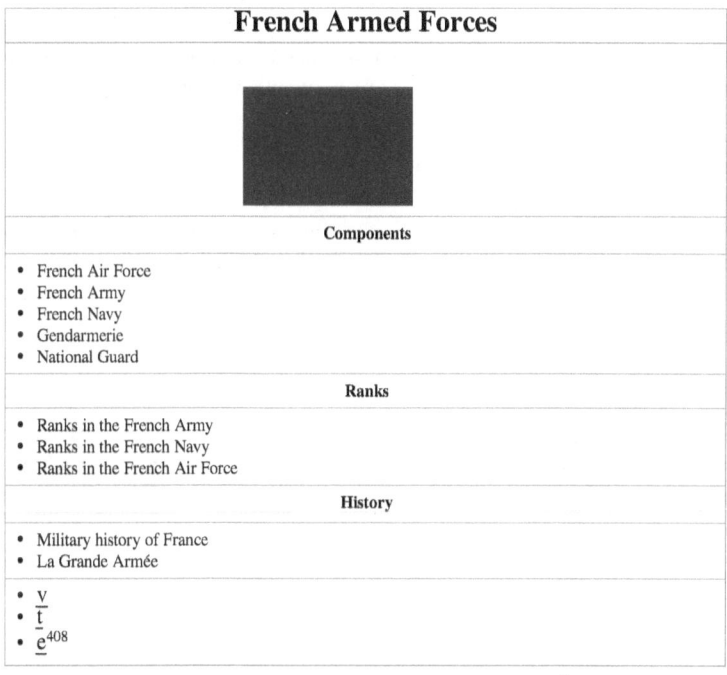

French Armed Forces
Components
• French Air Force • French Army • French Navy • Gendarmerie • National Guard
Ranks
• Ranks in the French Army • Ranks in the French Navy • Ranks in the French Air Force
History
• Military history of France • La Grande Armée
• v • t • e[408]

The Gendarmerie is the direct descendant of the **Marshalcy** of the ancien regime, more commonly known by its French title, the *Maréchaussée*.

During the Middle Ages, there were two Grand Officers of the Kingdom of France with police responsibilities: The Marshal of France and the Constable of France. The military policing responsibilities of the Marshal of France were delegated to the *Marshal's provost*, whose force was known as the Marshalcy because its authority ultimately derived from the Marshal. The marshalcy dates back to the Hundred Years War, and some historians trace it back to the early twelfth century.

Another organisation, the **Constabulary** (French: *Connétablie*), was under the command of the Constable of France. The constabulary was regularised as a military body in 1337.

In 1415 the Maréchaussée fought in the Battle of Agincourt and their commander, the "Prévôt des Maréchaux" (Provost of the Marshals), Gallois de Fougières, was killed in battle. His existence was rediscovered in 1934. Gallois de Fougières was then officially recorded as the first known gendarme to have died in the line of duty and his remains are now buried under the monument to the gendarmerie in Versailles.

Under King Francis I (French: François Ier, who reigned 1515–1547), the *Maréchaussée* was merged with the Constabulary. The resulting force was also known as the *Maréchaussée*, or, formally, the **Constabulary and Marshalcy of France** (French: *connétablie et maréchaussée de France*). Unlike the former constabulary the new *Maréchaussée* was not a fully militarized force.

In 1720, the *Maréchaussée* was officially attached to the Household of the King (*Maison du Roi*), together with the "gendarmerie" of the time, which was not a police force at all, but a royal bodyguard. During the eighteenth century, the marshalcy developed in two distinct areas: increasing numbers of **Marshalcy Companies** (*compagnies de marechaussée*), dispersed into small detachments, were stationed around the French countryside providing law and order, while specialist units provided security for royal and strategic sites such as palaces and the mint (e.g. the *garde de la prévôté de l'hôtel du roi* and the *prévôté des monnaies de Paris*).

While its existence ensured the relative safety of French rural districts and roads, the *Maréchaussée* was regarded in contemporary England, which had no effective police force of any nature, as a symbol of foreign tyranny. English visitors to France saw their armed and uniformed patrols as royal soldiers with an oppressive role. In 1789, on the eve of the French Revolution, the *Maréchaussée* numbered 3,660 men divided into small brigades (a "brigade" in this context being a squad of ten to twenty men.)

The Revolution

During the revolutionary period, the *Maréchaussée* commanders generally placed themselves under the local constitutional authorities. Despite their connection with the king, they were therefore perceived as a force favouring the reforms of the French National Assembly.

As a result, the *Maréchaussée Royale* was not disbanded but simply renamed as the *gendarmerie nationale* (Law of 16 February 1791). Its personnel remained unchanged, and the functions of the force remained much as before. However, from this point, the gendarmerie, unlike the *Maréchaussée* became a fully military force. During the revolutionary period, the main force responsible for policing was the National Guard. Although the *Maréchaussée* had been the main police force of the *ancien regime*, the gendarmerie was initially a full-time auxiliary to the National Guard militia.

In 1791 the newly named *gendarmerie nationale* was grouped into 28 divisions, each commanded by a colonel responsible for three départements. In turn, two companies of gendarmes under the command of captains were based in each department. This territorial basis of organisation continued throughout the 19th and 20th centuries.

Nineteenth century

Under Napoléon, the numbers and responsibilities of the gendarmerie, renamed **gendarmerie impériale**, were significantly expanded. In contrast to the mounted *Maréchaussée*, the gendarmerie comprised both horse and foot personnel; in 1800 these numbered approximately 10,500 of the former and 4,500, respectively.

In 1804 the first Inspector General of Gendarmerie was appointed and a general staff established—based in the *rue du Faubourg-Saint-Honoré* in Paris. Subsequently, special gendarmerie units were created within the Imperial Guard, and for combat duties in French occupied Spain.

Following the Second Restoration of 1815, the gendarmerie was reduced in numbers to about 18,000 and reorganised into departmental legions. Under King Louis Phillippe a "gendarmerie of Africa" was created for service in Algeria and during the Second Empire the Imperial Guard Gendarmerie Regiment was re-established. The majority of gendarmes continued in what was now the established role of the corps—serving in small sedentary detachments as armed rural police. Under the Third Republic the ratio of foot to mounted gendarmes was increased and the numbers directly incorporated in the French Army with a military police role reduced.[409]

In 1901, the École des officiers de la gendarmerie nationale was established to train its officers.

Battle honours

Five battles are registered on the flag of the Gendarmerie:

- **Battle of Hondschoote** (1793): Four hundred gendarmes of the 32nd *Division* (equivalent of a regiment under the Revolution) engaged in battle on the left wing of the army. They seized enemy artillery positions and lost 117 men.
- **Villodrigo** (1812): The 1st legion of Gendarmerie on horseback, belonging to the Brigade of Cavalry of the Army of the North, clashed with the British cavalry on 23 October 1812. Charging with sabres, they penetrated enemy lines, killing 250 and taking 85 prisoners. Colonel Béteille, commanding the brigade, received twelve sabre cuts, but he survived.
- **Taguin** (1843): Thirty gendarmes on horseback were mobilised to take part in tracking the tribe of the emir Abd-El-Kader and participated in his capture. In a painting by Horace Vernet, which immortalises the scene (and hangs in the Musée de Versailles), the gendarmes appear alongside the Algerian Governor-General, Henri d'Orléans, duc d'Aumale.
- **Sevastopol** (1855): Two infantry battalions of the Regiment of Gendarmerie of the Imperial Guard participated in taking the city. The 1st battalion seized a strategic position that contributed towards the final victory. A total of 153 Gendarmes fell.
- **Indo-China** (1945/1954): Three legions of infantrymen from the Republican Guard were formed at the end of 1946. Charged with the formation of the Cochin China Civil Guard, they assumed security roles and patrolled the borders, suffering heavy losses: 654 killed or missing, and 1,500 wounded.

The gendarmerie is still sometimes referred to as the *maréchaussée* (the old name for the service). The gendarmes are also occasionally called *pandores*, which is a slang term derived from an 18th-century Hungarian word for frontier guards. The symbol of the gendarmerie is a stylized grenade, which is also worn by the Italian Carabinieri and the Grenadier Guards in Britain. The budget in 2008 was approximately 7.7 billion euros.

Missions

In French, the term "police" not only refers to the forces, but also to the general concept of "maintenance of law and order" (policing). The Gendarmerie's missions belong to three categories:

- Administrative police (*police administrative*), upholding public order, safety checks and traffic controls, assistance to people in imminent danger, protection duties, etc.

Figure 240: *The French Republican Guard is part of the National Gendarmerie and provides security as guards of honour during official ceremonies.*

- Judicial police (*police judiciaire*), handling penal law enforcement and investigation of crimes and felonies
- Military and defense missions, including military police for the armed forces

These missions include:

- The policing of the countryside, rivers, coastal areas, and small towns with populations under 20,000, that are outside of the jurisdiction of the French National Police. The Gendarmerie's area of responsibility represents approx. 95% of the French territory and 50% of the population of France
- Criminal investigations under judiciary supervision
- Maintaining law and order in public gatherings and demonstrations, including crowd control and other security activities;
- Police at sea
- Security of airports, civil nuclear sites and military installations
- Provision of military police services to the French military—on the French territory as well as during foreign operations (OPEX)
- For the Republican Guard (*Garde républicaine*—which is part of the Gendarmerie), participation in the state's protocol and ceremonies

Organization

Basic principles

The Gendarmerie, while remaining part of the French armed forces, has been attached to the Ministry of the Interior since 2009. Criminal investigations are run under the supervision of prosecutors or investigating magistrates. Gendarmerie members generally operate in uniform, and, only occasionally, in plainclothes.

Director-General

The Director-general of the Gendarmerie (DGGN) is appointed by the Council of Ministers, with the rank of Général d'Armée. The current Director-General is Général Richard Lizurey who took office on September 1, 2016.

The Director-General organizes the operation of the Gendarmerie at two levels:

- at the operational level. The DGGN is in charge of plans, operations, procurement, training and support of the forces in the field.
- in an advisory position for government in all matters pertaining to the Gendarmerie.

Directorate-General

The Gendarmerie headquarters, called the Directorate-General of the National Gendarmerie (Fr: Direction générale de la Gendarmerie nationale (DGGN)[410]), long located in downtown Paris, had been relocated since 2012 to Issy-les-Moulineaux, a southern Paris suburb.

The Directorate-General of the national gendarmerie includes:

- The general staff, divided into offices and services,
- The inspector-general of the Gendarmerie (I.G.G.N.)
- Three main directorates
  - Human Resource directorate (D.P.M.G.N.)
  - Finance and Support directorate (D.S.F.)
  - Operations directorate (D.O.E.)—The general, chief of the Operations directorate, has authority on:
    - Organisation and evaluation subdirectorate,
    - International co-operation subdirectorate,
    - Defence and public order subdirectorate,
    - Public safety and road traffic safety subdirectorate,
    - Criminal Investigation subdirectorate.
- Two joint Gendarmerie/Police offices
  - Joint Information systems office (ST(SI)2)
  - Joint purchasing office (SAELSI)

Organization

The main components of the organization are the following:
- The Departmental Gendarmerie — organized in 13 Regions of the Departmental Gendarmerie (one for each of the 13 metropolitan Regions of France), each reporting directly to the Director General (DGGN)
- The Mobile Gendarmerie — organized in 7 Regions of the Mobile Gendarmerie (one for each of the 7 military regions of metropolitan France, called Zones of Defense and Security)
- The Republican Guard — organized as a separate military corps in one cavalry and two infantry regiments (all three battalion-sized) and specialized units for training and logistical support. It provides protection and ceremonial guard for the President of The Republic, the Prime Minister, their official residencies and both chambers of the French Parliament.
- The Overseas Gendarmerie — in charge of French overseas departments and territories, bringing together the different gendarmerie branches under unified commands in the respective overseas territories. It is also tasked with providing security to the French embassies and consulates overseas.
- Five specialized Gendarmerie branches:
  - Air Gendarmerie — military police for the French Air Force and crash scene investigations involving French military aircraft under the dual subordination of the National Gendarmerie and the Air Force.
  - Maritime Gendarmerie — military police for the French Navy and coast guard under the dual subordination of the National Gendarmerie and the Navy.
  - Air Transport — security force for the civil aviation under the dual subordination of the National Gendarmerie and the Ministry of Transportation.
  - Ordnance Gendarmerie — security and counter-intelligence force for the *Direction générale de l'armement* (*DGA*), the armament and equipment procurement, development and maintenance agency of the French Ministry of Defence.
  - Nuclear ordnance security — security force for the French nuclear arsenal directly subordinated to the Minister of Defence. (The security of the civil nuclear powerplants and research establishments is provided by specialised units of the Departmental Gendarmerie).
- The Provost Gendarmerie — military police for overseas deployments. (The functions of military police for the French Army on French soil are fulfilled by units of the Mobile Gendarmerie).
- Intervention Group of the National Gendarmerie (GIGN): One of the two premier Counter-terror formations of France. Its counterpart within the National Police is the RAID. Operatives from both formations make up the protective detail of the French President (the GSPR).

Figure 241: *Four Departmental Gendarmes.*

- Operational support formations, such as the Gendarmerie air service, the forensic teams, high mountain rescue platoons, canine units, riverine, lake and diver support units etc.
- The education and training establishment
- The administration and support establishment

The above-mentioned organizations report directly to the Director General (DGGN) with the exception of the Republican Guard, which reports to the Île-de-France region.

The reserve force numbers 25,000 (not included in the 100,000 total). It is managed by the Departmental Gendarmerie at the regional level.

Departmental Gendarmerie

The Departmental Gendarmerie, or *Gendarmerie Départementale*, also named «La Blanche»[411] *(The White)*, is the most numerous part of the Gendarmerie, in charge of police in small towns and rural areas. Its territorial divisions are based on the administrative divisions of France, particularly the departments from which the Departmental Gendarmerie derives its name. The Departmental Gendarmerie carries out the general public order duties in municipalities with a population of up to 20 000 citizens. When that limit is exceeded, the jurisdiction over the municipality is turned over to the National Police.

It is divided into 13 metropolitan regions[412] (including Corsica), themselves divided into *groupements* (one for each of the 100 *département*, thus the name), themselves divided into *compagnies* (one for each of the 342 arrondissements).

It maintains gendarmerie brigades throughout the rural parts of the territory. There are two kind of brigades:

- Large autonomous territorial brigades (BTAs)
- Brigade groups composed of smaller brigades supervised by a larger one (COBs).

In addition, it has specialised units:

- Research units, who conduct criminal investigations when their difficulty exceeds the abilities of the territorial units
- Surveillance and intervention platoons (PSIGs), who conduct roving patrols and reinforce local units as needed.
- Specialized brigades for prevention of juvenile delinquency
- Highway patrol units.
- Mountain units, specialised in surveillance and search and rescue operations, as well as inquiries in mountainous areas

In addition, the Gendarmerie runs a national criminal police institute (*Institut de recherche criminelle de la gendarmerie nationale*) specializing in supporting local units for difficult investigations.

The research units may be called into action by the judiciary even within cities (i.e. in the National Police's area of responsibility). As an example, the Paris research section of the Gendarmerie was in charge of the investigations into the vote-rigging allegations in the 5th district of Paris (see corruption scandals in the Paris region).

Gendarmes normally operate in uniform. They may operate in plainclothes only for specific missions and with their supervisors' authorisation.

Mobile Gendarmerie

The Mobile Gendarmerie, or *Gendarmerie Mobile*, also named « La Jaune » *(The Yellow)*, is currently divided into 7 Defense zones (*Zones de Défense*). It comprises 18 Groupings (*Groupements de Gendarmerie mobile*) featuring 109 squadrons[413] for a total of approx. 12,000 men and women.

Its main responsibilities are:

- crowd and riot control
- general security in support of the Departmental Gendarmerie
- military and defense missions

Figure 242: *GBGM riot control training*

- missions that require large amounts of personnel (Vigipirate counter-terrorism patrols, searches in the countryside...)

Nearly 20% of the Mobile Gendarmerie squadrons are permanently deployed on a rotational basis in the French overseas territories. Other units deploy occasionally abroad alongside French troops engaged in military operations (called external operations or OPEX).

The civilian tasks of the *gendarmes mobiles* are similar to those of the police units known as *Compagnies Républicaines de Sécurité* (CRS), for which they are often mistaken. Easy ways to distinguish them include:

- the uniform of the CRS is dark blue, the *gendarmes mobiles* are clad in black jackets and dark blue trousers;
- the CRS wear a big red CRS patch; the gendarmes have stylised grenades.
- the helmet of the *gendarmes mobiles* is blue. The CRS helmet is black with two yellow stripes

The Mobile Gendarmerie includes GBGM (*Groupement Blindé de la Gendarmerie Nationale*), an Armoured grouping composed of seven squadrons equipped with VXB armoured personnel carriers, better known in the Gendarmerie as VBRG (*Véhicule Blindé à Roues de la Gendarmerie*, "Gendarmerie armoured wheeled vehicle"). It is based at Versailles-Satory. The unit also specializes in CBRN defense.

Figure 243: *GIGN operators*

National Gendarmerie Intervention Group

GIGN (Groupe d'intervention de la Gendarmerie nationale) is an elite law enforcement and special operations unit numbering about 400 personnel. Its missions include counter-terrorism, hostage rescue, surveillance of national threats, protection of government officials and targeting of organized crime.

GIGN was established in 1974 following the Munich massacre. Created initially as a relatively small SWAT unit specialized in sensitive hostage situations, it has since grown into a larger and more diversified force of nearly 400 members.[414]

Many of its missions are classified, and members are not allowed to be publicly photographed. Since its formation, GIGN has been involved in over 1,800 missions and rescued more than 600 hostages, making it one of the most experienced counter-terrorism units in the world.[415] The unit came into prominence following its successful assault on a hijacked Air France flight at Marseille Marignane airport in December 1994.

Republican Guard

The Republican Guard is a ceremonial unit based in Paris. Their missions include:[416]

- Guarding important public buildings in Paris such as the Élysée Palace, the residence of the Prime Minister of France, Hôtel Matignon, the Senate, the National Assembly, the Hall of Justice, and keeping public order in Paris.
- Honour and security services for the highest national personalities and important foreign guests;
- Support of other law enforcement forces (with intervention groups, or horseback patrols);
- Staffing horseback patrol stations, particularly for the forests of the Île-de-France region;

Overseas Gendarmerie

The non-metropolitan branches include units serving in the French overseas *départements* and territories (such as the Gendarmerie of Saint-Pierre and Miquelon), staff at the disposal of independent States for technical cooperation, Germany, security guards in French embassies and consulates abroad.

Maritime Gendarmerie

Placed under the dual supervision of the Gendarmerie and the Navy, its missions include:

- police and security in the naval bases;
- maritime surveillance;
- police at sea;
- assistance and rescue at sea.

Air Transport Gendarmerie

The Air Transport Gendarmerie (*Gendarmerie des Transports Aériens*) is placed under the dual supervision of the Gendarmerie and the direction of civilian aviation of the transportation ministry, its missions include:

- police and security in civilian airfields and airports;
- filtering access to aircraft, counter-terrorism and counter-narcotic activities, freight surveillance;
- surveillance of technical installations of the airports (control tower...);
- traffic control on the roads within the airports;
- protection of important visitors;
- judiciary inquiries pertaining to accidents of civilian aircraft.

Air Gendarmerie

The Air Gendarmerie (*Gendarmerie de l'Air*) is placed under the dual supervision of the Gendarmerie and the Air Force, it fulfills police and security missions in the air bases, and goes on the site of an accident involving military aircraft.

Ordnance Gendarmerie

The Ordnance Gendarmerie (Gendarmerie de l'Armement) fulfills police and security missions in the establishments of the Délégation Générale pour l'Armement (France's defence procurement agency).

Nuclear ordnance security Gendarmerie

As the name implies, this branch is in charge of all security missions pertaining to France's nuclear forces.

Provost Gendarmerie

The Provost Gendarmerie (*Gendarmerie prévôtale*), created in 2013, is the military police of the French Army deployed outside metropolitan France.

Foreign service

Gendarmerie units have served in:

- Syria
- Lebanon
- Algeria
- Kosovo
- Rwanda
- Ivory Coast
- Bosnia-Herzegovina
- Haiti
- Central Africa
- Macedonia
- Afghanistan

Uniforms

The uniform of the Gendarmerie has undergone many changes since the establishment of the corps. Throughout most of the 19th century a wide bicorne was worn with a dark blue coat or tunic. Trousers were light blue. White aiguillettes were a distinguishing feature. In 1905 the bicorne was replaced by a dark blue kepi with white braiding, which had increasingly been worn as a service headdress. A silver crested helmet with plume, modelled on that of the French cuirassiers was adopted as a parade headdress until 1914. Following World War I a relatively simple uniform was adopted for the Gendarmerie, although traditional features such as the multiple-cord aiguillette and the dark blue/light blue colour combination were retained.

Since 2006 a more casual "relaxed uniform" has been authorised for ordinary duties (see photograph below). The kepi however continues in use for dress occasions. Special items of clothing and equipment are issued for the various functions required of the Gendarmerie. The cavalry and infantry of the Republican Guard retain historic ceremonial uniforms dating from the 19th century.

Figure 244: *Gendarmes in a relaxed uniform, with soft hats*

Figure 245: *Gendarmerie's motorcycles*

Figure 246: *Air Transport Gendarmerie Bastille Day 2013 Paris*

Figure 247: *Some gendarmes mobiles equipped with shields, FAMAS and gas mask*

Figure 248: *Riot control gear: body armour, shield, tear gas mask, apparatus for throwing tear gas canisters.*

National Gendarmerie

Ranks

Officiers Généraux (General Officers)

Grade (Rank)	Insignia Rank
Général d'Armée (Army General)	
Général de Corps d'Armée (Corps General)	
Général de Division (Divisional General)	
Général de Brigade (Brigade General)	

Officiers supérieurs (Senior Officers)

Grade (Rank)	Insignia Rank Départementale	Insignia Rank Mobile	Corps administratif et technique	Insignia Rank Garde républicaine
Colonel (Colonel)				
Lieutenant-Colonel (Lieutenant Colonel)				
Chef d'Escadron (Squadron Leader) (Major)				

Officers Subalternes (Junior Officers)

Grade (Rank)	Insignia Rank Départe-mentale	Insignia Rank Mobile	Corps administratif et technique	Insignia Rank Garde républicaine
Capitaine (*Captain*)	▬ |||	▬ |||	▬ |||	▬ ||
Lieutenant (*Lieutenant*)				
Sous-Lieutenant (*Sub-Lieutenant*) (*Second Lieutenant*)				
Aspirant (*Aspirant*)	colspan across middle			
Élève Officier (*Officer Cadet*)				

Sous-officers (*Sub-Officers*)

Grade (Rank)	Insignia Rank Départe-mentale	Insignia Rank Mobile	Insignia Rank Corps de soutien	Insignia Rank Garde républicaine
Major				
Adjudant-Chef (*Chief Adjutant*) (*Warrant Officer Class One*)	▬ ||	▬ ||	▬ ||	▬ ||
Adjudant (*Adjutant*) (*Warrant Officer Class Two*)	▬		▬ ||	▬		▬ ||
Maréchal des Logis-Chef (*Chief Marshal of Lodgings*) (*Staff Sergeant*)				
Gendarme (*Gendarme*) (*Sergeant*)	◀◀	◀◀		◀◀
Gendarme sous contrat (*Junior Gendarme*) (*Sergeant*)	◀	◀		◀◀
Élève Sous-officer (*Sub-Officer Cadet*)				

Militaire du Rang (*Serviceman of the Rank*)

Grade (Rank)	Insignia Rank Départementale & Mobile
Gendarme Adjoint Maréchal-des-logis (*Deputy Gendarme Marshal of Lodgings*) (*Sergeant*)	
Gendarme Adjoint Brigadier Chef (*Deputy Gendarme Chief-Brigadier*) (*Corporal*)	
Gendarme Adjoint Brigadier (*Deputy Gendarme Brigadier*) (*Lance Corporal*)	
Gendarme Adjoint 1ère Classe (*Deputy Gendarme First Class*)	
Gendarme Adjoint (*Deputy Gendarme*)	

Personnel

The National Gendarmerie consisted of approx. 103,481 personnel units in 2006. Career gendarmes are either commissioned or non-commissioned officers. The lower ranks consist of auxiliary gendarmes on limited-time/term contracts. The 103,481 military personnel of the National Gendarmerie is divided into:[417]

- 5,789 officers and 78,354 NCOs of gendarmerie;
- 237 officers and 3,824 NCOs of the technical and administrative body;
- 15,277 section volunteers, from voluntary gendarmes (AGIV) and voluntary assistant gendarmes (GAV);
- 1,908 civilian personnel are divided into civil servants, state workers and contracted workers;
- 40,000 reserve personnel. This reserve force had not yet reached the authorised size limit. Only 25,000 men and women were signed up for reserve engagements (E.S.R.).[418]

This personnel mans the following units:

Départemental Gendarmerie

- 1,055 Community brigades;
- 697 autonomous brigades ;
- 370 Surveillance and Intervention Platoons (PSIG);
- 271 Dog-handling Teams;

- 17 Mountain Platoons;
- 92 Departmental Brigades for Investigations and Judicial Services;
- 383 Research sections and brigades;
- 14 Air Sections;
- 7 River Brigades;
- 26 Coastal brigades;
- 93 departmental squadrons for roadway security;
- 136 Highway Platoons;
- 37 brigades for the prevention of juvenile delinquency;
- 21 Centers for Information and Recruitment.

Gendarmerie Mobile

- 108 squadrons
- 6 Special Security Platoons.

Special formations

- 5 squadrons and 10 companies of Republican Guard;
- 40 brigades of gendarmerie for air transports and research sections (BGTA);
- 8 Protection Units;
- 19 Air sections and detachments;
- 18 gendarmerie armament units.

Other units

- 3 673 personnel overseas posts;
- 74 brigades and postes of the maritime gendarmerie;
- 54 brigades of Air Gendarmerie;
- 23 schools and Instruction Centers.

Prospective Centre

The Gendarmerie nationale's Prospective Centre (CPGN), which was created in 1998 by an ordinance of the Minister for Defence, is one of the gendarmerie's answers to officials' willingness to modernise the State. Under the direct authority of the general director of the gendarmerie, it is located in Penthièvre barracks on avenue Delcassé in Paris and managed by Mr Frédéric LENICA, (assisted by a general secretary, Colonel LAPPRAND) "maître des requêtes" in the Conseil d'Etat.[419]

Equipment

Helicopters

The Gendarmerie has used helicopters since 1954. They are part of the Gendarmerie air forces (French: Forces aériennes de la Gendarmerie or FAG—not to be confused with the Air Gendarmerie or the Air Transport Gendarmerie). FAG units are attached to each of the seven domestic "zonal" regions and six overseas COMGEND (Gendarmerie commands). They also operate for the benefit of the National Police which owns no helicopters (the Police also has access to Civil Security helicopters).

Forces aériennes de la Gendarmerie (FAG) operate a fleet of 55 machines belonging to three types and specialized in two basic missions: surveillance/intervention and rescue/intervention.

- Eurocopter AS350 Écureuil: 26 machines (surveillance/intervention)
- Eurocopter EC135: 15 machines (surveillance/intervention)
- Eurocopter EC-145: 14 machines (rescue/intervention)

Figure 249: *AS350 Écureuil.*

Figure 250: *EC-135*

Figure 251: *EC-145*

References

- Gilbert MAUREL "la guerre d'un gendarme en Algérie" ed L'Harmattan. ISBN 978-2-336-00943-8.

External links

 Wikimedia Commons has media related to *Gendarmerie (France)*.

- Gendarmerie nationale official site at the French MoI[420] (in English)
- Gendarmerie nationale official site at the French MoI[407] (in French)
- Gendarmerie nationale official site at the French MoD[421] (in French)

National Guard

National Guard (France)

National Guard	
Garde Nationale	
Active	1789–1872 2016–present
Country	France
Type	National Guard Gendarmerie
Size	75,000
Part of	French Armed Forces
Motto(s)	*Honneur et Patrie* "Honour and Fatherland"
Engagements	• French Revolutionary Wars • Napoleonic Wars • Greek War of Independence • Conquest of Algeria • Crimean War • Franco-Austrian War • Franco-Prussian War • Paris Commune (List of wars involving France)
Website	www<wbr/>.gouvernement<wbr/>.fr<wbr/>/garde-nationale[422]
Commanders	
Minister of the Armed Forces	Florence Parly
Secretary General for the National Guard	General Gaëtan Poncelin de Raucourt
Notable commanders	Gilbert du Motier, marquis de Lafayette

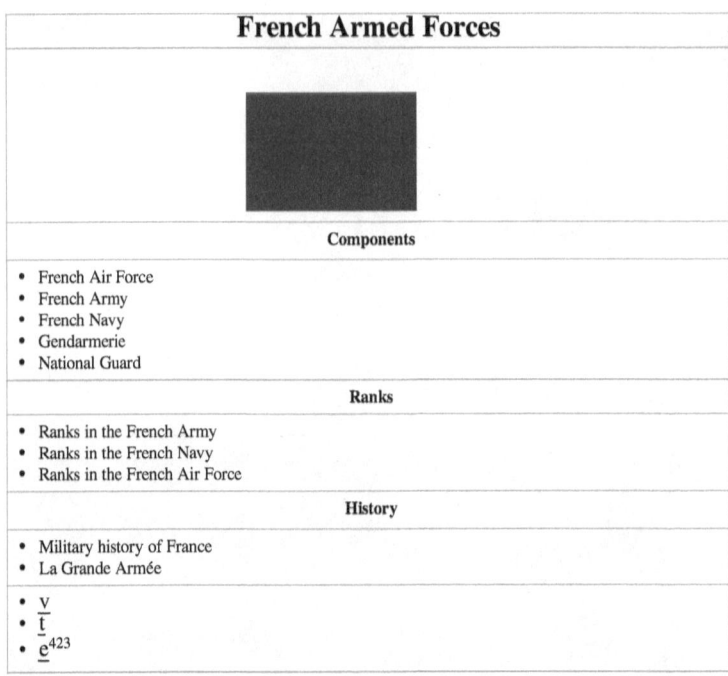

French Armed Forces
Components
• French Air Force • French Army • French Navy • Gendarmerie • National Guard
Ranks
• Ranks in the French Army • Ranks in the French Navy • Ranks in the French Air Force
History
• Military history of France • La Grande Armée
• v • t • e[423]

The **National Guard** (French: *la Garde nationale*) is a French gendarmerie that existed from 1789 to 1872, including a period of official dissolution from 1827 to 1830, re-founded in 2016. It was separate from the French Army and existed both for policing and as a military reserve. For most of its history the National Guard, particularly its officers, were widely viewed as loyal to middle-class interests. However, from 1792 to 1795, the National Guard was perceived as revolutionary and the lower ranks were identified with sans-culottes, and soon after the Franco-Prussian War of 1870-71, the National Guard in Paris became viewed as dangerously revolutionary, contributing to its dissolution.

In 2016, France announced the reestablishment of the National Guard in response to a series of terrorist attacks.

Creation

The raising of a "Bourgeois Guard" (*"garde bourgeoise"*) for Paris was discussed by the National Assembly on 11 July 1789 in response to the King's sudden and alarming replacement of prime minister Jacques Necker with the Baron de Breteuil on that day. The replacement caused rapidly spread anger and violence throughout Paris. The National Assembly declared the formation of a "Bourgeois Militia" (*"milice bourgeoise"*) on 13 July. In the early

National Guard (France) 407

Figure 252: *Philippe Lenoir, (1785–1867), French painter, in his National Guard uniform. By Horace Vernet (1789–1863)*

Figure 253: *Mssr. Hepp, commander of the National Guard of Strasbourg in 1790*

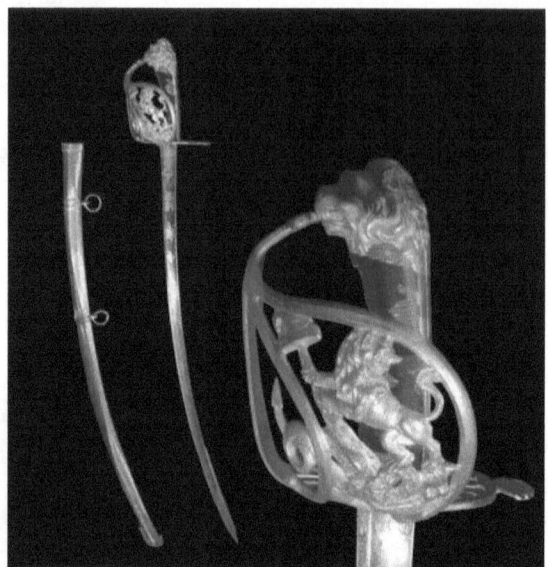

Figure 254: *Lafayette's sabre as general of the Garde nationale. On display at the Musée de l'Armée, Paris.*

morning of the next day, the search for weapons for this new militia led to the storming of the Hotel des Invalides and then the storming of the Bastille.

Lafayette was elected to the post of commander in chief of the Bourgeois Militia on 14 July, and it was renamed the "National Guard". Similar bodies were spontaneously created in the towns and rural districts of France in response to widespread fears of chaos or counter-revolution. When the French Guards mutinied and were disbanded during the same month, the majority of this former royal regiment's rank and file became the full-time cadre of the Paris National Guard.

Initially each city, town and village maintained its own National Guard, until they were united on 14 July 1790 under Lafayette, who was appointed "Commandant General of all the National Guards of the Kingdom".

Organization

The officers of the National Guard were elected. Under the law of 14 October 1791, all active citizens and their children over 18 years were obliged to enlist in the National Guard. Their role was the maintenance of law and order and,

Figure 255: *Soldiers of the Garde nationale of Quimper escorting royalist rebels in Brittany (1792). Painting by Jules Girardet.*

if necessary, the defence of the territory. Following a nationwide scheme decided on in September 1791, the National Guard was organised on the basis of district or canton companies. Five of these neighbourhood units (designated as fusiliers or grenadiers) made up a battalion. Eight to ten battalions comprised a *legion*. Districts might also provide companies of veterans and young citizens, respectively drawn from volunteers of over 60 or under 18. Where possible, there was provision for mounted detachments and artillerymen.[424]

The citizens kept their weapons and their uniforms at home, and set forth with them when required. The initially multi-coloured uniforms of the various provincial National Guard units were standardised in 1791, using as a model the dark blue coats with red collars, white lapels and cuffs worn by the Paris National Guard since its creation.[425] This combination of colours matched those of the revolutionary tricolour.

Role during the Revolution

The former Guet royal had held responsibility for the maintenance of law and order in Paris from 1254 to 1791, when the National Guard took over this role. In fact, the last commander of the Guet royal (*Chevalier du Guet*), de La Rothière, was elected to head the National Guard in 1791. In the summer

Figure 256: *The national Guard of Paris at the Battle of Paris, 1814*

of 1792, the fundamental character of the guard changed. The *fédérés* were admitted to the guard and the subsequent takeover of the guard by Antoine Joseph Santerre when Mandat was murdered in the first hours of the insurrection of 10 August placed a radical revolutionary at the head of the Guard. After the abolition of the monarchy (21 September 1792), the National Guard fought for the Revolution and it had an important role in forcing the wishes of the capital on the French National Assembly which was obliged to give way in front of the force of the "patriotic" bayonets.

After 9 Thermidor, year II (27 July 1794), the new government of the Thermidorian Reaction placed the National Guard under the control of more conservative leadership. Part of the National Guard then attempted to overthrow the Directory during the royalist insurrection on the 13 Vendémiaire, year IV (5 October 1795), but were defeated by forces led by Napoleon Bonaparte in the Battle of 13 Vendémiaire. The Paris National Guard thereafter ceased to play a significant political role.

First Empire

Napoleon did not believe that the middle-class National Guard would be able to maintain order and suppress riots. Therefore, he created a *Municipal Guard of Paris*, a full-time gendarmerie which was strongly militarised. However, he did not abolish the National Guard, but was content to partially disarm it. He kept the force in reserve and mobilised it for the defence of French territory in 1809 and 1814. In Paris during this period the National Guard comprised twelve thousand bourgeois property owners, serving part-time and equipped at their own expense, whose prime function was to guard public buildings on a roster basis.[426] Between 1811 and 1812 the National Guard, was organized in "cohorts" to distinguish it from the regular army, and for home defence *only*. By a skilful appeal to patriotism, and judicious pressure applied through the prefects, it became a useful reservoir of half-trained men for new battalions of the active army.

With the invasion of France by allied Austrian, Prussian, Russian and British armies in 1814, the National Guard was suddenly called on to provide support for regular Imperial forces. Existing National Guard units, such as those of Paris, were deployed as defence corps in their areas of recruitment. Mass conscription was extended to age groups previously exempt from military service, to provide more manpower for the expanded National Guard. Students and volunteers from gamekeepers and other professional groups formed separate units within the National Guard. Clothing and equipment was often in short supply and even the Paris National Guard was obliged to provide pikes as substitute weapons for some of its new recruits.[427]

Six thousand national guardsmen took part in the Battle of Paris in 1814. Following the occupation of the city by the allied armies, the National Guard was expanded to 35,000 men and became the primary force for maintaining order.[428]

The Restoration

Under the Restoration in 1814, the National Guard was maintained by Louis XVIII. Initially the Guard, purged of its Napoleonic leadership, maintained good relations with the restored monarchy. The future Charles X served as its Colonel-General, reviewed the force regularly and intervened to veto its proposed disbandment on the grounds of economy by the *Conseil Municipal* of Paris.[429] However, by 1827, the middle-class men who still composed the Guard had come to feel a degree of hostility towards the reactionary monarchy. Following hostile cries at a review on 29 April Charles X dissolved the Guard the following day, on the grounds of offensive behaviour towards the crown.[430] He neglected to disarm the disbanded force, and its muskets resurfaced in 1830 during the July Revolution.

Figure 257: *French Garde Nationale soldier with Tabatière rifle, 1870.*

National Guard following 1831

A new National Guard was established in 1831 following the July Revolution in 1830. It played a major role in suppressing the Paris June Rebellion of 1832 against the government of King Louis-Phillipe. However, the same National Guard fought in the Revolution of 1848 in favour of the republicans. This change in allegiance reflected a general erosion in the popularity of Louis-Phillipe and his "Bourgeois Monarchy", rather than any fundamental change in the make up of the National Guard, which remained a middle-class body.

Second Empire

Napoleon III confined the National Guard during the Second Empire to subordinate tasks to reduce its liberal and republican influence. During the Franco-Prussian War the Government of National Defense of 1870 called on the Guard to undertake a major role in defending Paris against the invading Prussian army. During the uprising of the Paris Commune, from March to May 1871, the National Guard in Paris was expanded to include all able-bodied citizens capable of carrying weapons. Following the Commune's defeat by the regular French Army, the National Guard was officially abolished and its units disbanded. Also disbanded was the Mobile National Guard (*Garde Nationale*

Mobile) raised in 1866 to provide personnel and officers for rapid deployment operations nationwide, as well as to provide reserve personnel for the armed forces.

End of the National Guard

Despite its major role in the Franco-Prussian War, the National Guard was disbanded soon after the establishment of the Third Republic. Having been converted from a volunteer reserve into a much larger force composed mainly of conscripts, the National Guard had lost its identity and *raison d'être*. It also faced opposition from the army which was opposed to such a large armed force outside its direct control. The role of the Paris units of the National Guard in the uprising of the Paris Commune led to a great degree of hostility towards the National Guard, especially from the army.

Perceived as an embodiment of the revolutionary republican "nation in arms" at the time of the Revolution of 1789, the National Guard was formally disbanded on 14 March 1872 as a threat to the security and order of the new Third Republic.

The National Guard was superseded by the creation of territorial regiments, made up of older men who had completed their period of full-time military service. These reserve units were embodied only in times of general mobilisation but remained an integral part of the regular army.

Recreation of the National Guard

After several terror attacks in France, which intensified in 2014 and 2015, French President François Hollande declared the total establishment of a new National Guard. By his words, the Guard will be formed using military reserve forces. Hollande expected to start parliamentary consultations on September 2016 about this matter.

On October 12, 2016, during a weekly meeting of the Cabinet, the National Guard was officially reconstituted after 145 years as the fifth service branch of the French Armed Forces under the Ministry of the Armed Forces.[431] The revitalized Guard will also reinforce elements of the National Gendarmerie and the National Police in securing major events nationwide while performing its historical responsibility as a national military and police reserve service.

It is expected that the new Guard will grow to a 72,500-member force in 2017 and grow to a 86,000-member national reserve in 2018.[432,433] The formation of the revived Guard will be assisted with a dedicated 311 million euro budget and its personnel will now come from the reserves, members from the private sector and active personnel seconded to the service. Unlike the Guard of the Revolutionary Wars, its officers are today seconded from both the Army and the National Gendarmerie and are graduates of their respective academies.

References

- Crowdy, Terry (2004). *French Revolutionary Infantry 1789–1802*. Oxford: Osprey. p. 14. ISBN 1-84176-660-7.
- Mansel, Philip (2003). *Paris Between Empires – Monarchy and Revolution 1814–1852*. New York: St. Martin's Press. pp. 13–14, 217–218. ISBN 0-312-30857-4.
- Maude, Frederic Natusch (1911). "Napoleonic Campaigns". In Chisholm, Hugh. *Encyclopædia Britannica*. **19** (11th ed.). Cambridge University Press. pp. 212–236.

Further reading

Wikimedia Commons has media related to *Garde nationale (Révolution française)*.

- Tulard, Jean; Fayard, Jean-François; Fierro, Alfred (1987). *Histoire et dictionnaire de la Révolution française, 1789–1799*. Bouquins (in French). Paris: Robert Laffont. ISBN 2-7028-2076-X.
- Bruce Vandervort, National Guard (France)[434], on the online Encyclopedia of 1848 Revolutions[435], James Chastain, ed.

External links

- Webpage of the reestablished National Guard[422]

Appendix

References

[1] http://www.lemonde.fr/international/article/2015/04/29/budget-de-la-defense-une-rallonge-de-3-8-milliards-d-euros_4624847_3210.html, lefigaro.fr
[2] //en.wikipedia.org/wiki/French_Armed_Forces#endnote_aid
[3] Official Presidential Website, Letter of Engagement to M. Jean-Claude Mallet, 31 July 2007 http//www.elysee.fr
[4] Jim Hoagland, "France's Whirlwind of Change", Real Clear Politics, 18 June 2008 http://www.realclearpolitics.com/articles/2008/06/sarkozy_on_the_move.html
[5] Gendarmerie - Workforce http://www.gendarmerie.interieur.gouv.fr/fre/Sites/Gendarmerie/Presentation/Effectifs, gendarmerie.interieur.gouv.fr, 2011
[6] http://www.defense.gouv.fr/
[7] http://www.cfr.org/france/french-military-strategy-nato-reintegration/p16619
[8] http://www.opoccuu.com/france-ranks-insignia.htm
[9] //en.wikipedia.org/wiki/Military_history_of_France#endnote_aid
[10] //en.wikipedia.org/wiki/Military_history_of_France#endnote_frontiers
[11] //en.wikipedia.org/wiki/Military_history_of_France#endnote_authority
[12] //en.wikipedia.org/wiki/Military_history_of_France#endnote_leadership
[13] //en.wikipedia.org/wiki/Military_history_of_France#endnote_rivalries
[14] //en.wikipedia.org/wiki/Military_history_of_France#endnote_collapse
[15] //en.wikipedia.org/wiki/Military_history_of_France#endnote_complaints
[16] //en.wikipedia.org/wiki/Military_history_of_France#endnote_nuclear
[17] //en.wikipedia.org/wiki/Military_history_of_France#endnote_avaricum
[18] //en.wikipedia.org/wiki/Military_history_of_France#endnote_force
[19] //en.wikipedia.org/wiki/Military_history_of_France#endnote_soissons
[20] //en.wikipedia.org/wiki/Military_history_of_France#endnote_spain
[21] //en.wikipedia.org/wiki/Military_history_of_France#endnote_admin
[22] //en.wikipedia.org/wiki/Military_history_of_France#endnote_motivation
[23] //en.wikipedia.org/wiki/Military_history_of_France#endnote_armies
[24] //en.wikipedia.org/wiki/Military_history_of_France#endnote_mounted
[25] //en.wikipedia.org/wiki/Military_history_of_France#endnote_component
[26] //en.wikipedia.org/wiki/Military_history_of_France#endnote_tactic
[27] //en.wikipedia.org/wiki/Military_history_of_France#endnote_castles
[28] //en.wikipedia.org/wiki/Military_history_of_France#endnote_feature
[29] //en.wikipedia.org/wiki/Military_history_of_France#endnote_internecine
[30] //en.wikipedia.org/wiki/Military_history_of_France#endnote_rejection
[31] //en.wikipedia.org/wiki/Military_history_of_France#endnote_plate
[32] //en.wikipedia.org/wiki/Military_history_of_France#endnote_little
[33] //en.wikipedia.org/wiki/Military_history_of_France#endnote_bungled
[34] //en.wikipedia.org/wiki/Military_history_of_France#endnote_suffered
[35] //en.wikipedia.org/wiki/Military_history_of_France#endnote_plans
[36] //en.wikipedia.org/wiki/Military_history_of_France#endnote_compagnies
[37] //en.wikipedia.org/wiki/Military_history_of_France#endnote_roman
[38] //en.wikipedia.org/wiki/Military_history_of_France#endnote_nobles
[39] //en.wikipedia.org/wiki/Military_history_of_France#endnote_gendarmes
[40] //en.wikipedia.org/wiki/Military_history_of_France#endnote_intercepting
[41] //en.wikipedia.org/wiki/Military_history_of_France#endnote_alliance
[42] //en.wikipedia.org/wiki/Military_history_of_France#endnote_vauban
[43] //en.wikipedia.org/wiki/Military_history_of_France#endnote_progress
[44] //en.wikipedia.org/wiki/Military_history_of_France#endnote_uniforms
[45] //en.wikipedia.org/wiki/Military_history_of_France#endnote_diplomaticrev
[46] //en.wikipedia.org/wiki/Military_history_of_France#endnote_modernwar

47 //en.wikipedia.org/wiki/Military_history_of_France#endnote_Chandler136
48 //en.wikipedia.org/wiki/Military_history_of_France#endnote_history
49 //en.wikipedia.org/wiki/Military_history_of_France#endnote_conscription
50 //en.wikipedia.org/wiki/Military_history_of_France#endnote_tore
51 //en.wikipedia.org/wiki/Military_history_of_France#endnote_nationalism
52 //en.wikipedia.org/wiki/Military_history_of_France#endnote_think
53 //en.wikipedia.org/wiki/Military_history_of_France#endnote_sevenpop
54 //en.wikipedia.org/wiki/Military_history_of_France#endnote_pop
55 //en.wikipedia.org/wiki/Military_history_of_France#endnote_replaced
56 //en.wikipedia.org/wiki/Military_history_of_France#endnote_food
57 //en.wikipedia.org/wiki/Military_history_of_France#endnote_decisive
58 //en.wikipedia.org/wiki/Military_history_of_France#endnote_system
59 //en.wikipedia.org/wiki/Military_history_of_France#endnote_colonialempire
60 //en.wikipedia.org/wiki/Military_history_of_France#endnote_confidence
61 //en.wikipedia.org/wiki/Military_history_of_France#endnote_dreyfus
62 //en.wikipedia.org/wiki/Military_history_of_France#endnote_competence
63 //en.wikipedia.org/wiki/Military_history_of_France#endnote_Strachan280
64 //en.wikipedia.org/wiki/Military_history_of_France#endnote_Keegan64
65 //en.wikipedia.org/wiki/Military_history_of_France#endnote_billion
66 //en.wikipedia.org/wiki/Military_history_of_France#endnote_maginot
67 //en.wikipedia.org/wiki/Military_history_of_France#endnote_ardennes
68 //en.wikipedia.org/wiki/Military_history_of_France#endnote_divisions
69 //en.wikipedia.org/wiki/Military_history_of_France#endnote_indicative
70 Royal Air Force Museum http://www.rafmuseum.org.uk/research/faq/roundel.cfm
71 //en.wikipedia.org/wiki/Military_history_of_France#endnote_aviation
72 //en.wikipedia.org/wiki/Military_history_of_France#endnote_operational
73 Jean-Claude Castex, *Dictionnaire des batailles navales franco-anglaises* https://books.google.com/books?id=U9tChhhw62AC&pg=PA18, Presses de l'Université Laval, 2004, p. 21
74 Jean-Claude Castex, *Dictionnaire des batailles navales franco-anglaises* https://books.google.com/books?id=U9tChhhw62AC&pg=PA18, Presses de l'Université Laval, 2004, p.21
75 //en.wikipedia.org/wiki/Military_history_of_France#endnote_performance
76 //en.wikipedia.org/wiki/Military_history_of_France#endnote_fleet
77 //en.wikipedia.org/wiki/Military_history_of_France#endnote_start
78 //en.wikipedia.org/wiki/Military_history_of_France#endnote_amalgamate
79 //en.wikipedia.org/wiki/Military_history_of_France#endnote_cameron
80 //en.wikipedia.org/wiki/Military_history_of_France#endnote_devils
81 //en.wikipedia.org/wiki/Military_history_of_France#endnote_spirited
82 //en.wikipedia.org/wiki/Military_history_of_France#endnote_exist
83 http://xenophongroup.com/montjoie/tilley.htm
84 http://www.turkishpress.com/news.asp?id=130761
85 https://www.amazon.com/gp/reader/0674027264/
86 http://www.chass.utoronto.ca/~cpercy/courses/6362Jurcic1.htm
87 http://www.onwar.com/aced/nation/fax/france/index.htm
88 http://napoleonistyka.atspace.com/FRENCH_ARMY.htm
89 http://xenophongroup.com/montjoie/oriflam.htm
90 http://www.americanrevolution.org/frcon.html
91 http://www.allworldwars.com/French%20Army%20from%20Revolution%20to%20the%20First%20Empire%20by%20Hippolyte%20Bellange.html
92 http://www.cfr.org/france/french-military-africa/p12578
93 pages 215, 217 and 218, Vol. XXX, Encyclopædia Britannica, 12th Edition, 1922
94 John Keegan, pages 300-308 "The First World War",
95 Bentley B.; Gilbert and Paul P. Bernard, "The French Army Mutinies of 1917," *Historian* (1959) 22#1 pp 24-41
96 Leonard V. Smith, "War and 'Politics': The French Army Mutinies of 1917," *War in History* (1995(2#2 pp 180-201.

[97] David French, "Watching the Allies: British Intelligence and the French Mutinies of 1917," *Intelligence & National Security* (1991) 6#3 pp 573-592
[98] Louis Delperier, pages 60-70 "Les Cuirassiers 1845-1918", Argout-Editions Paris 1981
[99] Sumner, Ian (2012), *They Shall Not Pass: The French Army on the Western Front 1914-1918*, Pen & Sword Military, (p. 85)
[100] Sumner, p. 86
[101] Barbara W. Tuchman, page 274 "The Guns of August", Constable & Co. Ltd 1962
[102] Sumner, p. 40 https//books.google.com
[103] Andre Jouineau, page 4 "Officers and Soldiers of the French Army 1915 to Victory,
[104] https://doi.org/10.2307/1987399
[105] https://www.jstor.org/stable/1987399
[106] https://www.amazon.com/gp/reader/0674027264/
[107] http://onlinelibrary.wiley.com/doi/10.1111/j.1540-6563.1959.tb01641.x/abstract
[108] https://doi.org/10.1111/j.1540-6563.1959.tb01641.x
[109] Martin Thomas, *The French Empire at War, 1940-1945* (Manchester University Press, 2007)
[110] Ian Sumner and François Vauvillier, *The French Army 1939–45 Vol. 2*, p. 38, London: Osprey, 1998.
[111] Horne, Alistair, "To Lose a Battle: France 1940", p.161-162, 229
[112] Christopher Lloyd, "Enduring Captivity: French POW Narratives of World War II 1." *Journal of War & Culture Studies* (2013) 6#1 pp: 24-39.
[113] Richard Vinen, *The Unfree French: Life under the Occupation* (2006) pp 183-214
[114] January 13, 1943 : junction between Franco-British troops in Libya http://www.ina.fr/economie-et-societe/vie-economique/video/I00009355/13-1-43-jonction-des-troupes-franco-britanniques-en-libye.fr.html, OFFICE FRANCAIS D'INFORMATIONS CINEMATOGRAPHIQUES – 1 January 1943
[115] Recruiting poster http://www.albert-arts-collections.com/_wp_generated/afiche_recrutement_hitler.jpg
[116] (Vigneras, Marcel, "Rearming the French", Office of the Chief of Military History, Dept. of the Army, (Washington, D.C. GPO) 1957, p. 244-246.)
[117] Free French origin
[118] Formed with FFI personnel.
[119] Did not see combat during the Second World War
[120] http://www.ina.fr/histoire-et-conflits/seconde-guerre-mondiale/video/AFE86002013/voyage-de-m-de-brinon-a-l-est.fr.html
[121] DES JEUNES DES CHANTIERS DE LA JEUNESSE EN STAGE CHEZ LES POMPIERS http://www.ina.fr/economie-et-societe/vie-sociale/video/AFE85000716/des-jeunes-des-chantiers-de-la-jeunesse-en-stage-chez-les-pompiers.fr.html, newsreel of French youth workings alumni training with firefighters in 1942, *Les Actualités Mondiales* – 20 February 1942, French national audiovisual institute INA
[122] LE SERMENT DES CHEFS MUSULMANS http://www.ina.fr/histoire-et-conflits/seconde-guerre-mondiale/video/AFE85001101/le-serment-des-chefs-musulmans.fr.html, newsreel of French Algeria French youth workings Muslim locals giving the hand salute to Marshal Pétain, France Actualités – 9 October 1942, INA
[123] Eric T. Jennings, *Vichy in the Tropics: Pétain's National Revolution in Madagascar, Guadeloupe, and Indochina, 1940-44*. (Stanford University Press, 2004)
[124] See "Revue Historique des Armées" 1985/3 : http://commandantdelaubier.info/circonstances/article-RHA.PDF
[125] Pétain, June 17, 1940 appeal http://www.larousse.fr/encyclopedie/musique/P%C3%A9tain_Philippe_message_du_17_juin_1940/1102208, audio recording of Pétain's Appeal of June 17
[126] *The life and times of Pilot Officer Prune: being the official story of Tee Emm*, by Tim Hamilton, H.M.S.O., 1991, pages 105 & 106
[127] Philippe Carrard, *The French who Fought for Hitler: Memories from the Outcasts* (Cambridge University Press, 2010)
[128] John D. Clarke, *French Eagles, Soviet Heroes: The Normandie-Niemen Squadrons on the Eastern Front* (The History Press, 2013)

[129] history of Normandie-Niemen http://www.fncv.com/biblio/conflits/1939-1945/normandie-niemen/risso.html
[130]
[131] GUF, p. 989
[132] Southern France http://www.history.army.mil/brochures/sfrance/sfrance.htm
[133] Chronology, p. 261
[134] Riviera, pp. 431–432
[135] Riviera, p. 431
[136] Chronology, p. 398
[137] Chronology, pp. 448–452
[138] Chronology, p. 509
[139] Last Offensive, p. 433
[140] Histoire du sous-marin *Surcouf* http://netmarine.net/g/bat/surcouf/histoire.htm, netmarine
[141] Les bâtiments ayant porté le nom de *Léopard* http://www.netmarine.net/bat/be/leopard/ancien.htm
[142] Michael Clodfelter. *Warfare and Armed Conflicts- A Statistical Reference to Casualty and Other Figures, 1500–2000.* 2nd Ed. 2002 .
[143] Gregory, Frumkin. *Population Changes in Europe Since 1939*, Geneva 1951.
[144] Tim Benbow, "'Menace to Ironclad': The British Operations against Dakar (1940) and Madagascar (1942)." *Journal of Military History* 75.3 (2011).
[145] Martin Thomas, "Imperial backwater or strategic outpost? The British takeover of Vichy Madagascar, 1942." *Historical Journal* (1996) 39#4 pp: 1049-1074.
[146] Martin Thomas, "Silent Partners: SOE's French Indo-China Section, 1943–1945," *Modern Asian Studies* (2000) 34#4 pp. 943–976, in JSTOR https://www.jstor.org/stable/313136
[147] C.L.I. http://pagesperso-orange.fr/cli/, Amicale des Anciens Commandos du CLI., Pierre Guinet (CLI veteran)
[148] Adjudant Pierre GUINET, Avec le Corps Léger d'Intervention Aéroporté, GUERRE d'Indochine, Témoignage http://www.michel-elbaze.fr/index.py?page=view&id=115 NICE – Juin 1993
[149] *Au service de la France en Indochine : 1941–1945*, général Mordant, edition IFOM Saigon, 1950
[150] https://web.archive.org/web/20110628215323/http://www.questia.com/read/58600747
[151] https://www.amazon.com/Lose-Battle-France-1940-ebook/dp/B002RI9O4Q/
[152] https://www.amazon.com/dp/0393309991/
[153] https://www.jstor.org/stable/1872428
[154] http://www.army.mil/cmh/brochures/sfrance/sfrance.htm
[155] Jean-Claude Castex, *Dictionnaire des batailles navales franco-anglaises* https//books.google.com, Presses de l'Université Laval, 2004, p. 21
[156] Jean-Claude Castex, *Dictionnaire des batailles navales franco-anglaises* https//books.google.com, Presses de l'Université Laval, 2004, p.21
[157] « Les larmes de nos souverains ont le goût salé de la mer qu'ils ont ignorée ».
[158] Jenkins, History of the French Navy, p15-31,
[159] L'Art des Armées Navales ou Traité des Evolutions Navales, see Naval Warfare in the Age of Sail, Brian Tunstall, 1990, p59-64,
[160] Jenkins, History of the French Navy, p82-86,
[161] http://www.canalacademie.com/ida386-L-expedition-de-La-Perouse-1785.html
[162] Source http://xenophongroup.com/mcjoynt/marine.htm
[163] Later commentators state that the French gunners were adequate artillerymen but very poor naval gunners — that is they were incapable of compensating for the movements of their own ships
[164] S. A. Balakin: *VMS Francyy 1914-1918*, Morskaya Kollektsya 3/2000 (Russian)
[165] Description http://www.hazegray.org/navhist/carriers/france.htm#foud and photograph http://www.hazegray.org/navhist/carriers/images/europe/foudre-2.jpg of *Foudre*
[166] Clement Ader on the structure of the aircraft carrier:
"An airplane-carrying vessel is indispensable. These vessels will be constructed on a plan very different from what is currently used. First of all the deck will be cleared of all obstacles. It will

be flat, as wide as possible without jeopardizing the nautical lines of the hull, and it will look like a landing field." Military Aviation, p35
On stowage:
"Of necessity, the airplanes will be stowed below decks; they would be solidly fixed anchored to their bases, each in its place, so they would not be affected with the pitching and rolling. Access to this lower decks would be by an elevator sufficiently long and wide to hold an airplane with its wings folded. A large, sliding trap would cover the hole in the deck, and it would have waterproof joints, so that neither rain nor seawater, from heavy seas could penetrate below." Military Aviation, p36
On the technique of landing:
"The ship will be headed straight into the wind, the stern clear, but a padded bulwark set up forward in case the airplane should run past the stop line" Military Aviation, p37

[167] Reference http://www.sandcastlevi.com/sea/carriers/cvchap1b.htm
[168] http://xenophongroup.com/mcjoynt/marine.htm
[169] http://www.CityofArt.net/bship/frameset6.html
[170] http://marinepremierempire.free.fr/
[171] https://www.un.org/en/peacekeeping/missions/unifil/ United Nations Interim Force in Lebanon] Peacekeeping in between the Blue Line
[172] http://www.defense.gouv.fr/terre
[173] //en.wikipedia.org/w/index.php?title=French_Army&action=edit
[174] Original French : (...) *Maître de sa force, il respecte l'adversaire et veille à épargner les populations. Il obéit aux ordres, dans le respect des lois, des coutumes de la guerre et des conventions internationales. (...) Il est ouvert sur le monde et la société, et en respecte les différences. (...)* :
[175] Quid, ed. 2001, p.690, see also 'France, Soldiers, and Africa.'
[176] Jacques Marseille, " L'Empire ", dans *La France des années noires*, tome 1, Éd. du Seuil, rééd coll. " Points-Histoire ", 2000, p.282.
[177] Isby and Kamps, 1985, 106.
[178] Clayton, 'France, Soldiers, and Africa', Brassey's Defence Publishers, 1988, p.190
[179] Collectif, Histoire des parachutistes français, Société de Production Littéraire, 1975, 544.
[180] Alistair Horne, *The French Army and Politics, 1870–1970* (1984).
[181] J.F.V. Keiger, *France and the World since 1870* (Arnold, 2001) p 207.
[182] Martin Evans, "From colonialism to post-colonialism: the French empire since Napoleon." in Martin S. Alexander, ed., *French History since Napoleon* (1999) pp 410–11
[183] Anthony Clayton, *The Wars of French Decolonization* (1994) p 85
[184] David Isby and Charles Kamps, Armies of NATO's Central Front, Jane's Publishing Company, 1985
[185] Colonel Lamontagne G, CD http://www.cmp-cpm.forces.gc.ca/dsa-dns/sa-ns/ab/sobv-vbos-eng.asp?mAction=View&mBiographyID=844 , accessed June 2013.
[186] Isby and Kamps, 1984, p.111, 162
[187] In 1986, the 109th Infantry Division was restructured into the 109th Brigade de Zone. In 1992, as part of the " Armée 2000 " plan, the brigade became the 109th brigade régionale de défense (109th Regional Defence Brigade).
[188] French Army Terre magazine, 1998, see III Corps (France) article for reference.
[189] Jane's Defence Weekly 31 July 1996 and 13 March 1996, International Defence Review July 1998
[190] CDEF(R), no. R3222-3 Code de la défense, art. R.3222-3
[191] Charles R. Shrader, The First Helicopter War: Logistics and Mobility in Algeria, 1954–1962, Greenwood Publishing Group, 1999, 28–31.
[192] Isby and Kamps, Armies of NATO's Central Front, 131–133.
[193] Code de la défense - Article R1211-4 https://www.legifrance.gouv.fr/affichCodeArticle.do?cidTexte=LEGITEXT000006071307&idArticle=LEGIARTI000031599500&dateTexte=20160505 legifrance.gouv.fr
[194] *Chiffres clés de la Défense - 2016* http://www.defense.gouv.fr/content/download/482812/7732293/Les%20chiffres%20cl%C3%A9s%20%C3%A9dition%202016%20FR%20.pdf Retrieved 2017-03-06.
[195] http://www.defense.gouv.fr/sites/terre/

[196] http://www.carlisle.army.mil/usawc/Parameters/00summer/bloch.htm
[197] http://napoleonistyka.atspace.com/FRENCH_ARMY.htm
[198] https://www.legion-etrangere.com/
[199] https://www.legion-recrute.com/
[200] Jean-Dominique Merchet, La Légion s'accroche à ses effectifs http://secretdefense.blogs.liberation.fr/defense/2008/11/la-lgion-saccro.html
[201] The Duke of Orleans was a former Lieutenant-General.
[202]
[203] Porch p. 17–18
[204] In *Le livre d'or de la Légion étrangère*, page 66.
[205] René Chartrand, *The Mexican Adventure 1861-67*, page 19,
[206] Martin Windrow, page 5 "Our Friends Beneath the Sands",
[207] Cambridge history of Africa, p.530
[208] Musée de l'Armée exhibit, Paris
[209] Shortly before his death, Seeger wrote, "I have a rendez-vous with Death, at some disputed barricade. .. And I to my pledged word am true, I shall not fail that rendezvous."
[210] Porch p. 382–3
[211] Windrow
[212] Comor André-Paul, « La Légion étrangère dans la guerre d'Algérie, 1954–1962 », Guerres mondiales et conflits contemporains, 1/2010 (n° 237), p. 81-93.
[213] Note that in the French language, the designation of "Mounted Company" () means mounted and could be applied for both Motorized or Mounted by other means. The designation of "Motorized Company" () would be strictly limited to being motorized which is not the word being used even if it was motorized. The referral of "Mounted" Saharan Companies () is used instead of motorized strictly, even if these units were motorized, to also describe the packing of artillery. The companies could be described as Motorized Saharan Companies of the Legion; however their strict French limitation to motorized only in terms of translation and function would be incorrect as they should be referred to as "Mounted" which would apply for both Motorized or mounting other means.
[214] L. Lagneau, "En 2018, la Légion étrangère aura « retrouvé ses effectifs d'il y a 20 ans »", *Zone militaire* http://www.opex360.com/2017/04/28/en-2018-la-legion-etrangere-aura-retrouves-effectifs-dil-y-20-ans/
[215] http://www.legion-etrangere.com/mdl/info_seul.php?id=478&titre=Officier-servant-a-titre-etranger Les mots du général COM.LE (words of the general commanding the Legion, COMLE) The Commandant's Editorial, Foreign Legion Officers serving at Foreign Titles represent 10% of the Officers Corps of the Foreign Legion. Seconded from the ranks, they are the heirs to the Foreign Officers that have served France – Russian, Danish, Indochinese or Swiss – which they set and follow their example
[216] https://www.youtube.com/watch?v=CIGquKXtxgw | Video of French Foreign Legion reciting the "Legionnaire's Code of Honour" in French
[217] https://www.youtube.com/watch?v=e8z3pCTw1ag | Video of French Foreign Legion reciting the "Legionnaire's Code of Honour" in French
[218] http://www.legion-etrangere.com/mdl/info_seul.php?id=361&titre=More-Majorum, *More Majorum*, Général de division Jean Maurin Commandant la Légion étrangère (Képi-blanc Magazine).
[219] The French word "Anciens" means literary in English, that which is old (as in more senior) or ancient. In the context word in reference, the use of "Anciens" (plural form, singular form being "Ancien") is referring to that which is old and senior. For the Legion, the context word in reference is referencing the veterans () and veteran foreign regiments () of the Legion, in case of the CEPs, BEPs & REPs, the context reference is referring to the paratrooper veterans () and veteran foreign paratrooper companies (CEP)s, battalions (BEP) () and regiments (REP)s () of the Legion, in this case the 2e REP () of the Legion.
[220] Official Website of the 2nd Foreign Parachute Regiment, History of the 2e REP, the 3rd Foreign Parachute Battalion *3e Bataillon Etranger de Parachutistes* " http://2rep.legion-etrangere.com/mdl/info_seul.php?id=104&idA=47&block=16&idA_SM=43&titre=3e-bep

[221] No further promotions are given to non-French Legionnaires on attaining the rank of *Adjudant Chef*, unless they become naturalized citizens of France. In 2016, of those Foreign Legion Officers serving at Foreign Titles (French: *Officiers servant à titre étranger*), 10% were seconded officers from the ranks.<ref>http://www.legion-etrangere.com/mdl/info_seul.php?id=478&titre= Officier-servant-a-titre-etranger Les mots du général COM.LE (words of the general commanding the Legion, COMLE) The Commandant's Editorial, Foreign Legion Officers serving at Foreign Titles represent 10% of the Officers Corps of the Foreign Legion. Seconded from the ranks, they are the heirs to the Foreign Officers that have served France – Russian, Danish, Indochinese or Swiss – which they set and follow their example

[222] Since 1 January 2009, the French military rank of *major* has been included under the heading of *sous-officiers*. Previously, *Major* had been an independent rank positioned between NCOs and commissioned officers. It is an executive position within a regiment or demi-brigade having responsibility for administrative and disciplinary issues

[223] French rank Sergent-Major (similar to Sergeant Major), existed until 1971 and could come close to but is not like the French rank of Major. The last Sergent-Major retired in 1985

[224] Official Website of the General Command COMLE http://www.legion-etrangere.com/mdl/info_seul.php?id=399&block=17&titre=l-honorariat-a-la-legion-etrangere, Section L'honorariat à la Légion Etrangère (Honorary rank induction in the Foreign Legion)

[225] Douglas Porch, page 418, The French Foreign Legion. A Complete History,

[226] Szecsko, p. 17

[227] *Encyclopædia Britannica* 1911 Edition, page 587, Vol. 27

[228] Pages 26-29 "La Legion Etrangere 1831/1945, Raymond Guyader, Hors Serie No. 6 Gazette des Uniformes 1997

[229] Pages 38-41 "La Legion Etrangere 1831/1945, Raymond Guyader, Hors Serie No. 6 Gazette des Uniformes 1997

[230] Page 41 "La Legion Etrangere 1831/1945, Raymond Guyader, Hors Serie No. 6 Gazette des Uniformes 1997

[231] Frederic Martyn, *Life in the Legion: from a Soldier's Point of View* (New York: Charles Scribner's Sons, 1911), pp. 83-84. Read online at archive.org https://archive.org/stream/lifeinlegionfrom00martiala#page/58/mode/2up

[232] Pages 44-46 "La Legion Etrangere 1831/1945, Raymond Guyader, Hors Serie No. 6 Gazette des Uniformes 1997

[233] Pages 47-49 "La Legion Etrangere 1831/1945, Raymond Guyader, Hors Serie No. 6 Gazette des Uniformes 1997

[234] Page 42 "La Legion Etrangere 1831/1945, Raymond Guyader, Hors Serie No. 6 Gazette des Uniformes 1997

[235] Page 46 "La Legion Etrangere 1831/1945, Raymond Guyader, Hors Serie No. 6 Gazette des Uniformes 1997

[236] Lib.ru http://lib.ru/TXT/franclegion.txt_Piece100.01

[237] Lib.ru http://lib.ru/TXT/franclegion.txt_Piece100.02

[238] French Foreign Legion – Recruiting http://www.legion-recrute.com/en/carriere.php?SM=0

[239] " Frequently Asked Questions About the Foreign Legion (English) http://www.legion-recrute.com/en/faq.php ." French Foreign Legion. Retrieved on 4 April 2012.

[240] Sharpe, Michael. (2008) *Waffen SS Elite Forces 1: Leibstandarte and Das Reich* (p. 183) .

[241] Evan McGorman, *Life in the French Foreign Legion*, p. 21

[242] Rijksoverheid.nl http://www.rijksoverheid.nl/onderwerpen/nederlandse-nationaliteit/verliezen-nederlandse-nationaliteit

[243] Benny Morris, *1948*, 2008, p.85.

[244] http://www.legion-etrangere.com

[245] http://en.legion-etrangere.com/

[246] https://web.archive.org/web/20080714000329/http://www.legion-etrangere.fr/fr/samle/index.php

[247] http://www.amicale-daguet.com/

[248] http://foreignlegion.info/

[249] https://archive.org/details/inforeignlegion00roserich

[250] http://www.booksandwriters.co.uk/F/books-about-the-french-foreign-legion.html

[251] //tools.wmflabs.org/geohack/geohack.php?pagename=French_Foreign_Legion&params=43. 2925_N_5.5534_E_source:wikidata
[252] http://www.defense.gouv.fr/terre/decouverte/materiels
[253] http://www.senat.fr/rap/r01-350/r01-350.html
[254] http://www.senat.fr/rap/r05-215/r05-215.html
[255] http://www.senat.fr/rap/a02-071-6/a02-071-69.html
[256] http://www.senat.fr/rap/a06-081-5/a06-081-57.html#toc53
[257] http://www.nrdc.org/nuclear/nudb/datab14.asp
[258] //en.wikipedia.org/w/index.php?title=Template:Weapons_of_mass_destruction&action=edit
[259] //en.wikipedia.org/w/index.php?title=Template:Nuclear_weapons&action=edit
[260] Table of French Nuclear Forces http://www.nrdc.org/nuclear/nudb/datab16.asp (Natural Resources Defense Council, 2002)
[261] *Origin of the Force de Frappe* http://nuclearweaponarchive.org/France/FranceOrigin.html (Nuclear Weapon Archive)
[262] https://fas.org/nuke/guide/israel/nuke/farr.htm
[263] http://www.wrmea.org/wrmea-archives/95-washington-report-archives-1982-1987/december-1986/694-israels-nuclear-arsenal.html
[264] https://www.jstor.org/stable/30246784 Pinkus, Binyamin; Tlamim, Moshe (Spring 2002). "Atomic Power to Israel's Rescue: French-Israeli Nuclear Cooperation, 1949–1957". Israel Studies. 7 (1): 104–38.
[265] http://www.au.af.mil/au/awc/awcgate/cpc-pubs/farr.htm
[266] *Stuck in the Canal*, Fromkin, David - Editorial in *The New York Times*, 28 October 2006
[267] *Die Erinnerungen*, Franz Josef Strauss - Berlin 1989, p. 314
[268] Germany, the NPT, and the European Option http://www10.antenna.nl/wise/beyondbomb/4-2.html (WISE/NIRS Nuclear Monitor)
[269] Farr, Warner D (September 1999), The Third Temple's holy of holies: Israel's nuclear weapons, The Counterproliferation Papers, Future Warfare Series, 2, USAF Counterproliferation Center, Air War College, Air University, Maxwell Air Force Base, retrieved July 2, 2006 https://fas.org/nuke/guide/israel/nuke/farr.htm
[270] https://fas.org/nuke/guide/israel/nuke/
[271] BBC News: Neutron bomb: Why 'clean' is deadly http://news.bbc.co.uk/1/hi/sci/tech/395689.stm
[272] UK parliamentary question on whether condemnation was considered by Thatcher government http://hansard.millbanksystems.com/commons/1980/jul/16/french-neutron-bomb
[273] Treize ans après le dernier des essais nucléaires français, l'indemnisation des victimes en marche https://www.google.com/hostednews/afp/article/ALeqM5g-1ldRO7kq73hvOjv93wPTGz7j1Q. Hervé ASQUIN, AFP. 27 May 2009.
[274] Four decades of French nuclear testing http://www.france24.com/en/20090324-four-decades-french-nuclear-tests-atomic-bomb-gerboise-bleue-algeria-polynesia . Julien PEYRON, France24. Tuesday 24 March 2009.
[275] French Senate report #179: The first French tests in the Sahara http://www.senat.fr/rap/o97-179/o97-1799.html
[276] La bombe atomique en héritage http://www.humanite.presse.fr/journal/2007-02-21/2007-02-21-846342, *L'Humanité*, February 21, 2007
[277] 1960: France explodes third atomic bomb http://news.bbc.co.uk/onthisday/hi/dates/stories/december/27/newsid_2985000/2985200.stm, *BBC* On This Day
[278] France's Nuclear Weapons http://nuclearweaponarchive.org/France/FranceOrigin.html
[279] Dossier de présentation des essais nucléaires et leur suivi au Sahara http://www.defense.gouv.fr/content/download/60823/571529/file/SAHARA.pdf
[280] VIVE LA BOMBE! http://www.ecovisionfestival.com/edizione2007//index.php?option=com_content&task=view&id=337&Itemid=168&lang=english
[281] http://fuseurop.univ-perp.fr/sahara_e.htm
[282] " Nuclear submarines collide in Atlantic' https://www.theguardian.com/uk/2009/feb/16/nuclear-submarines-collide". The Guardian, February 16th, 2009
[283] " France 'would use nuclear arms' http://news.bbc.co.uk/2/hi/europe/4627862.stm". BBC News, Thursday 19 January 2006

[284] Nucléaire : Mise à l'eau du terrible devant Sarkozy - France - LCI http://tf1.lci.fr/infos/france/politique/0,,3784844,00-mise-eau-terrible-devant-sarkozy-.html

[285] "France cuts its nuclear weapons by a third" https://www.telegraph.co.uk/news/main.jhtml?xml=/news/2008/03/22/wsarko222.xml. *The Daily Telegraph* (London).

[286] *Question of French nuclear tests in the Sahara.* GA Res. 1379 (XIV). UNGA, 14th Sess. UN Doc A/4280 (1959). http://www.un.org/documents/ga/res/14/ares14.htm

[287] *Les essais nucleaires* http://www.senat.fr/rap/o97-179/o97-1798.html#toc32—report of the French Senate (in French)

[288] Les victimes des essais nucléaires enfin reconnues http://www.lamontagne.fr/editions_locales/montlucon/les_victimes_des_essais_nucleaires_enfin_reconnues@CARGNjFdJSsHFh8MBxg-.html . Marie-Christine Soigneux, Le Montange (Clermont-Ferrand). 27 May 2009.

[289] « J'ai participé au premier essai dans le Sahara » DANIEL BOURDON, 72 ans, de Thourotte http://www.leparisien.fr/abo-oise/j-ai-participe-au-premier-essai-dans-le-sahara-24-05-2009-524072.php. Le Parisien. 24 May 2009.

[290] Government earmarks €10 million for nuclear test victims http://www.france24.com/en/20090324-govt-earmarks-10-million-euros-compensate-nuclear-test-victims-france-algeria-polynesia . France 24. Tuesday 24 March 2009.

[291] Court denies nuclear test victims compensation http://www.france24.com/en/20090522-france-denies-reparations-victims-nuclear-tests-1960s-algeria . France 24. Friday 22 May 2009

[292] Essais nucléaires français au sud de l'Algérie: La France définit six critères http://actualite.el-annabi.com/article.php3?id_article=9477. "La voix de l'oranie" (Oran, Algeria). 21 May 2009.

[293] Nuclear compensation bill falls short of expectations http://www.france24.com/en/20090527-nuclear-compensation-bill-disappoints-victims-france-justice . France24. Wednesday 27 May 2009

[294] VICTIMES ALGÉRIENNES DES ESSAIS NUCLÉAIRES FRANÇAIS. Sur quels critères sera évalué le handicap? http://www.lexpressiondz.com/article/2/2009-05-18/63841.html. L'Expression (Algeria), 18 May 2009, p.24

[295] http://firstworldwar.com/weaponry/gas.htm

[296] https://fas.org/nuke/guide/france/cbw/

[297] https://www.scribd.com/doc/56032100/France-and-Greatness-the-Development-of-the-French-Nuclear-Program

[298] http://sonicbomb.com/modules.php?name=Content&pa=showpage&pid=112

[299] http://www.sonicbomb.com

[300] http://www.isria.com/en/free/0000024.php

[301] https://web.archive.org/web/20060110012010/http://www.nti.org/e_research/profiles/France/index_2701.html

[302] http://www.thebulletin.org

[303] http://thebulletin.metapress.com/content/k01h5q0wg50353k5/fulltext.pdf

[304] http://thebulletin.metapress.com/content/f81x51w723j70458/?p=5a349b234b2a4525b6455a8c6ab292b6&pi=11

[305] https://books.google.com/books?id=TQkAAAAAMBAJ&pg=PA39

[306] http://video.google.com/videoplay?docid=4363730934900311131

[307] http://www.nuclearfiles.org/menu/key-issues/nuclear-weapons/basics/nuclear-stockpiles.htm

[308] https://web.archive.org/web/20081121020036/http://www.point-zero-penelope.org/

[309] http//alsos.wlu.edu

[310] http://www.wilsoncenter.org/nuclear-history-documents/

[311] Official Presidential Website, Letter of Engagement to M. Jean-Claude Mallet, 31 July 2007 http//www.elysee.fr

[312] http://merln.ndu.edu/whitepapers/france_english2008.pdf

[313] Rapid Fire April 29, 2013: With New Defense Whitepaper, France Dodges Necessary Tradeoffs http://www.defenseindustrydaily.com/france-whitepaper-livre-blanc-012462/

[314] http://www.lefigaro.fr/conjoncture/2013/04/29/20002-20130429ARTFIG00357-defense-les-cinq-elements-marquants-du-livre-blanc.php

[315] http://www.lepoint.fr/editos-du-point/jean-guisnel/hollande-sanctuarise-la-dissuasion-05-07-2012-1481026_53.php

[316] //en.wikipedia.org/w/index.php?title=Template:History_of_the_Arm%C3%A9e_de_l%27Air&action=edit
[317] Andre. Van Haute, *Pictorial History of the French Air Force: 1909–40*; *Pictorial History of the French Air Force: 1941–1974* (2 vol. 1975)
[318] "France: Air Force (Armée de l'Air), in Christopher H. Sterling, *Military Communications: From Ancient Times to the 21st century* (ABC-CLIO, 2008) p168
[319] Davilla, James J., and Arthur M. Soltan. *French Aircraft of the First World War*. Stratford, CT: Flying Machines Press, 1997.
[320] WWI Aircraft Profile Gallery: France http://www.wwiaviation.com/gallery-france.html *An Illustrated History of World War I* Accessed on 27 December 2013.
[321] Christienne, Charles, and Pierre Lissarrague. *A History of French Military Aviation*. Washington, D.C.: Smithsonian Institution Press, 1986.
[322] http://www.theaerodrome.com/aces/france/index.php?pageNum_names=12&totalRows_names=182 Retrieved on 24 June 2010.
[323] http://aerostories.free.fr/1940/page8.html
[324] http://www.dtic.mil/dtic/tr/fulltext/u2/a382183.pdf
[325] http://www.acepilots.com/wwi/lafayette.html
[326] http://www.acepilots.com/wwi/us_lufbery.html
[327] http://www.ville-reims.fr/contenu/tourisme/aviation.htm
[328] http//www.defense.gouv.fr
[329] http//www.defense.gouv.fr
[330] http//www.defense.gouv.fr
[331] http://perso.wanadoo.fr/aero.slhada/accueil.htm
[332] http://www.spartacus-educational.com/FWWfaas.htm
[333] http://www.wwiaviation.com/gallery-france.html
[334] //en.wikipedia.org/w/index.php?title=Template:History_of_the_Arm%C3%A9e_de_l%27Air&action=edit
[335] Ehrengardt, Christian J. and Shores, Christopher. (1985) L'Aviation de Vichy au combat: Tome 1: Les campagnes oubliées, 3 juillet 1940 - 27 novembre 1942. Charles-Lavauzelle.
[336] Young, Edward M. (1995) Aerial Nationalism: A History of Aviation in Thailand. Smithsonian Institution Press.
[337] Royal Thai Air Force. (1976) The History of the Air Force in the Conflict with French Indochina. Bangkok.
[338] Young, Edward M. (1995) Aerial Nationalism: A History of Aviation in Thailand. Smithsonian Institution Press.
[339] Elphick, Peter. (1995) Singapore: the Pregnable Fortress: A Study in Deception, Discord and Desertion. Coronet Books.
[340] Ehrengardt, Christian J. and Shores, Christopher. *op. cit.*
[341] Royal Thai Air Force. (1976) The History of the Air Force in the Conflict with French Indochina. Bangkok.
[342] Young, Edward M. (1995) Aerial Nationalism: A History of Aviation in Thailand. Smithsonian Institution Press.
[343] Hesse d'Alzon, Claude. *op. cit.*
[344] Young, Edward M. (1995) Aerial Nationalism: A History of Aviation in Thailand. Smithsonian Institution Press.
[345] Ehrengardt, Christian J. and Shores, Christopher. *op. cit.*
[346] http://perso.wanadoo.fr/paqsenior/aL'armee%20de%20l'air%20en%20IndochineE.htm
[347] https://web.archive.org/web/20070425142600/http://www.ambafrance-us.org/news/statmnts/2005/levitte_cat-022405.asp
[348] http://www.vva.org/theveteran/2002_08/mechanics.htm
[349] http://www.thehistorynet.com/vn/blsettingthestage/
[350] http://www.onwar.com/aced/chrono/c1900s/yr45/findochina1946.htm
[351] http://aerostories.free.fr/events/algerie/algerie07
[352] http://aerostories.free.fr/events/algerie/algerie06
[353] http://www.b26.com/marauderman/louis_morin.htm

[354] http://www.defense.gouv.fr/content/download/511454/8625925/Les%20chiffres%20cle%CC%81s%20de%20la%20D%C3%A9fense%20%C3%A9dition%202017%20EN.pdf

[355] *Faire face* (French is an action or behavior of being straight forward and being honest, truthful and correct regardless the environment).

[356] http://www.defense.gouv.fr/air

[357] "Annuaire statistique de la défense 2013–2014" http://www.defense.gouv.fr/content/download/290329/3770640/file/Annuaire%20statistique%20de%20la%20défense%202013-2014.pdf 10 July 2014 (in French)

[358] "Annuaire statistiques de la défense 2012–2013" http://www.defense.gouv.fr/content/download/210241/2333433/file/Annuaire%20statistiques%20de%20la%20défense%202012-2013.pdf 4 June 2013 (in French)

[359] ()

[360] //en.wikipedia.org/w/index.php?title=Template:French_military&action=edit

[361] http://gallica.bnf.fr/ark:/12148/bpt6k6335889t/f20.item.r=A%C3%A9ronautique, Law of March 29, 1912 organizing the *Military Aeronautics*, published in Journale Officiel of March 31, 1912, Editor BNF-Gallica, gallica.bnf.fr

[362] History of light aviation of the French Army 1794–2008, Lavauzelle, Collection of History, Memory and Patrimony, Général André Martini, 2005, Paris, pages 36,42,

[363] http://www.hydroretro.net/etudegh/glevy.pdf, Hydroplanes Georges Lévy, Gérard Hartmann, 2011, The Schneider cup and veteran hydroplanes.

[364] http://gallica.bnf.fr/ark:/12148/bpt6k64542845/f2.item.r=a%C3%A9ronautique, Law on the creation of the Aeronautics Arm on December 8, 1922 published in JO on December 9, 1922, BNF-Gallica, gallica.bnf.fr

[365] Young(ed),"Command in NATO after the Cold War", 96.

[366] "Sarkozy confirmed that France will soon return to NATO's integrated command" https://web.archive.org/web/20080618161517/http://sweetness-light.com/archive/sarkozy-confirms-france-will-rejoin-nato 17 June 2008

[367] "Report Hubert Védrine" http://www.defense.gouv.fr/content/download/190042/2094793/file/Rapport%20Védrine_GBR_DEU.pdf 12 November 2012 (in English)

[368] Légifrance, base CDEF(R), numéro R3224-8, Code de la Défense, Art. R.3224-8

[369] http://www.legifrance.gouv.fr/affichTexte.do;jsessionid=5F076BBA16987B447BFCB1DAA0CFCD22.tpdjo13v_2?cidTexte=JORFTEXT000000274513&categorieLien=id, Décret n° 2007-601 du 26 avril 2007, modifiant la première partie du code de la Défense (partie réglementaire), Légifrance, Jacques Chirac, April 26, 2007

[370] Décret du 26 avril 2007 http://www.legifrance.gouv.fr/affichTexte.do;jsessionid=5F076BBA16987B447BFCB1DAA0CFCD22.tpdjo13v_2?cidTexte=JORFTEXT000000274513&categorieLien=id.

[371] "The Military Balance 2013". http://www.tandfonline.com/toc/tmib20/current, 14 March 2013.

[372] http://www.defense.gouv.fr/sca/metiers-et-expertise-du-sca, Métiers et expertise du SCA, defense.gouv.fr, February 11, 2015.

[373] Nouvelles escadres aériennes : une cohérence opérationnelle accrue, des valeurs renforcées http://www.defense.gouv.fr/air/actus-air/nouvelles-escadres-aeriennes-une-coherence-operationnelle-accrue-des-valeurs-renforcees. Site de l'Armée de l'air accessed 16 November 2015.

[374] designations of Escadrilles composed of the identifying number of material devices (for instance SPA for escadrille equipped with SPAD, N for Nieuport, SAL for Salmson,etc.) and an order number

[375] http://www.defense.gouv.fr/air/activites/unites-au-sol/les-fusiliers-commandos/les-fusiliers-commandos, Les fusiliers commandos, February 10, 2015, August 2, 2010, defense.gouv.fr; Officier commando de l'air http://www.nae.fr/wp-content/uploads/2014/07/OFFICIER-COMMANDO-PARACHUTISTE-DE-LAIR.pdf.

[376] "France faced with developments in the international and strategic context" http://www.defense.gouv.fr/english/content/download/160035/1649050/file/Doc_preparatoire_LBDSN_UK-2012-V2_WEB_Protected.pdf 3 April 2012 (in English)

[377] Scramble http://www.scramblemagazine.nl/orbats/france/airforce. Scramblemagazine.nl. Retrieved on 2013-08-16.
[378] http://alert5.com/2018/06/22/french-air-force-retires-the-mirage-2000n/
[379] https://www.dassault-aviation.com/wp-content/blogs.dir/2/files/2018/07/Dassault-Aviation-Press-Conference-July-19-2018.pdf
[380] Wikipedia lede, French Air Force
[381]
[382] http://www.avionslegendaires.net/2018/02/actu/super-king-air-350-alsr-des-shadow-r-mk-1-a-la-francaise/
[383] Michel L. Martin, Le déclin de l'armée de masse en France. Note sur quelques paramètres organisationnels,Revue française de sociologie, volume 22, number 22-1, year 1981, pages 87–115 [www.persee.fr/web/revues/home/prescript/article/rfsoc 0035-2969 1981 num 22 1 3390]
[384] Bilan social 90, Editor : Direction de la fonction militaire et du personnel civil, 1990, total pages 62, passage 6 to 8 format=PDF http://www.defense.gouv.fr/content/download/13304/122222/file/1990.pdf.
[385] http://www.defense.gouv.fr/english/air
[386] http://www.senat.fr/rap/a05-102-6/a05-102-616.html
[387] (download PDF file or see HTML version https://www.defense.gouv.fr/content/download/400382/6028076/file/Chiffrescle%CC%81s2015GB.PDF)
[388] French Navy http://www.defense.gouv.fr/marine/organisation/forces/force-d-action-navale/forces-de-surface/forces-de-surface, defense.gouv.fr
[389] http://www.etremarin.fr
[390] L'Ordonnance royale de 1772 prévoit le port de l'ancre d'or sur les tenues des régiments des ports constituant le corps royal de la Marine, implantés à Toulon, Brest, Rochefort, Saint-Malo, Bordeaux, Le Havre, Bayonne et Cherbourg.
[391] //en.wikipedia.org/w/index.php?title=Template:French_military&action=edit
[392] Wawro, Geoffrey: *The Franco-Prussian War: The German conquest of France in 1870–1871*
[393] Wilhelm Rustow and John Layland Needham: *The Way for the Rhine Frontier, 1870: Its Political and Military History*
[394] Description http://www.hazegray.org/navhist/carriers/france.htm#foud and photograph http://www.hazegray.org/navhist/carriers/images/europe/foudre-2.jpg of *Foudre*
[395] T.D. Young, *Command in NATO after the Cold War*, Carlisle Barracks, 1997
[396] *Chiffres clés de la Défense - 2016* http://www.defense.gouv.fr/content/download/482812/7732293/Les%20chiffres%20cl%C3%A9s%20C%3%A9dition%202016%20FR%20.pdf Retrieved 2017-03-06.
[397] Rapport sur la féminisation des noms de métier, fonction, grade ou titre – La diversité des usages http://www.culture.gouv.fr/culture/dglf/cogeter/feminisation/5diversite.html#ancre1064047
[398] Projet De Loi De programmation Militarie 2014/2019 http://www.infosdefense.com/wp-content/uploads/2013/08/LPM-DT.pdf (in French) August 2013
[399] http://www.defense.gouv.fr/marine
[400] http://fr.calameo.com/read/00033187617b5e26f6f56/
[401] http://fr.calameo.com/read/00033187619f879f74b63/
[402] http://www.netmarine.net/
[403] http://www.meretmarine.com/
[404] http://www.ffaa.net
[405] http://www.worldwar1atsea.net/WW1NavyFrench.htm
[406] MEMOGENDV6 information brochure edited by SIRPA-G, the Gendarmerie information bureau. The 100,000 figure includes approx 3,600 civilians.
[407] http://www.gendarmerie.interieur.gouv.fr/
[408] //en.wikipedia.org/w/index.php?title=Template:French_military&action=edit
[409] "Edouard Detaille, pages 281-293, "L'Armee Francaise",
[410] fr:Direction générale de la Gendarmerie nationale
[411] After the colour of the silver stripes that the gendarmes wear on their kepis, as opposed to the golden stripes of the Mobile Gendarmerie.

[412] Since 2016, metropolitan France has been divided into 12 administrative regions.
[413] Squadron in the British sense of the term. The equivalent US unit would be a troop or a company.
[414] circa 570 with the regional branches.
[415] *Gend'Info* (the Gendarmerie's information magazine) December 2014 issue
[416] http://www.defense.gouv.fr/gendarmerie/votre_espace/contents_in_english/organisation/special_branches/special_branches
[417] http://www.defense.gouv.fr/gendarmerie/votre_espace/contents_in_english/personnel/personnel
[418] http://www.defense.gouv.fr/gendarmerie/decouverte/moyens/effectifs/repartition/repartition_des_effectifs
[419] http//www.defense.gouv.fr
[420] https://archive.is/20121218092644/http://www.gendarmerie.interieur.gouv.fr/eng/
[421] http://www.defense.gouv.fr/gendarmerie/
[422] http://www.gouvernement.fr/garde-nationale
[423] //en.wikipedia.org/w/index.php?title=Template:French_military&action=edit
[424] Crowdy 2004, p. 14.
[425] Philip Haythornthwaite, page 87 "Uniforms of the French Revolutionary Wars,
[426] Mansel 2003, p. 4.
[427] E.G. Hourtouille, page 127 "1814 The Campaign for France",
[428] Mansel 2003, p. 13.
[429] Mansel 2003, p. 217.
[430] Mansel 2003, p. 218.
[431]
[432] *La « garde nationale », un vivier de 72 000 réservistes en 2017*, Le Monde, October 12, 2016 issue http://www.lemonde.fr/societe/article/2016/10/12/la-garde-nationale-nouveau-label-des-reserves-operationnelles_5012062_3224.html
[433] *Garde nationale, la génération « Charlie Hebdo »*, Le Monde, October 27, 2016 issue http://www.lemonde.fr/societe/article/2016/10/27/garde-nationale-la-generation-charlie-hebdo_5021169_3224.html
[434] https://web.archive.org/web/20060117210944/http://www.cats.ohiou.edu/~Chastain/ip/natguard.htm
[435] https://web.archive.org/web/20051202085301/http://www.cats.ohiou.edu/~Chastain/index.htm

Article Sources and Contributors

The sources listed for each article provide more detailed licensing information including the copyright status, the copyright owner, and the license conditions.

French Armed Forces *Source:* https://en.wikipedia.org/w/index.php?oldid=851663703 *License:* Creative Commons Attribution-Share Alike 3.0 *Contributors:* 19est66, 7Sidz, Absolutelypuremilk, Adavidb, AdjectivesAreBad, Aldred1208, Amaury, Anjosebeth, Anotherclown, Antiochus the Great, Artur Andrzej, Asire123, BU Rob13, Barek, Barjimoa, Basuel.jan133, Beyond My Ken, Bgwhite, Billymccoy1776, Blaue Max, Blaylockjam10, Bonadea, Caftaric, Chaserockstar, Ckrish, ClueBot NG, Colonestarrice, Coltsfan, Conboy456, Crazywarz, Crystallizedcarbon, Cyberbot II, Davemck, DavisAndrew416, Dirkbb, Douglas the Comeback Kid, Dragonefly777, Editor abcdef, El cid, el campeador, Erdic, Eric0928, Excirial, Fabsss, Flyer22 Reborn, Fraggle81, Frenzie23, Fuortu, General Ization, Gilliam, Glacierfairy, HMSLavender, Hayman30, Hcobb, Histoire476, Ian Dalziel, Iceonthemoon, Ifnord, InterestingCircle, J947, JMRAMOS0109, JayCoop, Jmcdon10, K6ka, Kaloyan34-FR, Kind Tennis Fan, Kosack, KylieTastic, Lemnaminor, LilHelpa, Lojbanist, LordHello1, LunchBuddies, Marc123456, Materialscientist, McMemelord, Md3l3t3, Mediavalia, Meters, Michealdasanta, Mikewood192, MilborneOne, Mollolkg, Mosper, Mother Gota, Mz7, Nath1991, Necrid Master, Nick-D, NicoScribe, Nikkimaria, Niko67000, Noclador, Nopphan, Norman21, NyggerHoleos69, OJOM, Oshwah, Pantegral, Pearce10123, PedalFuriously!, Pompomlover71, Qzd, RakMed, Red Rudy, Redalert2fan, Reordcraeft, RicJac, Rjensen, Rob984, Rocoro965, Rsrikanth05, Russ3Z, SantiLak, Sarahj2107, Skjoldbro, Slazenger, Ssolbergj, TechnicianGB, The Happy New Yorker, Themilitaryjunkie, Thorkall, Tornado chaser, Torvalu4, TwoTwoHello, Unicornpankakes, Username900122, Wrestlingring, Yamaguchi先生, Zocke1r, 180 anonymous edits 1

Military history of France *Source:* https://en.wikipedia.org/w/index.php?oldid=850895073 *License:* Creative Commons Attribution-Share Alike 3.0 *Contributors:* 099jallen, 5 albert square, Alixandah, Andres rojas22, Anotherclown, AustralianRupert, BD2412, Beland, Bender235, Betterbinder, Blaue Max, Borhammer, Brandmeister, Buckshot06, Chewings72, ClueBot NG, Cowlibob, DITWIN GRIM, Dainomite, Dead Mary, DegenFarang, DeltaQuad, Dewritech, Diefre, Don Brunett, Dreck123, Drmies, Droyselich, EBY3221, Eelamme, Epbr123, Epicgenius, Erielhonan, EternalFlare, Excirial, EyeInTheSky118, FactsOnly2014, Favonian, Fishbox123, Fjlgsjlagfjlgs, Fram, Frietjes, G.Fryer, Gadget850, Gogo Dodo, Gravuritas, Guanaco, Harry-, Hazhk, Histoire476, Historiansunite, Hmains, Hmainsbot1, Howitshouldhavebeen, Hutcher, I dream of horses, Ian Dalziel, Italia2006, Jackfork, JamesBWatson, Jdaloner, Johnbod, Jonathon A H, Jprg1966, Keukati, Khazar2, Kingolf, Krakkos, Kudzu1, KylieTastic, L Kensington, L'amateur d'aéroplanes, Lepsyleon, LindsayH, Magioladitis, Magnolia677, Malizengin, Marechal Ney, Materialscientist, Mean as custard, Mlkj, Modest Genius, Moe Epsilon, Mogism, Nev1, Noclador, Northern Muriqui, OJOM, OffsBlink, Omar77, Optakeover, Palindromedairy, Peregrine981, Pharaoh of the Wizards, Philip Trueman, PinkAmpersand, Qwertzy, R'n'B, RekishiEJ, Renaud Houdinet, Rich Farmbrough, Rjensen, Robina Fox, Royalmate1, Rsrikanth05, SantiLak, SchreiberBike, SheriffIsInTown, Shnowemehou, Sirtywell, Smallkupo, Steve Quinn, SteveStrummer, Sun Creator, Swagmuncher911, Tancrede de Lentaigne, TerinHD, The High Fin Sperm Whale, The Thing That Should Not Be, Thetweaker2017, Tide rolls, Tommy2010, Twobells, UberCryxic, UltimaRatio, Uncle Dick, Username900122, Utcursch, VEBott, Vinse14, Violetriga, Vrenator, Wayne Slam, WikHead, Wikipelli, Zocke1r, ▯, 170 anonymous edits 13

French Army in World War I *Source:* https://en.wikipedia.org/w/index.php?oldid=853059574 *License:* Creative Commons Attribution-Share Alike 3.0 *Contributors:* 72, Alansplodge, Asclepias, Auntieruth55, AustralianRupert, Berean Hunter, Berserker276, Bigger digger, Binksternet, Blaue Max, Buistr, CAPTAIN RAJU, CLCStudent, Chase me ladies, I'm the Cavalry, ClueBot NG, CommonsDelinker, Cst17, Cyclopaedic, DITWIN GRIM, DMorpheus, DMorpheus2, DadaNeem, Declanus, Dewritech, Diewelt, Don Durandal, Donner60, Drewmutt, Filiep, Fladrif, Gilliam, Guigui169, Hamish59, Hengistmate, History man lasacawac, Howicus, I dream of horses, Iohannes Animosus, Italia2006, JeffTheMudkip1, Jianhui67, Jprg1966, Jrt989, Justin15w, K6ka, Keith Johnston, Keith-264, Kiore, LtNOWIS, Mad Man American, MagSumner, Magioladitis, Marek69, Mkruglova, MusikAnimal, Mynameinc, Naraht, Nick-D, Oenie, Oshwah, Otto Didakt, Paulturtle, Piotrus, Pluma, Pmj, Qzd, R'n'B, RASAM, RaiderAspect, Ralphiethedinosaur, Rich Farmbrough, Rjensen, Scartboy, Skizzik, Tabletop, Tarheel95, Tobby72, TrollKaiser177, Ttom, Ulric1313, UltimaRatio, Vijay rath, Woogie10w, Woohookitty, YUL89YYZ, ВикиДо, 100 anonymous edits 51

Military history of France during World War II *Source:* https://en.wikipedia.org/w/index.php?oldid=849998559 *License:* Creative Commons Attribution-Share Alike 3.0 *Contributors:* A412, Addeamarielle1, Addihockey10, Anotherclown, Anselmelt, Arrowban, Athaenara, Avoided, Aymatth2, BD2412, Banak, Bentogoa, Bgwhite, Bilorv, Brenont, Brian Crawford, Carlroddam, Ccgrimm, Cgschmidt3169, ChoraPete, Chris the speller, Cliché Online, ClueBot NG, Cnwilliams, Colonies Chris, CommonsDelinker, Cyfal, DASHBotAV, DITWIN GRIM, Dead Mary, Denniss, Derekbridges, Dewritech, DexDor, Diwas, DocYako, Doctor Papa Jones, Donner60, Download, DuncanHill, Eastfarthingan, Ein Stein Drei, Emeraldflames, Equendil, Eumolpo, Fnorp, Fraggle81, Frania Wisniewska, Fustos, Gaius Cornelius, Gidonb, Giraffedata, GraemeLeggett, Gravuritas, Gregthebunny, Guigui169, Half4me, Heywoodg, Hutcher, Innotata, Italia2006, Jdaloner, John of Reading, Josve05a, Jss199, Just a guy from the KP, K6ka, Keith-264, Khazar2, Kubek15, Lear's Fool, Lepsyleon, LilHelpa, Lisiate, LittleWink, Look2See1, Lotje, LtNOWIS, Lyndaship, Magioladitis, Manxruler, Mark Arsten, Materialscientist, Matthew Proctor, Michaelhurwicz, Mild Bill Hiccup, MisterBee1966, Motacilla, Moustachioed Womanizer, MrNimbo, Mscuthbert, Mustangmike, Mynameisgavin15, NFD9001, Naraht, NearEMPTiness, NewEnglandYankee, Niceguyedc, Nick Number, Noclador, Nono64, Northumbrian, Op47, PMLawrence, Paulturtle, QMarion II, RandomCritic, Reatlas, Rhododendrites, Rich Farmbrough, Rjensen, Rpclod, Rstrong1234, RudyReis, Ryk72, Sadads, Sharkb, SteveStrummer, Sue Rangell, Tatrgel, The Utahraptor, Thetweaker2017, UY Scuti, UberCryxic, UltimaRatio, Valenciano, Victor falk, Vuvar1, W. B. Wilson, Wavelength, Welsh, Wishva de Silva, Woohookitty, Wtripley, XPTO, Y, YSSYguy, ÄDA - DÄP, Сергей Шумаков, 128 anonymous edits 72

History of the French Navy *Source:* https://en.wikipedia.org/w/index.php?oldid=852683160 *License:* Creative Commons Attribution-Share Alike 3.0 *Contributors:* Aldis90, Attilios, BD2412, Bender235, Blaue Max, Blaylockjam10, BoH, Bobblehead, Buckshot06, Chris the speller, ClueBot NG, CommonsDelinker, DITWIN GRIM, Darklilac, David Trochos, Derekbridges, Dewritech, Dpm64, Drmies, Echuck215, Esw01407, Felix505, Ground Zero, Iberville, Indubitably, Italia2006, J04n, John of Reading, Johnbod, King JohnCAPTCHA, Knife-in-the-drawer, Korrigan, Lacrimosus, LandedEagle, Larryneilson, Llammakey, Lyndaship, M-le-mot-dit, Marc-AntoineV, Mccapra, Med, Mike riversdale, Mild Bill Hiccup, Mkpumphrey, Mr ed2, NYArtsnWords, Neddyseagoon, Neilc, Per Honor et Gloria, Petrusbarbygere, Rabbabodrool, Rama, Rif Winfield, Rjensen, Rjwilmsi, Sobolewski, SteveStrummer, Steven J. Anderson, Student7, The Bushranger, TheLongTone, Tim!, UberCryxic, UltimaRatio, YUL89YYZ, ÄDA - DÄP, 47 anonymous edits 154

French Army *Source:* https://en.wikipedia.org/w/index.php?oldid=852791866 *License:* Creative Commons Attribution-Share Alike 3.0 *Contributors:* 1q2wegfhjuyt5r, 331dot, AXB, Abyssmeister, Agtx, America789, Anotherclown, Antiochus the Great, Arne6664, B.Velikov, Bandaidsplus, Basilicofresco, Berserker276, Binabik80, Blaue Max, Bsadowski1, Buckshot06, Buistr, Byteflush, CLCStudent, Caballero1967, Caddycracker, Camyoung54, Citadel48, Clean Copy, Closedmouth, ClueBot NG, CommonsDelinker, Comp.arch, Cowlibob, Creuzbourg, DVdm, Danbag65, Degen Earthfast, DelftUser, Dewritech, Doctor Poodle-doo, Dormskirk, Douglas the Comeback Kid, Dragonefly777, Dungeontrial, Eat me, I'm an azuki, Eat my mr coccy, Ebyabe, El C, Entranced98, Faizan, Favonian, FrenchArmy, Fugitron, Gadget850, Garuda28, Giraffedata, Gladamas, Grible, Hammersfan, HarryKernow, Hede2000, Hibernian, Hmainsbot1, Huehuelol, HugoAWB, Illegitimate Barrister, Incorrecthighleft, Infamousx99x, Ira Leviton, Iridescent, Italia2006, JCO312, Jack Greenmaven, Jessicapierce, John of Reading, Jperrylsu, Jpv123456, Julius.kusuma, Kaoh, Keith-264, Kent Krupa, Klemen Kocjancic, Koolmath, Kwamikagami, L'amateur d'aéroplanes, Lepsyleon, LittleWink, LlywelynII, Lovley Jubley, Lucifero4, MB298, Magioladitis, Mandruss, Marcus Cyron, MarksmanWonder, Mesoso2, Michael dingo, Mmortal03, Mogism, Mztourist, Natyayl, NawlinWiki, Nefja, Niko67000, Noclador, OJOM, Oshwah, Padfoot79, Quercus solaris, RaphaelQS, Relentlessly, Rjensen, Rob984, SchreiberBike, Seaphoto, ShakespeareFan00, Simplexity22, Souslegionersoul, Squids and Chips, Srdjan m, Strike Eagle, TMDF44, TheBaron0530, TheTallSomething, Thetweaker2017, Tom.Reding, Tony1, Tpbradbury, Transphasic, Trappist the monk, Troll3454, Tttttttttt23443443, TwoTwoHello, Widr, Wikipelli, ZappaOMati, Zausek, Zigzig20s, 140 anonymous edits 181

French Foreign Legion *Source:* https://en.wikipedia.org/w/index.php?oldid=852683458 *License:* Creative Commons Attribution-Share Alike 3.0 *Contributors:* Al83tito, Alanobrien, Ansh666, Antiqueight, Arjayay, Artaxus, Attilios, B****n, BD2412, Bender235, BigHaz, Blairall, Blaue Max, Buistr, ClueBot NG, Colonies Chris, CompliantDrone, Davhamil, Dewritech, Dinosaur192, DocWatson42, E to the Pi times i, Eksummer, Finnusertop, Frap, Frédérique Macaron, Giraffedata, GizzyCatBella, Grye, HJ Mitchell, Hohum, Iareallknowing, Italia2006, J04n, JB4340, JJMC89, Jbourboncole, John of Reading, Just a guy from the KP, Keith D, Kelisi, Kintetsubuffalo, Kostja, LilHelpa, Litlok, Loginnigol, LukeSurl, MAINEiac4434, Madreterra, Magioladitis, Maximajorian Viridio, Mbarland, Mccapra, Me, Myself, and I are Here, Michael Devore, Mndata, Mojowiha, NFLisAwesome, Neptune's Trident, Niteshift36, NorthCoastReader, NousEssayons, OJOM, Olli Niemitalo, Onel5969, OpesMentis, Orenburg1, Oshwah, Paul2520, Quickbar, QuiteUnusual, RAF910, RPH, Randy Kryn, Richard Keatinge, Russ3Z, SantiLak, Sct72, Seligne, Shellwood, Sietse, Sjö, Soetermans, Stuntman104, The Banner, The Quixotic Potato, The Sage of Stamford, TheFarix, Tintin nap, Tobby72, Trappist the monk, Twillisjr, Vihelik, WOSlinker, WereSpielChequers, WhisperToMe, WickWrite, Yosy, ZappaOMati, Кирова, 72 anonymous edits 203

Modern equipment of the French Army *Source:* https://en.wikipedia.org/w/index.php?oldid=851721836 *License:* Creative Commons Attribution-Share Alike 3.0 *Contributors:* America789, Antiochus the Great, Arjayay, Arnaud Lambert, BD2412, Blaue Max, BrookKoorb, Buistr, Cavalryman V31, Clevelander09, ClueBot NG, CommonsDelinker, Courcelles, Cyberbot II, DITWIN GRIM, DemFail, Dl2000, Dragonefly777, EditorDB, Evertatops, Faceless Enemy, FrenchArmy, GeorgeBarnick, Gilliam, Goldenbirdman, Hibernian, Hsinchong, I dream of horses, IheartIcebeams, John of Reading, Jonesey95, Jules Brunet, Kaloyan34-FR, Kaloyan99, Keith D, KylieTastic, L'amateur d'aéroplanes, LibyanMercenary, Lignières, LittleWink, LordHello1, Marcus Cyron, Mark Ekimov, MarnetteD, Molinaro787, Mortartroop, Mpawluk, Mr.Strat Starky, NahidSultan, Niceguyedc, Nickel nitride, Noclador, Northamerica1000, Novarupta, ObscureReality, Ohconfucius, Rachmat04, Ragnord, Rurickovich, Scotteaton92, Shaunak patel, Sirtywell, Smalljim, Straken, Sémhur, The Showgun Master, TheFuzzyOne, Thom2002, Thoms.l, Underlying lk, WikHead, 木の枝, 233 anonymous edits 273

France and weapons of mass destruction *Source:* https://en.wikipedia.org/w/index.php?oldid=852147216 *License:* Creative Commons Attribution-Share Alike 3.0 *Contributors:* 18Things, 219.106の者, A p3rson, Abattoir666, Alan G. Archer, Ancylostomiasis, Angusmclellan, Arado, Arunsingh16, Atomicgurl00, BD2412, Bambuway, Banedon, Belovedfreak, Bender235, Benea, Biem, BorgQueen, Buckshot06, Chumash11, Cliché Online, ClueBot

NG, Cnwilliams, Coffee, Colonies Chris, CoolieCoolster, Crosbiesmith, DadaNeem, Danlaycock, Dawkeye, Dcirovic, Deepred6502, Deineka, Der Statistiker, Deyoea, DocWatson42, Double Plus Ungood, Dziban303, Ebehn, EdC~enwiki, Enthusiast01, Erdic, Esurnir, Fasettle, FiveFourTwo, Freddie Scowen, Frietjes, Gnomsovet, Hawkeye7, Headbomb, Hibernian, Hugginsian, Hugo999, ISOGuru, Ingolfson, Ira Leviton, Italia2006, J.delanoy, Jarble, Jean.julius, John, John Vandenberg, Johnfos, Julesd, KAMiKAZOW, Kharkiv07, Khazar2, Kipoc, Ktr101, Legobot II, Lemmey, Leosls, LilHelpa, Limnalid, Lpele, Madcoverboy, Magioladitis, Malcolmx15, Mattflaschen, Matthew, Maurice Carbonaro, Max rspct, MeekSaffron, Mkolberg, Mombas, Moshe Constantine Hassan Al-Silverburg, Mouloud47, MrTranscript, Mynameinc, N.MacInnes, Natobxl, Newsnightmelrion, Nick Number, Nick D, Nirvana2013, Oh358chang, OlEnglish, Poliphile, Poolcode, Puddhe, Rich Farmbrough, Rickyrab, Rjwilmsi, Rotblats09, Rwendland, Sailsbystars, Sardanaphalus, Scorpionman, Shame On You, SkoreKeep, StjJackson, T L Miles, Tabletop, Tazmaniacs, Technopat, The PIPE, The Random Editor, TheSandDoctor, Tim!, TommyStevensLndn, Trusilver, Tssha, Tweenk, WC Jay, West.andrew.g, Ylee, Zarcademan123456, Zoe0, 136 anonymous edits 283
2008 French White Paper on Defence and National Security *Source:* https://en.wikipedia.org/w/index.php?oldid=786228836 *License:* Creative Commons Attribution-Share Alike 3.0 *Contributors:* Antiochus the Great, Bearcat, Green Giant, IRISZOOM, Marek69, Mcewan, Noclador, ObscureReality, Wilhelmina Will, 5 anonymous edits .... ??
2013 French White Paper on Defence and National Security *Source:* https://en.wikipedia.org/w/index.php?oldid=749149801 *License:* Creative Commons Attribution-Share Alike 3.0 *Contributors:* Antiochus the Great, Crazyforreading, Green Giant, IRISZOOM, Mogism, Nohomers48, OccultZone, Phd8511, That-Vela-Fella, TheFuzzyOne, 5 anonymous edits .... ??
History of the Armée de l'Air (1909–1942) *Source:* https://en.wikipedia.org/w/index.php?oldid=843574577 *License:* Creative Commons Attribution-Share Alike 3.0 *Contributors:* Aileron, Aldis90, Alkivar, Andycjp, Angusmclellan, Anotherclown, Ardfern, Articseahorse, Binksternet, Brickie, Buckshot06, CTF83!, Carabinieri, Cedrus-Libani, Chelnar, Chris the speller, Christopher Crossley, Cnwilliams, Coll7, CommonsDelinker, DITWIN GRIM, Dabbler, Danceswithzerglings, Darkstar8799, Davidcannon, Dewritech, Dl2000, FJM, Fairsing, Fixer88, Gavbadger, Georgejdorner, Good Olfactory, GracchusB, GraemeLeggett, Grant's ghost, Greenshed, Greyengine5, Gsl, Harris7, Harryurz, Jdaloner, Julius.kusuma, Karl Dickman, Keith-264, Kusma, Legotech, Letdorf, Lfgnyc, Lockley, Logologist, Lommer, Mack2, Magus732, Mandsford, Mark83, Matt Crypto, Maximus Rex, Mieciu K, Mikeo1938, Motacilla, Moverton, Mrtrey99, Neddyseagoon, Neopeius, NiD.29, Niceguyedc, Olivier, Orenburg1, Paul A, Paul Foxworthy, Picaballo, PrimeHunter, Rama, Reedmalloy, Rich Farmbrough, Richard Keatinge, Rjensen, Rlandmann, Russ3Z, Sensor, Sherurcij, Shyam, Snowmanradio, Spicemix, Srnec, SteveStrummer, Sus scrofa, TAnthony, Tassedethe, Tazmaniacs, Template namespace initialisation script, Thadius856, The PIPE, The Rambling Man, TheLongTone, Threecharlie, Tim!, TopLelKek, Topbanana, Trekphiler, UberCryxic, Vardion, Vgy7ujm, Whosasking, Wieralee, ÁDA - DÁP, 48 anonymous edits 303
History of the Armée de l'Air in the colonies (1939–62) *Source:* https://en.wikipedia.org/w/index.php?oldid=828772077 *License:* Creative Commons Attribution-Share Alike 3.0 *Contributors:* Ahoerstemeier, Ardfern, Bporopat, Buckshot06, CalJW, Carl Logan, Cedrus-Libani, Chris the speller, Christopher Crossley, Daniel J. Leivick, Deacon of Pndapetzim, Descendall, DocWatson42, GVP Webmaster, Gimme danger, Good Olfactory, Graeme374, Hmains, IAC-62, Jarnalhe, Jason Quinn, Jop2~enwiki, JoshuaZ, Julius.kusuma, Kelisi, Kevin Murray, Krellis, L'amateur d'aéroplanes, Lommer, MilborneOne, Miq, Mrtrey99, Neddyseagoon, Osomec, Pekinensis, Picaballo, Rbeas, SJC, Spot87, Srnec, Tassedethe, Tazmaniacs, The ed17, Trekphiler, Whosasking, 19 anonymous edits 321
French Air Force *Source:* https://en.wikipedia.org/w/index.php?oldid=852871320 *License:* Creative Commons Attribution-Share Alike 3.0 *Contributors:* Anotherclown, Antiochus the Great, Arnaud Lambert, Arpingstone, Aumnamahashiva, B.Velikov, BD2412, BilCat, Buckshot06, ClueBot NG, Colonel67, CommonsDelinker, Counny, Cype, David Biddulph, Dawneeker2000, Dnemiss, Droit Comparé, Duboka, Frietjes, Garuda28, Greenshed, GüniX, Illegitimate Barrister, Irondome, Kaoh, Le Addeur noir, Lignières, Lttradiumlevans77, McSly, Mesoso2, MilborneOne, Molinaro787, Narky Blert, Noclador, OJOM, Onel5969, Orenburg1, PeterWD, Plandu, Rcbutcher, Redalert2fan, Skjoldbro, TAnthony, Tom.Reding, Trappist the monk, Vanguard10, Vrnavanti, Yintan, Zausek, 118 anonymous edits 332
French Navy *Source:* https://en.wikipedia.org/w/index.php?oldid=852863838 *License:* Creative Commons Attribution-Share Alike 3.0 *Contributors:* 3primetime3, AXB, Aednichols, Aledownload, Anotherclown, Antiochus the Great, Arado, arne6664, Attilios, Beagel, BilCat, Blaue Max, Blaylockjam10, Brozozo, BubbleEngineer, Buckshot06, Buistr, Chris the speller, ClueBot NG, Cnwilliams, Creuzbourg, Cyfal, DITWIN GRIM, David Biddulph, Deadbeef, Deb, Derekbridges, Dewritech, DocWatson42, Download, Dragnadh, EdgyWashington, Editorjohn112, Euroflux, Fanx, Felix505, Frietjes, Frosty, Fry1989, Garuda28, Gbawden, GroveGuy, Hibernian, Hmains, I, Englishman, Indy beetle, Iridescent, IronGargoyle, Italia2006, J04n, JMRAMOS0109, Jim1138, John of Reading, Jop2~enwiki, Joseph Solis in Australia, KTo288, Kaloyan34-FR, Kaoh, Keith-264, Ketiltrout, Languid Scientist, Llammakey, Lockesdonkey, Luis99omg, Magioladitis, Magging34555, MarksmanWonder, Masterblooregard, Materialscientist, Mccapra, Mimich, Mogism, Molinaro787, Morningstar1814, Mr Xaero, Naraht, Noclador, OJOM, PaulinSaudi, Phd8511, PhnomPencil, Pjposullivan, Pkbwcgs, Plastikspork, Pol098, Pontus1974, Popo le Chien, Quercus solaris, Rama, RickinBaltimore, Rif Winfield, Rob984, Seren Dept, Shuipzv3, SimonTrew, Ska;sdlhasj, Skjoldbro, SoLando, Speltdecca, Steel1943, Steve92341, SteveStrummer, StjJackson, Sun Creator, Taketa, Tbritt333, Tech77, The PIPE, TheFeds, TheLongTone, Thewolfchild, Tom.Reding, Trappist the monk, UnsungKing123, Wbm1058, Widr, Zausek, Zeamays, ÁDA - DÁP, 147 anonymous edits 359
National Gendarmerie *Source:* https://en.wikipedia.org/w/index.php?oldid=852792434 *License:* Creative Commons Attribution-Share Alike 3.0 *Contributors:* Adamanthenes, Aesopos, Aextan, Alan, Alansplodge, Albertyanks, Aldis90, Alfion, AndrewHowse, Android Mouse Box 3, Andy Marchbanks, Antholintello, Antiochus the Great, Archolman, Awg1010, B.Velikov, BD2412, Ben Ben, BilCat, Blaue Max, Bri, Buistr, Calamarain, CharlieEchoTango, Chris the speller, Cliché Online, CommonsDelinker, Comp25, Consciousnessbliss, Couteausuisse, Creuzbourg, Curtainrail, Cyrille13140, Cyrius, DITWIN GRIM, Dan653, Dave1185, David.Monniaux, Davix, Degen Earthfast, Derim Hunt, Dewritech, DocWatson42, Demedend, Dumelow, Dumond.stephane, ES Vic, Euroflux, Formicarius, Frietjes, Garuda28, George Burgess, GiW, Gradac, Grafen, Graham87, Hairy Dude, Hibernian, IM-yb, Iridescent, Iuio, JMRAMOS0109, JamesBWatson, JayCoop, Jimmy, Jimmy Pitt, John of Reading, Jop2~enwiki, Joseph Solis in Australia, KTo288, Kaloyan34-FR, Kaltenmeyer, Kaoh, Ketiltrout, Kyah117, LairepoNite, Liam987, LilHelpa, Lordsketor, LukasMatt, Lutskovp, M-le-mot-dit, Mach1988, Mandarax, Martarius, MaithieuN, Mauls, Max rspct, Mesoso2, Michael Hardy, MichaelRD, Mjmarcus, Mr. Neutron, MrRadioGuy, Niceguyedc, Nick Number, Ninetyone, OJOM, ObiOne, Octane, Otto Didakt, PKT, PeterHuntington, Phonemonkey, Pogo-Pogo-Pogo, Qwyrxian, R'n'B, Rama, RedSoxFan274, Rezonansowy, Rich Farmbrough, Rjwilmsi, Rob3512, Rob984, Rojomoke, Rthorton, Russia 55, SJK, Saint Fnordius, SamuelTheGhost, SchreiberBike, Scott Roy Atwood, Selket, Ser Amantio di Nicolao, Shuipzv3, SilkTork, Sinaloa, Sleigh, Sm8900, StjJackson, Stymphal, Superzohar, Tabletop, Techhead7890, There'sNoTime, ThunderingTyphoons!, Tim!, Tomtom9041, Trappist the monk, UltimaRatio, Usama ibn Saddam ben Yorik, Vrac, WereSpielChequers, WhatsUpWorld, WhisperToMe, Woohookitty, YUL89YYZ, Yamastick, Zausek, 阿文, 173 anonymous edits 379
National Guard (France) *Source:* https://en.wikipedia.org/w/index.php?oldid=852792434 *License:* Creative Commons Attribution-Share Alike 3.0 *Contributors:* AManWithAFace, Alai, Aldis90, Arthistorian1977, BD2412, Bgwhite, BilCat, Blaue Max, Blaylockjam10, Bluemoose, Broomwick, Buistr, CCBuhr, Caerwine, Carl Logan, ClueBot NG, Cnwilliams, CommonsDelinker, DITWIN GRIM, DJ202667, DanMS, DangerouslyPersuasiveWriter, Degen Earthfast, Duffman~enwiki, Funnyhat, Gaia Octavia Agrippa, Gaius Octavius Princeps, Garuda28, Gonim, Grahamec, Huangdi, ISuredI, Indopug, J.delanoy, JMRAMOS0109, Jalen~enwiki, Jdaloner, Jmabel, JohnRamos1989, JorisEnter, JustJust51, Jvhertum, Jytdog, Kaceythekc, KylieTastic, Lazuillasher, LordAmeth, M-le-mot-dit, MB298, Mach1988, Macofe, Magioladitis, Marek69, Matt Crypto, Mesoso2, Meters, Midas02, Mitch Ames, Neddyseagoon, Nev1, OJOM, PBS, Paul August, Per Honor et Gloria, Philg88, Polylerus, Prinsgezinde, Qwerty0, Rama, Raven in Orbit, Rjwilmsi, Rmontijo, SchreiberBike, Seaphoto, Shuipzv3, Skaanadog, SkateTier, Spangineer, StjJackson, Stoicjoe, Sychonic, TaBOT-zerem, Tazmaniacs, Thatdog, The Captain Justice, Thebigdeal1776, Tordail, Trainik, Trappist the monk, UberCryxic, Widr, Zmflavius, 67 anonymous edits 405

Image Sources, Licenses and Contributors

The sources listed for each image provide more detailed licensing information including the copyright status, the copyright owner, and the license conditions.

Image *Source:* https://en.wikipedia.org/w/index.php?title=File:Logo_of_the_French_Armed_Forces.svg *License:* Creative Commons Attribution-Sharealike 3.0 *Contributors:* User:Julien1978 1
Image *Source:* https://en.wikipedia.org/w/index.php?title=File:MarquePresident.svg *License:* Public Domain *Contributors:* User:Superbenjamin 1
Image *Source:* https://en.wikipedia.org/w/index.php?title=File:Marque_mindef.svg *Contributors:* User:Auguel 1
Image *Source:* https://en.wikipedia.org/w/index.php?title=File:Marque_CEMA.svg *License:* Creative Commons Attribution-Sharealike 2.0 *Contributors:* User:Rama 2
Image *Source:* https://en.wikipedia.org/w/index.php?title=File:Flag_of_Austria.svg *License:* Public Domain *Contributors:* User:SKopp 2
Image *Source:* https://en.wikipedia.org/w/index.php?title=File:Flag_of_Belgium_(civil).svg *License:* Public Domain *Contributors:* Allforrous, Andres gb.ldc, Bean49, Cathy Richards, David Descamps, Dbenbenn, Denelson83, Evanc0912, FreshCorp619, Fry1989, Gabriel trzy, Howcome, IvanOS, Jdx, Mimich, Ms2ger, Nightstallion, Oreo Priest, Pitke, Ricordisamoa, Rocket000, Rodejong, Sarang, SiBr4, Sir Iain, ThomasPusch, Warddr, Zscout370, 15 anonymous edits 2
Image *Source:* https://en.wikipedia.org/w/index.php?title=File:Flag_of_Germany.svg *License:* Public Domain *Contributors:* Anomie, Jo-Jo Eumerus 2
Image *Source:* https://en.wikipedia.org/w/index.php?title=File:Flag_of_Italy.svg *License:* Public Domain *Contributors:* Anomie, Jo-Jo Eumerus 2
Image *Source:* https://en.wikipedia.org/w/index.php?title=File:Flag_of_Sweden.svg *License:* Public Domain *Contributors:* Anomie, Jo-Jo Eumerus, Mr. Stradivarius 2
Image *Source:* https://en.wikipedia.org/w/index.php?title=File:Flag_of_the_United_Kingdom.svg *License:* Public Domain *Contributors:* Anomie, Good Olfactory, Jo-Jo Eumerus, MSGJ, Mifter 2
Image *Source:* https://en.wikipedia.org/w/index.php?title=File:Flag_of_the_United_States.svg *License:* Public Domain *Contributors:* Anomie, Jo-Jo Eumerus, MSGJ, Mr. Stradivarius 2
Figure 1 *Source:* https://en.wikipedia.org/w/index.php?title=File:Free_French_Foreign_Legionnairs.jpg *License:* Public Domain *Contributors:* CatMan61, Common Good, Docu, Fæ, Graphium, Jim Sweeney, Thib Phil, 1 anonymous edits 3
Figure 2 *Source:* https://en.wikipedia.org/w/index.php?title=File:Opérations_extérieures_depuis_2001.png *Contributors:* User:Blaue Max 6
Figure 3 *Source:* https://en.wikipedia.org/w/index.php?title=File:Leclerc-openphotonet_PICT6015.JPG *License:* Creative Commons Attribution-Sharealike 2.5 *Contributors:* Daniel Steger (Lausanne,Switzerland) 8
Figure 4 *Source:* https://en.wikipedia.org/w/index.php?title=File:Charles_De_Gaulle_(R91)_underway_2009.jpg *License:* Public Domain *Contributors:* USN 9
Figure 5 *Source:* https//en.wikipedia.org *License:* Public Domain *Contributors:* Ariadacapo, Fæ, Joshbaumgartner, JotaCartas, L'amateur d'aéroplanes, Mike-tango, Milru, Zhuyifei1999 10
Image *Source:* https://en.wikipedia.org/w/index.php?title=File:Flag_of_France.svg *License:* Public Domain *Contributors:* Anomie, Fastily, Jo-Jo Eumerus 13
Figure 6 *Source:* https://en.wikipedia.org/w/index.php?title=File:Battle_of_Castillon.jpg *License:* Public Domain *Contributors:* -Ilhador-, Bom-Bom, BotMultichill, Brian Ammon, Eamezaga, Ecummenic, Evrik, Julien Demade, Kilom691, Lomita, Man vyi, Rolling Bone, Soerfm, Tar Lócesilion, Zhuyifei1999, 1 anonymous edits 14
Figure 7 *Source:* https://en.wikipedia.org/w/index.php?title=File:Frontiere_francaise_985_1947_small.gif *License:* Creative Commons Attribution 3.0 *Contributors:* Obscurs 16
Figure 8 *Source:* https://en.wikipedia.org/w/index.php?title=File:French_Empire_evolution.gif *License:* GNU Free Documentation License *Contributors:* User:Roke∼commonswiki 17
Figure 9 *Source:* https://en.wikipedia.org/w/index.php?title=File:Paul_Jamin_-_Le_Brenn_et_sa_part_de_butin_1893.jpg *License:* Public Domain *Contributors:* AnonMoos, BotMultichill, Charvex, Cristiano64, Dmitry Rozhkov, Kilom691, Mattes, Schmarrnintelligenz, TwoWings, Underwaterbuffalo, Zolo, 3 anonymous edits 18
Figure 10 *Source:* https://en.wikipedia.org/w/index.php?title=File:Franks_expansion.gif *License:* GNU Free Documentation License *Contributors:* User:Roke∼commonswiki 19
Figure 11 *Source:* https://en.wikipedia.org/w/index.php?title=File:Bayeux_Tapestry_WillelmDux.jpg *License:* Public Domain *Contributors:* alipaiman 20
Figure 12 *Source:* https://en.wikipedia.org/w/index.php?title=File:SiegeAvignon1226.jpg *License:* Public Domain *Contributors:* Acoma, Bohème, JuTa, Mel22, Shakko 21
Figure 13 *Source:* https://en.wikipedia.org/w/index.php?title=File:Cannons_abandonded_by_Thomas_Scalles_at_Mont_Saint-Michel.jpg *License:* Public Domain *Contributors:* Greenshed 22
Figure 14 *Source:* https://en.wikipedia.org/w/index.php?title=File:Francis_at_Marignan.jpg *License:* Public Domain *Contributors:* BotMultichill, Ghirlandajo, Mattes, Moagim, Revent, Siren-Com, Tangopaso, Xaviateur 23
Figure 15 *Source:* https://en.wikipedia.org/w/index.php?title=File:Rocroi.jpg *License:* Public Domain *Contributors:* Basvb, Blue Tulip, Bukk, Carolus, Jcb, Krun, Olivier, Pline, Rythin∼commonswiki, Schmelzle, 2 anonymous edits 24
Figure 16 *Source:* https://en.wikipedia.org/w/index.php?title=File:Battle-of-Fontenoy.jpg *License:* Public Domain *Contributors:* BotMultichill, Centenier, ChristianT, Hohum, Labattblueboy, Lotje, Soerfm, Ster3oPro, Thib Phil, 1 anonymous edits 25
Figure 17 *Source:* https://en.wikipedia.org/w/index.php?title=File:Yorktown80.JPG *License:* Public Domain *Contributors:* -Strogoff-, Alensha, BotMultichill, Cplakidas, Garitan, Goldfritha∼commonswiki, Infrogmation, Itsmine, J.-H. Janßen, JamieS93, Jarekt, Man vyi, Mbdortmund, Morgan Riley, Nonenmac, Royalbroil, Shakko, The Red Hat of Pat Ferrick, Un1c0s bot∼commonswiki, Zolo 26
Figure 18 *Source:* https://en.wikipedia.org/w/index.php?title=File:Bataille_Jemmapes.jpg *License:* Public Domain *Contributors:* inc 27
Figure 19 *Source:* https://en.wikipedia.org/w/index.php?title=File:Mort_Beaupuy.jpg *License:* Public Domain *Contributors:* AnRo0002, Anne97432, AnonMoos, Barbe-Noire, Fab5669, Karldupart, Khaerr∼commonswiki, Kilom691, Mathiasrex, Ramessou Mériamon, Schekinov Alexey Victorovich, Tan Khaerr, Thib Phil, VIGNERON 28
Figure 20 *Source:* https://en.wikipedia.org/w/index.php?title=File:Ulm_capitulation.jpg *License:* Public Domain *Contributors:* Alonso de Mendoza, AnRo0002, Auntieruth55, BotMultichill, BrokenSphere, Fma12, Hohum, Jappalang, Kilom691, Martin', Soerfm, UberCryxic, Wknight94 30
Figure 21 *Source:* https://en.wikipedia.org/w/index.php?title=File:Iena.jpg *License:* Public Domain *Contributors:* AYE R, Anne97432, Bohème, BotMultichill, Bukk, Ecummenic, Equendil, FDRMRZUSA, Fma12, Hohum, Soerfm, Tpbradbury, Wikid77 30
Figure 22 *Source:* https://en.wikipedia.org/w/index.php?title=File:Europe_map_Napoleon_1811.svg *License:* Public Domain *Contributors:* Europe_map_Napoleon_1811.png: OwenBlacker derivative work: Mnmazur (talk) 31
Figure 23 *Source:* https://en.wikipedia.org/w/index.php?title=File:131Etendue_de_l'Empire_Français.png *License:* Public Domain *Contributors:* Gd21091993 33
Figure 24 *Source:* https://en.wikipedia.org/w/index.php?title=File:Zouaves_de_la_Garde_pendant_la_campagne_d'Italie.jpg *License:* Public Domain *Contributors:* Moustachioed Womanizer, Thib Phil, Zaccarias 34
Figure 25 *Source:* https://en.wikipedia.org/w/index.php?title=File:French_87th_Regiment_Cote_34_Verdun_1916.jpg *License:* Public Domain *Contributors:* BrokenSphere, Giorgiomonteforti, Gsl∼commonswiki, JMCC1, Jibi44, Jkelly, Marcus Cyron, Rcbutcher, Svencb, 2 anonymous edits 35
Figure 26 *Source:* https://en.wikipedia.org/w/index.php?title=File:Free_French_Foreign_Legionnairs.jpg *License:* Public Domain *Contributors:* CatMan61, Common Good, Docu, Fæ, Graphium, Jim Sweeney, Thib Phil, 1 anonymous edits 36
Figure 27 *Source:* https://en.wikipedia.org/w/index.php?title=File:RHP_Cote_d'ivoire_2003.jpg *License:* Creative Commons Attribution-Sharealike 3.0,2.5,2.0,1.0 *Contributors:* Supercopter 37
Figure 28 *Source:* https://en.wikipedia.org/w/index.php?title=File:French-roundel.svg *License:* Public Domain *Contributors:* Nichalp 40
Figure 29 *Source:* https://en.wikipedia.org/w/index.php?title=File:BattleOfVirginiaCapes.jpg *License:* Public Domain *Contributors:* AYE R, AnRo0002, Anne97432, Bukk, Common Good, Ecummenic, Garitan, Gcal1971∼commonswiki, Jafeluv, Leyo, Magicpiano, Man vyi, Mattes, Morgan Riley, Rama, World Imaging, 4 anonymous edits 41
Figure 30 *Source:* https://en.wikipedia.org/w/index.php?title=File:Charles_De_Gaulle_(R91)_underway_2009.jpg *License:* Public Domain *Contributors:* USN 41
Figure 31 *Source:* https://en.wikipedia.org/w/index.php?title=File:French_Foreign_Legion_dsc06878.jpg *License:* Creative Commons Attribution-Sharealike 2.0 *Contributors:* User:David.Monniaux 43
Image *Source:* https://en.wikipedia.org/w/index.php?title=File:Commons-logo.svg *License:* logo *Contributors:* Anomie, Callanecc, CambridgeBayWeather, Jo-Jo Eumerus, RHaworth 51

Figure 32 *Source:* https://en.wikipedia.org/w/index.php?title=File:Poilusrepos.jpg *Contributors:* Asclepias, Catfishmo, Ctruongngoc, Jibi44, Président, Rcbutcher, Rosenzweig, Thib Phil, Tinodela, Yann, Zeugma fr, 1 anonymous edits ... 52
Figure 33 *Source:* https://en.wikipedia.org/w/index.php?title=File:Jean-Baptiste-Édouard_Detaille_Champigny_Décembre_1870_(1879).jpg *License:* Public Domain *Contributors:* Chabe01, FA2010, Howicus, Águila bambata ... 52
Figure 34 *Source:* https://en.wikipedia.org/w/index.php?title=File:Reservists_at_Gare_de_L'est,_Paris_(LOC).jpg *License:* Public Domain *Contributors:* Paris 16, Tangopaso ... 54
Figure 35 *Source:* https://en.wikipedia.org/w/index.php?title=File:Guarding_subway_entrance,_Paris_(LOC).jpg *License:* Public Domain *Contributors:* Fæ, Gérald Garitan, Jeriby, Olivier, Paris 16, Paris 17 ... 55
Figure 36 *Source:* https://en.wikipedia.org/w/index.php?title=File:Schlieffen_Plan_fr.svg *License:* Creative Commons Attribution-Sharealike 3.0,2.5,2.0,1.0 *Contributors:* Tinodela ... 55
Figure 37 *Source:* https://en.wikipedia.org/w/index.php?title=File:Joseph_Joffre.jpg *License:* anonymous-EU *Contributors:* Andros64, AusTerrapin, Beroesz, Coloniale, Dancer, Dowew~commonswiki, Jb1902, Leyo, Palamède, Stanmar ... 57
Figure 38 *Source:* https://en.wikipedia.org/w/index.php?title=File:French_87th_Regiment_Cote_34_Verdun_1916.jpg *License:* Public Domain *Contributors:* BrokenSphere, Giorgiomonteforti, Gsl~commonswiki, JMCC1, Jibi44, Jkelly, Marcus Cyron, Rcbutcher, Svencb, 2 anonymous edits 58
Figure 39 *Source:* https://en.wikipedia.org/w/index.php?title=File:Georges_Scott,_A_la_baïonnette_!.jpg *License:* Public Domain *Contributors:* Lvcvlvs ... 60
Figure 40 *Source:* https://en.wikipedia.org/w/index.php?title=File:River_Crossing_NGM-v31-p338.jpg *License:* Public Domain *Contributors:* - 61
Figure 41 *Source:* https://en.wikipedia.org/w/index.php?title=File:1917_-_Execution_à_Verdun_lors_des_mutineries.jpg *License:* Public Domain *Contributors:* AndreasPraefcke, Catsmeat, Emijrp, Garitan, Hohum, Juiced lemon, KoS, Quibik, Sherbrooke, Siebrand, Skimel, Stas1995, Svencb, Timeshifter, 2 anonymous edits ... 63
Figure 42 *Source:* https://en.wikipedia.org/w/index.php?title=File:El_114_de_infantería,_en_París,_el_14_de_julio_de_1917,_León_Gimpel.jpg *License:* Public Domain *Contributors:* Avron, Blaue Max, Catfishmo, Catsmeat, Centenier, M11rtinh, Olivier, Olybrius, Ultimate Destiny, 2 anonymous edits ... 64
Figure 43 *Source:* https://en.wikipedia.org/w/index.php?title=File:French_troops_going_to_Gallipoli_IWM_Q_13411.jpg *License:* Public Domain *Contributors:* Labattblueboy, Rcbutcher ... 65
Figure 44 *Source:* https://en.wikipedia.org/w/index.php?title=File:French_75_gun_at_Cape_Helles_1915.jpg *License:* Public Domain *Contributors:* Ernest Brooks (1876–1957), official Admiralty photographer ... 66
Figure 45 *Source:* https://en.wikipedia.org/w/index.php?title=File:French_heavy_cavalry_Paris_August_1914.jpg *License:* Public Domain *Contributors:* Dominic, Garitan, Gérald Garitan, Trex2001 ... 68
Figure 46 *Source:* https://en.wikipedia.org/w/index.php?title=File:French_heavy_cavalry_Paris_August_1914.jpg *License:* Public Domain *Contributors:* Bohème, Gsl~commonswiki, Ketamino, Nilfanion, Rcbutcher, SoLando, Tangopaso, Thib Phil ... 69
Figure 47 *Source:* https://en.wikipedia.org/w/index.php?title=File:Musée_de_l'Armée_-_Février_2011_(21).jpg *License:* Public Domain *Contributors:* Edouard Detaille ... 70
Figure 48 *Source:* https://en.wikipedia.org/w/index.php?title=File:Second_model_LVF_(reverse).jpg *License:* Public Domain *Contributors:* BotMultichill, Cirt, Florival fr, Fornax, Zscout370, 1 anonymous edits ... 74
Figure 49 *Source:* https://en.wikipedia.org/w/index.php?title=File:1er_régiment_parachutiste_d'infanterie_de_marine_-_drapeau.svg *License:* Creative Commons Attribution-Share Alike *Contributors:* Badzil, Cerveaugeïne, Coloniale, Fantasn 72, MGA73bot2, O (bot), Sarang, Sémhur, Thomas-Pusch, 3 anonymous edits ... 74
Figure 50 *Source:* https://en.wikipedia.org/w/index.php?title=File:7e_régiment_de_chasseurs_d'Afrique-drapeau.svg *License:* Creative Commons Attribution-Share Alike *Contributors:* , ... 75
Figure 51 *Source:* https://en.wikipedia.org/w/index.php?title=File:Churchill_De_Gaulle_HU_60057.jpg *License:* Public Domain *Contributors:* British Government ... 76
Figure 52 *Source:* https://en.wikipedia.org/w/index.php?title=File:Piorun1.jpg *License:* Public Domain *Contributors:* Andros64, Belissarius, Havang(nl), Jarekt, Romary, Siebrand, 1 anonymous edits ... 77
Figure 53 *Source:* https://en.wikipedia.org/w/index.php?title=File:De_Gaulle_shot0064.png *License:* Public Domain *Contributors:* Lokal Profil, Palamède, Rama, Zscout370 ... 78
Figure 54 *Source:* https://en.wikipedia.org/w/index.php?title=File:Insigne_du_1°_BCCP_SAS.jpg *License:* Public Domain *Contributors:* BrunoLC 79
Figure 55 *Source:* https://en.wikipedia.org/w/index.php?title=File:3rd_4th_sas_tarbes_1945.jpg *License:* Public Domain *Contributors:* Barker (Lt) No 5 Army Film & Photographic Unit ... 81
Figure 56 *Source:* https://en.wikipedia.org/w/index.php?title=File:Logo-2eDB-p1000401.jpg *Contributors:* User:Rama ... 83
Figure 57 *Source:* https://en.wikipedia.org/w/index.php?title=File:Bundesarchiv_Bild_101I-141-1258-15,_Russland-Mitte,_Soldaten_der_französischen_Legion,_Fahne.jpg *License:* Creative Commons Attribution-Sharealike 3.0 Germany *Contributors:* BotMultichill, Cirt, Florival fr, Lomita, Martin H., 3 anonymous edits ... 84
Figure 58 *Source:* https://en.wikipedia.org/w/index.php?title=File:Bundesarchiv_Bild_101I-720-0318-04,_Frankreich,_Parade_der_Milice_Francaise.jpg *License:* Creative Commons Attribution-Sharealike 3.0 Germany *Contributors:* BotMultichill, Catsmeat, Jarekt, Martin H., Melanom, Pgautl305, Thib Phil ... 85
Figure 59 *Source:* https://en.wikipedia.org/w/index.php?title=File:Bundesarchiv_Bild_183-J15385,_Katyn,_Öffnung_der_Massengräber,_Gräber_polnischer_Generale.jpg *License:* Creative Commons Attribution-Sharealike 3.0 Germany *Contributors:* Balcer~commonswiki, Dezidor, Dodsosk~commonswiki, Ilmari Karonen, Lowdown, PaterMcFly, Ras67, Túrelio, ~Pyb, 5 anonymous edits ... 86
Figure 60 *Source:* https://en.wikipedia.org/w/index.php?title=File:Bundesarchiv_Bild_101I-027-1475-37,_Marseille,_deutsch-französische_Besprechung.jpg *License:* Creative Commons Attribution-Sharealike 3.0 Germany *Contributors:* Alonso de Mendoza, Baronnet, BotMultichill, Gkml, Goesseln, Lucarelli, Marianne Casamance, Martin H. ... 85
Figure 61 *Source:* https://en.wikipedia.org/w/index.php?title=File:Bundesarchiv_Bild_101III-Apfel-017-30,_Frankreich,_Paris,_deutsche_Besatzung.jpg *License:* Creative Commons Attribution-Sharealike 3.0 Germany *Contributors:* AnRo0002, BotMultichill, Cliché Online~commonswiki, DIREKTOR, Mbdortmund, Ras67, Thgoiter, Wolfmann ... 89
Figure 62 *Source:* https://en.wikipedia.org/w/index.php?title=File:Flag_of_Free_Republic_of_Vercors.svg *License:* Creative Commons Attribution-Sharealike 3.0 *Contributors:* Vectorized by Froztbyte ... 90
Figure 63 *Source:* https://en.wikipedia.org/w/index.php?title=File:Chadian_soldier_of_WWII.jpg *License:* Public Domain *Contributors:* Free French press. Transfer: United States Office of War Information. ... 91
Figure 64 *Source:* https://en.wikipedia.org/w/index.php?title=File:Eisenhower_giraud_salute_flag.jpg *License:* Public Domain *Contributors:* Library of Congress Prints and Photographs Division Washington, D.C. 20540 ... 92
Figure 65 *Source:* https://en.wikipedia.org/w/index.php?title=File:Degaulle-freefrench.jpg *License:* Public Domain *Contributors:* Frank Capra (film) ... 93
Figure 66 *Source:* https://en.wikipedia.org/w/index.php?title=File:World_war_two_algiers_luftwaffe_raid_french_algeria_1943.JPEG *License:* Public Domain *Contributors:* Lt. W. R. Wilson. (Army) ... 94
Figure 67 *Source:* https://en.wikipedia.org/w/index.php?title=File:Freefrench_british_captured_hms_CHARLES_PLUMIER.jpg *License:* Public Domain *Contributors:* Hampton, J A (Lt) Royal Navy official photographer ... 95
Figure 68 *Source:* https://en.wikipedia.org/w/index.php?title=File:Normandie_fire.jpg *License:* Public Domain *Contributors:* US National Archives photo ... 96
Figure 69 *Source:* https://en.wikipedia.org/w/index.php?title=File:1939-1940-battle_of_france-plan-evolution.jpg *License:* Public Domain *Contributors:* 1989, Bkeli, Diannna, Dove, Herbythyme, Incnis Mrsi, Kingruedi~commonswiki, McZusatz, Mtsmallwood, Priim, 1 anonymous edits ... 97
Figure 70 *Source:* https://en.wikipedia.org/w/index.php?title=File:16May-21May1940-Fall_Gelb.svg *License:* Public Domain *Contributors:* The History Dept at the United States Army Academy ... 101
Figure 71 *Source:* https://en.wikipedia.org/w/index.php?title=File:British_prisoners_at_Dunkerque,_France.jpg *License:* Public Domain *Contributors:* AnRo0002, Catsmeat, Courcelles, G.dallorto, Gaius Cornelius, Kilom691, Kjetil r, Man vyi, Moonik, Nortmannus, Olybrius, PpPachy, Rama, SoLando, SterkeBak, Themightyquill, Thib Phil, W.wolny, 2 anonymous edits ... 105
Figure 72 *Source:* https://en.wikipedia.org/w/index.php?title=File:13June_25June1940_FallRot.svg *License:* Public Domain *Contributors:* History Dept of United States Military Academy ... 108
Figure 73 *Source:* https://en.wikipedia.org/w/index.php?title=File:French_troops_barricades2_paris_1940.png *Contributors:* Frank Capra (film) 109
Figure 74 *Source:* https://en.wikipedia.org/w/index.php?title=File:Dewoitine_D.520_Le_Bourget_02.JPG *License:* Creative Commons Attribution-Sharealike 3.0,2.5,2.0,1.0 *Contributors:* PpPachy ... 109
Figure 75 *Source:* https://en.wikipedia.org/w/index.php?title=File:Bundesarchiv_Bild_183-H25217,_Henry_Philippe_Petain_und_Adolf_Hitler.jpg *License:* Creative Commons Attribution-Sharealike 3.0 Germany *Contributors:* Althiphika, BotMultichill, Daniel*D, Drdoht, Gkml, Herr Satz, Kaiser-Begemot, Klemen Kocjancic, Lupo, Mogelzahn, Mtsmallwood, Rrohdin, Teofilo, YMS, 2 anonymous edits ... 111
Figure 76 *Source:* https://en.wikipedia.org/w/index.php?title=File:Spitfire_Musee_du_Bourget_P1010977.JPG *License:* Creative Commons Attribution-ShareAlike 3.0 Unported *Contributors:* Pline ... 112

Figure 77 *Source:* https://en.wikipedia.org/w/index.php?title=File:Emile_Fayolle_portrait_battle_of_britain_free_french_RAF.jpg *License:* Public Domain *Contributors:* Battle of Britain Monument Archives 113
Figure 78 *Source:* https//en.wikipedia.org *License:* Creative Commons Attribution-Sharealike 3.0 Germany *Contributors:* BotMultichill, Cirt, Florival fr, Martin H., Pgautl35, Wieralee, 2 anonymous edits 114
Figure 79 *Source:* https://en.wikipedia.org/w/index.php?title=File:Yak_3_Musee_du_Bourget_P1010974.JPG *License:* Creative Commons Attribution-ShareAlike 3.0 Unported *Contributors:* Pline 116
Figure 80 *Source:* https://en.wikipedia.org/w/index.php?title=File:Elba_1944.png *License:* Public Domain *Contributors:* () 117
Figure 81 *Source:* https://en.wikipedia.org/w/index.php?title=File:FFI_voiture.jpg *License:* GNU Free Documentation License *Contributors:* Ain92, Bilou~commonswiki, ComputerHotline, HAF 932, Historicair, MGA73bot2, OgreBot 2, Olybrius, Paris 16, PpPachy, TCY, Tiraden, 1 anonymous edits 117
Figure 82 *Source:* https://en.wikipedia.org/w/index.php?title=File:Sherman-french-army-normandy.jpg *License:* Public Domain *Contributors:* Ain92, Botteville, Bukvoed, Catsmeat, Cliché Online~commonswiki, Florival fr, KTo288, Makthorpe, PpPachy, Stunteltje, Thib Phil, 2 anonymous edits 120
Figure 83 *Source:* https://en.wikipedia.org/w/index.php?title=File:Crowds_of_French_patriots_line_the_Champs_Elysees-edit2.jpg *License:* Public Domain *Contributors:* Jack Downey, U.S. Office of War Information 121
Figure 84 *Source:* https://en.wikipedia.org/w/index.php?title=File:Logo-2eDB-p1000401.jpg *Contributors:* User:Rama 122
Figure 85 *Source:* https://en.wikipedia.org/w/index.php?title=File:Free_French_armoured_car_which_participated_to_the_liberation_of_La_Rochelle_in_1945.jpg *License:* Creative Commons Attribution-Sharealike 3.0 *Contributors:* Uploadalt 123
Figure 86 *Source:* https://en.wikipedia.org/w/index.php?title=File:M10_destroyer_du_8e_RCA,_Illhauesern_1.JPG *License:* Public Domain *Contributors:* Rémi Stosskopf 123
Figure 87 *Source:* https//en.wikipedia.org *License:* Public Domain *Contributors:* - 124
Figure 88 *Source:* https://en.wikipedia.org/w/index.php?title=File:Jean_Sassi_001.jpg *License:* Public Domain *Contributors:* Renée Sassi 124
Figure 89 *Source:* https://en.wikipedia.org/w/index.php?title=File:Sherman-french-army-normandy.jpg *License:* Public Domain *Contributors:* Ain92, Botteville, Bukvoed, Catsmeat, Cliché Online~commonswiki, Florival fr, KTo288, Makthorpe, PpPachy, Stunteltje, Thib Phil, 2 anonymous edits 125
Figure 90 *Source:* https://en.wikipedia.org/w/index.php?title=File:Leclerc-p011247.jpg *License:* Public Domain *Contributors:* Carl Logan~commonswiki, Florival fr, Garitan, Oursmili, Rama, Teofilo 126
Figure 91 *Source:* https://en.wikipedia.org/w/index.php?title=File:French_us_arms_1944.jpg *Contributors:* Conseil Régional de Basse-Normandie / National Archives USA 127
Figure 92 *Source:* https://en.wikipedia.org/w/index.php?title=File:JACQUESLECLERC.JPG *License:* Public Domain *Contributors:* Photographer working for the United States military 128
Figure 93 *Source:* https://en.wikipedia.org/w/index.php?title=File:Liberation_of_Marseille,_August_1944.jpg *Contributors:* User:Rama 129
Figure 94 *Source:* https//en.wikipedia.org *License:* Public Domain *Contributors:* Ain92, Florival fr, NearEMPTiness, Pedro Xing, Pibwl, Qwirkle, Wieralee 130
Figure 95 *Source:* https://en.wikipedia.org/w/index.php?title=File:Free_french_navy_triomphant_1940.jpg *License:* Public Domain *Contributors:* Tomlin, H W (Lt) Royal Navy official photographer 133
Figure 96 *Source:* https://en.wikipedia.org/w/index.php?title=File:Free_french_navy_sloop_1940.jpg *License:* Public Domain *Contributors:* Tomlin, H W (Lt) Royal Navy official photographer 135
Figure 97 *Source:* https://en.wikipedia.org/w/index.php?title=File:French_navy_aa_1940_1941.jpg *License:* Public Domain *Contributors:* Tomlin, H W (Lt) Royal Navy official photographer 136
Figure 98 *Source:* https://en.wikipedia.org/w/index.php?title=File:P-38_Parked.jpg *Contributors:* BLueFiSH.as, FAEP, Karl Dickman, Makthorpe, Svensson1 138
Figure 99 *Source:* https://en.wikipedia.org/w/index.php?title=File:General_Spears_and_General_de_Gaulle.jpg *License:* Public Domain *Contributors:* Lt L C Priest 139
Figure 100 *Source:* https://en.wikipedia.org/w/index.php?title=File:Georges-Leygues-1.jpg *License:* Public Domain *Contributors:* Alexpl, Rama, Rcbutcher 139
Figure 101 *Source:* https://en.wikipedia.org/w/index.php?title=File:Africa1940.png *License:* Creative Commons Attribution-Sharealike 3.0,2.5,2.0,1.0 *Contributors:* Jackaranga 142
Figure 102 *Source:* https://en.wikipedia.org/w/index.php?title=File:P-40F_GCII-5_Casablanca_9Jan43.jpg *License:* Public Domain *Contributors:* USAAF 142
Figure 103 *Source:* https://en.wikipedia.org/w/index.php?title=File:B-26_Le_Bourget_01.JPG *License:* Creative Commons Attribution-Sharealike 3.0,2.5,2.0,1.0 *Contributors:* User:PpPachy 143
Figure 104 *Source:* https://en.wikipedia.org/w/index.php?title=File:French_sas_north_africa_1943.jpg *License:* Public Domain *Contributors:* Currey (Sgt) No 2 Army Film & Photographic Unit 144
Figure 105 *Source:* https://en.wikipedia.org/w/index.php?title=File:Free_French_Foreign_Legionnairs.jpg *License:* Public Domain *Contributors:* CatMan61, Common Good, Docu, Fæ, Graphium, Jim Sweeney, Thib Phil, 1 anonymous edits 147
Figure 106 *Source:* https://en.wikipedia.org/w/index.php?title=File:AWM_009747.jpg *License:* Public Domain *Contributors:* not stated 148
Figure 107 *Source:* https://en.wikipedia.org/w/index.php?title=File:Gcma_commando_french_indochina_japanese.jpg *License:* Public Domain *Contributors:* Cliché Online 150
Image *Source:* https://en.wikipedia.org/w/index.php?title=File:PD-icon.svg *License:* Public Domain *Contributors:* Alex.muller, Anomie, Anonymous Dissident, CBM, Jo-Jo Eumerus, MBisanz, PBS, Quadell, Rocket000, Strangerer, Timotheus Canens, 1 anonymous edits 153
Image *Source:* https://en.wikipedia.org/w/index.php?title=File:Civil_and_Naval_Ensign_of_France.svg *License:* Public Domain *Contributors:* created by User: David Newton 154
Figure 108 *Source:* https://en.wikipedia.org/w/index.php?title=File:Jacob_Gerritz._Loef_-_Frans_oorlogsschip.jpg *License:* Public Domain *Contributors:* BoH, BotMultichill, Bukk, Mattes, Vincent Steenberg 157
Figure 109 *Source:* https://en.wikipedia.org/w/index.php?title=File:White_ensign_Battle_martinique_1779_img_9388.jpg *License:* Creative Commons Attribution-Sharealike 3.0 *Contributors:* Med 158
Figure 110 *Source:* https://en.wikipedia.org/w/index.php?title=File:Quibcardinaux2.jpg *License:* Public Domain *Contributors:* Anne97432, Barbe-Noire, BotMultichill, Botaurus, Bukk, Dormskirk, Mattes, Rama, Rsteen 160
Figure 111 *Source:* https://en.wikipedia.org/w/index.php?title=File:Bataille-Cardinaux.jpg *License:* Public Domain *Contributors:* AYE R, Anne97432, Arnaud Palastowicz, Bohème, BotMultichill, Botaurus, Broichmore, Bukk, Ecummenic, Korrigan, Mattes, Postdlf, Rama, Revent, 2 anonymous edits 160
Figure 112 *Source:* https://en.wikipedia.org/w/index.php?title=File:HMS_Monmouth_and_Foudroyant_1758.jpg *License:* Public Domain *Contributors:* AYE R, BotMultichill, Botaurus, Bukk, Docu, Ecummenic, File Upload Bot (Magnus Manske), Ibn Battuta, Korrigan, Mattes, P4K1T0, Postdlf, Rama, Rsteen, SchipperAnnetje, Stunteltje, Takeaway, 1 anonymous edits 160
Figure 113 *Source:* https://en.wikipedia.org/w/index.php?title=File:Scale_model_of_Royal_Louis-MnM2_13_MG_32-mg_6991.jpg *Contributors:* AYE R, Paris 16, Rama, S. DÉNIEL 161
Figure 114 *Source:* https://en.wikipedia.org/w/index.php?title=File:BattleOfVirginiaCapes.jpg *License:* Public Domain *Contributors:* AYE R, AnRo0002, Anne97432, Bukk, Common Good, Ecummenic, Garitan, Gcal1971~commonswiki, Jafeluv, Leyo, Magicpiano, Man vyi, Mattes, Morgan Riley, Rama, World Imaging, 4 anonymous edits 161
Figure 115 *Source:* https://en.wikipedia.org/w/index.php?title=File:Etat_de_la_Marine_royale_de_France,_1785..jpg *License:* Public Domain *Contributors:* AYE R, KTo288, Petrusbarbygere 162
Figure 116 *Source:* https://en.wikipedia.org/w/index.php?title=File:BattleOfVirginiaCapes.jpg *License:* Public Domain *Contributors:* AYE R, AnRo0002, Anne97432, Bukk, Common Good, Ecummenic, Garitan, Gcal1971~commonswiki, Jafeluv, Leyo, Magicpiano, Man vyi, Mattes, Morgan Riley, Rama, World Imaging, 4 anonymous edits 163
Figure 117 *Source:* https://en.wikipedia.org/w/index.php?title=File:Map_Battle_of_Basques_Roads_1809.jpg *License:* Creative Commons Attribution-Sharealike 3.0 *Contributors:* PHGCOM 164
Figure 118 *Source:* https://en.wikipedia.org/w/index.php?title=File:Épisode_de_l'expédition_du_Mexique_en_1838.jpg *License:* Public Domain *Contributors:* BotMultichill, Bukk, Fab5669, HombreDHojalata, J. K. H. Friedgé, Jospe, Rama 165
Figure 119 *Source:* https://en.wikipedia.org/w/index.php?title=File:Napoleon(1850).jpg *License:* Public Domain *Contributors:* Bukk, Ibn Battuta, Kertraon, Makthorpe, Mu, Rama, Stunteltje, TomTheHand, World Imaging 166
Figure 120 *Source:* https://en.wikipedia.org/w/index.php?title=File:Plongeur.jpg *License:* Public Domain *Contributors:* Infrogmation, Juiced lemon, Rcbutcher, World Imaging 166
Figure 121 *Source:* https://en.wikipedia.org/w/index.php?title=File:Gloire.jpg *License:* Public Domain *Contributors:* Bukk, Denniss, Djembayz, GeorgHH, Joshbaumgartner, Makthorpe, Pibwl, Rama, Rüdiger Wölk, Stan Shebs, Un1c0s bot~commonswiki, World Imaging 167
Figure 122 *Source:* https://en.wikipedia.org/w/index.php?title=File:LeRedoutablePhoto.jpg *License:* Public Domain *Contributors:* BotMultichill, DieBuche, Makthorpe, RSteen, Rcbutcher, World Imaging, 1 anonymous edits 167
Figure 123 *Source:* https://en.wikipedia.org/w/index.php?title=File:T-jaureg.JPG *License:* Public Domain *Contributors:* Larryneilson 168

Figure 124 *Source:* https://en.wikipedia.org/w/index.php?title=File:LaGuerriere.jpg *License:* Public Domain *Contributors:* KTo288, Pibwl, Rama, Rsteen, World Imaging, 1 anonymous edits 169
Figure 125 *Source:* https://en.wikipedia.org/w/index.php?title=File:Le_Vauban_(cuirassé).jpg *License:* Public Domain *Contributors:* User:Esby 170
Figure 126 *Source:* https://en.wikipedia.org/w/index.php?title=File:Equipage.jpg *Contributors:* - 172
Figure 127 *Source:* https://en.wikipedia.org/w/index.php?title=File:Branlebas_de_combat.jpg *License:* Public Domain *Contributors:* unknown 172
Figure 128 *Source:* https://en.wikipedia.org/w/index.php?title=File:LeFoudre.jpg *License:* Public Domain *Contributors:* Rcbutcher, World Imaging, 2 anonymous edits 173
Figure 129 *Source:* https://en.wikipedia.org/w/index.php?title=File:Fantasque.jpg *License:* Public Domain *Contributors:* U.S. Military 175
Figure 130 *Source:* https://en.wikipedia.org/w/index.php?title=File:Naval_Ensign_of_Free_France.svg *License:* GNU Free Documentation License *Contributors:* User: David Newton 176
Figure 131 *Source:* https://en.wikipedia.org/w/index.php?title=File:Temeraire1048.jpg *Contributors:* Denniss, Hohum, Juiced lemon, Rama .. 178
Image *Source:* https://en.wikipedia.org/w/index.php?title=File:Logo_of_the_French_Army_(Armee_de_Terre).svg *License:* Creative Commons Attribution-Sharealike 3.0 *Contributors:* User:Cheposo 181
Figure 132 *Source:* https://en.wikipedia.org/w/index.php?title=File:Villars_a_Denain1.jpg *License:* Public Domain *Contributors:* Adam Cuerden, Alonso de Mendoza, BotMultichill, Bukk, Durero, Ecummenic, Ermanarih, Jimmy44, Louis le Grand∼commonswiki, Martin H., Mmm448∼commonswiki, Moagim, Mu, Rebel Redcoat∼commonswiki, Thib Phil, WolfDW 184
Figure 133 *Source:* https://en.wikipedia.org/w/index.php?title=File:Battle-of-Fontenoy.jpg *License:* Public Domain *Contributors:* BotMultichill, Centenier, ChristianT, Hohum, Labattblueboy, Lotje, Soerfm, Ster3oPro, Thib Phil, 1 anonymous edits 185
Figure 134 *Source:* https://en.wikipedia.org/w/index.php?title=File:Bataille_Jemmapes.jpg *License:* Public Domain *Contributors:* inc 186
Figure 135 *Source:* https://en.wikipedia.org/w/index.php?title=File:Charles_Meynier_-_Napoleon_in_Berlin.png *License:* Public Domain *Contributors:* Anne97432, BlackIceNRW, BotMultichill, Bukk, Coyau, FDRMRZUSA, Frank Schulenburg, Jörg Zägel, Kilom691, Kirtap, Kurpfalzbilder.de, Man vyi, Mathiasrex, Moustachioed Womanizer, Savh, Srittau, Tpbradbury, Trzęsacz, Wst, 1 anonymous edits 187
Figure 136 *Source:* https://en.wikipedia.org/w/index.php?title=File:Prise_de_la_Zaatcha_(1849).png *License:* Public Domain *Contributors:* Ashashyou, DenghiùComm, Dzlinker, Labattblueboy, Moustachioed Womanizer, Pe-Jo, Robert Weemeyer 188
Figure 137 *Source:* https://en.wikipedia.org/w/index.php?title=File:Napoléon_III_et_l'Italie_-_Gerolamo_Induno_-_La_bataille_de_Magenta_-_001.jpg *License:* Creative Commons Attribution-Sharealike 3.0 *Contributors:* BotMultichill, Thesupermat 188
Figure 138 *Source:* https://en.wikipedia.org/w/index.php?title=File:El_114_de_infantería,_en_París,_el_14_de_julio_de_1917,_León_Gimpel.jpg *License:* Public Domain *Contributors:* Avron, Blaue Max, Catfishmo, Catsmeat, Centenier, M11rtinb, Olivier, Olybrius, Ultimate Destiny, 2 anonymous edits 190
Figure 139 *Source:* https://en.wikipedia.org/w/index.php?title=File:Free_French_Foreign_Legionnairs.jpg *License:* Public Domain *Contributors:* CatMan61, Common Good, Docu, Fæ, Graphium, Jim Sweeney, Thib Phil, 1 anonymous edits 191
Figure 140 *Source:* https://en.wikipedia.org/w/index.php?title=File:Commando_de_chasse_V66_du_4me_Zouaves.jpg *License:* Public Domain *Contributors:* Ardfern, Beyond My Ken, Garitan, Gbfffdsc, Madame Grinderche, Peroxide, Thib Phil 192
Figure 141 *Source:* https://en.wikipedia.org/w/index.php?title=File:Chars_AMX-30_francais.jpg *License:* Public Domain *Contributors:* INeverCry, L'amateur d'aéroplanes, Tacuru87 193
Figure 142 *Source:* https://en.wikipedia.org/w/index.php?title=File:RHP_Cote_d'ivoire_2003.jpg *License:* Creative Commons Attribution-Sharealike 3.0,2.5,2.0,1.0 *Contributors:* Supercopter 194
Figure 143 *Source:* https://en.wikipedia.org/w/index.php?title=File:HK416.jpg *License:* Creative Commons Attribution-Sharealike 2.0 *Contributors:* Dybdal. 200
Figure 144 *Source:* https://en.wikipedia.org/w/index.php?title=File:Leclerc-openphotonet_PICT6015.JPG *License:* Creative Commons Attribution-Sharealike 2.5 *Contributors:* Daniel Steger (Lausanne,Switzerland) 200
Figure 145 *Source:* https://en.wikipedia.org/w/index.php?title=File:AMX_AuF1,_40e_régiment_d'artillerie,_Implementation_Force,_1996.jpg *License:* Public Domain *Contributors:* Ain92, BotMultichill, High Contrast, Kyah117, L'amateur d'aéroplanes, Marcus Cyron, Rama 200
Figure 146 *Source:* https://en.wikipedia.org/w/index.php?title=File:Eurocopter_Tiger_p1230203.jpg *License:* Creative Commons Attribution-ShareAlike 3.0 Unported *Contributors:* User:David.Monniaux 201
Image *Source:* https://en.wikipedia.org/w/index.php?title=File:Flag_of_legion.svg *License:* Public Domain *Contributors:* SuperManu 203
Image *Source:* https://en.wikipedia.org/w/index.php?title=File:Grenade_legion.svg *License:* Public Domain *Contributors:* Infographie Képi blanc 205
Image *Source:* https://en.wikipedia.org/w/index.php?title=File:BananeLEor.jpg *License:* Public Domain *Contributors:* davric 205
Figure 147 *Source:* https://en.wikipedia.org/w/index.php?title=File:Légion_Étrangère_1852.png *License:* Public Domain *Contributors:* Jean Sorieul 209
Figure 148 *Source:* https://en.wikipedia.org/w/index.php?title=File:Légionnaire-Mexique.JPG *License:* Public Domain *Contributors:* davric 210
Figure 149 *Source:* https://en.wikipedia.org/w/index.php?title=File:Main_Danjou.gif *License:* Public Domain *Contributors:* davric 211
Figure 150 *Source:* https://en.wikipedia.org/w/index.php?title=File:Legion_sniper,_Tuyen_Quang.jpg *License:* Public Domain *Contributors:* Auntof6, File Upload Bot (Magnus Manske), Garitan, Gérald Garitan, OgreBot 2, Quibik 212
Figure 151 *Source:* https://en.wikipedia.org/w/index.php?title=File:Bonifacio_Légion_JPG1.jpg *License:* Creative Commons Attribution 3.0 *Contributors:* Jean-Pol GRANDMONT 213
Figure 152 *Source:* https://en.wikipedia.org/w/index.php?title=File:RMLE_-_1918.jpg *License:* Public Domain *Contributors:* Léna, OgreBot 2, Palamède, Patrub01 215
Figure 153 *Source:* https://en.wikipedia.org/w/index.php?title=File:Americans_in_French_Foreign_Legion_1916.jpg *License:* Public Domain *Contributors:* Author: Morlae, Edward 215
Figure 154 *Source:* https://en.wikipedia.org/w/index.php?title=File:Alan_seeger_foreign_legion.jpg *License:* Public Domain *Contributors:* Halsey, Francis Whiting 216
Figure 155 *Source:* https://en.wikipedia.org/w/index.php?title=File:Paul-Frédéric_Rollet.jpg *License:* Public Domain *Contributors:* Alfvanbeem, Gérald Garitan, Ji-Elle, Rcbutcher 217
Figure 156 *Source:* https://en.wikipedia.org/w/index.php?title=File:Bundesarchiv_Bild_102-00723,_Marokko,_Fremdenlegionäre.jpg *License:* Creative Commons Attribution-Sharealike 3.0 Germany *Contributors:* Ain92, D.W., Karat, Manxruler, Thib Phil, Tresckow 218
Figure 157 *Source:* https://en.wikipedia.org/w/index.php?title=File:Free_French_Foreign_Legionnairs.jpg *License:* Public Domain *Contributors:* CatMan61, Common Good, Docu, Fæ, Graphium, Jim Sweeney, Thib Phil, 1 anonymous edits 219
Figure 158 *Source:* https://en.wikipedia.org/w/index.php?title=File:Cie_para_3REI.JPG *License:* Public Domain *Contributors:* Lieutenant Morin 220
Figure 159 *Source:* https://en.wikipedia.org/w/index.php?title=File:Insigne_du_1°_REP.jpg *License:* Public Domain *Contributors:* reprise de l'insigne du 1er BEP 221
Figure 160 *Source:* https://en.wikipedia.org/w/index.php?title=File:Monument_aux_morts_legion_para.jpg *License:* Public Domain *Contributors:* Aschroet, Davric∼commonswiki, 1 anonymous edits 223
Figure 161 *Source:* https://en.wikipedia.org/w/index.php?title=File:CSPLE-tenue-parade.jpg *License:* Public Domain *Contributors:* davric .. 224
Figure 162 *Source:* https://en.wikipedia.org/w/index.php?title=File:Prince_Aage_of_Denmark.jpg *License:* Public Domain *Contributors:* Bain News Service, publisher 225
Figure 163 *Source:* https://en.wikipedia.org/w/index.php?title=File:Legion1PW.jpg *License:* Public Domain *Contributors:* Richard Bareford 226
Figure 164 *Source:* https://en.wikipedia.org/w/index.php?title=File:DesertStormMap_v2.svg *License:* Creative Commons Attribution-Share Alike *Contributors:* Jeff Dahl 227
Figure 165 *Source:* https://en.wikipedia.org/w/index.php?title=File:FFLegion.JPEG *License:* Public Domain *Contributors:* TECH. SGT. H. H. DEFFNER 228
Figure 166 *Source:* https://en.wikipedia.org/w/index.php?title=File:Patrol_paratroopers_foreign_legion_paris_notre_dame.jpg *License:* Creative Commons Zero *Contributors:* Jebulon 231
Figure 167 *Source:* https://en.wikipedia.org/w/index.php?title=File:ERC_90_ER.JPG *License:* Public Domain *Contributors:* davric 231
Figure 168 *Source:* https://en.wikipedia.org/w/index.php?title=File:French_Milouf_070308-N-3884F-003.JPEG *License:* Public Domain *Contributors:* Department of Defense photo by: MCC PHILIP A. FORTNAM 231
Figure 169 *Source:* https://en.wikipedia.org/w/index.php?title=File:TE_2REI_Afghanistan.jpg *License:* Creative Commons Attribution-Sharealike 3.0 *Contributors:* davric 232
Figure 170 *Source:* https://en.wikipedia.org/w/index.php?title=File:Cal50_Browning_2REI_2.jpg *License:* Creative Commons Attribution-Sharealike 3.0 *Contributors:* davric 232
Figure 171 *Source:* https://en.wikipedia.org/w/index.php?title=File:FRF2_Afghanistan.JPG *License:* Creative Commons Attribution-Sharealike 3.0 *Contributors:* davric 233
Figure 172 *Source:* https://en.wikipedia.org/w/index.php?title=File:Marche_Fourragére_02.jpg *License:* Public Domain *Contributors:* davric 235
Figure 173 *Source:* https://en.wikipedia.org/w/index.php?title=File:Aerocordage-calvi.jpg *License:* Public Domain *Contributors:* davric 235
Figure 174 *Source:* https://en.wikipedia.org/w/index.php?title=File:DLEM_tir.JPG *License:* Public Domain *Contributors:* davric 236
Figure 175 *Source:* https://en.wikipedia.org/w/index.php?title=File:Parachutistes_Balagne.jpg *License:* Public Domain *Contributors:* Davric 236

Figure 176 *Source:* https://en.wikipedia.org/w/index.php?title=File:Largage_parachutistes.JPG *License:* Public Domain *Contributors:* Davric 237

Figure 177 *Source:* https://en.wikipedia.org/w/index.php?title=File:ORANGE_Camerone2010.jpg *License:* Creative Commons Attribution-Sharealike 3.0,2.5,2.0,1.0 *Contributors:* Jeanlouiszimmermann ... 239

Figure 178 *Source:* https://en.wikipedia.org/w/index.php?title=File:Drapeaux_1RE_et_2REI_Paris_2003.jpg *License:* Public Domain *Contributors:* davric ... 239

Image *Source:* https://en.wikipedia.org/w/index.php?title=File:Insigne_du_COMLE.jpg *License:* Public Domain *Contributors:* BrunoLC ... 240

Image *Source:* https://en.wikipedia.org/w/index.php?title=File:Insige_de_béret_COMLE_Type_2.jpg *License:* Public Domain *Contributors:* BrunoLC ... 240

Image *Source:* https://en.wikipedia.org/w/index.php?title=File:Drapeau-1RE-verso.jpg *License:* Public Domain *Contributors:* davric ... 241

Image *Source:* https://en.wikipedia.org/w/index.php?title=File:Insigne_1er_régiment_étranger-transparent.png *License:* Public Domain *Contributors:* Medium69, OgreBot 2 ... 241

Image *Source:* https://en.wikipedia.org/w/index.php?title=File:Pionniers.png *License:* Public Domain *Contributors:* Superwikifan ... 241

Image *Source:* https://en.wikipedia.org/w/index.php?title=File:Insign_de_béret_1er_RE_Type_3.jpg *License:* Public Domain *Contributors:* BrunoLC ... 241

Image *Source:* https://en.wikipedia.org/w/index.php?title=File:Insigne_régimentaire_du_4e_régiment_étranger_(1937).jpg *License:* Public Domain *Contributors:* inconnu sous le commandement du lieutenant-colonel Lorillard ... 241

Image *Source:* https://en.wikipedia.org/w/index.php?title=File:Insigne_de_béret_du_4e_RE.jpg *License:* Public Domain *Contributors:* BrunoLC 241

Image *Source:* https://en.wikipedia.org/w/index.php?title=File:Insigne-GRLE.jpg *License:* Public Domain *Contributors:* User:Davric ... 241

Image *Source:* https://en.wikipedia.org/w/index.php?title=File:GRLE-béret.png *License:* Public Domain *Contributors:* Davric, improved by Garfieldairlines and Poke2001 ... 241

Image *Source:* https://en.wikipedia.org/w/index.php?title=File:DCRE.png *License:* Public Domain *Contributors:* davric ... 241

Image *Source:* https://en.wikipedia.org/w/index.php?title=File:Insigne_du_1°_REI.JPG *License:* Public Domain *Contributors:* BrunoLC ... 241

Image *Source:* https://en.wikipedia.org/w/index.php?title=File:1er_régiment_étranger_de_cavalerie-drapeau.svg *License:* GNU Free Documentation License *Contributors:* Fantassin 72 (Coloniale) ... 242

Image *Source:* https://en.wikipedia.org/w/index.php?title=File:Insigne_1er_régiment_étranger_de_cavalerie.jpg *License:* Public Domain *Contributors:* Lieutenant colonel Berger cdt PI le régiment ... 242

Image *Source:* https://en.wikipedia.org/w/index.php?title=File:Insigne_de_béret_du_1er_REC.JPG *License:* Public Domain *Contributors:* BrunoLC 242

Image *Source:* https://en.wikipedia.org/w/index.php?title=File:CERA.JPG *License:* Public Domain *Contributors:* BrunoLC ... 242

Image *Source:* https://en.wikipedia.org/w/index.php?title=File:Parachutiste_métropolitain_légion-béret.jpg *License:* Public Domain *Contributors:* BrunoLC ... 242

Image *Source:* https://en.wikipedia.org/w/index.php?title=File:Insigne1erBEP.jpg *License:* Public Domain *Contributors:* Cba Segrétain ... 242

Image *Source:* https://en.wikipedia.org/w/index.php?title=File:Insigne_1°CEPML.jpg *License:* Public Domain *Contributors:* Lieutenant Molinier 242

Image *Source:* https://en.wikipedia.org/w/index.php?title=File:1er_régiment_étranger_de_génie-drapeau.svg *License:* GNU Free Documentation License *Contributors:* Fantassin 72 (Coloniale) ... 242

Image *Source:* https://en.wikipedia.org/w/index.php?title=File:1reg.JPG *License:* Public Domain *Contributors:* d'après le modèle de l'insigne du 6e REI au Levant (1939) Fabrication artisanale puis Drago ... 242

Image *Source:* https://en.wikipedia.org/w/index.php?title=File:Insigne_de_béret_du_1er_REG.jpg *License:* Public Domain *Contributors:* BrunoLC 242

Image *Source:* https://en.wikipedia.org/w/index.php?title=File:Insigne_2e_régiment_étranger_de_génie.jpg *License:* Public Domain *Contributors:* davric ... 243

Image *Source:* https://en.wikipedia.org/w/index.php?title=File:Insigne_de_béret_du_2e_RE_Type_3.jpg *License:* Public Domain *Contributors:* BrunoLC ... 243

Image *Source:* https://en.wikipedia.org/w/index.php?title=File:2e_REC.jpg *License:* Public Domain *Contributors:* BrunoLC ... 243

Image *Source:* https://en.wikipedia.org/w/index.php?title=File:2REI.jpg *License:* Public Domain *Contributors:* davric ... 243

Image *Source:* https://en.wikipedia.org/w/index.php?title=File:2rei.jpg *License:* Public Domain *Contributors:* Insigne créée en 1957 par le colonel Goujon, commandant le 2e REI ... 243

Image *Source:* https://en.wikipedia.org/w/index.php?title=File:2rep.jpg *License:* Public Domain *Contributors:* créé en 1949 au Cambodge (inconnu) 243

Image *Source:* https://en.wikipedia.org/w/index.php?title=File:2e_régiment_étranger_de_parachutistes-drapeau.svg *License:* Creative Commons Attribution-Share Alike *Contributors:* , ... 243

Image *Source:* https://en.wikipedia.org/w/index.php?title=File:RMLE.jpg *License:* Public Domain *Contributors:* davric ... 244

Image *Source:* https://en.wikipedia.org/w/index.php?title=File:3rei.jpg *License:* Public Domain *Contributors:* Inconnu - Homologation n° G 3426 le 25 mars 1987. ... 244

Image *Source:* https://en.wikipedia.org/w/index.php?title=File:Insigne_de_béret_du_3e_RE.jpg *License:* Public Domain *Contributors:* BrunoLC 244

Image *Source:* https://en.wikipedia.org/w/index.php?title=File:1°_-_21°_RMVE.JPG *License:* Public Domain *Contributors:* BrunoLC ... 244

Image *Source:* https://en.wikipedia.org/w/index.php?title=File:2°_-_22°_RMVE.JPG *License:* Public Domain *Contributors:* BrunoLC ... 244

Image *Source:* https://en.wikipedia.org/w/index.php?title=File:Insigne3REP.jpg *License:* Public Domain *Contributors:* Capitaine Darmuzai ... 244

Image *Source:* https://en.wikipedia.org/w/index.php?title=File:5e_régiment_étranger_d'infanterie-drapeau.svg *License:* Creative Commons Attribution-Share Alike *Contributors:* , ... 244

Image *Source:* https://en.wikipedia.org/w/index.php?title=File:5°_REI_Type_1.jpg *License:* Public Domain *Contributors:* Créée en 1942 par le colonel Marcel Alessandri - Insigne non homologué ... 244

Image *Source:* https://en.wikipedia.org/w/index.php?title=File:5°_REI_béret_Type_2.jpg *License:* Public Domain *Contributors:* BrunoLC ... 244

Image *Source:* https://en.wikipedia.org/w/index.php?title=File:6e_régiment_étranger_d'infanterie-drapeau.svg *License:* Creative Commons Attribution-Share Alike *Contributors:* Fantassin 72 (Coloniale) ... 245

Image *Source:* https://en.wikipedia.org/w/index.php?title=File:6°_régiment_étranger_d'infanterie.jpg *License:* Public Domain *Contributors:* Ltn Bonchard et Lt F. (au Levant) ... 245

Image *Source:* https://en.wikipedia.org/w/index.php?title=File:6°_REG_Type_1.jpg *License:* Public Domain *Contributors:* BrunoLC ... 245

Image *Source:* https://en.wikipedia.org/w/index.php?title=File:11°_Régiment_étranger_d'Infantrie.JPG *License:* Public Domain *Contributors:* BrunoLC ... 245

Image *Source:* https://en.wikipedia.org/w/index.php?title=File:12°_Régiment_étranger_d'Infantrie.JPG *License:* Public Domain *Contributors:* BrunoLC ... 245

Image *Source:* https://en.wikipedia.org/w/index.php?title=File:13e_demi-brigade_de_légion_étrangère-drapeau.svg *License:* Creative Commons Attribution-Share Alike *Contributors:* Fantassin 72 (Coloniale) ... 245

Image *Source:* https://en.wikipedia.org/w/index.php?title=File:Insigne_régimentaire_de_la_13e_Demi-brigade_de_Légion_étrangère.jpg *License:* Public Domain *Contributors:* Davric~commonswiki, DragonflySixtyseven, INeverCry, Leyo, Richard Harvey, 2 anonymous edits ... 245

Image *Source:* https://en.wikipedia.org/w/index.php?title=File:Insigne_de_béret_du_13e_DBLE.jpg *License:* Public Domain *Contributors:* BrunoLC ... 245

Image *Source:* https://en.wikipedia.org/w/index.php?title=File:Dlem.jpg *License:* Public Domain *Contributors:* Caporal-chef Pardel sur concours organisé par CBA Racaud ... 245

Image *Source:* https://en.wikipedia.org/w/index.php?title=File:Insigne_de_béret_du_DLEM.JPG *License:* Public Domain *Contributors:* BrunoLC 245

Figure 179 *Source:* https://en.wikipedia.org/w/index.php?title=File:Foreign_Legion_Chinese_hat_Bastille_Day_2008.jpg *License:* Creative Commons Attribution 2.5 *Contributors:* Bohème, Creuzbourg, Davric~commonswiki, Florival fr, Jastrow, O (bot), Thib Phil, Wolfmann ... 246

Image *Source:* https://en.wikipedia.org/w/index.php?title=File:Première_classe_Légion.PNG *License:* Creative Commons Attribution-ShareAlike 3.0 Unported *Contributors:* Première_classe.png: Rama derivative work: Moustachioed Womanizer ... 248

Image *Source:* https://en.wikipedia.org/w/index.php?title=File:Caporal_Légion.png *License:* Creative Commons Attribution-ShareAlike 3.0 Unported *Contributors:* Caporal.png: Rama derivative work: Moustachioed Womanizer (talk) ... 248

Image *Source:* https://en.wikipedia.org/w/index.php?title=File:Caporal-chef_Legion.png *License:* Creative Commons Attribution-ShareAlike 3.0 Unported *Contributors:* Caporal-chef.png: Rama derivative work: Moustachioed Womanizer (talk) ... 248

Figure 180 *Source:* https://en.wikipedia.org/w/index.php?title=File:Foreign_Legion_bugler_Bastille_Day_2008.jpg *License:* Creative Commons Attribution 2.5 *Contributors:* Blaue Max, Davric~commonswiki, Florival fr, Jastrow, MrPanyGoff, O (bot), Rama, Tangopaso, 1 anonymous edits ... 248

Figure 181 *Source:* https://en.wikipedia.org/w/index.php?title=File:Pionnier-legion.JPG *License:* Public Domain *Contributors:* davric ... 248

Figure 182 *Source:* https://en.wikipedia.org/w/index.php?title=File:SCH_manchegauche.jpg *License:* Public Domain *Contributors:* davric ... 251

Image *Source:* https://en.wikipedia.org/w/index.php?title=File:Sergent.png *License:* GNU Free Documentation License *Contributors:* Bilou~commonswiki, BotMultichill, BotMultichillT, MGA73bot2, Oursmili, Rama, Zscout370 ... 249

Image Source: https://en.wikipedia.org/w/index.php?title=File:Sergent-chef.png License: GNU Free Documentation License Contributors: Bilou~commonswiki, BotMultichill, BotMultichillT, MGA73bot2, Oursmili, Rama, Zscout370 249
Image Source: https://en.wikipedia.org/w/index.php?title=File:Adjudant.png License: Public Domain Contributors: Bilou~commonswiki, BotMultichill, F l a n k e r, Oursmili, Rama, Rocket000 250
Image Source: https://en.wikipedia.org/w/index.php?title=File:Adjudant-chef.png License: Public Domain Contributors: Bilou~commonswiki, BotMultichill, F l a n k e r, Oursmili, Rama, Rocket000 250
Image Source: https://en.wikipedia.org/w/index.php?title=File:Major-French-Army.png License: GNU Free Documentation License Contributors: Bilou~commonswiki, BotMultichill, BotMultichillT, MGA73bot2, Oursmili, Rama, Steinbeisser~commonswiki, Zscout370 250
Image Source: https://en.wikipedia.org/w/index.php?title=File:Sous-lieutenant.png License: GNU Free Documentation License Contributors: Bilou~commonswiki, BotMultichill, BotMultichillT, MGA73bot2, Oursmili, Rama, Zscout370 250
Image Source: https://en.wikipedia.org/w/index.php?title=File:Lieutenant.png License: GNU Free Documentation License Contributors: Bilou~commonswiki, BotMultichill, BotMultichillT, MGA73bot2, Oursmili, Rama, Zscout370 250
Image Source: https://en.wikipedia.org/w/index.php?title=File:Capitaine.png License: Public Domain Contributors: Bilou~commonswiki, BotMultichill, BotMultichillT, F l a n k e r, Ilmari Karonen, Oursmili, Rama, Rocket000, Zil 250
Image Source: https://en.wikipedia.org/w/index.php?title=File:Commandant.png License: GNU Free Documentation License Contributors: Cornelis 250
Image Source: https://en.wikipedia.org/w/index.php?title=File:Lieutenant-colonel.png License: GNU Free Documentation License Contributors: Bilou~commonswiki, BotMultichill, BotMultichillT, MGA73bot2, Oursmili, Rama, Zscout370 250
Image Source: https://en.wikipedia.org/w/index.php?title=File:Colonel.png License: GNU Free Documentation License Contributors: Avron, Bilou~commonswiki, CommonsDelinker, F l a n k e r, MGA73bot2, Oursmili, Rama, 1 anonymous edits 250
Image Source: https://en.wikipedia.org/w/index.php?title=File:Insigne_général_de_brigade.svg License: Public Domain Contributors: Elgewen, Sarang 250
Image Source: https://en.wikipedia.org/w/index.php?title=File:Insigne_général_de_division.svg License: Public Domain Contributors: Sarang 250
Figure 183 Source: https://en.wikipedia.org/w/index.php?title=File:Pionniers-Cameroné.jpg License: Public Domain Contributors: davric .. 252
Figure 184 Source: https://en.wikipedia.org/w/index.php?title=File:MLE02.jpg License: Public Domain Contributors: davric 253
Figure 185 Source: https://en.wikipedia.org/w/index.php?title=File:2june_2007_296.jpg License: Creative Commons Attribution-Sharealike 2.5 Contributors: Utente:Jollyroger 254
Figure 186 Source: https://en.wikipedia.org/w/index.php?title=File:French_Foreign_Legion_dsc06878.jpg License: Creative Commons Attribution-Sharealike 2.0 Contributors: User:David.Monniaux 255
Figure 187 Source: https://en.wikipedia.org/w/index.php?title=File:Flmorocco.png Contributors: Le Petit Journal newspaper 256
Image Source: https://en.wikipedia.org/w/index.php?title=File:Jean_Olié_(1961).jpg Contributors: AWossink, Tekstman 259
Image Source: https://en.wikipedia.org/w/index.php?title=File:GMP_Bastille_Day_2008-crop.jpg License: Creative Commons Attribution 2.5 Contributors: Jastrow, O (bot), Rama, Thesupermat 260
Figure 188 Source: https://en.wikipedia.org/w/index.php?title=File:Monument_morts_legion.JPG License: Public Domain Contributors: davric 262
Figure 189 Source: https://en.wikipedia.org/w/index.php?title=File:Insigne_du_COMLE.jpg License: Public Domain Contributors: BrunoLC 262
Figure 190 Source: https://en.wikipedia.org/w/index.php?title=File:1er_RE.JPG License: Public Domain Contributors: davric 263
Figure 191 Source: https://en.wikipedia.org/w/index.php?title=File:Képi_Blanc_profile.jpg License: Public Domain Contributors: davric .. 263
Figure 192 Source: https://en.wikipedia.org/w/index.php?title=File:FAMAS-img_1018.jpg License: Creative Commons Attribution-Sharealike 2.0 Contributors: Rama 263
Figure 193 Source: https://en.wikipedia.org/w/index.php?title=File:Béret_vert_de_la_Légion_étrangère.jpg License: Public Domain Contributors: BrunoLC 264
Figure 194 Source: https://en.wikipedia.org/w/index.php?title=File:Insigne_de_béret_légion_Type_1.JPG License: Public Domain Contributors: BrunoLC 264
Figure 195 Source: https://en.wikipedia.org/w/index.php?title=File:Insigne_de_béret_de_la_Légion_étrangère.jpg License: Public Domain Contributors: BrunoLC 265
Image Source: https://en.wikipedia.org/w/index.php?title=File:EU-France.svg License: Creative Commons Attribution-Sharealike 3.0 Contributors: NuclearVacuum 283
Image Source: https://en.wikipedia.org/w/index.php?title=File:WMD_world_map.svg License: Creative Commons Attribution-Sharealike 2.5 Contributors: User:Andux, User:Simon, User:Vardion 283
Image Source: https://en.wikipedia.org/w/index.php?title=File:Symbol_book_class2.svg License: Creative Commons Attribution-Sharealike 2.5 Contributors: Lokal_Profil 285
Image Source: https://en.wikipedia.org/w/index.php?title=File:Folder_Hexagonal_Icon.svg License: GNU Free Documentation License Contributors: Anomie, Jo-Jo Eumerus, Mifter 285
Image Source: https://en.wikipedia.org/w/index.php?title=File:Fat_man.jpg License: Public Domain Contributors: U.S. Department of Defense 285
Figure 196 Source: https://en.wikipedia.org/w/index.php?title=File:USS_Enterprise_FS_Charles_de_Gaulle.jpg License: Public Domain Contributors: U.S. Navy photo by Photographer's Mate Airman Doug Pearlman. 291
Figure 197 Source: https://en.wikipedia.org/w/index.php?title=File:Protestations_australie_essais_nucleaires021996_part.jpg Contributors: User:Lpele 292
Figure 198 Source: https://en.wikipedia.org/w/index.php?title=File:Leclerc-openphotonet_PICT6015.JPG License: Creative Commons Attribution-Sharealike 2.5 Contributors: Daniel Steger (Lausanne,Switzerland) 299
Figure 199 Source: https://en.wikipedia.org/w/index.php?title=File:French-roundel.svg License: Public Domain Contributors: Nichalp .. 304
Figure 200 Source: https://en.wikipedia.org/w/index.php?title=File:Ferte-Alais_Air_Show_2004_20.jpg License: Creative Commons Attribution-Sharealike 3.0,2.5,2.0,1.0 Contributors: Lionel Allorge 304
Figure 201 Source: https://en.wikipedia.org/w/index.php?title=File:Morane-Saulnier_L_drawing.jpg Contributors: User:NiD.29 306
Figure 202 Source: https://en.wikipedia.org/w/index.php?title=File:1915VoisinLA5B2.jpg Contributors: User:Thierry~commonswiki 306
Figure 203 Source: https://en.wikipedia.org/w/index.php?title=File:Nieuport_23_colour_photo.jpg License: Public Domain Contributors: Asclepias, Catfishmo, Leyo, NiD.29, Pazuzu, SCDBob~commonswiki 307
Figure 204 Source: https://en.wikipedia.org/w/index.php?title=File:SPAD_S_XIII_Right_Rear.jpg License: Public Domain Contributors: Air Service, United States Army 307
Figure 205 Source: https://en.wikipedia.org/w/index.php?title=File:Charupien_Biplan_Bréguet_8-03-18_-_Fonds_Berthelé_-_49Fi1098.jpg Contributors: Mk-II, NiD.29, Prüm 308
Figure 206 Source: https://en.wikipedia.org/w/index.php?title=File:NiD.29_du_33e_RAM.jpg License: Public Domain Contributors: Jelob . 309
Figure 207 Source: https://en.wikipedia.org/w/index.php?title=File:Nieuport-Delage_NiD.62_C1.JPG License: Creative Commons Attribution-Sharealike 3.0,2.5,2.0,1.0 Contributors: User:Peyot 310
Figure 208 Source: https://en.wikipedia.org/w/index.php?title=File:Dewoitine_BA_112.JPG License: Creative Commons Attribution-Sharealike 3.0 Contributors: inconnu ; G.Garitan pour les modifications et le téléversement 311
Figure 209 Source: https://en.wikipedia.org/w/index.php?title=File:MS_406_fighters_in_Syria_July_1941.jpg License: Public Domain Contributors: Australian armed forces 312
Figure 210 Source: https://en.wikipedia.org/w/index.php?title=File:D.520_in_museum.jpg License: Creative Commons Attribution-Sharealike 2.5 Contributors: D.520_Le_Bourget_01.jpg: User:PpPachy 313
Figure 211 Source: https://en.wikipedia.org/w/index.php?title=File:Bloch_MB.200.png License: Public Domain Contributors: GifTagger, Petebutt 313
Figure 212 Source: https://en.wikipedia.org/w/index.php?title=File:AMIOT_143_M_06763_copie.jpg License: Creative Commons Attribution-Sharealike 3.0 Contributors: User:Garitan 314
Figure 213 Source: https://en.wikipedia.org/w/index.php?title=File:A-26C_loaned_to_France_in_Indochina.jpg License: Public Domain Contributors: USAF 324
Figure 214 Source: https://en.wikipedia.org/w/index.php?title=File:French_F8F_Bearcats_at_Tourane_c1954.jpg License: Public Domain Contributors: U.S. Navy (Copied from CVL-48-1229 (L) in Naval Attache Report) 326
Image Source: https://en.wikipedia.org/w/index.php?title=File:Logo_of_the_French_Air_Force_(Armee_de_l'Air).svg License: Public Domain Contributors: User:Cheposo ....
Figure 215 Source: https://en.wikipedia.org/w/index.php?title=File:C02797Watt1915.jpg License: Public Domain Contributors: Unknown (lent by Chaplain the Reverend E N Merrington) 334
Figure 216 Source: https://en.wikipedia.org/w/index.php?title=File:NA_T28_Fennec.jpg License: GNU Free Documentation License Contributors: Kogo 335
Figure 217 Source: https://en.wikipedia.org/w/index.php?title=File:Dassault_Mirage_IIIC_France_-_Air_Force_AN0695826.jpg Contributors: Articseahorse, Fæ, Helmy oved, L'amateur d'aéroplanes, LittleWink, OT38 336
Figure 218 Source: https://en.wikipedia.org/w/index.php?title=File:Two_French_air_force_Dassault_Mirage_F1C_aircraft.jpg License: Public Domain Contributors: USAF 337

Figure 219 *Source:* https://en.wikipedia.org/w/index.php?title=File:André_Lanata_-_Cérémonie_présentation_et_de_passation_du_drapeau_à_la_promotion_2016_X_2016.jpg *License:* Creative Commons Attribution-Sharealike 2.0 *Contributors:* Ecole polytechnique Université Paris-Saclay . 339
Figure 220 *Source:* https://en.wikipedia.org/w/index.php?title=File:Bases-aeriennes-france.jpg *License:* Public Domain *Contributors:* Mike-tango 20:37, 13 November 2006 (UTC) ... 344
Figure 221 *Source:* https://en.wikipedia.org/w/index.php?title=File:Crotale_missile_launchers_DSC00866.jpg *License:* Creative Commons Attribution-ShareAlike 1.0 Generic *Contributors:* User:David.Monniaux ... 345
Figure 222 *Source:* https://en.wikipedia.org/w/index.php?title=File:Ba117.jpg *License:* Creative Commons Attribution-Share Alike *Contributors:* Mike-tango ... 346
Figure 223 *Source:* https://en.wikipedia.org/w/index.php?title=File:AWAC-IMG_1410.jpg *License:* Creative Commons Attribution-Sharealike 2.0 *Contributors:* User:Rama ... 348
Figure 224 *Source:* https://en.wikipedia.org/w/index.php?title=File:French_Armed_Forces2.JPEG *License:* Public Domain *Contributors:* SRA ESPERANZA BERRIOS, USA ... 351
Figure 225 *Source:* https://en.wikipedia.org/w/index.php?title=File:Ecole_Air_Bastille_Day_2007.jpg *License:* Creative Commons Attribution 2.5 *Contributors:* Blaue Max, Jastrow, Man vyi, Rama, Verdy p ... 352
Image *Source:* https://en.wikipedia.org/w/index.php?title=File:French_Air_Force-général_d'armée_aérienne.svg *License:* Creative Commons Attribution-Sharealike 2.0 *Contributors:* Rama ... 354
Image *Source:* https://en.wikipedia.org/w/index.php?title=File:French_Air_Force-général_de_corps_aérien.svg *License:* Creative Commons Attribution-Sharealike 2.0 *Contributors:* Rama ... 354
Image *Source:* https://en.wikipedia.org/w/index.php?title=File:French_Air_Force-général_de_division_aérienne.svg *License:* Creative Commons Attribution-Sharealike 2.0 *Contributors:* Rama ... 354
Image *Source:* https://en.wikipedia.org/w/index.php?title=File:French_Air_Force-général_de_brigade_aérienne.svg *License:* Creative Commons Attribution-Sharealike 2.0 *Contributors:* Rama ... 354
Image *Source:* https://en.wikipedia.org/w/index.php?title=File:French_Air_Force-colonel.svg *License:* Creative Commons Attribution-Sharealike 2.0 *Contributors:* Rama ... 354
Image *Source:* https://en.wikipedia.org/w/index.php?title=File:French_Air_Force-lieutenant-colonel.svg *License:* Creative Commons Attribution-Sharealike 2.0 *Contributors:* Rama ... 354
Image *Source:* https://en.wikipedia.org/w/index.php?title=File:French_Air_Force-commandant.svg *License:* Creative Commons Attribution-Sharealike 2.0 *Contributors:* Rama ... 354
Image *Source:* https://en.wikipedia.org/w/index.php?title=File:French_Air_Force-capitaine.svg *License:* Creative Commons Attribution-Sharealike 2.0 *Contributors:* Rama ... 354
Image *Source:* https://en.wikipedia.org/w/index.php?title=File:French_Air_Force-lieutenant.svg *License:* Creative Commons Attribution-Sharealike 2.0 *Contributors:* Rama ... 354
Image *Source:* https://en.wikipedia.org/w/index.php?title=File:French_Air_Force-sous-lieutenant.svg *License:* Creative Commons Attribution-Sharealike 2.0 *Contributors:* Rama ... 354
Image *Source:* https://en.wikipedia.org/w/index.php?title=File:French_Air_Force-aspirant.svg *License:* Creative Commons Attribution-Sharealike 2.0 *Contributors:* Rama ... 354
Image *Source:* https://en.wikipedia.org/w/index.php?title=File:French_Air_Force-élève_officier.svg *License:* Creative Commons Attribution-Sharealike 2.0 *Contributors:* Rama ... 354
Image *Source:* https://en.wikipedia.org/w/index.php?title=File:French_Air_Force-aspirant_élève.svg *License:* Creative Commons Attribution-Sharealike 2.0 *Contributors:* Rama ... 356
Image *Source:* https://en.wikipedia.org/w/index.php?title=File:French_Air_Force-aspirant_EOPN.svg *License:* Creative Commons Attribution-Sharealike 2.0 *Contributors:* Rama ... 357
Image *Source:* https://en.wikipedia.org/w/index.php?title=File:French_Air_Force-major.svg *License:* Creative Commons Attribution-Sharealike 2.0 *Contributors:* Rama ... 355
Image *Source:* https://en.wikipedia.org/w/index.php?title=File:French_Air_Force-adjudant-chef.svg *License:* Creative Commons Attribution-Sharealike 2.0 *Contributors:* Rama ... 355
Image *Source:* https://en.wikipedia.org/w/index.php?title=File:French_Air_Force-adjudant.svg *License:* Creative Commons Attribution-Sharealike 2.0 *Contributors:* Rama ... 355
Image *Source:* https://en.wikipedia.org/w/index.php?title=File:French_Air_Force-sergeant-chef.svg *License:* Creative Commons Attribution-Sharealike 2.0 *Contributors:* Rama ... 355
Image *Source:* https://en.wikipedia.org/w/index.php?title=File:French_Air_Force-sergeant.svg *License:* Creative Commons Attribution-Sharealike 2.0 *Contributors:* Rama ... 355
Image *Source:* https://en.wikipedia.org/w/index.php?title=File:French_Air_Force-caporal-chef.svg *License:* Creative Commons Attribution-Sharealike 2.0 *Contributors:* Rama ... 355
Image *Source:* https://en.wikipedia.org/w/index.php?title=File:French_Air_Force-caporal.svg *License:* Creative Commons Attribution-Sharealike 2.0 *Contributors:* Rama ... 355
Image *Source:* https://en.wikipedia.org/w/index.php?title=File:French_Air_Force-aviateur_de_première_classe.svg *License:* Creative Commons Attribution-Sharealike 2.0 *Contributors:* Rama ... 355
Image *Source:* https://en.wikipedia.org/w/index.php?title=File:French_Air_Force-aviateur.svg *License:* Creative Commons Attribution-Sharealike 2.0 *Contributors:* Rama ... 355
Image *Source:* https://en.wikipedia.org/w/index.php?title=File:Logo_of_the_French_Navy_(Marine_Nationale).svg *License:* Creative Commons Attribution-Sharealike 3.0 *Contributors:* User:Cheposo ... 359
Figure 226 *Source:* https://en.wikipedia.org/w/index.php?title=File:Ancre_Marine_nationale.svg *License:* Creative Commons Attribution-Sharealike 2.0 *Contributors:* Rama ... 363
Figure 227 *Source:* https://en.wikipedia.org/w/index.php?title=File:Richelieu_1943.jpg *License:* Public Domain *Contributors:* Hohum, The ed17, Zeugma fr ... 366
Figure 228 *Source:* https://en.wikipedia.org/w/index.php?title=File:French_navy_facilities_in_metropolitan_France_corrected_2.svg *Contributors:* User:Pontus1974 ... 367
Figure 229 *Source:* https://en.wikipedia.org/w/index.php?title=File:Chevalier_Paul_(D_621).jpg *License:* Creative Commons Attribution 2.0 *Contributors:* https://www.flickr.com/people/42274124@N05/ Michael Davies ... 368
Figure 230 *Source:* https://en.wikipedia.org/w/index.php?title=File:Rafale_070412-N-8157C-542.JPEG *License:* Public Domain *Contributors:* U.S. Navy photo by Mass Communication Specialist 1st Class Denny Cantrell ... 369
Figure 231 *Source:* https://en.wikipedia.org/w/index.php?title=File:Jean-Bart_seaman_Bastille_Day_2008.jpg *License:* Creative Commons Attribution 2.5 *Contributors:* Badzil, Bohème, Ctruongngoc, Jastrow, O (bot), WakuTEST, 3 anonymous edits ... 372
Figure 232 *Source:* https://en.wikipedia.org/w/index.php?title=File:Charles-de-Gaulle_seaman_Bastille_Day_2008.jpg *License:* Creative Commons Attribution 2.5 *Contributors:* Badzil, Blaue Max, Cobatfor, Ctruongngoc, High Contrast, Jastrow, Mattes, O (bot), SunOfErat, WakuTEST, 1 anonymous edits ... 372
Figure 233 *Source:* https://en.wikipedia.org/w/index.php?title=File:Matelot.jpg *License:* Creative Commons Attribution-Sharealike 3.0 *Contributors:* Marine nationale/Seurot Franck ... 373
Figure 234 *Source:* https://en.wikipedia.org/w/index.php?title=File:Quartier_maitre.jpg *License:* Creative Commons Attribution-Sharealike 3.0 *Contributors:* Marine nationale/Cavallo, Christian ... 373
Figure 235 *Source:* https://en.wikipedia.org/w/index.php?title=File:FREMM_Mohammed_VI_-_Lorient_2013-05.JPG *License:* Creative Commons Attribution-Sharealike 3.0 *Contributors:* User:XIIIfromTOKYO ... 374
Figure 236 *Source:* https://en.wikipedia.org/w/index.php?title=File:Barracuda-Suffren.svg *License:* Creative Commons Attribution-Sharealike 2.0 *Contributors:* Rama ... 375
Figure 237 *Source:* https//en.wikipedia.org *Contributors:* Official Navy Page from United States of America MC2 Tom Gagnier/U.S. Navy ... 375
Figure 238 *Source:* https://en.wikipedia.org/w/index.php?title=File:Gengarmerie_img_1069.jpg *License:* Creative Commons Attribution-Sharealike 2.0 *Contributors:* Rama ... 380
Figure 239 *Source:* https://en.wikipedia.org/w/index.php?title=File:Garde_républicaine_cavalry_squadron_-_Paris.jpg *License:* Creative Commons Attribution-Sharealike 3.0 *Contributors:* User:Domenjod ... 380
Figure 240 *Source:* https://en.wikipedia.org/w/index.php?title=File:French_Republican_Guard_Bastille_Day_2007_n2.jpg *License:* Creative Commons Attribution 2.5 *Contributors:* Marie-Lan Nguyen ... 385
Figure 241 *Source:* https://en.wikipedia.org/w/index.php?title=File:Gendarmes_501585_fh000019.jpg *License:* Creative Commons Attribution-ShareAlike 3.0 Unported *Contributors:* User:David.Monniaux ... 388
Figure 242 *Source:* https://en.wikipedia.org/w/index.php?title=File:GBGM5F_Domenjod_160316.jpg *Contributors:* User:Domenjod ... 390
Figure 243 *Source:* https://en.wikipedia.org/w/index.php?title=File:GIGN4_Domenjod_160316.jpg *Contributors:* User:Domenjod ... 391
Figure 244 *Source:* https://en.wikipedia.org/w/index.php?title=File:Gengarmerie_img_1069.jpg *License:* Creative Commons Attribution-Sharealike 2.0 *Contributors:* Rama ... 394

Figure 245 *Source:* https://en.wikipedia.org/w/index.php?title=File:Gendarmerie_BMW_R1100RT.jpg *License:* Creative Commons Attribution-Sharealike 2.0 *Contributors:* User:Rama ... 395
Figure 246 *Source:* https://en.wikipedia.org/w/index.php?title=File:Air_Transport_Gendarmerie_Bastille_Day_2013_Paris_t110557.jpg *License:* Creative Commons Attribution 2.5 *Contributors:* Jastrow, Rama ... 395
Figure 247 *Source:* https://en.wikipedia.org/w/index.php?title=File:Gendarmes_mobiles_FAMAS.jpg *License:* GNU Free Documentation License *Contributors:* Beorhtwulf, David.Monniaux, Rama, Sfan00 IMG ... 396
Figure 248 *Source:* https://en.wikipedia.org/w/index.php?title=File:Gendarmes_mobiles_p1200789.jpg *License:* Creative Commons Attribution-ShareAlike 3.0 Unported *Contributors:* User:David.Monniaux ... 396
Image *Source:* https://en.wikipedia.org/w/index.php?title=File:Général_armée_gend.svg *License:* Creative Commons Attribution-Sharealike 3.0,2.5,2.0,1.0 *Contributors:* Mangouste35 ... 397
Image *Source:* https://en.wikipedia.org/w/index.php?title=File:Général_corps_d'armée_gend.svg *License:* Creative Commons Attribution-Sharealike 3.0,2.5,2.0,1.0 *Contributors:* Mangouste35 ... 397
Image *Source:* https://en.wikipedia.org/w/index.php?title=File:Général_division_gend.svg *License:* Creative Commons Attribution-Sharealike 3.0,2.5,2.0,1.0 *Contributors:* Mangouste35 ... 397
Image *Source:* https://en.wikipedia.org/w/index.php?title=File:Général_brigade_gend.svg *License:* Creative Commons Attribution-Sharealike 3.0,2.5,2.0,1.0 *Contributors:* Mangouste35 ... 397
Image *Source:* https://en.wikipedia.org/w/index.php?title=File:Col_gd.svg *License:* Creative Commons Attribution-Sharealike 3.0,2.5,2.0,1.0 *Contributors:* Mangouste35 ... 397
Image *Source:* https://en.wikipedia.org/w/index.php?title=File:Col_gm.svg *License:* Creative Commons Attribution-Sharealike 3.0,2.5,2.0,1.0 *Contributors:* Mangouste35 ... 397
Image *Source:* https://en.wikipedia.org/w/index.php?title=File:Col_cta.svg *License:* Creative Commons Attribution-Sharealike 3.0,2.5,2.0,1.0 *Contributors:* Mangouste35 ... 397
Image *Source:* https://en.wikipedia.org/w/index.php?title=File:Col_gr.svg *License:* Creative Commons Attribution-Sharealike 3.0,2.5,2.0,1.0 *Contributors:* Mangouste35 ... 397
Image *Source:* https://en.wikipedia.org/w/index.php?title=File:Lcl_cta.svg *License:* Creative Commons Attribution-Sharealike 3.0,2.5,2.0,1.0 *Contributors:* Mangouste35 ... 397
Image *Source:* https://en.wikipedia.org/w/index.php?title=File:Cen_gd.svg *License:* Creative Commons Attribution-Sharealike 3.0,2.5,2.0,1.0 *Contributors:* Mangouste35 ... 397
Image *Source:* https://en.wikipedia.org/w/index.php?title=File:Cen_gm.svg *License:* Creative Commons Attribution-Sharealike 3.0,2.5,2.0,1.0 *Contributors:* Mangouste35 ... 397
Image *Source:* https://en.wikipedia.org/w/index.php?title=File:Cdt_cta.svg *License:* Creative Commons Attribution-Sharealike 3.0,2.5,2.0,1.0 *Contributors:* Mangouste35 ... 397
Image *Source:* https://en.wikipedia.org/w/index.php?title=File:Cen_gr.svg *License:* Creative Commons Attribution-Sharealike 3.0,2.5,2.0,1.0 *Contributors:* Mangouste35 ... 397
Image *Source:* https://en.wikipedia.org/w/index.php?title=File:Cne_gd.svg *License:* Creative Commons Attribution-Sharealike 3.0,2.5,2.0,1.0 *Contributors:* Mangouste35 ... 398
Image *Source:* https://en.wikipedia.org/w/index.php?title=File:Cne_gm.svg *License:* Creative Commons Attribution-Sharealike 3.0,2.5,2.0,1.0 *Contributors:* Mangouste35 ... 398
Image *Source:* https://en.wikipedia.org/w/index.php?title=File:Cne_cta.svg *License:* Creative Commons Attribution-Sharealike 3.0,2.5,2.0,1.0 *Contributors:* Mangouste35 ... 398
Image *Source:* https://en.wikipedia.org/w/index.php?title=File:Cne_gr.svg *License:* Creative Commons Attribution-Sharealike 3.0,2.5,2.0,1.0 *Contributors:* Mangouste35 ... 398
Image *Source:* https://en.wikipedia.org/w/index.php?title=File:Aspirant_gend.svg *License:* Creative Commons Attribution-Sharealike 3.0,2.5,2.0,1.0 *Contributors:* Mangouste35 ... 398
Image *Source:* https://en.wikipedia.org/w/index.php?title=File:Adc_gd.svg *License:* Creative Commons Attribution-Sharealike 3.0,2.5,2.0,1.0 *Contributors:* Mangouste35 ... 398
Image *Source:* https://en.wikipedia.org/w/index.php?title=File:Adc_gm.svg *License:* Creative Commons Attribution-Sharealike 3.0,2.5,2.0,1.0 *Contributors:* Mangouste35 ... 398
Image *Source:* https://en.wikipedia.org/w/index.php?title=File:Adc_cstag.svg *License:* Creative Commons Attribution-Sharealike 3.0,2.5,2.0,1.0 *Contributors:* Mangouste35 ... 398
Image *Source:* https://en.wikipedia.org/w/index.php?title=File:Adc_gr.svg *License:* Creative Commons Attribution-Sharealike 3.0,2.5,2.0,1.0 *Contributors:* Mangouste35 ... 398
Image *Source:* https://en.wikipedia.org/w/index.php?title=File:Adj_gd.svg *License:* Creative Commons Attribution-Sharealike 3.0,2.5,2.0,1.0 *Contributors:* Mangouste35 ... 398
Image *Source:* https://en.wikipedia.org/w/index.php?title=File:Adj_gm.svg *License:* Creative Commons Attribution-Sharealike 3.0,2.5,2.0,1.0 *Contributors:* Mangouste35 ... 398
Image *Source:* https://en.wikipedia.org/w/index.php?title=File:Adj_cstag.svg *License:* Creative Commons Attribution-Sharealike 3.0,2.5,2.0,1.0 *Contributors:* Mangouste35 ... 398
Image *Source:* https://en.wikipedia.org/w/index.php?title=File:Adj_gr.svg *License:* Creative Commons Attribution-Sharealike 3.0,2.5,2.0,1.0 *Contributors:* Mangouste35 ... 398
Image *Source:* https://en.wikipedia.org/w/index.php?title=File:Gend_gd.svg *License:* Creative Commons Attribution-Sharealike 3.0,2.5,2.0,1.0 *Contributors:* Mangouste35 ... 398
Image *Source:* https://en.wikipedia.org/w/index.php?title=File:Gend_gm.svg *License:* Creative Commons Attribution-Sharealike 3.0,2.5,2.0,1.0 *Contributors:* Mangouste35 ... 398
Image *Source:* https://en.wikipedia.org/w/index.php?title=File:Gend_gr.svg *License:* Creative Commons Attribution-Sharealike 3.0,2.5,2.0,1.0 *Contributors:* Mangouste35 ... 398
Image *Source:* https://en.wikipedia.org/w/index.php?title=File:Gend_sc_gd.svg *License:* Creative Commons Attribution-Sharealike 3.0,2.5,2.0,1.0 *Contributors:* Mangouste35 ... 398
Image *Source:* https://en.wikipedia.org/w/index.php?title=File:Gend_sc_gm.svg *License:* Creative Commons Attribution-Sharealike 3.0,2.5,2.0,1.0 *Contributors:* Mangouste35 ... 398
Image *Source:* https://en.wikipedia.org/w/index.php?title=File:Gend_sc_gr.svg *License:* Creative Commons Attribution-Sharealike 3.0,2.5,2.0,1.0 *Contributors:* Mangouste35 ... 398
Image *Source:* https://en.wikipedia.org/w/index.php?title=File:Gav_mdl.svg *License:* Creative Commons Attribution-Sharealike 3.0,2.5,2.0,1.0 *Contributors:* Mangouste35 ... 399
Image *Source:* https://en.wikipedia.org/w/index.php?title=File:Gav_bch.svg *License:* Creative Commons Attribution-Sharealike 3.0,2.5,2.0,1.0 *Contributors:* Mangouste35 ... 399
Image *Source:* https://en.wikipedia.org/w/index.php?title=File:Gav_bri.svg *License:* Creative Commons Attribution-Sharealike 3.0,2.5,2.0,1.0 *Contributors:* Mangouste35 ... 399
Image *Source:* https://en.wikipedia.org/w/index.php?title=File:Gav_1cl.svg *License:* Creative Commons Attribution-Sharealike 3.0,2.5,2.0,1.0 *Contributors:* Mangouste35 ... 399
Image *Source:* https://en.wikipedia.org/w/index.php?title=File:Gav_gav.svg *License:* Creative Commons Attribution-Sharealike 3.0,2.5,2.0,1.0 *Contributors:* Mangouste35 ... 399
Figure 249 *Source:* https://en.wikipedia.org/w/index.php?title=File:Helicopter_rescue_sancy_takeoff.jpg *License:* Creative Commons Attribution-Sharealike 2.0 *Contributors:* Fabien1309 ... 401
Figure 250 *Source:* https://en.wikipedia.org/w/index.php?title=File:Eurocopter_EC-135_T2+.jpg *License:* Creative Commons Attribution-Sharealike 2.0 *Contributors:* Alexandre Prévot ... 402
Figure 251 *Source:* https://en.wikipedia.org/w/index.php?title=File:Eurocopter_EC_145._France_-_Gendarmerie_JP6591482.jpg *Contributors:* Ariadacapo, Fæ, LittleWink, 1 anonymous edits ... 402
Figure 252 *Source:* https://en.wikipedia.org/w/index.php?title=File:Philippe_Lenoir_by_Horace_Vernet.jpg *License:* Creative Commons Attribution-Sharealike 2.0 *Contributors:* User:Rama ... 407
Figure 253 *Source:* https://en.wikipedia.org/w/index.php?title=File:Monsieur_Hepp-Jean-Daniel_Heimlich_f4651969.jpg *License:* Creative Commons Attribution-Sharealike 2.0 *Contributors:* User:Rama, User:Rama/use_my_images ... 407
Figure 254 *Source:* https://en.wikipedia.org/w/index.php?title=File:Lafayette_sabre-IMG_0755_0770-black.jpg *License:* Creative Commons Attribution-Sharealike 2.0 *Contributors:* Rama ... 408
Figure 255 *Source:* https://en.wikipedia.org/w/index.php?title=File:Révolte_Fouesnant.jpg *License:* Public Domain *Contributors:* Anne97432, BotMultichill, Bukk, Bzh-99, Ecummenic, Fab5669, Hohum, Hsarrazin, Khaerr~commonswiki, O (bot), Radarm, Rich Farmbrough, Thib Phil, Underwaterbuffalo, VIGNERON, 2 anonymous edits ... 409

Figure 256 *Source:* https://en.wikipedia.org/w/index.php?title=File:Horace_Vernet_-_La_Barrière_de_Clichy.jpg *License:* Public Domain *Contributors:* Blaue Max, Bohème, BotMultichill, DutchHoratius, Equendil, GeorgHH, Kilom691, Mu, Neuceu, Paris 16, Thib Phil, Zolo, Иван Дулин, 1 anonymous edits 410
Figure 257 *Source:* https://en.wikipedia.org/w/index.php?title=File:French_Garde_Nationale_soldier_with_Tabatiere_rifle_1870.jpg *License:* Public Domain *Contributors:* Avron, Bennylin, Gérald Garitan, Hoodinski, Jordi, Tatesic, Zolo 412
Image *Source:* https://en.wikipedia.org/w/index.php?title=File:Wikisource-logo.svg *License:* Creative Commons Attribution-Sharealike 3.0 *Contributors:* ChrisiPK, Guillom, INeverCry, Jarekt, JuTa, Leyo, Lokal Profil, MichaelMaggs, NielsF, Rei-artur, Rocket000, Romaine, Steinsplitter 414

License

Creative Commons Attribution-Share Alike 3.0
//creativecommons.org/licenses/by-sa/3.0/

Index

.50 BMG, 276

A-20 Havoc, 119
A400M Atlas, 346
AA-52 machine gun, 276
Aaron Bank, 127
Abbeville, 105
Abd al-Qadir al-Jazairi, 384
Abdelaziz Bouteflika, 293
Abomey, 213
Abraham Duquesne, 377
Absolute monarchy, 34
Abu Dhabi, 348, 360, 368
Acadia, 157
Ace pilot, 110
Achnacarry, 118
ACMAT, 279
Active citizen, 408
Ad hoc, 137
Adjudant, 234, 250
Adjudant-chef, 234
Adjutant, 398
Administrative divisions of France, 388
Admiral, 371, 377
Admiral of France, 371
Admiral of the Fleet, 371
Admiral of the Fleet (Royal Navy), 371
Adolf Hitler, 86
Adolphe Messimy, 69
Adrian helmet, 70, 189, 258
Adriatic, 135
Adriatic Sea, 19
Aerial warfare, 332
Aéronautique Navale, 303
Aérospatiale Alouette III, 360
Aérospatiale Gazelle, 282
Aérospatiale SA 330 Puma, 236, 281, 340
Aérospatiale SA330 Puma, 349
Afghanistan, 6, 206, 229, 230, 336, 393
AFHQ, 126
Africa, 5, 38, 317
Afrika Korps, 147
Agadir, 317
Ahaggar Mountains, 290

Aiguillettes, 394
Air Base 115 Orange-Caritat, 347
Air Base 120 Cazaux, 347
Air Base 125 Istres, 347
Air Base 126 Solenzara, 347
Air Base 942 Lyon-Mont Verdun, 347
Air Base 943 Nice, 347
Air Battalion Royal Engineers, 305
Airborne early warning and control, 340, 348
Air-Britain, 355
Airbus 310, 333
Airbus 340, 333
Airbus A310, 340, 343, 349
Airbus A330 MRTT, 298, 300
Airbus A340, 343, 349
Airbus A400, 333
Airbus A400M, 39, 338
Airbus A400M Atlas, 349
Air campaign, 228
Aircraft carrier, 42, 140, 177, 291, 369
Aircraft pilot, 334
Air Defence, 10, 369
Air Defense and Air Operations Command, 339
Air force, 39, 332, 333
Air Force Aerial Weapon Systems Brigade, 340
Air Force Maneuver Support Brigade, 340
Air Forces Command (France), 340
Air Force Security and Intervention Forces Brigade, 340
Air Force Training Command (France), 338
Air France Flight 8969, 391
Air Gendarmerie, 10
Airport crash tender, 279
Airship, 334
Air-Sol Moyenne Portée, 340
Airspace Control Brigade, 340
Air supremacy, 308
Air traffic controller, 353
Air Transport Auxiliary, 314
Air Transport Gendarmerie, 10
Aisne River, 59
Alain Bouquin, 261
Alain Delon, 377

441

Alain Richard, 266
Alamanni, 18
Alan Seeger, 216, 244
Alaric II, 19
Albania and weapons of mass destruction, 284
Albert II, Prince of Monaco, 377
Albert Kesselring, 315
Albert, Somme, 59
Alexandria, 177
Algeciras Campaign, 364
Algeria, 37, 42, 205, 217, 221, 289, 295, 316, 329, 393
Algeria and weapons of mass destruction, 284
Algerian independence movement, 290
Algerian War, 7, 37, 190, 192, 198, 204, 206, 222, 288, 332, 351, 366
Algerian War of Independence, 289
Algeria War, 336
Algiers, 87, 92, 94, 207, 214
Algiers putsch, 191
Algiers putsch of 1961, 192, 206, 223, 224
Alistair Horne, 417
Aliyah Bet, 268
Allied Forces Central Europe, 190
Allied Occupation Zones in Germany, 15
Allied-occupied Austria, 37
Allied-occupied Germany, 4, 37
Allies of World War I, 51, 56, 57
Allies of World War II, 4, 15, 72, 125, 138
All-terrain vehicle, 280
Almería, 134
Alpes-Maritimes, 111
Alpha Jet, 333, 347, 349
Alphonse Georges, 76
Alphonse Juin, 80, 143
Alps, 15, 17, 80, 290
Al Qaeda, 6
Alsace, 59, 80, 122, 124, 214, 267
Alsace-Lorraine, 34, 47, 51, 53, 54, 219
Ambérieu-en-Bugey, 347
Amédée Courbet, 377
American Civil War, 31
American-led intervention in Iraq (2014–present), 6
American Revolution, 185
American Revolutionary War, 4, 15, 27, 163, 182, 363
American Volunteer Group, 328
American War of Independence, 163
AMGOT, 73
Amiens, 75, 105
Amiot 143, 314
Ammunition, 147
Amphibious assault ship, 369
Amphibious transport dock, 369
AMX 10 RC, 277

AMX-56 Leclerc, 200, 297
AMX Leclerc, 277, 299
Anchor, 361
Ancien Régime, 23, 253
Ancien Régime in France, 381
Andre Gaston Pretelat, 110
André Lanata, 332
André Marty, 377
Angkor, 323
Anglo-French blockade of the Río de la Plata, 364
Anglo French Supreme War Council, 97
Anglo-French War (1202–1214), 22
Anglo-French War (1627–1629), 362
Anglo-French War (1778–1783), 363
Anglo-French War (1778–83), 4
Anglo-Iraqi War, 317
Annaba, 93
Anne Hilarion de Tourville, 159, 377
Annus Mirabilis of 1759, 159
Antananarivo, 214
Anthony Fokker, 308
Anti-aircraft, 94
Anti-aircraft gun, 136
Anti-communism, 269
Anticommunist, 86
Anti-Gaddafi forces, 7
Anti-materiel rifle, 276
Anti-nuclear movement, 285
Anti-submarine, 369
Anti-tank, 106
Anti-tank guided missile, 276
Anti-tank weapon, 276
Antoine Béthouart, 143
Antoine de Saint-Exupéry, 138
Antoine Joseph Santerre, 410
Appeal of 18 June, 37, 111, 176
Appeal of June 18, 77
Aqua-lung, 177
Arabic language, 21
Arc de Triomphe, 121
Archduke Franz Ferdinand of Austria, 53
Ardennes, 60, 99, 314
Argentina, 280
Argentina and weapons of mass destruction, 284
Ariovistus, 17
Aristide Aubert du Petit Thouars, 376
Aristide Briand, 62
Armand Blanquet du Chayla, 376
Armand Jean du Plessis, Cardinal Richelieu, 155
Armand Jean du Plessis de Richelieu, 361
Armed forces, 8
Armed Forces of the Russian Federation, 269
Armée de lAir, 303, 321, 322

Armée de lAir (Part II: Fighting for Free France, 1940-1945), 325
Armée de Libération Nationale, 222
Armée de terre, 8
Armistice, 217, 310
Armistice with France (Second Compiègne), 110, 176
Armistice with Germany (Compiègne), 56, 110
Armored car (military), 56, 146, 147
Armored fighting vehicle, 278
Armored personnel carrier, 390
Armored Train of the Foreign Legion, 221
Armoured and Cavalry Branch Training School, 193
Armoured car, 278
Armoured Cavalry Arm, 196
Armoured Cavalry Branch, 195, 273
Armoured cruiser, 173, 365
Armoured engineering vehicle, 278
Armoured fighting vehicle, 277
Armoured personnel carrier, 277, 278
Armoured recovery vehicle, 278
Armoured warfare, 390
Arms race, 53
Army, 181, 182
Army General, 397
Army General (France), 354, 379, 386
Army Group B, 99
Army Human Resources Directorate, 197
Army of Africa (France), 33, 75, 93, 187, 207, 209, 213, 224, 248, 255
Army of the Levant, 148, 182, 204, 335
Arnaud de Tarlé, 367
Arras, 59, 61
Arrondissement in France, 389
Artillery, 22, 58, 67, 100, 214, 227, 334
Artois, 59
Aspirant, 354, 398
Assault rifle, 275
Aster (missile family), 376
AT4 CS, 276
ATGM, 278
Athens, 365
Atlantic campaign of May 1794, 364
Atlantic Ocean, 155, 361
Atlantique 2, 360
Atomic Energy Act of 1946, 288
Attack aircraft, 360
Attack helicopter, 281
Attack on Mers-el-Kébir, 316, 366
Aubagne, 229, 262, 263
Auckland, 293
Australia, 292
Australia and weapons of mass destruction, 284
Australia Group, 5
Australian Army, 267

Australian Defence Force, 269
Austrasia, 19
Austria, 2, 274
Austria–Hungary, 53
Austrian Empire, 4, 15, 30, 209
Austrian Succession, 185
Austro-Hungarian Navy, 365
Austro-Sardinian War, 34
Avenue Delcassé, 400
Aviatik, 305
Aviation Navale, 9, 367
Avions Amiot, 310
Aviso, 134, 135
Avisos, 369
Avord Air Base, 342, 347
Axis powers, 4, 15, 73, 110, 145, 147, 174, 219, 317, 321
Azawad, 38

B-24 Liberator, 81
B-26 Invader, 330
Babemba Traoré, 214
Bachelor of science, 371
Bachelors degree, 199
Backhoe loader, 279
Bắc Ninh Campaign, 212
Bahamas, 157
Balkans, 5
Balkans Campaign (World War I), 35
Ballistic missile defence, 374
Ballistic missiles, 336
Ballistic missile submarine, 370
Ballistic missile submarines, 361
Baltiysk, 115
Bandvagn 206, 278
Bangkok, 322
Banlieue, 192
Banque de France, 138
Barbara Tuchman, 50
Barrow-in-Furness, 134
Bashar al-Assad, 38
Basques, 19
Basra, 317
Bastille Day Military Parade, 248, 253, 348, 352
Bat dAf, 207
Bâtiment multi-mission, 374
BATRAL-class landing ship, 374
Battalion, 210, 250
Battambang, 322
Battle dress uniform, 201
Battle for Paris, 83
Battle of Agincourt, 22, 382
Battle of Agosta, 377
Battle of Albert (1914), 60
Battle of Alesia, 18

443

Battle of Algiers (1957), 206
Battle of Alma, 208
Battle of Arnemuiden, 40, 156
Battle of Arras (1914), 60
Battle of Arras (1940), 106
Battle of Beachy Head (1690), 159, 362, 377
Battle of Berlin, 114
Battle of Bir Hakeim, 3, 36, 43, 147, 191, 218, 219
Battle of Bouvines, 22
Battle of Britain, 110, 112, 113
Battle of Cádiz (1640), 157
Battle of Camarón, 43, 204, 210, 217, 239
Battle of Cape Finisterre (1761), 363
Battle of Cape Finisterre (disambiguation), 363
Battle of Cape Henry, 363
Battle of Cap-Français, 363
Battle of Caporetto, 66
Battle of Cassel 1328, 22
Battle of Castillon, 14, 23
Battle of Charleroi, 59
Battle of Chesapeake, 41
Battle of Dakar, 137, 138, 175
Battle of Damascus (1941), 218
Battle of Denain, 184
Battle of Dien Bien Phu, 44, 151, 206, 220
Battle of Dieppe, 113
Battle of Dunkirk, 107
Battle of Entrames, 28
Battle off Ist, 135
Battle of Fontenoy, 25, 185
Battle of Foochow, 42, 166
Battle of Formigny, 23
Battle of France, 4, 15, 36, 73, 77, 190, 314, 335
Battle of Fuzhou, 365
Battle of Gabon, 141
Battle of Gergovia, 18
Battle of Grand Port, 364
Battle of Grenada, 363
Battle of Groix, 364
Battle of Guise, 58
Battle of Hastings, 20, 21
Battle of Hondschoote, 384
Battle of Iena, 30
Battle of Jemappes, 27, 186
Battle of Jena-Auerstedt, 187
Battle of Kinburn (1855), 364
Battle of Koh Chang, 175
Battle of Kolwezi, 226
Battle of Königsberg, 131
Battle of Lagos, 159
Battle of Lagos (1693), 362
Battle of La Rochelle, 40
Battle of Le Cateau, 59
Battle of Lissa (1811), 364
Battle of Lorraine, 59
Battle of Magenta, 43, 188, 209
Battle of Marignan, 23
Battle of Martinique (1780), 158
Battle of Mers-el-Kebir, 132
Battle of Mons, 59
Battle of Monte Cassino, 75, 88, 115
Battle of Moscow, 114
Battle of Mulhouse, 59
Battle of Navarino, 364
Battle of Palermo, 40, 158
Battle of Paris (1814), 410, 411
Battle of Patay, 22, 23
Battle of Quiberon Bay, 159, 363
Battle of Rocroi, 24
Battle of Sedan (1870), 211
Battle of Shipu, 365
Battle of Sluys, 40
Battle of Soissons (486), 18
Battle of Solferino, 209
Battle of Texel (1694), 362
Battle of the Allia, 17, 18
Battle of the Ardennes, 59
Battle of the Atlantic, 134, 365
Battle of the Basque Roads, 164, 364
Battle of the Bulge, 132
Battle of the Chesapeake, 42, 163, 363, 377
Battle of the Frontiers, 35, 59
Battle of the Golden Spurs, 22
Battle of the Malta Convoy (1800), 364
Battle of the Mediterranean, 135, 366
Battle of the Netherlands, 99
Battle of the Nile, 364
Battle of the Smala, 384
Battle of the Somme, 59, 216
Battle of the Tagus, 364
Battle of the Yser, 61
Battle of Thuận An, 365
Battle of Tolbiac, 18
Battle of Tory Island, 364
Battle of Toulouse (721), 19
Battle of Tours, 19, 45
Battle of Trafalgar, 42, 164, 165, 364, 377
Battle of Ulm, 30
Battle of Ushant (disambiguation), 363
Battle of Veracruz (1838), 165, 364
Battle of Verdun, 35, 56, 61, 216, 308
Battle of Vigo Bay, 363
Battle of Vouillé, 19
Battle of Waterloo, 32
Battleship, 133, 140, 365
Battles of Barfleur and La Hougue, 159, 362
Bayeux Tapestry, 20
Bayonet, 210
Bayonne, 75
BBC, 77, 422

BBC News, 422
Beard, 252
Beau Geste, 256
Béchar, 289, 290
Béhanzin, 213
Beijing, 168
Belfort, 131
Belgium, 2, 51, 56, 58, 275, 276
Belloy-en-Santerre, 216
Benelli M3, 275
Berchtesgaden, 132
Beret, 201, 258
Béret, 87
Beretta 92, 274
Berezina, 115
Berliet VXB-170, 390
Bernard B. Fall, 266
Bernard Colcomb, 260
Bernard Giraudeau, 377
Bernard Goupil, 260
Bernard Grail, 260
Bernard Janvier, 226, 227
Bernard Montgomery, 144
Bersaglieri, 226
Berthier carbine, 68
Berthier rifle, 68
Bertrand Goldschmidt, 286
Beryl incident, 289
Besançon, 75
Betrayal, 134
Bicarbonate of soda, 68
Bicorne, 394
Bienwald, 131
Biological agent, 283
Biological and Toxin Weapons Convention, 294
Biological weapons, 286
Biological Weapons Convention, 286
Bishara, 146
Black Forest, 131
Black Hand (Serbia), 53
Blaise Cendrars, 244
Blériot Flying School, 305
Blériot XI, 304, 305
Blitzkrieg, 98
Bloch, 311
Bloch MB.170, 311
Bloch MB.200, 313
Blockade, 98, 157
Blue-water navy, 361
Bob Denard, 377
Boeing C-135 Stratolifter, 340
Boeing E-3, 349
Boeing E-3 Sentry, 332, 347
Boeing KC-135 Stratotanker, 340
Bolshevism, 86

Bombardment of Shimonoseki, 364
Bombard (weapon), 22
Bombay, 151
Bomber, 312
Book:Weapons of mass destruction, 285
Bordeaux, 14, 59, 75, 90, 108, 198, 337, 347
Bordeaux-Beauséjour, 347
Bordeaux-Mérignac Air Base, 340
Bordeaux-Mérignac Airport, 347
Boshin war, 169
Bosnia-Herzegovina, 393
Boulogne-sur-Mer, 106
Bourbon monarchy, 34
Bourbon Restoration, 411
Bourges, 18, 75
Bourrasque-class destroyer, 134
Brazil and weapons of mass destruction, 284
Breakwater (structure), 119
Breguet 14, 308
Brennus (4th century BC), 17, 18
Brest Arsenal, 360, 368
Brest, France, 107, 159, 164, 362, 370
Bretagne-class battleship, 171
Brétigny-sur-Orge Air Base, 348
Breton people, 118
Briare, 110
Brigade, 209, 250
Brigade General, 397
Brigadier, 399
Brigadier General, 250
British 1st Army, 144
British 2nd Parachute Brigade, 127
British 7th Armoured Division, 147
British Armed Forces, 226, 268, 269
British Army, 267
British Commandos, 118
British Commonwealth, 317
British Eighth Army, 147
British Expeditionary Force (World War I), 58
British Expeditionary Force (World War II), 97, 99
British India, 81
Brittany, 80, 118, 409
Bruni dEntrecasteaux, 376
Bruno Dary, 260
Brussels, 99
Buffalo (mine protected vehicle), 278
Bulgaria and weapons of mass destruction, 284
Bulldozer, 279
Bullpup, 258
Bulson, 102
Bureau Central de Renseignements et dAction, 79, 122
Burgonet, 70
Burnous, 201
BvS 10, 278

445

C-130, 333
C-130 Hercules, 346
C-135F, 337, 347, 349
C-47 Skytrain, 324
Cabinet (government), 77
Cabinet of France, 7, 293
Cadet, 398
Caen, 75, 115
CAESAR self-propelled howitzer, 280
Calais, 23, 106
Calvi, Haute-Corse, 203, 229, 236
Cambodia, 33, 37, 151, 206, 228, 321, 322
Cambrai, 105
Cambrai - Épinoy Air Base, 349
Cameroon, 33, 94
Camouflage Centre Europe, 201
Camp Larzac, 229
Camp Raffalli, 237
Canada, 157
Canada and weapons of mass destruction, 284
Cannes, 125
Cannon, 157
Canon de 75 modèle 1897, 66, 420
Canopus (nuclear test), 291
Caproni, 145
Captain Danjou, 211
Captain (land), 354, 398
Captain (naval), 376
Captain (OF-2), 250
Carabinieri, 384
Carbine, 68
Cardinal de Richelieu, 156
Cardinal Richelieu, 25, 155
Cargo aircraft, 333
Caribbean, 33, 157
Carlingue, 88
Carlism, 208
Carlist Wars, 43
Carl von Clausewitz, 29
Carolingian Empire, 19
Carpet bombing, 101
Casabianca (Q183), 176
Casablanca, 90, 142, 317
Casablanca Conference, 73
Casablanca Conference (1943), 93
CASA CN-235, 349
Case Anton, 93, 175, 366
Cassard-class frigate, 300, 374
Castelnaudary, 229
Castle, 21
Castle of San Juan de Ulúa, 165
Category:Weapons of mass destruction, 285
Caterpillar D6, 279
Catholic Church, 19
Catholicism, 25
Caudron G.III, 305

Cavalaire-sur-Mer, 126
Cavalry, 145, 334
Cazaux Air Base, 342
CBRN defense, 390
Central Africa, 33, 205, 393
Central African Republic, 206, 228
Central African Republic conflict (2012–present), 204
Central African Republic conflict under the Djotodia administration, 6, 182
Central Army Group, 192
Central Directorate of Telecommunications and Informatics, 198
Central Engineering Directorate, 198
Central Intelligence Agency, 328
Central Powers, 35, 51
Centre Saharien d.27Exp.C3.A9rimentations Militaires, 287
César Campinchi, 90
Ceylon, 81, 151
Chacal-class destroyer, 133
Chad, 91, 141, 145, 205, 226, 336, 348
Chadian Civil War (2005–10), 6
Chadian–Libyan conflict, 38, 206, 332
Chainmail, 21
Châlons-en-Champagne, 75
Champs Élysées, 121
Champs-Élysées, 352
Chandler, David G., 48
Char B1 bis, 104
Charente-Maritime, 123
Charisma, 91
Charlemagne, 3, 14, 19, 88
Charlemagne-class battleship, 171
Charleroi, 60
Charles de Gaulle, 6, 37, 72, 76, 93, 176, 286, 288, 291, 366, 377
Charles de Gaulle (R 91), 291
Charles Delvert, 71
Charles de Tricornot de Rose, 305
Charles Hector, comte dEstaing, 164, 377
Charles Huntziger, 102
Charles Lanrezac, 60
Charles Mangin, 189
Charles Nungesser, 308
Charles V, Holy Roman Emperor, 23
Charles VII of France, 23, 183
Charles X, 364
Charles X of France, 34, 411
Chassepot, 189
Chasseurs Alpins, 110, 195, 196, 201, 273
Chasseurs dAfrique, 255
Châteaudun Air Base, 347
Chauchat, 67
Chef des armées, 2, 7
Chemical cartridge respirators, 68

446

Chemical warfare, 67, 68
Chemical weapon, 283, 286, 294
Chemical weapon proliferation, 284
Chemical weapons, 286
Chemical Weapons Convention, 5, 286, 294
Cherbourg, 159, 360
Cherbourg Naval Base, 368
Cherchell, 143
Cher (department), 88
Chernyakhovsk, 115
Chevron (insignia), 248, 250
Chevrons danciennete (chevrons of seniority), 249
Chief of staff, 379
Chief of Staff of the French Air Force, 332, 333, 338, 339
Chief of Staff of the French Army, 182, 183, 195, 273
Chief of Staff of the French Navy, 182, 360, 361
Chief of the Defence Staff (France), 2, 183, 333, 338, 339
Chieftain, 17
Chief Warrant Officer, 234, 250
China, 321, 325
China and weapons of mass destruction, 284, 286
Chindits, 81, 151
Chlorine, 59, 68, 295
Cholera, 208
Christian Piquemal, 260
Christophe de Saint-Chamas, 261
Christophe Prazuck, 360
CIEES, 287, 290
Circassians, 148
CITEREFCrowdy2004, 427
CITEREFMansel2003, 427
Citizenship, 265
Civil Air Transport, 328
Civil war in Côte dIvoire, 38
Claire Lee Chennault, 150, 328
Classe préparatoire aux grandes écoles, 199, 371
Claude de Forbin, 159
Clearance Diving Team (RAN), 227
Clément Ader, 174
Clermont-Ferrand, 75
C.L.I., 150
Clipperton Island, 289
Clovis I, 3, 14, 15, 19
CND, 292
Coalition, 227
Coalition of the Gulf War, 227
Cochinchina, 168
Cochinchina Campaign, 364
Cognac – Châteaubernard Air Base, 347

Cold War, 4, 5, 192, 351
Collaborationism, 111
Colleville-sur-Mer, 119
Colmar – Meyenheim Air Base, 337
Colmar-Meyenheim Air Base, 348
Colmar Pocket, 123, 131
Colombo, 151
Colonel, 57, 67, 217, 250, 259, 354, 397
Colonialism, 145
Combat engineer, 252
Combat helmet, 258
Combat search and rescue, 340
Command and Control, 277
Commandant (rank), 354
Commandement Air des Forces de Défense Aérienne, 336
Commandement de la force daction terrestre, 194
Commandement de La Légion Étrangère, 204
Commander-in-Chief of the French Armed Forces, 1
Commando Parachute Group, 234
Commandos Marine, 154, 367
Commissariat, 342
Commissariat à lÉnergie Atomique, 287
Commission de Paris, 166
Commissioner, 342
Commons:Category:Air force of France, 356
Commons:Category:French Army, 202
Commons:Category:Garde nationale (Révolution française), 414
Commons:Category:Gendarmerie (France), 403
Commons:Category:Military of France, 51
Commons:Category:Navy of France, 378
Commons:French Foreign Legion, 271
Commonwealth of Independent States, 269
Communal Depot of the Foreign Regiments, 241
Compagnies dordonnance, 23, 183
Compagnies Républicaines de Sécurité, 88, 390
Company (military unit), 242, 250
Compiègne, 110
Comprehensive Nuclear-Test-Ban Treaty, 286
Comprehensive Test Ban Treaty, 5, 293
Conical Asian hat, 246
Conscription, 7, 56, 87, 183, 207
Constable of France, 381, 382
Constabulary, 382
Copyright status of work by the U.S. government, 153
Corporal, 399
Corps, 54, 209
Corps General, 397
Corps Léger dIntervention, 81
Corruption scandals in the Paris region, 389

447

Corsica, 111, 126, 229, 290
Corsica 1943, 137
Corvette, 164
Côte dIvoire, 37, 38
Cotonou, 213
Cotton, 68
Coulommiers, Seine-et-Marne, 76
Council of Ministers of France, 386
Count Aage of Rosenborg, 224, 225, 244
Counter-terrorism, 387, 391
Courbet-class battleship, 133, 171
Courseulles-sur-Mer, 119
Court-martial, 63
Couterne, 127
Creil, 6
Creil Air Base, 349
Crete, 137
Crimea, 205
Crimean Peninsula, 208
Crimean War, 4, 15, 34, 168, 182, 204, 206, 254, 364, 405
Croix de Guerre, 155, 196, 274
Cross of Lorraine, 112, 122, 176
Crotale (missile), 345
Crown of Castile, 40
Cruiser, 140
Cruiser tanks, 107
Crusades, 21, 45
Cuirassiers, 69, 394
Current French Navy ships, 360
Curtiss P-36 Hawk, 322
Curtiss P-40, 137, 142
Curt von Jesser, 116
Curzio Malaparte, 244
Cybercrime, 381

Dahomey, 213
Dahomey Amazons, 213
Dakar, 136–138, 175, 177, 317, 348, 360, 368
Damascus, 148
Dassault Aviation, 338
Dassault Falcon 20, 360
Dassault Falcon 2000, 333, 350
Dassault Falcon 50, 340
Dassault Falcon 7X, 333, 349
Dassault Falcon 900, 333, 349
Dassault Mirage 2000, 333, 340, 347, 348
Dassault Mirage F1, 337, 338
Dassault Mirage III, 39, 336, 338
Dassault Mirage IV, 336, 337
Dassault Rafale, 10, 177, 298, 300, 333, 338, 340, 346, 369, 370
David McTaggart, 292
David Stirling, 78, 137
DCL, 278
D-Day, 120, 126

De Bello Gallico, 44
Declaration of war, 53
Decolonisation, 191
Decolonization, 37
Defence Historical Service, 197
Degrad des Cannes, 360, 368
De Havilland Mosquito, 325
Délégation générale pour larmement, 7, 393
Delta-wing, 338
Demi-brigade, 250
Democratic Republic of the Congo, 206
Demographic crisis of Russia, 269
Demographics, 29
Denis Béraud, 360
Departmental Gendarmerie, 10, 387, 388
Departments of France, 137, 383, 388, 389
Deployments of the French military, 6
Destroyer, 77, 133, 134, 140, 173, 174, 365
Destruction of the French Fleet at Mers-el-Kebir, 42, 136, 156, 175
Dewoitine D.500, 311
Dewoitine D.520, 109, 110, 311, 313, 317
DHC-6 Twin Otter, 350
Diamond HK36 Super Dimona, 350
Dien Bien Phu, 151, 328
Dietrich von Choltitz, 121
Digital object identifier, 70, 71
Dijon, 75, 128
Dijon Air Base, 349
Dinant, 103
Diocese of the French Armed Forces, 198
Diplomatic Revolution, 27
Direction centrale du service dinfrastructure de la défense, 198
Direction Générale de la Sécurité Extérieure, 293
Director-general, 386
Dive bomber, 101, 322
Divisional general, 204, 354, 397
Division Daguet, 206, 227
Division (military), 62, 83, 190, 196, 209, 250
Djibouti, 205, 229, 348, 360
Djiboutian Civil War, 38
Djibouti (city), 368
Douaumont, 62
Douglas Haig, 62
Douglas SBD Dauntless, 318
Doullens Air Base, 348
Drachenbronn Air Base, 349
Dreadnought, 172, 173
Dreyfus Affair, 34
Duchy of Brittany, 361
Dump truck, 279
Dunkerque-class battleship, 174
Dunkirk evacuation, 132, 366
Dunkirk, France, 104, 107

Durance-class tanker, 376
Dushanbe, 345
Dutch East Indies, 268
Dwight David Eisenhower, 328
Dwight D. Eisenhower, 92, 121, 126
Dyatkovo, 114
Dzaoudzi, 360, 368

E-2 Hawkeye, 360
Early Modern Era, 51
Eastern Front (World War II), 72, 74, 98, 114, 115
East Indies campaign, 1778–1783, 42
EBRC Jaguar, 277

École de formation des sous-officiers de larmée de lair, 347
École de lair, 332, 352
École des officiers de la gendarmerie nationale, 383
École militaire interarmes, 199
École Navale, 361, 371
École Polytechnique, 201
École Spéciale Militaire de Saint-Cyr, 199, 201

Edgard de Larminat, 129

Édith Piaf, 224
Édouard Barès, 305
Édouard Daladier, 97, 98

Edouard Detaille, 70

Édouard Nieuport, 303

Edward Gibbon, 44
Edward Hughes (admiral), 164
Edward Spears, 139
EFA (mobile bridge), 279
Effects of nuclear explosions, 285
Egypt, 177
Egypt and weapons of mass destruction, 284
Eighty Years War, 25
El Alamein, 147
Elan-class minesweeping sloops, 134
Elba, 117
Elba 1944, 116
Elbląg, 115
Electronic warfare, 332, 360

Élysée Palace, 392

Embargo, 293
Embraer EMB 121 Xingu, 350, 360

Émile Bertin, 171

Émile Muselier, 134, 176

Emmanuel Macron, 1
Empire of Japan, 72
Ems Dispatch, 51
Encyclopædia Britannica Eleventh Edition, 414
Engin Blindé du Génie, 278
Engin de débarquement amphibie rapide, 375
Engineering Arm, 196
Engineers, 334
English Channel, 60, 95, 105, 108, 361
English language, 290, 332
English Navy, 40, 156
English people, 265
Enhanced radiation bomb, 288
Enlisted personnel, 371
Entente Cordiale, 364
Epaulette, 201, 255

Épinal, 75

ERC 90 Sagaie, 37, 194, 231, 277
Erich von Falkenhayn, 61
Erich von Manstein, 99
Eric Tabarly, 377
Eritrea, 141
Ernest Doudart de Lagrée, 376
Erwan Bergot, 242
Erwin Rommel, 103, 106, 147
Erwin von Witzleben, 97
ERYX, 276
Escadrilles, 312
Escadron de Chasse 01-007 Provence, 346
Escadron de chasse 02.005, 347
Escadron de transport 50, 348
Escort carriers, 127
Estimated worldwide nuclear stockpiles, 286
Ethiopia, 141

Étienne François, duc de Choiseul, 155

Eugene Bullard, 244, 309
Eugène Étienne, 69
Eugène Sue, 377
Euphrates, 45
Euro, 379, 384
Eurocopter AS332 Super Puma, 340
Eurocopter AS350 Écureuil, 401
Eurocopter AS532 Cougar, 282, 333, 350
Eurocopter Dauphin, 360
Eurocopter EC120 Colibri, 282
Eurocopter EC135, 401
Eurocopter EC-145, 401
Eurocopter EC725, 282, 333, 350
Eurocopter Fennec, 282, 333, 340, 350
Eurocopter Lynx, 360

Eurocopter Panther, 360
Eurocopter Tiger, 197, 201, 281
Eurocorps, 39
Europe, 13, 41, 156, 281, 282, 321
European Atomic Energy Community, 287
European integration, 4, 15
European Union, 2, 298
Eurozone crisis, 374
Eustache Bruix, 376
Ever Victorious Army, 268
Evian agreements, 289

Évreux-Fauville Air Base, 342, 343, 346

Excavator, 279
Exocet, 376
Expeditionary warfare, 73
Extra EA-300, 333, 350

Faaa International Airport, 290
Fabre Hydravion, 173, 365
Facing colour, 184
Falcon 10, 360
Falcon 50, 360
Falklands War, 338
Fall of France, 156, 322, 366
Fallschirmjäger (Nazi Germany), 100
FAMAS, 255, 258, 264, 275
FAMAS (rifle), 43, 396
Fangataufa, 291, 293
Fantasque-class destroyer, 133, 174, 175, 365
Farman MF.11, 305
Fast battleship, 174
Fech Fech, 145
Fédéré, 410
FEFEO, 81, 150
FÉLIN, 258, 277
Ferdinand Foch, 57, 189
Ferdinand VII of Spain, 34
Fernand de Brinon, 86
Fernando Pereira, 293
Fez (hat), 256
Fezzan, 145
FGM-148 Javelin, 276
Fiat, 146
Fiat BR.20, 110
Fiat CR.42, 110
Fieseler Fi 156, 325
Fifth Army (France), 56, 58
Fighter aircraft, 39, 291, 308, 333, 338, 360
Fighter Brigade (France), 340
File:France location map-Regions and departements-2016.svg, 75
Financial crisis of 2007–08, 39
Fire ships, 159
First Army (France), 54, 82, 219

First Battle of Champagne, 59
First Battle of the Aisne, 59
First Battle of the Marne, 35, 56, 58
First Battle of Ypres, 61
First Canadian Division, 107
First Carlist War, 4, 15, 34, 204, 206
First Coalition, 29
First French Empire, 31, 155, 361
First Gulf War, 201
First Indochina War, 33, 37, 190, 206, 220, 222, 266, 336, 384
First Ivorian Civil War, 194, 204
First Lieutenant, 199, 250
First Sino-Japanese War, 171
First World War, 15, 305, 334
Flag of France, 40, 362
Flamethrower, 116
Fleet Air Arm, 140
Floréal-class frigate, 298, 300
Florence Parly, 1, 7, 405
Florent de Varennes, 377
Flotte du Ponant, 361
Flying aces, 309
Flying Tigers, 328
FN 5.7×28mm, 275
FNFL, 133
FN MAG, 276
FN Minimi, 276
FN P90, 275
FN SCAR, 275
Fokker Eindecker fighters, 308
Fokker M.5K, 308
Folgore Brigade, 226
Foot arms and horse arms, 248
Force 136, 81, 150
Force daction navale, 10, 360, 367
Force de dissuasion, 336
Force de frappe, 4, 38, 286, 288, 295
Forced labour under German rule during World War II, 76
Force H, 316
Force océanique stratégique, 360, 370
Forces Sous-marines, 367
Ford Ranger (T6), 280
Foreign Air Supply Company, 242
Foreign Legion Command, 203, 217, 224, 225, 240, 250, 262, 420, 421
Foreign Legion Detachment in Mayotte, 203, 230, 236, 240, 241, 245
Foreign Legion Pioneers (Pionniers), 203, 204, 229, 230, 241, 249
Foreign Legion Recruiting Group, 203, 229, 240, 241
Forest of Argonne, 56
FORFUSCO, 154, 359
Former Soviet Republics, 286

450

Formiguière, 235
Fort de Nogent, 229
Fort Eben-Emael, 101
Fortifications of Vauban, 26
Fort Saint Louis (Martinique), 360, 368
Foudre-class landing platform dock, 300
Fourragère, 201, 221
Fourth Army (France), 56
Fourth French Republic, 16
Fr:109e division dinfanterie (France), 193
Fr:61e escadre de transport, 343
Fr:Adieu vieille Europe, 246
Fr:Administration et administrateurs de la Marine royale française, 178
Franc, 36
Françafrique, 38
France, 4, 8, 13, 56, 181, 195, 250, 274–282, 286, 305, 332, 354, 355, 359, 379, 405
France 1944, 131
France and weapons of mass destruction, **283**, 284, 286
France–Habsburg rivalry, 23
France in the American Revolutionary War, 4, 15, 27, 155, 363
France in the Seven Years War, 27
Frances nuclear testing series, 288
Franchet dEsperey, 189
Francisco Franco, 311
Francis Garnier, 376
Francis I of France, 23, 382
Francis Perrin, 287
Franco-Austrian War, 34
Franco-Dutch War, 25, 158, 362
Franco-German Brigade, 39, 196
François Achille Bazaine, 241
François Certain Canrobert, 243
François Darlan, 90, 93, 110, 143, 371
François Hollande, 38, 413
François Joseph Paul de Grasse, 377
François Joseph Paul, marquis de Grasetilly, comte de Grasse, 42, 155, 163
François Lecointre, 2
François Sevez, 73
François Thurot, 376
Francophone Africa, 5
Francophone countries, 265
Franco-Polish Military Alliance, 97
Franco-Prussian War, 4, 15, 34, 47, 52, 53, 182, 189, 204, 206, 207, 303, 364, 405, 406, 412
Franco-Siamese War, 365
Franco-Spanish War (1635–1659), 157
Franco-Spanish War (1635–59), 362
Francs-Tireurs et Partisans, 89
Franks, 3, 14, 18
Franz Halder, 105

Franz Josef Strauss, 422
Fr:Armée française de la Libération, 219
Fr:base aérienne 115 Orange-Caritat, 353
Fr:Base aérienne 186 Nouméa, 348
Fr:brigade aérienne des forces de sécurité et dintervention, 340
Fr:Camp de Carpiagne, 229
Fr:Clément Maudet, 210
Fr:code de la Défense, 338
Fr:Commandos parachutistes de lair, 351, 353
Fr:commissaire des armées, 351
Fr:contrôleur aérien, 351
Fr:convoyeur de lair, 352
Fr:Der gute Kamerad, 247
Fr:Détachement air 181 La Réunion, 348
Fr:Direction générale de la Gendarmerie nationale, 426
Fr:École de formation des sous-officiers de lArmée de lair, 353
Fr:École de lair, 352
Fr:École denseignement technique de lArmée de lair, 353
Fr:École de pilotage de lArmée de lair, 352
Fr:École des commissaires des armées, 352
Fr:École militaire de lair, 352
Frédéric Joliot-Curie, 286
Free Belgian Forces, 97
Free France, 133, 136, 182, 366
Free French, 77, 116, 135, 138, 147, 218, 219
Free French Air Force, 79, 115, 303, 321
Free French Air Forces, 335
Free French Flight, 141
Free French Forces, 3, 4, 15, 36, 37, 72, 79, 111, 175, 176, 191, 218, 219, 317
Free French Naval Air Service, 79, 141
Free French Naval Forces, 79, 133, 134, 366
Free French Navy, 118, 134–136
Free Republic of Vercors, 90, 116
Freetown, 138
Fréjus, 361
FREMM, 369
FREMM multipurpose frigate, 178, 298, 300, 374
French, 182, 205, 333, 379
French 2nd Division (World War II), 83
French aircraft carrier Charles de Gaulle, 41, 42, 369
French aircraft carrier Charles de Gaulle (R91), 9, 177, 298
French aircraft carrier PA2, 300, 369, 374
French air defense radar systems, 345
French Air Force, 1, 2, 7, 10, 39, 40, 182, 303, **332**, 333, 355, 362, 372, 381, 387, 406
French Algeria, 37, 92–94, 112, 187, 198, 206, 207, 223, 225, 229, 289
French-American, 150

French and Indian War, 155
French and Indian Wars, 4, 15
French Armed Forces, **1**, 61, 181, 182, 189, 222, 226, 258, 275, 297, 298, 332, 333, 351, 360, 362, 381, 405, 406, 413
French Army, 1, 2, 7, 51, **181**, 195, 203, 205, 234, 273, 274, 332–334, 362, 372, 381, 387, 406
French Army in World War I, **51**, 189
French Army Light Aviation, 9, 195–197, 227, 273, 279
French Army Mutinies, 57
French Army Mutinies (1917), 62
French Army of Alsace (WWI), 60
French Army Special Forces Brigade, 9
French aviso Commandant Duboc, 134
French Barracuda class submarine, 375
French Barracuda-class submarine, 178, 298, 300, 376
French battleship Bouvet, 170
French battleship Courbet (1911), 133, 177
French battleship Jauréguiberry, 168, 170
French battleship Lorraine, 127
French battleship Masséna, 170
French battleship Napoléon, 365
French battleship Paris, 133, 177
French battleship Redoutable (1876), 365
French battleship Richelieu, 140, 177, 366
French campaign against Korea, 204
French Campaign against Korea, 1866, 169, 364
French colonial empire, 2, 3, 14, 17, 25, 33, 34, 72, 91, 182, 190, 206, 207, 213, 310, 335, 336, 360, 364, 381
French colonial empires, 15
French Colonial Forces, 33
French conquest of Algeria, 33, 93, 182, 204, 405
French Consulate, 29
French corvette Aconit, 177
French cruiser Dupuy de Lôme (1887), 365
French cruiser Georges Leygues, 140, 177
French cruiser Gloire (1935), 140, 177
French cruiser Montcalm, 140, 177
French cruiser Suffren, 177
French Defence Health service, 7, 197
French destroyer La Combattante, 119
French destroyer L'Audacieux, 140
French destroyer Le Malin, 135
French destroyer Léopard, 133, 177
French destroyer Le Terrible, 135
French destroyer Le Triomphant, 133, 177
French destroyer Ouragan, 134
French Directory, 410
French ensigns, 154, 158
French Equatorial Africa, 92, 94, 111

French Évian Accords referendum, 1962, 37
French Expeditionary Corps (1943-1944), 80
French expedition to Ireland (1796), 364
French Fifth Republic, 371
French First Army, 97, 115, 128
French fleets, 154
French Forces in Germany, 190
French Forces of the Interior, 72, 79, 219, 417
French Foreign Legion, 3, 9, 36, 42, 147, 148, 183, 187, 191, 195–197, 201, **203**, 273, 323
French Foreign Legion Veteran Societies Federation (Légion étrangère), 240, 420
French Fourth Republic, 73, 287
French–German enmity, 4, 15
French Guards, 408
French Guiana, 203, 229, 230, 235, 348
French India, 32, 94
French Indochina, 33, 73, 80, 81, 94, 111, 150, 190, 221, 321, 336
French interior ministers, 90
French intervention in Mexico, 4, 15, 43, 169, 189, 204, 206, 364
French ironclad Gloire, 166, 167, 365
French ironclad Redoutable, 166, 167
French language, 2, 42, 82, 205, 219, 223, 234, 332, 333, 335, 336, 338–344, 351–353, 360, 361, 379, 421, 425
French Mandate for Syria and the Lebanon, 148
French military, 200
French Military Mission to Japan (1867), 169
French military mission to Japan (1867–68), 189
French Military Mission to Poland, 97
French monarchy, 156
French Morocco, 310
French National Assembly, 382, 392, 410
French National Guard, 2
French nationality law, 205
French National Police, 385
French Naval Aviation, 154, 334, 359, 361
French Navy, 1, 2, 7, 40, 110, 207, 208, 212, 218, 226, 333, **359**, 362, 381, 387, 406
French Ninth Army, 97
French nobility, 361
French North Africa, 92, 93, 175, 190, 341, 366
French Parliament, 183, 387
French patrol vessel L'Adroit, 374
French Polynesia, 94, 288, 289, 292, 348
French presidential election, 2012, 38
French Renaissance, 23
French Republic, 2, 111
French Republican Guard, 385

French Resistance, 73, 77, 86, 90, 127, 177, 219
French Revolution, 27, 47, 155, 361, 363, 382
French Revolutionary Army, 29, 185, 186
French Revolutionary Wars, 4, 15, 182, 364, 405
French Revolution of 1848, 187
French Royal Army (1652–1830), 184
French Sahara, 287
French seaplane carrier Foudre, 173, 365
French Senate, 357, 392, 423
French Seventh Army, 97
French ship Ça Ira (1781), 164
French ship Couronne (1636), 157
French ship Héros (1752), 160
French ship Jean Bart (1852), 208
French ship Le Foudroyant (1751), 161
French ship Napoléon (1850), 166
French ship Royal Louis (1758), 161
French ship Siroco (L9012), 300
French ship Soleil-Royal (1670), 158
French ship Soleil-Royal (1749), 160
French ship Tourville, 159
French ship Ville de Paris (1764), 162
French Somaliland, 141
French State, 111
French submarine Plongeur, 166, 167, 365
French submarine Surcouf, 133, 174, 177, 365
French submarine Surcouf (N N 3), 96
French submarine Téméraire (S617), 178
French Third Republic, 51, 72, 211, 365, 371, 383, 413
French Wars of Religion, 3, 14, 24
French West Africa, 92, 138
French West Indies, 32
Fr:Escadre aérienne de commandement et de conduite projetable, 343
Fr:Escadron de formation des commandos de lair, 353
FR F2 sniper rifle, 232, 233, 276
Fr:groupe de ravitaillement en vol 02.091 Bretagne, 343
Frigate, 164, 361, 369
Fri (yacht), 293
Fr:Jean Vilain, 210
Fr:Légion étrangère, 205
Fr:mécanicien daéronefs, 351
Fr:météorologue, 351
Fr:militaire technicien de lair, 353
Fr:Navigateur aérien, 352
Fr:Officier mécanicien navigant, 352
Fr:officiers des bases de lair, 353
Fronde, 155
Front Algérie Française, 38
Front line, 57
Fr:Ordre de Saint-Jean de Jérusalem, 361
Fr:Pierre Sergent (militaire), 242
Fr:Région militaire, 198
Fr:Sarie Marais, 247
Fr:service du commissariat des armées, 342
Fr:Service industriel de laéronautique, 341
Fr:Structure intégrée de maintien en condition opérationnelle des matériels aéronautiques de la Défense, 341
Fr:Zone de défense et de sécurité, 198, 387
Fusiliers Commandos de lAir, 10, 337, 338, 340, 344, 351
Fusiliers de Marine, 164
Fusiliers Marins, 9, 148, 154, 361, 367
Future French aircraft carrier, 298
Future of the French Navy, 154

Gabès, 144
Gabon, 205, 214, 230, 348
Gabriel Auphan, 176
Gabriel Voisin, 303
Gaëtan Poncelin de Raucourt, 405
Gaiter, 70
Galley, 156
Galley slave, 157
Gallic Wars, 3, 13
Gallipoli, 208
Gallipoli Campaign, 65, 216
Gallo-Roman culture, 18
Garde Mobile, 412
Gardes françaises, 184, 185
Gare de Paris-Est, 54
Garigliano, 88
Garin Tzabar, 268
Gas mask, 135, 396
Gaston Palewski, 290
Gaul, 3, 14
Gaur, 81
GCT 155mm, 200, 280
Gebel Sherif, 146
Gendarme (historical), 24
Gendarmerie, 379, 381, 398, 405, 410
Gendarmerie maritime, 367
General, 59, 66, 147, 148, 303
Général, 217, 240, 259–261
General Atomics MQ-9 Reaper, 350
Général darmée aérienne, 332
Général de brigade, 227
Général de brigade aérienne, 354
Général de corps aérien, 354
Général de division, 420
General Leclerc, 83, 126
Generaloberst, 147
General Patton, 120
General purpose machine gun, 276
General staff, 386
Geneva, 329

453

Geneva Protocol, 286, 294
Genoa, 174
Geographic coordinate system, 271
George Jellicoe, 2nd Earl Jellicoe, 137
Georges Bergé, 78, 137
Georges Catroux, 148
Georges Guingouin, 116
Georges Guynemer, 308
Georges Hamacek, 243
Georges Leygues-class frigate, 374
Georges Madon, 308
Georges Mandel, 90
Gerboise Bleue, 289
Gerboise Rouge, 289
Gerd von Rundstedt, 99
German Army (German Empire), 67, 295, 305
German Empire, 34, 267, 295
Germanic peoples, 3, 14, 18
German Instrument of Surrender, 73
German occupation of France during World War II, 111
German submarine U-564, 134
German Unification, 53
Germany, 2, 274–277, 279, 321
Germany 1945, 131
Germany and weapons of mass destruction, 284
Gestapo, 177
Ghana, 289
Gibraltar, 44, 95, 112, 316
GIGN, 10, 387, 391
Gilbert du Motier, marquis de Lafayette, 405, 408
Global power, 287
Global War on Terror, 226
Global War on Terrorism, 182, 204
Glock 17, 274
Glorious First of June, 364
Glorious Revolution, 25
Gold Beach, 119
Golden Cavalry of St George, 26
Government agency, 379
Government of France, 182
Government of National Defense, 412
Gowind-class corvette, 374
Grande Armée, 30, 186, 187, 333, 362, 381, 406
Grandes Unités Françaises, 153
Great Britain, 15, 168, 338
Great Officers of the Crown of France, 381
Greek War of Independence, 182, 405
Green beret, 204
Greenock, 95
Greenpeace, 292
Grenade, 67, 384, 390
Grenade (insignia), 203, 249

Grenade launcher, 277
Grenadier Guards, 384
Grenoble, 75, 347
Groupe, 312
Groupe de Ravitaillement en Vol 02.091 Bretagne, 343
Groupe de sécurité de la présidence de la République, 387
Groupement, 312
Groupement de Commandos Mixtes Aéroportés, 151
Grumman F4F Wildcat, 318
Grumman F8F Bearcat, 326
Guadeloupe, 33, 94, 157
Guard of honour, 228
Guerrilla warfare, 325
Guet royal, 409
Guiana Space Centre, 229
Guise, 58
Gulf War, 38, 39, 182, 204, 206, 227, 332, 338, 366
Gunboat diplomacy, 364
Gun synchronizer, 308
Günther von Kluge, 113, 114
Gustave Fourreau, 260
Gustav Line, 115
Gustavus Adolphus of Sweden, 32
Guy Pedroncini, 63

H, 134
Habsburg, 24
Haiti, 6, 393
HALO jump, 237
Hammaguir, 290
Hammoudia, 289
Hand grenade, 67
Hanoi, 326
Harki, 38
Harkis, 192
Hauptsturmführer, 114
Hawker Hurricane, 107
Heavy cruiser, 140
Heavy machine gun, 276
Hebrew language, 268
Heckler & Koch AG36, 277
Heckler & Koch MP5, 275
Heckler & Koch PSG1, 276
Heckler & Koch USP, 274
Hectare, 221
Heil Hitler, 89
Heilongjiang, 321
Heinkel He 111, 315
Heinz Guderian, 102
Helicopter, 333, 360
Hélie de Saint Marc, 242
Helmuth von Moltke the Younger, 59

Henri dAstier de la Vigerie, 143
Henri Dentz, 148
Henri dOrléans, duc dAumale, 384
Henri Farman, 303
Henri Giraud, 93, 97
Henri Gouraud (French Army officer), 214
Henri Honoré dEstienne dOrves, 177
Henri Honoré Giraud, 92
Henri Joseph Fenet, 114
Henri-Joseph Paixhans, 166
Henri Lafont, 88
Henri Rol-Tanguy, 121
Henry II of France, 184
Henry IV of France, 156
Henry Maitland Wilson, 126
Henschel Hs 126, 315
Heraklion, 137
Herbert Kitchener, 1st Earl Kitchener, 241
Hermann Göring, 107
Hermanville-sur-Mer, 119
Hervé Morin, 294
Hew Strachan, 50
Hexagone Balard, 339
High Commissioner for Atomic Energy, 286
Highway patrol, 389
Hiroshima, 289
Historian, 44
History, 32
History of France, 26
History of nuclear weapons, 285
History of the Armée de lAir (1909–1942), 56, 303, **303**, 321
History of the Armée de lAir in the colonies (1939–62), 303, 321, **321**
History of the French Navy, 154, **154**
History of the Netherlands (1939–1945), 100
Hitler, 310
HK416, 200, 275
HK 417, 276
HMAS Australia (D84), 140
HMAS Supply, 293
HMNB Devonport, 134
HMNZS Canterbury (F-421), 293
HMNZS Otago (F111), 293
HMS Ark Royal (91), 317
HMS Dreadnought (1906), 171
HMS Faulknor, 95
HMS Hermes (95), 140
HMS Largs, 95, 96
HMS Ramillies (07), 127
Ho Chi Minh City, 324
Hoggar Mountains, 289
Holy Roman Emperor, 19, 23
Holy Roman Empire, 3, 14, 23
Honneur et Fidélité, 203, 238, 240
Honneur, patrie, valeur, discipline, 360

Horace Vernet, 384, 407
Horizon-class frigate, 178, 300, 368
Horne, Alistair, 71
Hostage, 391
Hotchkiss M1909 Benet-Mercie machine gun, 305
Hotchkiss M1914 machine gun, 67
Hotel des Invalides, 408
Hôtel Matignon, 392
Hôtel Meurice, 121
House of Bourbon, 29, 158
House of Capet, 21
House of Valois, 29
Howitzer, 66, 280
Hubert Lyautey, 62
Hué, 326
Huguenots, 24
Humanitarian aid, 38
Hundred Days Offensive, 35
Hundred Thousand Sons of Saint Louis, 34, 182, 187
Hundred Years War, 3, 14, 22, 40, 182, 183, 381
Hydrogen bomb, 291

Iberian Peninsula, 155
I Corps (France), 82, 137
II Corps (France), 82
II Corps (United States), 144
III Corps (France), 82, 419
Ile dAix, 164
Île-de-France, 347, 392
Ile Longue, 368
Île Longue, 360

Imperial Guard (Napoleon I), 31, 383
Imperial Japanese Navy, 171
Imperial Russia, 15
India and weapons of mass destruction, 284, 286
Indian Army (1895–1947), 317
Indian Ocean, 38
Indian Ocean in World War II, 149
Indochina, 217, 222
Indo-China, 205
Indochina War, 151, 204, 332, 366
Indonesia, 268
In Ekker, 290
Infantry, 9, 67, 100, 226, 334
Infantry fighting vehicle, 277
In France, 185
Infrastructure service defense, 198
In-Salah, 290

Inspection of the Foreign Legion, 217
Inspector-general, 386
Institut National de la Santé et de la Recherche Médicale, 293
Intercontinental ballistic missile, 193
International Court of Justice, 292
International Standard Book Number, 48–50, 71, 270, 295, 355, 378, 402, 414
Interwar period, 39
Invasion of Algiers in 1830, 34, 187, 364
Invasion of Dominica (1778), 363
Invasion of French Indochina, 322
Invasion of Guadeloupe (1759), 159
Invasion of Poland, 97, 311
Investigating magistrate, 386
IPTN CN-235, 346
Iran and weapons of mass destruction, 284
Iraq, 228, 317, 336
Iraq and weapons of mass destruction, 284
Iraqforce, 317
Irish Armed Forces, 226
Ironclad, 166, 170
Ironclad warship, 365
Isabella II of Spain, 208
Isan, 322
Islamic, 19
Islamism, 38
Israel, 6, 268
Israel and weapons of mass destruction, 284
Israel Defense Forces, 268
ISRIA, 296
Issy-les-Moulineaux, 386
Istres-Le Tubé Air Base, 342
Italian Armed Forces, 226
Italian Campaign (World War II), 80, 115
Italian invasion of France, 110
Italian nuclear weapons program, 284
Italian Wars, 3, 14, 24, 182
Italia (Roman Empire), 17
Italy, 2, 27, 274, 275, 281, 338
Ivorian-French War, 38
Ivory Coast, 6, 206, 229, 393

Jacob Gerritz. Loef, 157
Jacob L. Devers, 126
Jacques Benoist-Méchin, 85
Jacques Cartier, 25
Jacques Cassard, 376
Jacques Chirac, 7, 292, 293
Jacques Duchesne, 212
Jacques Lefort, 260
Jacques Massu, 191, 222
Jacques Morin, 222, 242
Jacques Necker, 406
Jacques-Noël Sané, 163
Jacques-Yves Cousteau, 177, 377

James II of England, 25
James Somerville (admiral), 316
Janes Defence Weekly, 202, 419
January 2015 Île-de-France attacks, 195
Japan, 171, 321
Japan and weapons of mass destruction, 284
Japanese Instrument of Surrender, 75, 177, 366
Jean Armand de Maillé-Brézé, 157
Jean Baptiste Colbert, 362
Jean-Baptiste Colbert, 155, 158
Jean-Baptiste Colbert, Marquis de Seignelay, 362
Jean Baptiste Eugène Estienne, 67
Jean Bart, 159, 376
Jean-Claude Coullon, 240, 260
Jean Cocteau, 377
Jean Colonna dOrnano, 145
Jean Danjou, 204, 210, 223, 241, 243
Jean Decoux, 322
Jean de Laborde, 176
Jean de Lattre de Tassigny, 75, 129, 219, 327
Jean Deuve, 151
Jean de Vienne, 377
Jean du Casse, 376
Jean-François de Galaup, comte de Lapérouse, 163
Jean-François de Galaup, comte de La Pérouse, 376
Jean Gabin, 377
Jean Jules Henri Mordacq, 216
Jean Le Morillon, 151
Jean-Louis Franceschi, 260
Jean Louis Roué, 260
Jean-Luc Carbuccia, 243
Jean Maurin, 204, 261, 420
Jean Moulin, 90
Jean Olié, 259
Jean-Pierre Bosser, 182
Jean Sassi, 122, 124, 151
Jeep, 128, 130
Jeremy Black (historian), 48
Jeune École, 170
Jijel, 93
Jilin, 321
J. Lawton Collins, 132
Joan of Arc, 23
John Foster Dulles, 328
John Keegan, 49
John Roberts (historian), 50
John Vereker, 6th Viscount Gort, 99
Joint Directorate of Infrastructure Networks and Information Systems, 198, 340
Joint-service, 198
Joint Space Command (France), 341
Jordan, 149
José Aboulker, 143

Joseph Darnand, 86
Joseph de Goislard de Monsabert, 129
Joseph Gallieni, 214
Joseph Joffre, 54, 56, 57, 67, 189
Joseph Vuillemin, 76
JSTOR, 70
Jules Dumont dUrville, 165, 376
Jules Girardet, 409
Julius Caesar, 3, 14, 17
July Revolution, 34, 187, 411
June Days uprising, 188
June Rebellion, 412
Junkers Ju 52, 325
Junkers Ju 88, 137
Juno Beach, 119
Juvenile delinquency, 389

Kamerun, 66
Karl Mack von Leiberich, 30
Karlsruhe, 131
Katyn massacre, 86
KC-135, 333
Keelung Campaign, 212
Kepi, 43, 201, 254, 255, 394
Képi, 189
Képi Blanc (publication), 420
Khalid bin Sultan, 228
Killed in action, 220
King Clovis I, 18
Kingdom of France, 207
Kingdom of Italy (1861–1946), 53, 72, 77
Kingdom of Jerusalem, 21
Kirkuk, 317
Knight, 20
Knights Hospitaller, 361
Kolwezi, 206
Konrad Adenauer, 287
Koran, 45
Korea, 169, 325
Kosovo, 206, 393
Kosovo Force, 38, 228
Kosovo War, 182, 332, 366
Kriegsmarine, 175, 316, 366
Kuwait, 205

La Compania Sahariana de Cufra, 145
Laconia incident, 135
La Fayette-class frigate, 298, 300
Lafayette Escadrille, 347
La Ferme, 235
Lambaesis, 226
Lance Corporal, 399
Lances, 21
Lancia, 146
Landing craft infantry, 118
Landmine, 116

Land mine, 5
Land Rover Defender, 279
Land warfare, 181
Laos, 33, 37, 151, 321, 322
La Rochelle, 123
Last battle of the battleship Bismarck, 134
Latécoère, 310
Laudun-lArdoise, 229
Lauterbourg, 131
LAviation Militaire, 174
Law enforcement agency, 379, 391
Law enforcement in Saint Pierre and Miquelon, 392
Lazare Ponticelli, 244
League of Nations Mandate, 33
Lebanese Civil War, 182, 204, 226
Lebanon, 6, 33, 205, 217, 226, 317, 393
Lebel Model 1886 rifle, 67
Le Boudin, 204, 245, 253
Le Bourget, 115
Le Chant des Africains, 88
Leclerc, 8
Le Fantasque-class destroyer, 135
Légion des Volontaires Français, 74, 114
Légion nord-africaine, 89
Legion of French Volunteers Against Bolshevism, 84
Legion of Honour, 155, 196, 274
Legislative Assembly (France), 28
Le Havre, 115
Lend Lease, 82
Lend-Lease, 92, 95
Lens, Pas-de-Calais, 61
Leopold III of Belgium, 97
Léopold III of Belgium, 107
Le Petit Prince, 138
Les Invalides, 198
Leukemia, 290
Levant Fleet, 361
Levée en masse, 28
LGI Mle F1, 277
LHumanité, 289, 422
Liaoning, 321
Liberalism, 28, 34
Liberation of France, 72
Liberation of Paris, 80, 121
Liberté-class battleship, 171
Liberté, égalité, fraternité, 27
Libreville, 348
Libya, 7, 80
Libya and weapons of mass destruction, 284
Libyan no-fly zone, 7
Licata, 137
Lieutenant, 305, 335, 354, 398
Lieutenant Ballantyne, 145
Lieutenant colonel, 250, 354

Lieutenant commander, 377
Lieutenant-General (France), 420
Lieutenant junior grade, 371
Light cruiser, 172
Light machine gun, 276
Light tank, 231
Light Utility Vehicle, 279, 280
Lille, 75, 192, 198
Limoges, 75
Lingua franca, 21
List of aircraft carriers of France, 361
List of battleships of France, 154, 366
List of battles involving France, 2, 13
List of cruisers of France, 154
List of current French Navy ships, 154
List of destroyers of France, 154
List of estimated death tolls from nuclear attacks on cities, 285
List of former European colonies, 13
List of French armies in World War I, 13, 72
List of French armies in World War II, 13, 72
List of French Army regiments, 13, 72, 195, 273
List of French Commands and Army groups, 13, 72
List of French corps in World War I, 13, 72
List of French corps in World War II, 13, 72
List of French divisions in World War I, 13, 72
List of French divisions in World War II, 13, 72
List of French monarchs, 207
List of French Navy ship names, 154
List of French Paratrooper Units, 9, 10, 196, 203, 206, 220–223, 226, 227, 234, 246, 335, 340, 420
List of French sail frigates, 154
List of missiles by country, 284
List of Naval Ministers of France, 154
List of nuclear weapons, 285
List of senior officers of the French Army, 195, 274
List of ships of the Forces navales françaises libres, 176
List of ships of the Free French Naval Forces, 136
List of ships of the line of France, 154
List of states with nuclear weapons, 285
List of submarines of France, 154, 361
List of wars involving France, 182, 405
List of weapons of mass destruction treaties, 285
Liverpool, 112
LLR 81mm, 280
Lockheed C-130 Hercules, 340, 350
Lockheed C-130J Super Hercules, 350
Loire River, 44
Lombards, 19

Longbowmen, 22
Long Range Desert Group, 146
Lord Cornwallis, 26
Lorient, 164, 360
Lorraine (region), 122, 214
Louis Aleno de St Aloüarn, 376
Louis Antoine de Bougainville, 155, 159, 376
Louis-Antoine Gaultier, 241
Louis Auguste Le Tonnelier de Breteuil, 406
Louis Béchereau, 303
Louis Blériot, 303
Louis-Claude de Saulces de Freycinet, 376
Louis Darquier de Pellepoix, 87
Louis Faury, 97
Louis Philippe I, 34, 207, 364, 420
Louis-Philippe of France, 42
Louis-Phillipe, 412
Louis Phillippe, 383
Louis Pichot de Champfleury, 261
Louis-René Levassor de Latouche Tréville, 165, 376
Louis the Pious, 20
Louis Thomas Villaret de Joyeuse, 376
Louis XIII, 184
Louis XIII of France, 155, 157, 361
Louis XIV, 3, 14, 25, 51, 184
Louis XIV of France, 155
Louis XVIII of France, 411
Louis XVI of France, 155, 162
Louis XV of France, 155, 159
Low Countries, 27, 99
Loyada, 205
Luang Prabang, 151
Luc-Julien-Joseph Casabianca, 376
Luc Ravel, 198
Luftstreitkräfte, 305
Luftwaffe, 39, 93, 100, 107, 112, 147
Lunéville, 75
Luxembourg, 25, 51, 100
Luxeuil, 337
Luxeuil Air Base, 342, 346
Lyon, 75, 131
Lyon-class battleship, 174

M10 tank destroyer, 123
M16A2 rifle, 275
M1917 Browning machine gun, 135
M203 grenade launcher, 277
M270 MLRS, 280
M2 Browning, 276
M2 Half Track Car, 121
M4 Sherman, 80, 125
M51 (missile), 178, 283
Macedonian front (World War I), 216
Machine gun, 56, 59, 67, 135, 308
MAC Mle 1950, 274

Madagascar, 149, 157, 205
Maghreb, 33
Maginot Line, 36, 97
Mahal (Israel), 268
Main battle tank, 277
Mainland France, 203
Maison militaire du roi de France, 184
Major, 86, 250, 397
Major (France), 234, 250, 398, 421
Major-General, 148
Malagasy Uprising, 192
Malgré-nous, 73, 219
Mali, 7, 38, 206, 289, 336
Man-at-arms, 22
Manchuria, 321
Mandingo Wars, 204, 206
Manhattan Project, 287
Man-of-war, 157
Manstein Plan, 36
Maquis du Vercors, 90
Maquis (World War II), 86
Marcel Beau, 335
Marcel Bigeard, 222
Marcel-Bruno Gensoul, 316
Marcel Cerdan, 377
Marcel Letestu, 260
March battalion, 148
Marche Képi Blanc, 235
Marching Regiment of the Foreign Legion, 215, 216, 218, 225, 244
Marching Regiments of Foreign Volunteers, 244
Marcoule Nuclear Site, 287
Marie Émile Fayolle, 112
Marie Louis Henry de Granet-Lacroix de Chabrières, 243
Marie Pierre Koenig, 147
Marie Skłodowska Curie, 286
Marine nationale, 9
Marine royale (France), 361
Marines, 227, 361
Maritime Gendarmerie, 10, 154, 359, 361
Maritime Prefect, 154
Marle, Aisne, 103
Marne River, 58
Marrakech, 317
Marseille, 87, 125, 229, 361, 391
Marseille Marine Fire Battalion, 10, 359, 361
Marseille Provence Airport, 391
Marseilles, 129
Marshal of France, 57, 371, 381
Marshal of Lodgings, 398, 399
Martin B-10, 322
Martin B-26 Marauder, 143
Martinique, 33, 94, 157, 348
Martin Maryland, 317

Masters degree, 199
Matériel, 196
Matériel (French Army), 9
Matilda II, 106
Maubeuge, 58
Maurice Challe, 206
Maurice Gamelin, 97
Maurice Sarrail, 189
Mauritania, 336
Mauritius campaign of 1809–11, 364
Maxime Weygand, 91, 106
May 1958 crisis, 192, 288
Mayotte, 203, 230
Médaille militaire, 155, 196, 221, 274
Medieval, 40
Mediterranean, 155
Mediterranean, Middle East and African theatres of World War II, 135, 138, 148
Mediterranean Sea, 42, 226, 361
Mediterranean Theatre of World War II, 126
Medium bomber, 143
Meerkat (vehicle), 279
Mehariste, 145
Méhariste, 258
Meknès, 317
Mekong, 322
Melun, 75
Mèo, 151
Merina Kingdom, 214
Mers-el-Kebir, 175
Mers-el-Kébir, 316
Mers El Kébir, 136
Meteorology, 351
Metropolitan France, 111, 207, 211, 290
Metz, 56, 75
Metz-Frescaty Air Base, 348
Meuse, 99
Meuse River, 101
Mexico, 205, 210
Mexico and weapons of mass destruction, 284
Michel Serres, 377
Michiel de Ruyter, 40
Middle Ages, 3, 14, 21, 361, 381
Middle East, 5
Middle-East, 141
Mike Calvert, 81
Milan, 209, 276
Milice, 85, 86
Militarism, 53
Military Affairs: The Journal of Military History, Including Theory and Technology, 70
Military Air Transport Command, 336, 337
Military band, 253
Military doctrine, 338
Military Fuel Service (France), 7, 197

Military history of France, 2, **13**, 195, 273, 333, 362, 381, 406
Military history of France during World War II, **72**
Military intervention against ISIL, 332
Military of France, 286, 293, 385, 386
Military police, 203, 223, 383, 385, 393
Military port of Toulon, 360, 368
Military rank, 371
Military recruitment, 205
Military reserve, 406
Military reserve force, 53
Military reserve forces of France, 8, 183, 333, 361
Military tradition, 252
Militia, 86
Minesweeper (ship), 134, 135
Minibus, 280
Minié rifle, 189
Minister of the Armed Forces (France), 1, 7, 405, 413
Minister of the Interior (France), 379
Minister of the Navy and Colonies, 90
Minister of Transportation (France), 392
Minister of War (France), 69
Ministry of Defence (France), 333
Ministry of the Armed Forces (France), 183
Ministry of the Interior, 386
Mirage 2000, 333, 349
Mirage 2000-5F, 346
Mirage 2000C, 347
Mirage 2000D, 346
Mirage 2000N, 347
Mirage 5, 337
Mirage F.1, 337
Mirage IV, 337
MIRV, 288
Missile Moyenne Portée, 276
Missile Technology Control Regime, 5
Missing in action, 221
Mission Héraclès, 38, 345
Mistral-class amphibious assault ship, 298, 300, 374
Mistral (missile), 280
Mitrailleuse, 189
Mitsubishi Ki-21, 322
Mitsubishi Ki-30, 322
Mobile Gendarmerie, 10, 88, 387, 389
Modern equipment and uniform of the French Army, 195, 273
Modern equipment of the French Army, **273**
Mont de Marsan, 337
Mont-de-Marsan Air Base, 343, 347
Monthermé, 102
Montoire, 111
Montpellier, 75

Montreal Laboratory, 287
Mont-Saint-Michel, 22
Morale, 205
Morane-Saulnier, 310, 325
Morane-Saulnier L, 305
Morane-Saulnier MS.406, 312
Morhange, 56
Morocco, 53, 205, 217, 218, 256, 270, 289, 316, 317, 329
Mortar (weapon), 67, 280
Mortier 120mm Rayé Tracté Modèle F1, 280
Mororoa, 293
Mororoa e tatou, 293
Mossberg 500, 275
Mosul, 317
Motto, 79
MRAP, 278
Muammar Gaddafi, 7, 38
Mudry CAP 10, 360
Muhammad, 45
Mulhouse, 54, 75
Multinational Force in Lebanon, 182, 204, 206, 226
Multiple rocket launcher, 280
Munich massacre, 391
Mururoa, 5, 291, 293
Murzuk, 145
Musée de lArmée, 408, 420
Musée de Versailles, 384
Musketeers of the Guard, 185
Mustang (military officer), 234, 421
Myanmar, 325
Myanmar and weapons of mass destruction, 284

Nagasaki, Nagasaki, 169
Namur (city), 100
Nancy, France, 75, 336
Nancy - Ochey Air Base, 346
Nancy-Ochey Air Base, 342
Nantes, 75, 107
Napoleon, 364
Napoleon Bonaparte, 4, 15, 29, 410
Napoleon I, 30, 51, 185
Napoleonic Campaigns, 414
Napoleonic Era, 29, 252
Napoleonic France, 32
Napoleonic Wars, 4, 15, 67, 182, 185, 364, 405
Napoleon III, 364
Napoléon III, 156
Napoleon III of France, 412
Napoleons invasion of Russia, 31
National Convention, 28, 164
National Council of the Resistance, 90
National Gendarmerie, 1, 2, 8, 10, 11, 226, 333, 362, 367, **379**, 381, 406, 413

National Guard (disambiguation), 405
National Guard (France), 1, 8, 185, 333, 362, 381, 383, **405**, 406
National Guard of the United States, 267
Nationalism, 29
National Liberation Front (Algeria), 222
National markings, 317
National Police (France), 379, 387, 413
National Territory Land Command (France), 196
NATO, 4, 6, 15, 16, 38, 73, 190, 286, 288, 295, 297, 298, 336, 343
NATO Military Command Structure, 190, 338
Naturalization, 421
Natural Resources Defense Council, 422
Naval Action Force, 154, 359
Naval artillery, 365
Naval Battle of Casablanca, 366
Naval commandos (France), 9, 79, 177, 361
Naval doctrine, 369
Naval operations in the Dardanelles Campaign, 173, 365
Naval warfare, 359
Navy, 359
Nazi, 132
Nazi Germany, 72, 77, 98, 175
Nazis, 77
Nazi salute, 86
NDjamena, 345
Nec pluribus impar, 240, 242
Negev Nuclear Research Center, 287
Neman River, 115
Netherlands and weapons of mass destruction, 284
Neustria, 19
Neutral country, 58
Neutron bomb, 288
Neville Chamberlain, 97
New Caledonia, 94, 289, 348
New France, 4, 15, 32, 159
New Hebrides, 94
New York harbour, 96
New York Herald Tribune, 286
New Zealand, 5
New Zealand Army, 267
New Zealand Defence Force, 269
New Zealand Prime Minister, 293
Nexter Aravis, 278
N'Djamena, 348
NH90, 360
NHIndustries NH90, 281
Niall Ferguson, 2, 13
Nice, 75
Nicolas Baudin, 376
Nicolas Sarkozy, 5, 292, 297
Niemen, 115

Nieuport 11, 308
Nieuport 16, 308
Nieuport 17, 308
Nieuport 23, 307
Nieuport-Delage, 310
Niger, 214
Nigeria, 289
Nile, 45
Nîmes, 229
Nine Years War, 25, 158, 185, 362
Ninth Army (France), 102
Nivelle Offensive, 57, 62
Nixon administration, 288
NKVD, 86
No. 13 Group RAF, 113
No. 242 Group RAF, 137
No. 327 Squadron RAF, 113
No. 329 Squadron RAF, 119
No. 340 Squadron RAF, 112, 113, 119
No. 341 Squadron RAF, 113, 119
No. 342 Squadron RAF, 119
No. 4 Commando, 118
Non-commissioned officer, 42, 247, 257, 399
Non, je ne regrette rien, 224, 245
Norman Conquest, 3, 14
Normandie-Niemen, 114–116, 131
Normandy, 107, 118, 125, 130, 361
Normandy Invasion, 118
Normandy Landings, 37
Norman Kirk, 293
Normans, 21
Norman Schwarzkopf, Jr., 228
North African Campaign, 141, 144, 206
North American T-28 Trojan, 335
North Atlantic Treaty Organisation, 4
Northern Army Group, 193
Northern France Campaign (1944), 37
Northern Mali conflict, 6, 182, 204, 207, 229
Northern Mali conflict (2012–present), 38
North Korea and weapons of mass destruction, 284, 286
North Sea, 19, 190
Northwest African Photographic Reconnaissance Wing, 137
Norwegian Campaign, 206, 365
Nouméa, 360, 368
November 2015 Paris attacks, 195, 229
Noyelles-lès-Humières, 105
Nuclear arms race, 285
Nuclear deterrence, 286
Nuclear deterrent, 2, 370
Nuclear disarmament, 285
Nuclear espionage, 285
Nuclear ethics, 285
Nuclear explosion, 285
Nuclear labor issues, 285

Nuclear marine propulsion, 361
Nuclear Non-Proliferation Treaty, 5, 283
Nuclear power in France, 287
Nuclear proliferation, 284, 285
Nuclear terrorism, 285
Nuclear test, 289, 293
Nuclear testing, 292, 293
Nuclear Threat Initiative, 296
Nuclear warfare, 285
Nuclear warhead, 286
Nuclear weapon, 283, 285
Nuclear weapon design, 285
Nuclear weapons and Israel, 286
Nuclear weapons and the United Kingdom, 286, 288
Nuclear weapons and Ukraine, 284, 286
Nuclear weapons delivery, 285
Nuclear weapons testing, 285
Nuclear weapon yield, 285
Nuclear winter, 285

Oberkommando des Heeres, 105
Occupation of the Ruhr, 35
Océan-class ship of the line, 163
Office of Strategic Services, 127
Office of the Chief of Military History, 417
Officer (armed forces), 371
Officer Cadet, 354, 398
Officer candidate, 354
Officers, 265
Old French, 21
Old Sarum, 112
Omaha Beach, 119
Open city, 108, 109
Operational Mentoring and Liaison Team, 230
Operation Barbarossa, 113, 114
Operation Catapult, 95, 132, 177
Operation Cobra, 120
Operation Daguet, 201
Opération Daguet, 206, 227
Operation Desert Shield, 228
Operation Diadem, 115
Operation Dove, 128
Operation Dragoon, 75, 80, 88, 122, 177
Operation Enduring Freedom, 182, 197, 204, 207, 229
Operation Enduring Freedom – Horn of Africa, 6
Opération Épaulard I, 226
Opération Épervier, 345
Opération Harmattan, 7, 332, 367
Operation Husky, 137, 138
Operation Jedburgh, 124, 151
Operation Jumelles, 206, 222
Opération Licorne, 6
Operation Neptune, 119, 177

Operation Nordwind, 122
Operation Overlord, 82, 118, 120, 177
Operation Pugilist, 144
Opération Sentinelle, 195
Operation Serval, 7, 207, 229
Operation Span, 128
Operation Torch, 84, 93, 141, 143, 317
Operation Unicorn, 207, 229
Operation Unified Protector, 338
Oran, 87, 112, 316
Orange-Caritat Air Base, 353
Orange, Vaucluse, 239
Organisation de larmée secrète, 38
Organisation for Security and Co-operation in Europe, 4
Origins of the French Foreign Legion, 205, 207
Orléans, 75
Orléans – Bricy Air Base, 343, 346
Orne, 127
ORP Piorun (G65), 77
Oryol, 115
Oscar de Négrier, 212
Osprey Publishing, 71
Ottoman Empire, 24, 168
Ottoman military band, 246
Otto von Bismarck, 51
Oubangui-Chari, 148
Ouistreham, 118
Overseas collectivity, 229, 348
Overseas departments and territories of France, 33, 360
Overseas France, 290
Overseas territory (France), 229

P-36 Hawk, 315
P-38 Lightning, 137, 138
Pacific, 5
Pacification of Algeria, 206, 207, 213
Pacific Ocean, 5
Pacific War, 366
Paixhans gun, 365
Pakistan and weapons of mass destruction, 284, 286
Pannonian Avars, 19
Papeete, 360, 368
Parabellum MG14, 308
Parachute Company of the 3rd Foreign Infantry Regiment, 222, 242
Paramilitary, 86
Paris, 1, 4, 58, 75, 156, 338, 379
Paris Air Base, 339
Paris Commune, 182, 211, 405, 412, 413
Paris Fire Brigade, 9, 183
Paris Hall of Justice, 392
Partial Nuclear Test Ban Treaty, 286
Pas-de-Calais, 107

Passage Company of the Foreign Legion (CPLE), 221
Pastry War, 42, 165, 166
Pat Clayton, 145
Patrice de Mac-Mahon, Duke of Magenta, 209
Patrice de MacMahon, Duke of Magenta, 243
Patrol aircraft, 360
Patrol boat, 361
Paul Arnaud de Foïard, 242, 243
Paul Aussaresses, 122, 222
Paul Emile Victor, 377
Paul-Frédéric Rollet, 204, 217, 224, 240, 241, 244, 251, 259
Paul Gardy, 259, 260
Paul Gauguin, 377
Paul Hoste, 158
Paul Lardry, 260
Paul Legentilhomme, 148
Paul Ludwig Ewald von Kleist, 106
Paul Pau, 59
Paul Reynaud, 77, 103
Paul Teste, 377
Pau, Pyrénées-Atlantiques, 305
Peacekeeping, 226
Penal military unit, 208
Pen & Sword Military, 71
Penthièvre, 400
Peppino Garibaldi, 244
Perfidious Albion, 134
Periscope, 68
Permanent residence (United States), 267
Persian Gulf, 206, 227, 336
Pescadores Campaign, 365
Peter I of Serbia, 241
Petitions, 292
Petit Véhicule Protégé, 278
Peugeot P4, 279
PGM Hécate II, 232, 276
PGM Ultima Ratio, 276
Phalange africaine, 88
Philippe de Gaulle, 377
Philippe de Hauteclocque, 118
Philippe II, Duke of Orléans, 155
Philippe Kieffer, 118, 177
Philippe Lavigne, 340
Philippe Leclerc de Hauteclocque, 75
Philippe Lenoir, 407
Philippe Pétain, 57, 62, 189
Philippines and weapons of mass destruction, 284
Phoney War, 72
Phosgene, 295
Picardy, 99, 312
Pieds-Noirs, 37
Pierre André de Suffren de Saint Tropez, 42, 163
Pierre Bouvet, 376
Pierre-Charles Villeneuve, 377
Pierre Jeanpierre, 221, 222, 241–243, 245
Pierre Joseph Jeanningros, 241, 243
Pierre Lancelot, 135
Pierre Laval, 85
Pierre Le Gloan, 109, 110
Pierre Le Moyne dIberville, 376
Pierre Loti, 377
Pierre Loutrel, 88
Pierre Marie Gallois, 289
Pierre Messmer, 290
Pierre Paoli, 88
Pierre Roques, 303
Pierre Savorgnan de Brazza, 376
Pierre Segrétain, 241–243, 245
Pilatus PC-21, 333, 350
Pilatus PC-6 Porter, 281
Pioneer (military), 252
Pith helmet, 255, 257
Planned French Invasion of Britain (1759), 159
Plan XVII, 54, 56, 59
Plate armour, 22
Plateau dAlbion, 193
Platoon, 242, 250
Platoon leader, 199
Plutonium, 287
Plymouth, 95, 135, 177
Poilus, 52, 190
Poitiers, 75
Poland, 44, 267, 311, 321
Poland and weapons of mass destruction, 284
Police, 379, 406
Polish government in exile, 138
Polish Navy, 77, 133, 134
Pope, 19
Porch, Douglas, 71
Port, 347
Port des Galets, 360, 368
Portoferraio, 117
Porto-Novo, 213
Port Said, 151
Portsmouth, 133, 177
Poznań, 115
Praetorian Guard, 266
Prague, 115
Pre-dreadnought, 173
Prefect (France), 411
Préfet, 87
President of France, 1, 2, 7, 111, 183, 291, 292, 387
President of the French Republic, 38
Prime Minister of France, 7, 98, 387, 392
Projection and Support Air Force Brigade, 340
Propaganda, 140
Protected cruiser, 173

Protestants, 25
Provence, 17
Provisional Government of the French Republic, 73, 75
Provost (military police), 393
Prussia, 4, 15, 27, 30, 412
Pump-action shotgun, 275
Puttee, 70
Pyrenees, 15, 235, 290

Quasi-War, 364
Quebec, 159
Queen Elizabeth-class aircraft carrier, 369
Quid (encyclopedia), 419
Quimper, 409

R.530, 336
Rabat, 317
Race to the Sea, 60
Radar, 177
Radiation, 290
Radiation hardening, 288
Radioactive, 290
Radiological warfare, 283
Rafale, 39, 333, 347, 349, 360
RAF Habbaniya, 317
RAID (French Police unit), 387
Raid Marche, 235
Rainbow Warrior (1978), 293
Ranavalona III, 214
Ranks and insignia of NATO armies enlisted, 248, 249
Ranks and insignia of NATO armies officers, 250
Ranks in the French Air Force, 2, 333, 351–353, 362, 381, 406
Ranks in the French Army, 2, 182, 196, 210, 224–226, 234, 242, 247–250, 274, 333, 362, 381, 406, 421
Ranks in the French Navy, 2, 154, 333, 360, 362, 381, 406
Raoul Lufbery, 309
Raoul Magrin-Vernerey, 240, 259
Raphaël Vienot, 229, 241
Rapid Action Force (France), 193
Rapid deployment force, 206
Rashid Ali Al-Gaylani, 317
Raymond Le Corre, 260
Razzia, 213
RCA, 207, 229
Rear admiral, 376
Reconnaissance, 146
Reconnaissance vehicle, 277, 278
Red army, 113
Redoutable-class submarine (1967), 177
Ref admin, 45

Ref aid, 44
Ref alliance, 46
Ref amalgamate, 48
Ref ardennes, 47
Ref armies, 45
Ref artilleryreforms, 46
Ref authority, 44, 46
Ref avaricum, 44
Ref aviation, 47
Ref billion, 47
Ref bulk, 47
Ref bungled, 45
Ref cameron, 48
Ref castles, 45
Ref Chandler136, 46
Ref collapse, 44
Ref colonialempire, 47
Ref compagnies, 46
Ref competence, 47
Ref complaints, 44
Ref component, 45
Ref confidence, 47
Ref conscription, 46
Ref decisive, 47
Ref devils, 48
Ref diplomaticrev, 46
Ref divisions, 47
Ref dreyfus, 47
Ref exaggerated, 45
Ref exist, 48
Ref feature, 45
Ref fleet, 47
Ref food, 47
Ref force, 44
Ref frontiers, 44
Ref gendarmes, 46
Ref history, 46
Ref important, 44
Ref indicative, 47
Ref intercepting, 46
Ref internecine, 45
Ref Keegan64, 47
Ref leadership, 44
Ref little, 45
Ref maginot, 47
Ref modernwar, 46
Ref motivation, 45
Ref mounted, 45
Ref nationalism, 46
Ref nature, 46
Ref nobles, 46
Ref nuclear, 44
Ref operational, 47
Ref performance, 47
Ref plans, 46
Ref plate, 45

Ref pop, 46
Ref progress, 46
Ref rejection, 45
Ref replaced, 47
Ref rivalries, 44
Ref roman, 46
Ref sevenpop, 46
Ref soissons, 44
Ref spain, 44
Ref spirited, 48
Ref start, 48
Ref Strachan280, 47
Ref suffered, 45
Ref system, 47
Ref tactic, 45
Ref think, 46
Ref tore, 46
Ref uniforms, 46
Ref vauban, 46
Régence, 155
Reggane, 289, 290
Regia Aeronautica, 108
Regiment, 57, 62, 250
Régiment dinfanterie-chars de marine, 227
Régiments de marche de volontaires étrangers, 244
Regions of France, 387, 389
Reims, 62, 75, 303
Reims – Champagne Air Base, 349
Rémy Raffalli, 243
Renault FT, 67
Renault GBC 180, 281
Renault Kangoo, 280
Renault Kerax, 281
Renault R35, 137
Renault Trafic, 280
Renault TRM 10000, 281
René Bousquet, 87, 88
René Coty, 287
René Duguay-Trouin, 159, 376
René Fonck, 308
René Lennuyeux, 259, 260
René Morel (Légion étrangère), 260
René Mouchotte, 112, 335
Rennes, 75, 198
Republican Guard (France), 10, 201, 384, 385, 387
Republic of Congo, 206
Republic of Macedonia, 228, 393
Republic of the Congo, 206, 228
Reservist, 190
Réunion, 289, 348
Revanchism, 34, 47
Revolutionary France, 29
Révolution nationale, 85
Revolutions of 1848 in France, 412

Rheims, 73
Rhine River, 15, 121, 131
Rhodesian Bush War, 269
Rhodesian Light Infantry, 269
Rhodesian Security Forces, 269
Rhodesia Regiment, 269
Rhone River, 19
Ribbons of the French military and civil awards, 155, 196, 274
Richard Lizurey, 379, 386
Richelieu-class battleship, 174, 365
RICM, 197
Rifle, 67
Rifled musket, 31
Rifle grenade, 67
Rif War, 204, 217, 310
Rimailho Model 1904TR, 67
River Dyle, 99
River Thames, 45
Road–rail vehicle, 279
Robert A. Doughty, 71
Robert Cowley, 48
Robert Daniel Murphy, 143
Robert Nivelle, 57, 62, 189
Robert Surcouf, 165, 376
Rochefort, Charente-Maritime, 164, 347
Roger Blaizot, 81
Rogue state, 17
Roland Garros (aviator), 305
Roman Empire, 3, 14, 18, 19, 239
Romania and weapons of mass destruction, 284
Romania during World War I, 56
Rome, 17
Romorantin, 347
Rotterdam, 100
Rouen, 115
Rouffach, 124
Roundel, 40
Round shot, 157
Royal Air Force, 39, 81, 147, 317
Royal Australian Navy, 227, 293
Royal Flying Corps, 305
Royal Navy, 26, 40, 136, 156, 158, 159, 164, 300, 316, 366, 371
Royal Netherlands East Indies Army, 268
Royal Netherlands Navy, 40, 158
Royal Tank Regiment, 107
Royal Thai Air Force, 322
Royal Thai Army, 322
Royal Thai Navy, 322
Royan, 122
Rue Royale, Paris, 156
Rufisque, 140
Russia, 2, 16, 168
Russia and weapons of mass destruction, 284, 286

Russian Empire, 4, 53
Russo-Japanese war, 67
Rwanda, 205, 206, 228, 393

S2 (missile), 337
S3 (missile), 193, 337
Saarland, 97
Saar Offensive, 97
Saclay Nuclear Research Centre, 287
SAGEM Patroller, 282
SAGEM Sperwer, 282
Sahara, 225, 289
Sahara Desert, 289
Saharan Companies of the French Foreign Legion, 224
Saharan Méharistes Companies (méharistes sahariennes), 223–225
Sahariana, 146
Sahel, 206
Saigon, 326
Sailors, 361
Saint-Christol, Vaucluse, 229
Saint-Dizier, 39, 338
Saint-Dizier – Robinson Air Base, 346
Saint-Domingue, 33
Saintes, Charente-Maritime, 347
Saint-Laurent-sur-Mer, 119
Saintonge War, 22
Saint-Pierre and Miquelon, 94
Saint-Raphaël, Var, 126
Saint Tropez, 125
Saint-Tropez, 126
Salon-de-Provence Air Base, 347
Salonika Front, 56
Sambre, 103
Samori Ture, 214
Samuel de Champlain, 25, 376
SAN Jodel D.140 Mousquetaire, 333, 350
San Marco Regiment, 226
Sans-culotte, 406
Sans-culottes, 185
Sapper, 252
Saracens, 44
Sarajevo, 206, 228
Sarrebourg, 54
Sash, 201, 255
Satory, 390
Saudi Arabia, 228
Saudi Arabia and weapons of mass destruction, 284
Saumur, 193
Saverne, 122
Saxons, 19
Scania PRT-range, 279
Scharführer, 88
Scheldt, 105

Schlieffen Plan, 55, 59, 97, 98
Schneider CA1, 67
Scottish Highlands, 44
Scout Movement, 87
Scramble for Africa, 33
Scuttling of the French fleet in Toulon, 96, 156, 176, 366
Seaplane, 173, 365
Seaplane carrier, 173, 365
Search and rescue, 389
Seawall, 157
Second Anglo-Dutch War, 362
Second Armistice at Compiègne, 76, 133
Second Army (France), 56
Second Battle of Artois, 59, 216
Second Battle of Champagne, 59, 216
Second Battle of Orléans (1870), 211
Second Battle of the Aisne, 35, 62, 67, 216
Second Battle of the Marne, 35
Second Battle of Ypres, 59, 68, 295
Second Coalition, 29
Second Franco-Dahomean War, 204, 206
Second French colonial empire, 4
Second French Empire, 207, 211, 361, 371, 383, 412
Second generation (1998–2012), 280
Second Italian War of Independence, 4, 15, 34, 182, 189, 204, 206, 405
Second Ivorian Civil War, 38, 182, 204
Second Lieutenant, 199, 250, 398
Second Madagascar expedition, 204, 206
Second Opium War, 168, 189, 364
Second Restoration, 383
Second Sino-Japanese War, 321
Second World War, 15
Security Council, 15, 16
Sedan, France, 53, 101
Self-propelled artillery, 280
Semi-automatic pistol, 274
Semi-automatic shotgun, 275
Senegal, 138, 317
SEPECAT Jaguar, 39
Sergeant, 398, 399
Sergeant Major, 421
Service de maintenance industrielle terrestre, 197
Service du commissariat des armées, 198
Service rifle, 200, 275
Sétif and Guelma massacre, 191
Sevastopol, 208, 384
Seventh Army (France), 97
Seventy-four (ship), 163
Seven Years' War, 363
Seven Years War, 4, 15, 28, 32, 155, 159, 182, 185
Shaba II, 38, 204

SHAEF, 126
Shako, 254
Sheet (sailing), 361
S-Hertogenbosch, 104
Shield, 396
Ship of the line, 164
Ship prefix, 134
Sicherheitspolizei, 87
Sidi Bel Abbès, 223, 229, 262
Siege, 26, 32
Siege of Calais (1558), 23
Siege of La Rochelle, 157
Siege of Maubeuge, 58
Siege of Orléans, 23
Siege of Paris (1870–1871), 211
Siege of Petropavlovsk, 364
Siege of Sevastopol (1854–1855), 208, 384
Siege of Tuyên Quang, 212, 223
Siege of Yorktown, 26, 42, 163
Siegfried Line, 131
Siem Reap, 323
Sievert, 290
Sigmaringen, 73
Sikasso, 214
Simon Fraser, 15th Lord Lovat, 118
Sinking of the Rainbow Warrior, 5, 293, 296
Sino-French War, 204, 206, 212, 365
Sisophon, 322
Sister ship, 133
Six-Day War, 39, 338
Sixth Army (France), 58
Smolensk, 115
Sniper, 67
Sniper rifle, 276
Snipers, 232
Socata Rallye, 360
Socata TB 30 Epsilon, 333, 350
Socata TB-30 Epsilon, 347
SOCATA TBM, 281, 333, 340
Socata TBM 700, 350
Socialist Party (France), 38
Soissons, 312
Somalia, 206, 228
Somme (river), 105
Somme River, 59
SOMUA S35, 104
Sơn Tây Campaign, 212
Sous-officiers – Sub-officers, 421
South Africa, 279
South Africa and weapons of mass destruction, 284, 286
South-East Asian theatre of World War II, 149
South Korea and weapons of mass destruction, 284
South Vietnam, 329
Soviet anti-missile defences, 288
Soviet Union, 33
SPAD S.XIII, 308
Spahi, 201, 246
Spahis, 191, 256
Spain, 23, 377
Spanish Civil War, 270, 311
Spanish Empire, 24
Spanish Legion, 207, 216, 270
Spanish Netherlands, 25
Special Air Service, 78, 81, 84, 132
Special forces, 6, 116
Special operations, 391
Special Operations Command (France), 340
SPECTRA helmet, 258, 277
Speyer, 131
Spitfire, 112, 113, 137
Squadron (aviation), 312
Squadron Leader, 397
SS Alhama, 134
SS Ariosto, 134
SSBN, 370
SS Carsbreck, 134
SSN (hull classification symbol), 361, 369
SS Normandie, 96
Staff Sergeant, 398
Standing French Navy Deployments, 154
States of emergency in France, 195
St Chamond (tank), 67
Stele, 221
St. Étienne Mle 1907, 67
Stockpile (military), 286
Stokes Mortar, 67
Storming of the Bastille, 408
Storm Shadow, 178, 376
Strasbourg, 75, 122, 131
Strategic Air Forces Command, 336, 337, 340, 349
Strategic Oceanic Force, 154
Strike Force (France), 15
Structure of the French Army, 195, 273
Sturmbannführer, 86
Stuttgart, 115, 131
Sub-Lieutenant, 354, 398
Submachine gun, 275
Submarine, 173, 177, 365
Submarine forces (France), 10, 154, 359, 360
Sub-Officer, 398
Sub-Saharan Africa, 206, 213
Suebi, 17
Suez Crisis, 206, 287, 336
Sui generis collectivity, 348
Summit (meeting), 4
Supermarine Spitfire, 325
Susan Travers, 265
SWAT, 391
Sweden, 2, 276, 278, 279, 281

Sweden and weapons of mass destruction, 284
Sweden during World War II, 75
Switzerland, 281
Switzerland and weapons of mass destruction, 284
Syagrius, 18
Syria, 33, 205, 217, 317, 393
Syria and weapons of mass destruction, 284
Syria–Lebanon Campaign, 182, 204, 218
Syria-Lebanon Campaign, 206, 317
Syrian Civil War, 6, 38
Système de Commandement et de Conduite des Opérations Aérospatiales, 340

Tabatière rifle, 412
Tabun (nerve agent), 295
Taiwan and weapons of mass destruction, 284
Tajikistan, 345
Taliban, 6
Tamanrasset, 290
Tan Afella, 290
Tanezrouft, 289, 290
Tank, 56, 67, 277
Tarbes, 81
Tarragona, 208
Taverny Air Base, 349
Tchad, 345
T. C. W. Blanning, 46
Tear gas, 68, 295
Template:French military, 333, 362, 381, 406
Template:Nuclear weapons, 286
Template talk:French military, 333, 362, 381, 406
Template talk:Nuclear weapons, 286
Template talk:Weapons of mass destruction, 285
Template:Weapons of mass destruction, 285
Ten days campaign, 15, 34
Ten Days Campaign, 4
Territorial waters, 369
Terrorism, 195
Terrorist, 5
Thai people, 151
Thales Watchkeeper WK450, 300
The Daily Telegraph, 266, 423
The Guardian, 422
The Hague, 100
The Historian (journal), 71
The Lancaster House Treaties (2010), 39, 298
The New York Times, 422
Thermidorian Reaction, 410
Third Army (France), 56
Third Battle of the Aisne, 57
Third French Republic, 36
Thirty Years War, 3, 14, 157, 182
Thuringians, 18

Thyroid cancer, 293
Tirailleurs, 191, 256
TN 81, 292
TNT equivalent, 283, 291
Tobruk, 43
Togo, 33, 66
Tokyo, 323
Tokyo bay, 75, 177
Tonkin, 255
Tonkin Campaign, 206, 365
Torpedo, 134
Torpedo boat, 173
Tortuga (Haiti), 157
Toul, 75
Toulon, 75, 88, 137, 140, 159, 164, 175, 207, 211, 361, 362
Toulouse, 75
Toulouse - Francazal Air Base, 348
Tours, 293, 347
Towed artillery, 280
Tozeur, 144
Trainer (aircraft), 333, 360
Transall C-160, 237, 333, 340, 343, 346, 347, 350
Treaty of Verdun, 20
Treaty of Versailles, 35, 310
Treaty on the Non-Proliferation of Nuclear Weapons, 286
Trench warfare, 51, 59, 67, 68, 295
TRF1, 280
Tricolour (flag), 69
Triomphant-class submarine, 177, 178
Triple Entente, 35
Tripod, 68
Tripoli, 80
Troupes de Marine, 9, 148, 195–197, 201, 273
Troy H. Middleton, 132
Tubular magazine, 67
Tumble-home, 170
Tunisia, 144, 205, 217, 316, 329
Turban, 256
Turkish crescent, 246
Turnhouse, 113
Twenty Questions, 288

U-boat, 119
U-boat Campaign (World War I), 365
Ulm Campaign, 30
Uniform, 201
United Arab Emirates, 229
United Kingdom, 2, 53, 156, 278, 279, 281, 298, 299
United Kingdom and weapons of mass destruction, 284
United Kingdom of Great Britain and Ireland, 168

United Nations, 15
United Nations Assistance Mission for Rwanda, 38
United Nations Interim Force in Lebanon, 182, 204, 226
United Nations Protection Force, 38
United Nations Scientific Committee on the Effects of Atomic Radiation, 294
United Nations Security Council, 4
United States, 2, 16, 275–280, 299, 338
United States Air Force, 328
United States Air Force in France, 73
United States and weapons of mass destruction, 284, 286
United States Armed Forces, 268, 269
United States Army Air Service, 309
United States Army Center of Military History, 153
United States Marine Corps, 226
United States Navy, 226, 317
United States Third Army, 120
Universal Carrier, 147
University of Oxford, 45
Unmanned aerial vehicle, 299
UN Security Council Resolution 1973, 7
Urbain de Maillé-Brézé, 157
US 36th Infantry Division, 126
U.S. 3rd Infantry Division, 132
US 45th Infantry Division, 126
U.S. 6th Army Group, 126
USAF Counterproliferation Center, 287
U.S. Army, 227
USS Arkansas (BB-33), 127
USS Constellation vs La Vengeance, 364
USS Enterprise (CVN-65), 291
USS Enterprise vs Flambeau, 364
U.S. Seventh Army, 122
US Seventh Army, 128
USS Lafayette (AP-53), 96
USS Nevada (BB-36), 127
USSR, 86, 287, 289
USS Ranger (CV-4), 317
USS Sangamon (CVE-26), 317
USS Santee (CVE-29), 317
USS Suwannee (CVE-27), 317
USS Texas (BB-35), 127
Utah Beach, 118, 119
Utility helicopter, 360

Van, 280
Varennes-sur-Allier, 347
Variants, 278, 350
Vauban, 26
VBMR Griffon, 278
V Corps (United States), 119
Vehicle armour, 229

Véhicule blindé de combat dinfanterie, 277
Véhicule Blindé Léger, 278
Véhicule de lAvant Blindé, 278
Vel dHiv Roundup, 87
Vélizy – Villacoublay Air Base, 346
Veneti (Gaul), 18
Vercingetorix, 18
Verdun, 58, 61, 62
Versailles (city), 382, 390
Veteran, 268
Vice admiral, 371
Vice-admiral, 376, 377
Vichy, 78, 111, 316
Vichy France, 4, 37, 72, 111, 175, 176, 182, 190, 218, 219, 366
Vichy French Air Force, 303, 316, 321, 335
VI Corps (United States), 126
Victor Segalen, 377
Vienna, 30
Vientiane, 322
Vierville-sur-Mer, 119
Viet Minh, 44
Vietnam, 33, 37, 151, 168, 321
Vietnam veteran, 269
Vietnam War, 33
Vigipirate, 231, 390
VII Corps (United States), 132
VIII Corps (United States), 132
Villodrigo, 384
Vimy Ridge, 106
Visigoths, 19
Vive La Bombe, 290
Voisin III, 305
Voisin V, 306
Vo Nguyen Giap, 326
Vosges Mountains, 122, 131
Vought O2U Corsair, 322
VXB, 390

Wadi, 146
Waffen SS, 86, 89
Waffen-SS, 219
War in Afghanistan (1978–present), 182, 204
War in Afghanistan (2001–14), 6
War in Afghanistan (2001–2014), 332, 367
War in Afghanistan (2001–present), 38, 182, 204, 233
War memorial, 351
War Minister, 62
War of Devolution, 25
War of Saint-Sardos, 22
War of Spanish Succession, 185
War of the Austrian Succession, 4, 15, 25, 27, 182, 363
War of the Grand Alliance, 159
War of the League of Augsburg, 182

War of the Polish Succession, 4, 15, 27, 182
War of the Quadruple Alliance, 4, 15, 27
War of the Reunions, 25
War of the Spanish Succession, 3, 14, 25, 182, 363
War on Terror, 367
Warrant Officer, 234, 249, 250
Warrant Officer Class One, 398
Warrant Officer Class Two, 398
Wars of the Roses, 23
Washington Naval Treaty, 174, 365
Wassoulou Empire, 214
Water police, 392
Weapon of mass destruction, 283
Wehrmacht, 113, 266
Weimar Republic, 35
West Africa, 33
West Africa Campaign (World War I), 35
West Africa Campaign (World War II), 137
West Berlin, 37
Western Desert Campaign, 141
Western Europe, 16
Western Front (World War I), 35, 43, 51, 56, 59, 60, 189, 206, 216, 309
Western Front (World War II), 126
Western Sahara War, 38
West German Chancellor, 287
West Indies, 94
White Paper, 5, 297, 298
Wikipedia:Citation needed, 265, 267, 268, 270, 288, 305, 324
Wikipedia:Please clarify, 286
Wikt:camaraderie, 237
Wikt:capote, 189
Wikt:creed, 238
Wikt:esprit de corps, 237
William, German Crown Prince, 61
William III of England, 25
William the Conqueror, 361
Wing (military aviation unit), 312, 342
Winston Churchill, 76, 78, 103, 316
World War I, 51, 98, 182, 189, 190, 295, 332, 334, 365
World War II, 16, 36, 182, 190, 332, 365
Württemberg, 88, 132

Xavier Vallat, 85
X Corps (United Kingdom), 144
XIX Corps (France), 82, 93
XXI Corps (United States), 131

Yakovlev, 114
Yakovlev Yak-3, 116
Yom Kippur War, 338
Ypres, 59, 106
Yser River, 61

Yugoslavia, 206
Yugoslav Wars, 336
Yves Rocard, 177

Zaire, 206, 226, 228
Zaïre, 205
Zeeland, 100
Zone DOpérations Aériennes Alps, 312
Zone DOpérations Aériennes Est, 312
Zone DOpérations Aériennes Nord, 312
Zone DOpérations Aériennes Sud, 312
Zone rouge, 35
Zouave, 189, 192, 209, 255
Zouaves, 34

www.ingramcontent.com/pod-product-compliance
Lightning Source LLC
Chambersburg PA
CBHW030515230426
43665CB00010B/617